The Missionary Impact on Modern Nigeria
1842–1914

IBADAN HISTORY SERIES

General Editor J. F. A. Ajayi Ph.D.

The Missionary Impact on Modern Nigeria 1842–1914

A Political and Social Analysis

E. A. Ayandele PH. D.
Professor of History, University of Ibadan

Longman

LONGMAN GROUP LTD
London

*Associated companies, branches and representatives
throughout the world*

First published 1966
Third impression 1977
ISBN 0 582 64512 3

Printed in Hong Kong by
Commonwealth Printing Press Ltd

Contents

13221

8   Missionary Enterprise and the Awakening of Nigerian
     Cultural Nationalism, 1875–1914

9   The Missions and Education

List of Maps

Abbreviations

C.M.S.	Church Missionary Society Archives.
M.M.A.	Methodist Missionary Society Archives.
BMSS	Brooke's Manuscripts.
S.M.A.	Society of African Missions (Société des Missions Africains, Lyons).
U.P.	United Presbyterian Church of Scotland.
M.P.	Morel Papers.
L.P.	Lugard Papers.
A.P.S.	Aborigines Protection Society.
P.P.	Parliamentary Papers.
C.O.	Colonial Office.
F.O.	Foreign Office.
N.A.	National Archives, Nigeria.

Acknowledgements

We should like to make acknowledgement to the Controller of Her Majesty's Stationery Office for permission to use maps held under Crown Copyright in the Public Record Office, reference number S/0496 in S.O.403/71 as a basis for the map of the three Delta States of New Calabar, Bonny, Okrika, and oil markets.

To Aderẹmi

Introduction to the Ibadan History Series

The *Ibadan History Series* grew out of the efforts of some members of the Department of History, Ibadan University, Nigeria, to evolve a balanced and scholarly study of the history of African peoples south of the Sahara. In the years before the Second World War, the study of African history was retarded, and to some extent vitiated, by the assumption of many scholars that lack of written records in some areas of Africa meant also the absence of history. Documentary evidence had become so overwhelmingly important for the European scholar that he tended to equate written documents with history, and to take the absence of documents to mean the absence of events worthy of historical study. As a result in the nineteenth century, when Europe occupied Africa, her scholars did not attempt to understand or to build on the historical traditions in existence there; they sought instead to challenge and to supplant them. The history of European traders, missionaries, explorers, conquerors and rulers constituted, in their view, the sum total of African history.

Fortunately for the historian of today, African historical consciousness remained alive throughout the period of colonial rule: that tradition was too much a part of the African way of life to succumb to the attacks of the European scholar. Even in the heyday of white supremacy some educated Africans of the period were sufficiently dominated by their past to feel impelled to commit to writing the laws, customs, proverbs, sayings and historical traditions of their own communities. Notable among these may be mentioned James Africanus Horton of Sierra Leone, Reindorf and Sarbah of Ghana, Otomba Payne and Samuel Johnson of Nigeria, Apolo Kagwa of Uganda, to name but a few. The published works they left behind have become important sources of African history today; but they were swimming against the current of their time and made little impression on contemporaries. Historians continued to write as if Africans were not active participants in the great events that shaped their continent.

The decided change towards a new African historiography came with the movement towards independence. African nationalists rejected the European appraisal of their past. They demanded a new orientation and improved educational facilities to effect this reappraisal. With the establishment of new universities in Africa, it was inevitable that the teaching of history and the training of African historians would receive a new impetus. For obvious reasons the changeover was slow in coming. Even in the new universities the old theories for a time prevailed: besides European history, there were courses only on 'European activities in Africa' at the undergraduate level, and at the postgraduate level research was generally on British and French policy towards their African territories.

By the late 1940's, however, African research students were insisting that African history must be the history of Africans, not of Europeans *per se* in Africa; that local records and historical traditions must be used to supplement European metropolitan archives; in short, that Oral Tradition must be accepted as valid material for historical reconstruction. No doubt the validity of non-written sources for historical research had been pointed out before, but it was new for university departments of history to accept it, especially in relation to African Oral Tradition. Even then not everyone was happy about it. Anthropologists replied cautiously that Oral Tradition, even when seemingly factual, was not history and could only be interpreted in terms of its functions in society and within the particular culture. But this did not destroy its validity as material for history; it only argued for a return to the link between history and sociology advocated in the fourteenth century by the famous Tunisian historian, Ibn Khaldum.

Even in studies of European impact on African societies and cultures, where European archival material still remains our major source, this source should be checked and supplemented by Oral Tradition, material artefacts and other sources of history in Africa. The achievement of the present position in the study of African history has been the result of individual and co-operative efforts of many scholars in different parts of the world, but I think it is fair to say that the Universities in Africa, and Ibadan in particular, have played and are playing their part in this pioneering work.

The History Department here has always tried to reflect the new approach to African history. It has pioneered some of the recent studies into African indigenous history and culture. These include the scheme for the Study of Benin History and Culture and two other schemes now in progress, concerned with the cultural history of the peoples of Northern and Eastern Nigeria. Our staff now include the largest concentration of trained African historians to be found anywhere in a single institution. Our postgraduate school is also expanding.

Hitherto, the fruits of our research have been published largely in articles in the *Journal of the Historical Society of Nigeria*. The aim of the Ibadan History Series is to facilitate the publication in book form of some of the major works which are beginning to emerge from the

xiv

Ibadan School of History and to make available to a growing public, with the minimum of delay, the results of the latest contributions to our knowledge of the African past.

K. ONWUKA DIKE

Ibadan, Nigeria
18th January, 1965

Preface

Of the considerable number of studies which have been made on Christian Missions in Africa two have been of special interest to me, R. Oliver, *The Missionary Factor in East Africa* (Longmans, 1952) and J. F. Ade Ajayi, *Christian Missions in Nigeria 1841-1891* (Longmans, 1965). The former is a broad survey of the place of missionary enterprise in the phases of East African history, from the imperial viewpoint. The latter is an attempt to put in perspective the contributions of Christian Missions to the making of Nigeria, with emphasis on the emergence of the educated Africans.

The present work attempts an independent line of approach. The main emphasis is on the reaction of the various sections of the Nigerian community—chiefs, educated Africans, the ordinary people and slaves—to missionary activity. Mission policies and opinions at the headquarters in Europe and America have no place whatsoever, except when these affected the Nigerian peoples. Missionary enterprise is not examined to the exclusion of the other agencies—administration and European trading effort. For, as far as the Nigerian peoples were concerned, the administrator and the European missionary were birds of the same feather and they saw them really flocking together.

This subject has interested me particularly because it shows clearly that Nigerian history in the period with which this book deals is largely the history of the reaction of the Nigerian peoples to the three groups of intruders—missionaries, administrators and traders. For the Nigerian peoples, in the localities where they operated, the first group were by far the most important, not only because they preceded the two others but also because they were closest to the people. Moreover, it must be repeated, they were in a sense part of the administration as well.

Naturally, as with the majority of human beings, self-interest determined the reaction of each section of the Nigerian community to missionary propaganda. From the start, and throughout the period, the interests of the Nigerian peoples obviously differed widely from those of the missions. The main objective of the latter was spiritual success, a quick one that would make Nigeria a veritable kingdom of God on earth. The means of achieving this, they thought, was to be the secular arm of Britain. For the majority of Nigerians, however, the spiritual side of missionary enterprise was of the slightest weight. They mainly saw missionary enterprise simply as a suitable instrument for the achievement of their political and social aspirations. The Egba and Efik chiefs who invited missionaries to

Nigeria, hoping to use the latter for their political interest, found themselves hoist with their own petard; slaves and the under-privileged welcomed missionary enterprise to improve their social status. Also, to the consternation of the European missionaries, the educated Africans regarded the Church as a political and social instrument to exclude their white teachers from the Church, with the hope of doing likewise in the state. The white missionaries did not want to be excluded from the Church, nor did they wish British rule to come to an end. Missions, too, painfully discovered that the Nigerian peoples patronized their schools for the improvement of their social and material standing rather than for the edification of their souls. In effect it was the incidental aspects of missionary enterprise, not the moral or spiritual objectives of the missions, that attracted or repelled the various sections of the Nigerian community.

All missions are treated as a unit. The Nigerian peoples had no interest in doctrinal differences. They sought to use all missions for the same ends. Politically, doctrinal differences affected only the products of the Catholic Missions because Catholic teaching did not encourage political aspirations and stifled criticism. But in Yoruba-land the Society of African Missions, based in Lyons, arrived rather late in the interior. Statistically, socially and politically the Protestant missions became the most influential. The situation in Iboland was different. Spreading at an astonishing rate in that territory after 1902, the Society of the Holy Ghost Fathers, based in Paris, made an impact socially, but not politically until recent years, when the Eastern Nigerian Government began to be apprehensive of the potential political danger of the Catholic Church which controls a larger following than the Protestant Churches.

This book has grown out of my Ph.D. thesis for the University of London. The footnotes and bibliography indicate the range of my indebtedness to a large number of archivists and librarians in Nigeria, Britain and Italy. Lack of space prevents my listing all their names, so I hope they will pardon me for thanking them collectively. I appreciate immensely their kindness and co-operation, without which the collection of the materials for this book would have been delayed. I am grateful to the Nigerian Baptist Convention for releasing me to do the research and to lead the academic life that is so dear to my heart. My thanks are due to Professor Ajayi who supervised what I was able to do in Nigeria for a few months and made valuable suggestions; to Professor Roland Oliver of London University, Professor G. Shepperson and my kind friend, Mr Christopher Fyfe of Edinburgh University, Professor E. B. Idowu, Dr R. J. Gavin and

Mrs J. E. Pretty of the University of Ibadan, all of whom read parts or whole of the work and offered valuable advice; to Professor G. S. Graham for his unrelenting and sustaining prodding which hastened the production of this book and to Mr W. H. Stevenson who, at much expense to his time, read the manuscripts. I am deeply indebted to Dr J. E. Flint who supervised my thesis in London with a sympathy and encouragement that will be ever cherished. I take this opportunity to record my huge indebtedness to Professor J. C. Anene whose association since 1954 has meant more to me than can be expressed here. He not only intensified my interest in history but also introduced me into historical scholarship and gave me moral and material support, apart from valuable suggestions. I must also express my sense of appreciation to the University of Ibadan for generously financing this research. I am delighted to record here my gratitude to Professor K. O. Dike, General Editor of the *Ibadan History Series*, for his many kindnesses. Lastly, though not the least, I thank my wife who, in spite of the Devil's pranks on her health, shared with me the experience of this research work.

E. A. AYANDELE

History Department
University of Ibadan
23 June 1965

General Editor's Note

I would like to make a few remarks on this number of the Ibadan History Series. It is essential that readers should be advised that although this book and J. F. A. Ajayi's *Christian Missions in Nigeria 1841–1891; the making of a new élite* deal with missionary activity in Nigeria and are based on many common primary sources, yet they are independent studies. On going through them I have been impressed by the fact that the two works are so manifestly distinct in content, in emphasis, in scope and in perspective.

As is clear from its title, Professor Ajayi's work is primarily concerned with the emergence of educated Africans—a new élite—in pre-colonial Nigeria, which event the author regards as the greatest contribution of Christian missions to the history of Nigeria. In this book, on the other hand, Dr Ayandele concentrates on the political and social history of Nigeria from 1842 to 1914, through the mirror of missionary propaganda, as seen by the peoples themselves. This is the explanation for the fact that it is the key events in Nigeria's evolution in the period covered by this book that are analysed, and not missionary enterprise *per se.* This is a work on the resistance of Nigerian potentates—Ọbas, Chiefs and Emirs—to apprehended political results of missionary activity, the beginnings of Nigerian nationalism, the inevitable conflict and mixture of indigenous and European cultures, the hopes of the unprivileged in traditional Nigerian society that missionary enterprise would usher in the millennium, the contributions of Nigerians and Missions to educational development and the response of the Nigerian peoples to the moral and social programmes of missionaries.

The two works, although based on common sources, are thus seen to be complementary and I heartily recommend them to all students of African history, sociology, theology and political science in particular, and to the public in general.

K. ONWUKA DIKE

Ibadan
2 November 1965

The substitution of a civilized authority for the accursed despotism of Pagan and Mohammedan powers is a divine and gracious interposition.

J. T. F. Halligey,
Chairman of the Methodist Mission in
Yorubaland 1886–1890

1 The Beginnings, 1842–1875

Except for the futile, feeble and spasmodic attempts by the Portuguese to Christianize the peoples of Benin and Warri, European contact with the Bights of Benin and Biafra, dating back to the fifteenth century, was primarily commercial until about the middle of the nineteenth century. At first trade was in sylvan products, but in the sixteenth century, and for over 300 years, 'living tools' became the main export of the Niger Delta and provided the wealth upon which the 'city states' of Brass, Bonny, New Calabar and Old Calabar throve. In 1807, for both philanthropic and economic reasons, Britain abolished this nefarious traffic and in the next sixty years made strenuous efforts to see that this Act of Parliament was heeded in West Africa. The Niger Delta peoples were persuaded by treaties and compelled by the action of the British navy to resume legitimate trade, particularly in palm oil.[1]

Though significant, what is remarkable about this early European contact with the Niger Delta was not the mutual peacefulness in which transition from one commodity to the other was achieved, but the negligible impact made on the social and political institutions of the inhabitants. Records show that except in Old Calabar the cultural result of 400 years of European contact was the evolution of the bastardized 'pidgin' English which became the language of business. The Efik of Old Calabar seemed more accommodating to European civilization and, to the superficial observer, a blend of the European and indigenous was developing. The Efik, it is said, had schools in the eighteenth century. By the middle of the nineteenth century important Efik chiefs had learned to cherish 'Esquire' after their anglicized names, observed different 'Sundays' as part of their social life, imported European houses and luxurious articles, and knew the code of English table manners. It is recorded that King Eyamba V of Duke Town had journals recording events of the state in good

1 The best account of this economic contact is K. O. Dike: *Trade and Politics in the Niger Delta*, Oxford, 1956.

3

English, while Eyo Honesty II of Creek Town had a European clerk for his accounts.[1]

But all these were incidental aberrations, for the vital customs and institutions of the Efik were not affected. *Egbo*, the all-powerful freemasonry-like institution that united the tribe, slavery, immolation, substitutionary punishment, ordeal by the poison of the *esere* beans, and biennial human sacrifice, were still hallowed. Like the other Delta peoples the Efik sought to preserve their society and sovereignty by allowing no European settlement on their soil. Indeed, contemporary observers were stupefied by the apparent imperviousness of the Niger Delta peoples to European influence, but they came to the rash conclusion that these peoples were beyond the pale of 'civilization'.[2] They did not notice the fact that traders were not necessarily 'civilizers'. Their mission was exclusively to trade, and so long as the institutions of the Delta did not hamper trade the supercargoes had no interest in modifying them. This was a condition admirably fulfilled in the Niger Delta.

The introduction of missionary propaganda through the opposite ends of the Nigerian coast, Badagry and Old Calabar, in 1842 and 1846 respectively, altered the above situation and marked a turning-point in the political and social evolution of Nigeria. Missionary enterprise turned the white man's activity in Nigeria into a veritable political and social force. So formidable did it become that by the end of the nineteenth century it threatened to overthrow the Islamic revolution which had occurred between 1804 and 1831 in Northern Nigeria. The Fulani *jihad*, it should be noted, produced a minimum of political and social changes. Politically it changed the personnel but not the system of administration of the Hausa states itself. For in many ways Islam integrated and assimilated, preserving vital indigenous and social units like polygamy, slavery and the family. Also in the way it was propagated in Northern Nigeria, the higher classes—chiefs, district and village heads—were among the first converts to Islam and it was through them that households and the masses came under the banner of the Crescent. On the other hand, Christian missionaries, fired by the idealism of a faith to which they ascribed, rightly or wrongly, the enlightenment, progress and technological achievements of their countries, perceived no wisdom in compromising with indigenous customs and institutions: the new wine of European Christianity had to be put into new bottles.

1   In the National Library, Edinburgh, Hope Waddell: *Journals*, entries for 16, 17 April and 2 May 1846.
2   T. J. Hutchinson: *Ten Years' Wanderings Among the Ethiopeans*, London, pp. 79–80. P.P. 1863, LXXI Burton to Russell, 22 May 1862.

Furthermore missionaries sought to convert individuals, whose soul's relations with God was all that mattered, whilst the unprivileged classes were the object of their solicitude. They sought the creation of a completely new social order which would wipe away most of the customs and institutions of the old society. Allied with, and in many cases inseparable from the British secular arm, at least until the beginning of the twentieth century, missionary enterprise resulted, politically, in the supersession of Nigerian chiefs by 'Christian' white officials. For, declared a missionary, 'the substitution of a civilized authority for the accursed despotism of Pagan and Mohammedan powers is a divine and gracious interposition'.[1]

Thus ideologically, and to a certain extent in practice, a potentially violent intrusion was made into the social and political world of the Nigerian peoples with the advent of Christian missionaries. From about the middle of the nineteenth century until the First World War, the period covered in some detail by this book, missionary enterprise set in motion the processes towards which British administrators, and to some extent traders, were to contribute; it introduced the new era in Nigeria by which the dynamics of social, cultural and political changes were to be progressively more external than internal. It is clear, then, that in this study the missionary factor cannot be singled out to the complete exclusion of the secular arm of the British and British trade, both of which the missionary factor inspired to act in particular ways on many occasions.

In both Yorubaland and Old Calabar, missionary propaganda from its inception was inextricably bound up with political considerations. Starting with Yorubaland: the political situation was such that at the time the first missionaries arrived the traditional rulers in Badagry, in Lagos and in the interior were divided into factions. In all places one faction or the other favoured the advent of missionaries, whose presence, it was hoped, would confer definite political and military advantages on their patrons. In Badagry, Ipokia, Ado, Lagos and Abẹokuta there emerged pro-missionary and anti-missionary factions. The latter were led by Kosọkọ of Lagos and Gezo of Dahomey. The former was an energetic, ruthless, successful trader of royal blood, who before 1845 had cast anxious eyes on the throne which his less dynamic, peace-loving and rather pensive uncle, Akitoye, was at that time occupying. Gezo, who had ascended the Dahomian throne in 1818 and had liberated his country from the irksome Ọyọ yoke, had an interest in what was going on in the

1 J. T. F. Halligey: 'The Yoruba Country, Abeokuta and Lagos', *Work and Workers*, London 1899, p. 389.

Bight of Benin and the interior of Yorubaland. Rightly or wrongly, these two personalities believed that the missionaries, who began to denounce the slave trade, were not the genuine friends of Yorubaland and Dahomey. The pro-missionary factions were led by Akitoye, king of Lagos until he was forced into exile by Kosọkọ in 1845, Ṣodẹkẹ and Ogunbọna, leaders of the Ẹgba branch of the Yoruba tribe, and Wawu, chief of English Town in Badagry. All the latter professed hatred for the slave trade, love for legitimate trade and the warmest of friendliness towards the British.[1]

It would be misleading to accept unreservedly the missionary-inspired definition of the difference between the pro- and anti-missionary factions as being purely, or primarily, a moral one. The records make it abundantly clear that in spite of their moralistic professions the Ẹgba remained until 1891 slave-holders, slave-dealers and slave-hunters.[2] In fact human sacrifice was performed publicly in Abẹokuta, their capital, as late as 1887. In Badagry cases of surreptitious slave-dealing by pro-British and pro-missionary chiefs were reported in unpublished missionary journals and the dispatches of the British consuls in Lagos.

More to the point is the fact that the reaction of traditional rulers to missionaries depended on their political interests. In the case of Badagry the Wawu, who was traditionally fourth in rank to the Akran, chief of Portuguese Town, welcomed the missionaries and English traders in order to use them to claim a first-class status. The open arms with which the Ẹgba received the missionaries, too, must be seen against the background of their vicissitudes and political interests. No time could have been more opportune for the introduction of Christianity among this branch of the Yoruba tribe than the early forties of the nineteenth century. For years the position of the Ẹgba in Yorubaland had been insecure; their recent history one of unhappy encounters with their neighbours. Driven southwards from their once flourishing towns, over 100 townships had settled in the natural fortress of Abẹokuta about 1830 under the leadership of Ṣodẹkẹ.[3] The military state of Ibadan on the north-east and the relatively tranquil Ijẹbu state on the south-east, which had contributed to their misfortune, were still hostile neighbours. To the west lay the powerful military kingdom of Dahomey, under the ambitious Gezo, dedicated to their destruction. Although the Owiwi war of

1 C.M.S. CA2/031, S. A. Crowther: *Journals*, entries for 22 Dec. 1845, 12 Jan. 1846 and 13 Aug. 1846. C.M.S. CA2/07, Akitoye to Beecroft, 6 Jan. 1851.
2 Cf. J. B. Wood's article in the May issue of *Church Missionary Intelligencer*, 1893.
3 For detailed account of the Ẹgba in this period cf. S. O. Biobaku: *The Egba and their Neighbours 1842–72*, Oxford, 1957.

about 1833, in which they defeated the Ijẹbu and Ibadan, transformed them from the defensive to the offensive in their relations with their neighbours, yet they eagerly looked forward to an external agency to ensure their continued existence and sustain their solidarity. It was therefore natural that the political usefulness of the white man was uppermost in Ṣodẹkẹ's mind when in December 1842 he received Thomas Birch Freeman, the half-Negro half-English Wesleyan missionary who went to Abẹokuta on a reconnoitring visit. Ṣodẹkẹ lost no time in impressing upon him Ẹgba's desire for the white man's friendship. He was invited to settle in the town and bring others, missionaries and traders, with him.[1] A month later Henry Townsend, the Church Missionary Society missionary of Ẹgba fame, was also warmly received with the idea that he would stay, but he soon left. However, the Ẹgba were not to be discouraged. Through the educated Africans, the *Saros*, who had been settling in Abẹokuta since 1839, they succeeded in putting across to the British Government their pressing needs early in 1844. Ṣodẹkẹ asked for military help against Ado, a town about half-way between Abẹokuta and Badagry, with which war had broken out since 1841, petitioned for missionaries and traders and described himself and his people as crusaders against the slave trade in Yorubaland.[2]

Officials at the Colonial Office had shrewdly feared such political responsibility urged by Ṣodẹkẹ being thrust upon them. This was why they had been apprehensive of the absurd (as it seemed to them) nostalgia of liberated *Akus*, as the Yoruba were called in Sierra Leone, who preferred their fatherland, where they might find themselves in spiritual and physical bondage again, to the haven of Sierra Leone. The Colonial Office wondered whether these Akus would not claim the protection of the British Government and thus drag the latter into unsavoury 'interior' politics. Since the Government could not prevent their exodus, officials salved their conscience by leaving undefined the legal status of these emigrants. But a quite different situation arose when, in response to the pressure of these liberated Africans, missionaries followed them to Badagry and Abẹokuta. There could be no legal quibbling about the status of these missionaries as 'British subjects'. Indeed, unconvinced that the traditional rulers would give them satisfactory protection, the early missionaries demanded protection from the British Government as an inalienable right. Hope Waddell, the United Presbyterian Mission pioneer in Old Calabar, refused to leave Britain in December 1845 until the

1 F. D. Walker: *The Romance of the Black River*, London 1931, p. 42.
2 Ṣodẹkẹ to Macdonald, 7 Jan. 1844, quoted in J. F. Herskovits: *Liberated Africans and the History of Lagos Colony to 1866*, D. Phil. (Oxon), 1960, p. 104.

Government had given guarantee of 'every protection' to the missionary party.[1] The physical capacity of the secular arm, said the Foreign Mission Board in Edinburgh, must be impressed on the Efik and become a means of 'facilitating' success among them. Samuel Ajayi Crowther, later Bishop, made the same claim, demanding in the *civis Britannicus sum* manner of Palmerstonian days that Britain's 'anxious eye' should follow missionaries and the educated Africans wherever they went.[2]

From the start, then, missionary propaganda in Nigeria was not just a religious invasion. In effect it was associated with a political invasion as well. In the background was the secular arm of Britain, to be invoked when practicable. In Badagry, Lagos and Old Calabar missionaries did not hesitate to use the secular arm in the furtherance of their interests. But it is essential to understand the motive for missionary involvement in Yoruba and Efik politics. Their objective at all times remained constant—the Christianization of the Nigerian 'pagans'. But it was their considered judgment that the ultimate objective could not be achieved until certain conditions prevailed in both Yorubaland and Old Calabar. Among these were peace and stability, the abolition of the slave trade, the evolution of money economy, the creation in Nigeria of a society, industrial and 'civilized', similar to that of contemporary Europe. It should be borne in mind that in a sense the latter half of the nineteenth century was one in which people who had interest in Africans believed in, and advocated, the doctrine of the trinity of the Cs—Christianity, Commerce and Civilization. When therefore Thomas Birch Freeman urged George Maclean of the Gold Coast to protect the Christians in Badagry, and that the British should aid the Egba against all their enemies;[3] when the Reverend Gollmer of the C.M.S. asked that the Ijẹbu be attacked in 1856; when the same missionary saw the bombardment of Lagos as 'God's interposition for the good of Africa';[4] when Charles Phillips, the educated African pioneer of Christianity in Ondo, called upon a 'national calamity'[5] to befall the Ondo so that they might become Christians, they all believed that they were working for the spiritual salvation of the inhabitants and for their material well-being as well.

But, as has been mentioned, political thinking was not the monopoly of the pioneer missionaries. It was the primary motive of the

1   U.P. Minutes, 8 and 24 Dec. 1843.
2   Herskovits, op. cit., p. 106.
3   M.M.A., T. B. Freeman: 'Typescript of a Book', p. 421.
4   C.M.S. CA2/043 (a), Gollmer to Venn, 7 Jan. 1852.
5   C.M.S. G3/A2/02, Phillips to Wood, 23 Feb. 1822.

Nigerian chiefs who invited missionaries into the country. Neither the Egba nor the Efik chiefs had the least interest in the white man's creed *per se*; none of them wished the spiritual side of missionary enterprise any success. Indeed, as will be clear from this book, while a genuine quest for Christianity by individuals between 1842 and 1914 cannot be discounted, the majority of the Nigerian chiefs and people were either enamoured of, or repelled by, missionary enterprise for purely political or defined social reasons. The Egba and Efik chiefs who loom large in this chapter expected and tried to employ missionary propaganda strictly for their political ends, but did not anticipate that it would act as a political force in its own right.

That these two sets of political thinking are mutually incompatible is clear, but it was many years before clashes began to occur. It was natural that missionaries, reflecting the bounding self-confidence of mid-Victorian England, should work for a 'civilized' form of government. In the circumstances of work in Africa, however, they were usually cautious and sensible enough to keep their political ideas to themselves, or at most, partially to reveal them to British officers on the coast. On the other hand the Nigerian rulers often revealed much of their political thinking to the missionaries, seeing no particular reason for caution, and accepting the missionaries' disinterested motives.

Hardly had missionaries arrived in Badagry and Abeokuta in 1842 and 1846 respectively than the events which led to the British occupation of Lagos in 1851 were set loose. The politics of the three towns became a pro- and anti-missionary issue. As Jean Herskovits, Ajayi and Biobaku have touched on the decisive role of missionary enterprise in the events that led to the 1851[1] bombardment of Lagos, only the salient points need be noted here. Akitoye, who considered himself the rightful king of Lagos but, as noted already, had been deposed in 1845 by his more powerful nephew, Kosoko, saw the missionaries as the best instrument for his reinstatement. Kosoko, too, quickly discerned in these 'spiritual' intruders the real obstacle to his political ambitions. Both of them involved themselves in the politics of Badagry and Abeokuta, Akitoye siding with the missionary party and Kosoko with the anti-missionary group who wanted the missionaries expelled. In Abeokuta where the pro-missionary party was overwhelmingly strong, largely because of Egba need for British military aid against Dahomey, the anti-missionary group had no

1 Herskovits, op. cit., pp. 96–162. S. O. Biobaku: 'The Egba State and its Neighbours 1842–1872', London Ph.D., 1951, pp. 94–188. J. F. A. Ajayi, 'Christian Missions and the Making of Nigeria 1841–1891' London Ph.D., 1958, pp. 138–188.

effectual influence. In Badagry, too, largely through the frequent appearance of the British navy, the pro-missionary party was in the ascendant and all the anti-missionary chiefs and their followers were expelled from the town in 1851.

From 1846 to 1860 missionary propaganda played well the part expected of it by the Ẹgba: it kept Dahomey at bay without manifesting any imperialist intention. In 1851 Dahomey might have captured Abẹokuta but for the military defence organized by the missionaries and direct aid by the British Government. Henceforth, until the French attacked Dahomey in 1891, reliance on British military power remained the shibboleth of Ẹgba foreign policy. It had grave consequences for the Ẹgba. As will be shown in the next chapter it explains the decisive political assertiveness of the Protestant Christians, which became the thorn in the side of the Ẹgba authorities, from 1880 to 1891; it placed the Ẹgba under heavy obligations to the British Government. But we are here anticipating. Immediately the Dahomian menace was removed in 1851 the Ẹgba joined the missionaries in pressing for Kosọkọ's removal. Thus the bombardment of Lagos in 1851 was not an isolated event but the denouement of the first phase of British involvement in Yoruba politics and the territorial acquisition of Nigeria.

The lesson of the British succour for the Ẹgba was not lost on the Yoruba chiefs. Apart from military aid the missionaries were conferring material prosperity on the Ẹgba as part of their programme to make Abẹokuta a 'Sunrise within the Tropics'. Other Yoruba states came to look upon the patronage of missionaries as a matter of political prestige,[1] and began to hanker after them. Between 1852 and 1857 Ibadan, Ijaye, Ọyọ, Ilesha and Ogbomọshọ—all large towns—received missionaries.

But the other Yoruba states were denied the unique position of Abẹokuta: they lacked the large number of liberated Africans, the chief attraction of missionaries to Abẹokuta. Nor could missionary enterprise heal the political gangrene of Yoruba interstate warfare and intrigues from which the country had been suffering since the disintegration of the old Ọyọ Empire. Missionaries were few and far between; the territory was large and deterring to imperialist-minded adventurers. The humid atmosphere of the coastal areas was believed to be the cause of 'fever'; immediately behind the coast was a very thick insect-ridden vegetation, perforated by tortuous 18-inch 'routes'; the next layer, which stretched to a distance of over 200 miles away from the coast, was the open savannah, five to six days' trekking from the Atlantic seaboard. In the perilous circumstances

1   C.M.S. CA2/031, Ajayi Crowther to Chapman, 5 Jan. 1856.

10

just described missionaries could be put to death without the British Government being in a position to avenge them. The British had no footing yet on the Nigerian coast and no military power which missionaries could invoke to impose the political environment they wished. Yorubaland was not like contemporary China, where there was a central Chinese Government which, by means of treaties, was being held responsible for the lives of the European missionaries and Chinese converts in the interior.

In point of fact, rather than working for the political unity of Yorubaland, missionaries consciously encouraged interstate antagonism. Under the complete control of the chiefs missionaries were submissive and gave sentimental loyalty and approval to the policies of the states in which they were operating. The Ijaye war which broke out in March 1860 clearly illustrated this. In this war, in which the Egba and Ibadan fought on opposite sides, the missionaries in Ibadan attempted to justify the aggressive policy of that military state, while the missionaries in Abeokuta sided with the Egba.[1]

This is not to say that missionaries had no influence at all in the first decade of their activity; nor would it be true to say that none of them had a vision of a united Yorubaland. Indeed, on a limited scale, missionaries exercised political influence in Abeokuta. Foremost among them was Henry Townsend who had settled in Abeokuta since 1846. Said to be a member of *Ogboni*, a Yoruba freemasonry and 'senate' of the Egba, he became secretary to the *Alake*, the titular head of the Egba, in 1850, a position he held for over ten years. In this capacity he exercised a great deal of influence on the Alake and was the sole director of the Anglo-Egba policy from the Egba side. He aimed at supremacy in Abeokuta. In 1861 the British agent in Lagos observed that Townsend 'has been so long in the habit of directing the affairs of Abeokuta, that he would not brook any interference',[2] whether from the *Saros* or from the Negroes in America who wanted to settle in Abeokuta and wished to see created a centralized administration under the Alake, thus anticipating the much lauded G. W. Johnson. Townsend must however direct such a government. In his imagination too was the idea that his visionary Christian Egba theocracy must be the nucleus of a united Yoruba state. No other Yoruba state qualified to be the nucleus for such a creation because they lacked the prerequisites that so eminently fitted the Egba state for a decidedly 'Christian civilization'—large settlement of *Saros* and willingness to accept the white man's creed. In fact, said Townsend, 'the advance of Civilization and Christianity

1   J. F. A. Ajayi, op. cit., p. 397.
2   C.O. 147/2, McCoskry to Earl Russell, 2 Dec. 1861.

would be retarded'[1] by the emergence of a 'pagan' and Muslim state such as Ibadan under the control of Africans.

But Townsend was a dreamer. His vision was one thing, reality another. Indeed he exaggerated his influence with the Ẹgba and did not perceive that he and the other missionaries were, for the Ẹgba, only a tool for the advancement of purely Ẹgba interests. The Ẹgba would not accept his guidance whenever it conflicted with these interests. Townsend ought to have known this in the light of his experience among the Ẹgba. The latter demonstrated clearly that they had no modicum of interest in the missionaries' spiritual dispensation. They raised no objection to the adherence of the *Saros*, whom they regarded as 'white men', and the latter's slaves to the white man's faith but would not tolerate apostasy on the part of the real natives, and persecution of apostates was persistent and effectual.[2] Socially and materially they raised no objection to their children being initiated into the white man's mystery of reading and writing, and they themselves saw the advantages of imitating his technological superiority in house-building and cotton-ginning. On the other hand 'Christian' social laws must give way to indigenous customs and institutions that really mattered such as polygamy, burial rites, slavery and *Ogboni*.

The postponed conflict in the political ideas of the missionaries and their African patrons began to occur at the outbreak of the Ijaye war. In February 1860 the perennial Dahomian menace led to the usual appeal by the Ẹgba for British military aid through the missionaries. The British Consul, Brand, responded as usual and sent ammunition and volunteers; warning was sent by the British Government to Dahomey that an attack on the Ẹgba would be taken as declaration of war on Britain. As usual, again, Dahomey had to hold back. In March, however, at the outbreak of the Ijaye war, Townsend and the Lagos consular authority thought that the Ẹgba had been sufficiently groomed to behave like a 'Christian' state and work for peace. On Townsend's advice the Consul sent a deputation to instruct the Ẹgba on what the British Government expected of them; they were to join the deputation in mediating between Ibadan and Ijaye before hostilities broke out. It was then that the scales were removed from the eyes of the Consul and Townsend; the Ẹgba would brook no British interference, except militarily for Ẹgba ends. To the surprise of the C.M.S. and Townsend, Christianity had in no way tempered the patriotism of the Christians who became the most vocal

1 P.P. 1861 (LXIV), Townsend to Consul Brand, 12 Mar. 1860, enclosure in No. 3.
2 S. O. Biobaku, thesis cit., p. 124.

group, advocating war against the Ibadan on the grounds that a unique opportunity had arrived for the recovery of 'our father's land'.[1] Townsend himself swam with the tide and declared support for war because, as he put it, 'Ibadan is already too strong, and uses it to perpetuate war and kidnapping. In fact a balance of power is needed now.'[2] The Ẹgba refused to receive the Consul's deputation and would not allow it to proceed to Ibadan and Ijaye.[3] On the other hand the Ẹgba requested the British to destroy Whydah, Dahomey's chief port, stop importation of ammunition to Ibadan through the Ijẹbu territory and send military officers to defend Abẹokuta and aid the Ẹgba in launching war against all their enemies— Dahomey, Ibadan and Ijẹbu. The Ẹgba declared war against Ibadan.

Naturally the British Government demurred at this aggressive role the Ẹgba cast for it. Thus unbounded militarism and the refusal of the British to help the Ẹgba fight wars of revenge lay at the root of the strained Anglo-Ẹgba relations which reached the point of the Ẹgba offering their territory to France in 1891. From 1861 onwards anti-British and anti-missionary feelings began to gain ground among the Ẹgba. These feelings infected all Yoruba chiefs at the occurrence of the chief event of 1861. The chiefs became convinced that the supposed friends—the missionaries—who had been courting their favour with exciting European articles like silk umbrellas, looking-glasses, patent velvets, sugar and biscuits, were wolves in sheep's clothing. In that year King Dosunmu, Akitoye's successor, was forced to cede Lagos to the British Government, sign away his authority and become a pensioner.

This was an eventuality which even the chiefs who had been patronizing missionary enterprise had never conceived. Much as the various pro-missionary factions were delighted to use the missionaries for the fulfilment of their military and political purpose, they never wished to see the British establish themselves in any part of the Yoruba country. As the people with whom the chiefs had had direct and intimate dealings the missionaries were blamed for the British occupation of Lagos. 'This Government,' noted the first Governor of this new British Colony, 'is, in fact, an object of suspicion and mistrust to all the surrounding country . . . the general fear is that the territory of Lagos will gradually extend itself until it swallows up all the neighbouring states.'[4] Naturally, as the state that had erred most

1 C.M.S. CA2/017, Egba Christians to C.M.S., 1861.
2 P.P. 1861 (LXIV), Townsend to Consul Brand, 12 Mar. 1860, enclosure in No. 3.
3 Ibid. Brand to Earl Russell, 8 May 1860.
4 P.P. 1863 (LXXI), Freeman to Newcastle, 4 June 1862.

in patronizing missionary enterprise, the Ẹgba authorities were the most incensed. They began to regret that they had allowed missionaries to enter at all; some even began to wonder whether their patronage of the *Saros* was not a huge mistake. An educated African reported from the Ẹgba capital, 'the people in general now say that the white men are not to be trusted for they only come to take our country, to coax us and bye and bye they will take possession of it as they did Lagos'.[1]

This fear and distrust of the missionaries was clearly manifested when missionaries, the Lagos Government and educated Africans offered to intervene in the Ijaye war. All the combatants offered to destroy themselves rather than accept what they imagined as an ensnaring mediation.[2] After five years of desultory warfare they agreed to an uneasy peace in 1865 without outside intervention. The next twelve years accentuated rather than allayed anti-white suspicion. In 1867 a long looked for occasion was provided by Governor Glover's aggressive anti-Ẹgba policy. Ẹgba cumulative rage descended on the white missionaries whose property was either destroyed or looted. This was the *ifọle*. The white missionaries in the other stations in the interior withdrew voluntarily.

In Ogbomọshọ, further in the interior, where the Southern American Baptist Mission had established a station in 1855, the political and social results of missionary activity began to disconcert the traditionalists. For Barika, the first convert, began to defy the *Balẹ*, the chief of the town, over whom he began to assert superiority. The hostility of the traditionalists against the Christians developed into physical violence against the latter in 1879 when they attempted to bury a convert in the bush, and not in the house as was customary. According to the new-fangled Christian teaching burial in the house was 'heathenish' and unhygienic, but in the traditional concept the proper place where a man's soul was to reach out to those of his ancestors was in the house. It was only criminals who were buried in the bush. All the Christians were expelled from the town.[3]

Thus after 1867, to all outward appearances, the Yoruba chiefs could solace themselves with the thought that they had destroyed the nascent political dangers implied in missionary enterprise. Politically the Ẹgba did not yet fear the educated Africans. In fact among them they found ready allies in the anti-missionary group led by G. W. Johnson of the Ẹgba Board of Management. This group believed, like the chiefs, in the elimination of the political influence of the

1   C.M.S. CA2/o8o, H. Robbin to Venn, 7 Feb. 1863.
2   C.M.S. G3/A2/O1, Wood to the Secretaries, 14 Dec. 1881.
3   Ibid. 'Journal extracts for the half year ending Dec. 1879' by D. Olubi.

missionaries. Socially the *Saros* in Abẹokuta preferred to conform to indigenous pattern in all essentials. Many of them relapsed to polygamy, a large number joined *Ogboni* with its 'heathenish' rites and accepted titles. It is said that many did not find it difficult to relapse to idolatry. A contemporary reported that even the minority of Christians among the 3,000 *Saros* happily threw off 'what they felt to be its [Christianity's] trammels'.[1] In Ibadan, another place where there was a small concentration of *Saros*, the Christians were a tiny group with no political influence whatsoever. The Muslim and 'pagan' authorities nursed undisguised contempt for the under-privileged cowardly Christians who were not contributing to the achievement of the purpose of the military state.

As will be clear from the next chapter the chiefs were mistaken in assuming that the incipient British influence in Yorubaland had been destroyed by expulsion of the white missionaries only. As the Ẹgba were to learn belatedly, and as the Ijẹbu had discerned from the beginnings of missionary enterprise in Yorubaland, African mission-aries and their converts were unconsciously agents of British imperial-ism as well. In later years the Ẹgba were to regret the incompleteness of the *ifọle* which they discovered ought to have included the *Saros* as well. Christianity was allowed existence under the control of Africans.

British influence had come to stay in Yorubaland. The Colony of Lagos was henceforth a constant source of fear and irritation. Added to the sting of the refuge given to their slaves in Lagos, Glover's policy of pinpricks[2] increased the bitterness of the Ẹgba and Ijẹbu. If these tribal groups, whose territories were contiguous with the Lagos Colony, showed that they did not want the British by closing their routes to Lagos the British could not leave them alone because the colony depended upon the interior for economic survival. The interior chiefs were thus compelled to maintain an enforced contact with the British. So exasperated had the Ẹgba and Ijẹbu become that in 1872 these two tribal groups and Dosunmu planned to drive all the white men away from Lagos. The Ẹgba and the Ijẹbu, it is said, were to launch an orgy of human sacrifices by killing 130 freemen each. By doing this, they thought, the missionaries would be so disgusted that they would leave Lagos, the only haven left to them. Dosunmu and his anti-British supporters were to drive away all the other white men by force.[3] As for the other chiefs in the far interior, reported a white missionary on the spot, the paralysis inflicted on the

---

1 P.P. 1857 (XLIV), Consul Campbell to Clarendon, 18 Feb. 1856.
2 J. H. Glover, Governor of Lagos from 1865 to 1872; known to the chiefs as 'Goloba'. He was recalled in 1872 because of his expansionist policy.
3 C.M.S. CA2/096, Wood to Hutchinson, 4 Nov. 1872.

Ashanti Confederacy by the British in 1874 destroyed whatever remained of their faith in the white man.[1]

But the dreaded British establishment in Lagos, the contact they were compelled to have with it and distrust of the white missionaries made the chiefs change their attitude to the educated Africans. Somehow the chiefs came to think that the educated Africans belonged to them, would not betray their fatherland and could be trusted, and that their advice and guidance could be employed in their enforced contact with Lagos. They were now 'respected and esteemed'[2] instead of being held in contempt as before 1867.

This was the situation which veteran missionaries Hinderer and Townsend had to face in Ibadan and Abẹokuta respectively when they returned to the interior in 1875. To their chagrin they discovered that they were not wanted, and they voluntarily withdrew to Lagos. Hinderer noticed that all reverence for him had passed on to Daniel Olubi, at one time his houseboy and cook, but since 1869 the head of the Anglican churches in Ibadan, Ọyọ and Ogbomọshọ.[3] He recommended to Salisbury Square[4] that Bishop Crowther should take Yorubaland under his ecclesiastical supervision and evangelization be left in the hands of Africans. Townsend found himself 'so tormented' because he was no longer 'publicly recognized'.[5] The Ẹgba now shifted their confidence to the Saros who 'are now admitted to the native councils and have a large vote in all national concerns'.[6] He recommended that Abẹokuta and Ibadan be made a separate diocese under the episcopate of an able educated African, James Johnson.

But if in 1875 the Yoruba chiefs could delude themselves that they had eliminated a nascent British imperialism, the Efik of Old Calabar who were within reach of the men-of-war had a different experience. Within ten years of the coming of missionaries vital social customs and institutions were becoming unstable. Politically, through the efforts of the missionaries and traders, the Consul was already the ultimate sovereign by 1856. So effectual was the onslaught of missionary propaganda that in 1855, at the deliberate wish of missionaries and traders, Old Town, one of the three main settlements of the Efik was completely levelled because 'the total destruction of that place would be a great benefit to the other towns (and)

1 C.M.S. CA2/049 (a), Hinderer to Wright, 18 May 1875.
2 Ibid., same to same 15 July 1875.　　　　　3 Ibid.
4 Headquarters of the C.M.S.
5 C.M.S. CA2/99, Townsend to Wright, 29 Jan. 1875.
6 M.M.A. Minutes, 1875.

to the advancement of civilization'.[1] Socially the disappearance of their 'absurd' superstitions, customs and institutions, was only a matter of time. John Beecroft, the first British Consul in the Niger Delta, could say of the Efik in 1854 that 'when the old superstitious people now remaining go hence, there is every probability that the rising generation will throw to the winds those silly and cruel practices, the cause of unhappiness to thousands, and the curse, and bane of their country'.[2]

Unlike the Egba the persistent request of the Efik for missionaries in the early forties did not arise out of political extremities. They had no threatening neighbours. In fact the Efik were remarkably united under *Egbo*, their *Bene Esse*, by means of which they had extended their influence to the far interior. This institution was the only machine that held the Efik together, 'the want of which, though but a rude and insufficient system of order, would leave the country in anarchy'.[3] By it the chiefs increased their wealth and authority and reduced the great number of slaves to subjection. This is not to say that political motivation was absent: it was at the back of the minds of the two most important rivals, Eyo Honesty II of Creek Town and Eyamba V of Duke Town. Each of them sought to increase his political stature by outbidding the other in zeal for patronage of missionary propaganda.[4]

Efik desire for missionary enterprise must be seen in the light of their well-founded conviction that the supercargoes who made the suggestion would never make any harmful proposal to them. 'Every good thing we have comes from the white people because they know more than we', declared the most influential Efik in the middle of the nineteenth century.[5] This, in a nutshell, was Efik experience in their relations with Europeans for centuries. Economically, they had thrived on the transatlantic slave trade and, at the beginning of the nineteenth century, when the white man said he no longer wanted human cargoes but palm oil, they had found the changeover much easier and more profitable, than had the other Niger Delta tribes.[6] On the human plane the supercargoes in Old Calabar treated the Efik chiefs on terms of equality, if not with deference. They flattered the chiefs with frequent visits and patronized the kings' regular banquets of African dishes as a matter of respect. Even so masterful

1 P.P. 1854-5 (LVI), Masters and Supercargoes in Old Calabar to Lynslager, 15 Jan. 1855, enclosure 3 in No. 122.
2 Ibid. Consul Beecroft to Clarendon, 20 Feb. 1854.
3 Hope Waddell: *Journals*, 4 Dec. 1849.   4 Ibid. 11 May 1846.
5 Ibid. 21 Apr. 1846, quotes Eyo Honesty II.
6 K. O. Dike, op. cit., p. 67.

a man as John Beecroft dared not treat the Efik kings with disdain until he was appointed Consul in 1849. He was courteous, visited the kings and explained things to them in their houses (not in the gunboat as after 1849) and won their confidence by tact and persuasion. The hectoring, authoritarian and paternalistic treatment of the Niger Delta chiefs which is discernible in his subsequent consular dispatches was a new phenomenon.

It is therefore easy to understand Efik belief in the impeccability of the white man and their spontaneously favourable disposition to the idea of missionaries coming to work among them. Before 1846 attractive terms such as free land, protection and patronage had been offered. They expected nothing more than secular education from missionary enterprise. 'They (the white men) all get learning when young,' declared Efik spokesman for missionary propaganda, 'but our children grow up like the goats . . . a school in our town to teach our children to saby book like white people will be very good thing.'[1]

Meanwhile, the promises by the chiefs notwithstanding, the pioneering missionaries were aware that their social and political programme could not be carried out within the context of the indigenous society alone. Therefore, as has been mentioned, Waddell and his lieutenants left Britain in December 1845 only after the Admiralty had ordered the navy in West Africa to afford them 'every protection'. Also letters were obtained from 'influential parties in England'[2] to Beecroft, who landed the missionaries in Old Calabar in April 1846 in the *Ethiope*. The missionaries were conscious revolutionaries, seeing in their residence on Efik soil 'an era in the history of the country'.[3] It is essential to note that within ten days of the missionaries' arrival many chiefs had started to doubt the wisdom of their anxieties and hopes. 'Why do king give these people place to build house,' they began to ask with prophetic insight, 'by and by more will come and they will take the country.'[4] Revolution in Old Calabar, recorded Waddell, was inevitable. It was a sign of the progress of the Gospel when in the name of Christianity, slaves disobeyed their masters' orders, children were at loggerheads with their parents and women flouted the authority of *Egbo*. In was expected that within nine years the Efik would be completely converted and accept the moral and social codes of Europe.[5]

Inveterately set against the political intentions of the missionaries and their social revolutionary programme was the man who appeared to be their best friend, the little known Eyo Honesty II, King of

1 Hope Waddell: *Journals*, 21 Apr. 1846, quotes Eyo Honesty II.
2 Ibid. 1 Apr. 1846.   3 Ibid. 4 June 1846.
4 Ibid. 21 Apr. 1846.   5 Ibid. 19/22 Oct. 1854.

Creek Town. As the individual around whom the political and social implications of missionary enterprise among the Efik revolved in the most important years, 1846 to 1858, he deserves some attention. Born into an impoverished dynasty he had by rare commercial acumen and industry retrieved his family's fortune to the extent that by 1846 he was the wealthiest Efik and a formidable rival to Eyamba V of Duke Town. Creek Town, with a population of about 3,000, was an island, only a few miles away from Duke Town, its traditional rival on the mainland. John Young, who later became Eyamba V of Duke Town, had ascended the throne in 1834, and he increased the wealth which he had inherited. In fact the future Eyo Honesty II had had to serve in his employ. John Young acquired the highest title in the *Egbo* society, Eyamba, which name he consequently adopted and became the most powerful man among the Efik. .

This was the man with whom Eyo Honesty began to compete in political influence and wealth. Having obtained the necessary wealth he set about acquiring political influence by claiming the backing of missionaries and supercargoes. An attractive personality, he was admired and loved by missionaries and traders because of the many qualities he possessed. He spoke English intelligibly, neither smoked nor drank, and was honest and progressive in his outlook.[1] Confident that missionaries had no political intentions and believing that they had the key to future Efik prosperity—secular and industrial education—he backed them with a zeal he was to regret after a few years.

Like the Egba, Eyo Honesty sought to use missionaries for a political purpose—to extend his sovereignty to Duke Town, Old Town and beyond and thus occupy a position which no one before him had occupied. His enormous wealth, extensive trade and influence reduced the supercargoes to his 'humble servants';[2] by 1849 the Duke Town king, 'a large fat and rather aged man' who had succeeded Eyamba V, and chiefs were his debtors and therefore had to bow before his authority. His influence was great over Old Calabar and 'a very extensive tract of country up the river'. Even the missionaries were no more than his protégés in the first years of their activity. 'King Eyo is undoubtedly a ruler, and the principal ruler in the country,' declared Waddell, 'and as such must be respected by us. Our Christian principles, the interest of the country, the welfare of the Mission stations, require of us to respect him as a ruler of his people.'[3]

1 For excellent descriptions of Eyo cf. T. J. Hutchinson, *Impressions of Western Africa*, London 1858, pp. 151–4. Agnes Waddel: *Memorials of Mrs Sutherland of Old Calabar*, Paisley, 1883, pp. 26–8.
2 Hope Waddell: *Journals*, 28 Apr. 1846.   3 Ibid. 4 Dec. 1849.

However, much as Eyo incarnated the fanatical love of nineteenth-century Nigerian potentates for their sovereignty, he had a weakness: susceptibility to European ethical values, which he imbibed probably during his visits to the West Indies and Liverpool in his early days. Whilst the Ẹgba would have nothing to do with European morality and, as mentioned before, practised human sacrifice as late as 1887, Eyo believed that some Efik customs were 'fool things',[1] including human sacrifice which he would have liked scrapped. He did not perceive that by destroying these 'fool things', he would thereby demolish the foundation of his rule.

But it would be an error to conceive Eyo as a radical reformer. Indeed he never intended to go the length the missionaries wanted. He took a rational and practical view of missionary enterprise. In principle, he said, the missionary's doctrine and ideals were commendable; theoretically, too, he was not opposed to eventual Christianization of the Efik, but this could be left to a remote future. In practice, he believed, the Efik had no use for the missionary's social teachings *in toto*; conversion to Christianity would lead to a disregard of Efik laws and customs and result in eventual occupation of Old Calabar by the English; Efik customs and institutions were not ideal but were best for the Efik environment and had virtues and practical values which ought to commend them to missionaries, 'else no man can live in this country'.[2]

In a matter of two years Creek Town had become the centre of missionary activity in Old Calabar, to the chagrin of Eyamba V who had never liked the missionaries to establish themselves there. The king threw open his courtyard for Sunday services and was for many years the interpreter. Sunday markets were established and Efik religious beliefs demolished by the order he gave through *Egbo* that the *ekpeyong*, the guardian god of every Efik household, should be thrown into the river. His zeal for reform reached its climax in 1850, just after he had declared sovereignty over all Old Calabar with impunity. With the moral support of the missionaries and traders, who appealed to him to employ his 'almost unlimited' power in the interest of the gospel and 'humanity' by a stroke of the pen, Eyo put an end to immolation of slaves, by which the latter were believed by the Efik to accompany their masters to the other world. This was a practice common to all 'pagan' Africa, inculcating the essential religious tenet of immortality, and was a mark of respect to the masters. Henceforward, Eyo declared through *Egbo*, all immolation must cease; masters no longer had power of life and death over their

1 Agnes Waddel, op. cit., p. 27.
2 Hope Waddell: *Journals*, 4 Dec. 1849.

20

slaves; only criminals were to be put to death, not by masters, but by *Egbo* after due trial.

No contemporary Nigerian chief ever destroyed so important a religious and social basis of indigenous society as Eyo did. The *Egbo* law had far-reaching consequences. It made possible subsequent interference by Britain in Efik social laws and politics. The point must be emphasized that the stringent enforcement of the law of 1850 was due to its indigenous nature. No consul or gunboat could have achieved this. Apart from those relating to the slave trade, not a single one of the clauses of the humanitarian treaties Britain had negotiated with the Niger Delta states was carried out. Evidence shows clearly that such treaties were more honoured in their breach than in their observance. Much as the Foreign Office instructed the consuls to persuade the Niger Delta peoples to put an end to their 'barbarous' customs and 'abominable crimes' it would not order coercion for their suppression until the era of pacification. More than one consul could exclaim with Burton that 'a Consul's moral force without a man-of-war is a moral farce in these regions'.[1]

Like the Egba, by patronizing missionary enterprise in order to increase his political status and by carrying out the most revolutionary social legislation in Nigeria in the nineteenth century, Eyo made the missionaries' revolutionary programme possible in a short time. He opened the floodgate to further reforms soon demanded by the missionaries with the physical backing of the consular authority. Naturally Beecroft hastened to Old Calabar and obtained a treaty with Creek Town and Duke Town upon the basis of the *Egbo* Legislation.[2] Thus, ironically, though unwittingly, the individual who wished ardently to resist foreign political influence did most to lay the foundation of British rule in the Niger Delta.

Eyo was the first victim of his reforming zeal. Hardly had the law been passed than the missionaries and supercargoes seized the initiative from him. They formed the 'Society for the Abolition of Inhuman and Superstitious Customs and for promoting Civilization in Old Calabar'.[3] This was the first challenge to Eyo's supremacy in Old Calabar. Henceforth reforms were not to issue from Eyo himself. The new Society made itself the watchdog of the *Egbo* law and its stringent implementation, and dedicated itself to the demolition of one custom after another, especially the use of the *esere* beans, infanticide, twin-murder and substitutionary punishment. Consular support was secured by the enrolment of Beecroft as a member of the

1 P.P. 1863 (LXXI), Burton to Russell, 18 Dec. 1862.
2 W. Marwick: *William and Louisa Anderson*, Edinburgh, 1897, pp. 252–3.
3 Hope Waddell: *Journals*, 26 Feb. 1850.

Society.[1] Missionary enterprise began to undermine Eyo's authority. For the first time his orders were being disobeyed by slaves, who seized the *Egbo* law to embrace Christianity against his wish. Particularly galling was the newsmongering of the missionaries who sought to know everything and reported events to the traders and the Consul. Eyo had to protest at the missionaries' interference in 'matters of internal self-government'.[2] It is not surprising that he became so disillusioned as to plan an Egba-type expulsion of the missionaries but could not do so because of Old Calabar's vulnerability.[3] He knew the man-of-war's guns would back up the missionaries; already the Consul was imposing fines on Efiks for 'insulting' missionaries.[4]

But if Eyo's political vision was blurred by a sense of the irony of his situation, Old Town and Duke Town were greater sufferers. The former had never desired missionaries from the beginning because of 'excessive attachment to the native customs of the Calabar people';[5] the latter, described by a Consul as 'an African Sodom and Gomorrah', though it had accepted the *Egbo* law of 1850, was never responsive to the humanizing appeal of missionary endeavour. By 1856 both had become so embittered against the political and social implications of missionary enterprise that they wished the missionaries to leave. When Duke Town attempted to expel the missionaries, the chiefs discovered that they no longer had the power to do so, for by their anti-missionary manifestations 'the Queen of England be vexed too much'.[6] In 1855, for resisting the cultural and religious intrusion of missionaries Old Town was destroyed by the Royal Navy 'in the most able manner'.[7]

The destruction of Old Town was partly the logical consequence of the strained relations between Eyo and the missionaries, and partly due to the indiscretions of one missionary, Samuel Edgerley. Having discerned the political ambition of the missionaries, Eyo refused to 'blow *Egbo*' in Old Town, a measure that would have made the law of 1850 applicable there, in spite of pressure from the missionaries.[8] But it was singularly unfortunate that a missionary of Edgerley's temperament was located in Old Town. Most intolerant and tactless,

1   W. Marwick, op. cit., p. 248.
2   Hope Waddell: *Journals*, 14 Sept. 1850.
3   Ibid. 16/19 Oct. 1854; 28 Apr. 1856.
4   P.P. 1854–5 (LVI), Beecroft to Clarendon, 20 Feb. 1854.
5   *U.P. Missionary Record*, 1855, p. 307.
6   P.P. 1857 (XLIV), Consul Hutchinson to King Duke Ephraim, 4 June 1856, enclosure 4 in No. 70.
7   P.P. 1854–5 (LVI), Lieutenant Young to Commodore Adams, 24 Jan. 1855 enclosure 1 in No. 122.
8   Hope Waddell: *Journals*, 19 Mar. 1850.

he had no spark of sympathy for the religious and cultural susceptibilities of these 'degraded and heathen people'.[1] Hardly had he
arrived there in 1849 than he stirred up the bitterness of the people by
entering into the 'Palaver' house and kicking the *Egbo* drum. This
was an affront on the highest judicial and executive authority that
would have cost any Efik his life. Since Eyo's supremacy was acknowledged, Waddell, the leader of the Mission, apologized for Edgerley's
indiscretion and gave assurance that such would not happen again.[2]
But 1854 was different from 1849. Edgerley could now be sure of the
moral support of the other missionaries for his iconoclastic tendencies.
In August of that year he entered the shrine of *Anansa*, the titulary
guardian god of the town, broke its sacred egg and some images and
removed some for personal amusement. The people rose up in arms,
marched into the Mission House, and would have attacked Edgerley
but for the appeal made to Eyo who dispersed the infuriated people
with *Egbo*.[3] Nevertheless the missionaries were incensed at this
'assault' on the Mission; moreover they could not forget the humiliation of a white man standing before an African king, Eyo, and
judgment pronounced by the latter on a matter in which the white
man did not come out well. The missionaries and traders felt that a
decisive blow had been administered at their prestige and were bent
on having it retrieved. The latter considered calling in a man-of-
war.[4]

The missionaries found a *casus belli* in the immolation of about fifty
slaves which had accompanied the burial of King Willie Tom of
Old Town in February 1854. After the 'assault' on the Mission the
missionaries began to mobilize the opinion of the supercargoes and
the Consul against these people for alleged infringement of the *Egbo*
law of 1850. But according to Efik law the law of 1850 was not
binding on Old Town. This was because Willie Tom was absent at
the meeting in which Creek Town and Duke Town chiefs decided to
pass the *Egbo* law. The missionaries knew this.[5] No language was
spared by the missionaries to portray the people in the worst light in
their correspondence with the Consul.

At the appearance of Acting Consul Lynslager in February 1855
they drew his attention to the 'crimes' of the previous year and
furnished further evidence that also implicated Duke Town. The
Consul, they said, would be 'forwarding the work of Civilization' if
he suppressed in an 'effectual way' the 'horrid' practices in which

1 P.P. 1857 (XLIV), S. Edgerley to Hutchinson, 30 May 1856, enclosure 2 in
   No. 70.
2 Hope Waddell: *Journals*, 4 Dec. 1849.   3 Ibid. 28 Aug. 1854.
4 Ibid. 28 Aug. 1854.   5 Ibid. 22 Jan. 1855.

Old Town was pre-eminent.[1] The supercargoes echoed the same desire and Lynslager had to resolve that 'to put an end at once and for ever to these crimes it is absolutely necessary to destroy the town',[2] a task performed by *H.M.S. Antelope* on 18 February.

The significance of the destruction of Old Town is that it is one of the first examples of military action by the British, largely at the behest of the missionaries, designed to coerce traditional conservatives who resisted the penetration of European moral and Christian codes, even though the Africans in this case had not in fact committed themselves by treaty to such a course. A precedent was set for the future when Old Town was forced to accept missionaries and their revolutionary programme as the condition for the rebuilding of their town in 1856. They 'agreed' to protect the missionaries, abolish human sacrifice, hand over twins and orphans to missionaries, instead of killing them and administer the *esere* beans only through the supervision of the kings of Duke Town. It was appropriate that Consul Hutchinson who arranged these terms lectured the Efik that 'Queen Victoria and her gentlemen wish commerce and Christianity to flourish wherever the English flag waves'.[3]

The last desperate Efik resistance to the political and social consequences of missionary enterprise occurred in 1856. The Duke Town authorities were satisfied that the missionaries had forfeited their right to occupation of the land given them in 1846 and therefore sought to expel them. Efik laws had been deliberately broken and inroads made into the sovereignty of the chiefs. Without their consent, the town authorities alleged, the missionaries had settled educated Africans of Efik origin on 'Mission land' and had refused to allow the latter to be administered under Efik laws.[4] According to Efik land law the missionaries, by using the land given them for a purpose other than that for which it was given, automatically forfeited their right to the land. Not without some justification the chiefs feared that the settlement of these detribalized Efik would be the first step towards the annexation of their country. Moreover, the missionaries claimed that the Mission House constituted a sanctuary and that any Efik who broke tribal laws which were repugnant to the missionaries and who sought sanctuary with the missionaries, became

---

1   P.P. 1854–5 (LVI), Rev. W. Anderson to Acting Consul Lynslager, 15 Jan. 1855, enclosure 5 in No. 122. Rev. Edgerley to same, 16 Jan. 1855, enclosure 6 in No. 122.
2   Ibid. Lynslager to Lt. Young, 19 Jan. 1855, enclosure 2 in No. 122.
3   W. Marwick, op. cit., p. 309.
4   P.P. 1857 (XLIV), W. Anderson to Hutchinson, 30 May 1856, enclosure 1 in No. 70 same to same, 17 June 1856, enclosure 2 in No. 72.

automatically absolved from their tribal obligations.[1] This was the missionaries' bewildering political assertiveness with which the chiefs had to deal in the case of the three Efiks who were harboured by the missionaries. With Consul Hutchinson's consent the missionaries told the authorities that by escaping into the Mission House the refugees had asked for Consular protection. To prove their innocence, according to Efik custom, the refugees must take the usually fatal *esere* beans, and the chiefs insisted on their surrender. Of course the missionaries refused. Quite legitimately, as an independent state, the town authorities blew *Egbo*[2] on the Mission House, enunciating that all contact with the missionaries and the liberated Africans must cease, and that all Efiks who had children or slaves in the Mission must withdraw them. Even provisions were not to be sold to these unwanted foreigners.

To their consternation the town authorities discovered that they had lost both the right to legislate for their subjects, to whom the *Egbo* law applied, and the freedom to reject a foreign religion that had become an incubus. Within a short time Hutchinson appeared in the *H.M.S. Scourge* and summoned the authorities to the man-of-war. When the king, Duke Ephraim, described by the Consul as 'a stupid, sulky old man' and according to the missionaries a man unfit to rule Duke Town, saw the warlike demonstration being made, he came to 'his senses',[3] hastened to the gunboat and surrendered. By the 'paper' they had made with the missionaries in 1846, the chiefs, including Eyo Honesty II, came to understand they had given away their land 'for ever',[4] by inviting missionaries to their country, they were informed, they must patronize them; never again must they take anti-missionary measures; they could only 'molest' the missionaries and the educated Africans at the 'displeasure' of the Queen of England;[5] lastly, the Mission House was a sanctum to which all Efik could flee to escape unpleasant tribal obligations. Duke Ephraim and his chiefs were grateful that they had escaped the exemplary punishment of Old Town, changed their attitude to the missionaries and swore that they would henceforth make no more 'palaver' against the missionaries.[6]

It is not surprising that even the female missionaries began to defy the Efik authorities with impunity. Resentful of the clothing of the female slave converts in European gowns, an action that made the

1 Ibid. W. Anderson to Hutchinson, 30 May 1856.
2 i.e. proclaimed martial law. 3 Ibid. p. 351.
4 P.P. 1857 (XLIV), enclosure 5 in No. 70 Agreement signed.
5 W. Marwick, op. cit., p. 353.
6 W. Marwick, op. cit., p. 355.

slaves look superior to free women, the authorities blew the *Egbo* to forbid this. One of the female missionaries, Mrs Robb, instructed the slave converts to flout the authority of *Egbo*. A similar ban to prevent their going to church failed. Never had Efiks defied *Egbo* in such a manner. 'Fine ting dis be, white woman come make law for we,'[1] remarked the stupefied but powerless authorities.

The triumph of missionary enterprise among the Efik was henceforward assured. It may be said that between 1850 and 1875 there was a kind of rehearsal of Nigeria's later history in Old Calabar. Statistically, converts who numbered 200 in 1851 were over 1,671 in 1875, and stations rose from three to five with twenty-three outstations in the period. Politically, Efik sentiment and inclination became more and more British; *Pax Britannica* was *de facto* virtually established. In fact as early as 1856 the missionaries saw Old Calabar in terms of 'a free British Colony'.[2] On the social and cultural side the missionaries won more conquests: slaves gained more freedom and European form of marriage and inscribed graves were successfully introduced. In 1871 was born the missionary inspired *Young Calabar*,[3] imbued with a fierce type of idealism to wipe away overnight Efik religion and customs. Perhaps the most appropriate commentary on the social success of missionary enterprise and the consequent decline of Efik institutions was the following calvinistic law passed by Creek Town in 1873:

HENCEFORTH ON GOD'S DAY NO MARKET TO BE HELD IN ANY PART OF CREEK TOWN TERRITORY; NO SALE OF STRONG DRINK, EITHER NATIVE OR IMPORTED IN DOORWAYS OR VERANDAHS; NO WORK: NO PLAY; NO DEVIL MAKING: NO FIRING OF GUNS: NO EGBO PROCESSIONS: NO PALAVER.[4]

1 Agnes Waddel, op. cit., pp. 43–4.
2 Hope Waddell: *Journals,* Hope Waddell and others to Hutchinson, 16 June 1856.
3 W. Marwick, op. cit., p. 481.
4 H. M. MacGill, Report on Old Calabar Missions, 18 Dec. 1879.

The ease with which the white man has implanted himself in Africa, as governor, exploiter and teacher, is due more to the work of missionary societies than the use of machine guns. . . . But for the Christian missionary societies few of the modern Protectorates or Colonies could have been founded or maintained.

Sir H. H. Johnston

2 Missionary Enterprise and the Pacification of Yorubaland, 1875–1900

One of the most important features of the establishment of the *Pax Britannica* in Nigeria yet to be explained is why, broadly speaking, the British occupation of Yorubaland was more peaceful and more gradual than that of the rest of the country. The explanation lies in the fact that missionary propaganda had prepared the way for the 'governor, exploiter and teacher', a situation that did not exist in the other parts of the country. Except for one study,[1] which does not examine the aspect with which this chapter is concerned, the process of the white man's intrusion into Nigeria, indeed of Africa, has generally been analysed in the light of the administrator and trader, the missionary receiving no more than a casual observation.[2]

And yet, in the experience of the peoples of Yorubaland and the Niger Delta, as noted in the last chapter, missionaries were the pathfinders of British influence. It was a role they could not have escaped, partly because of the political environment in which they found themselves, partly because of their patriotic instincts and partly because it was the logical outcome of their activity. To take the last point first: the missionary, African or European, was the bearer of British influence in a subtle but sure manner. Unlike the administrator and trader, he lived among the people from the first, professed interest in their well-being and spoke their language. Although socially and religiously he was a nonconformist, unwary chiefs did not think at first that he was necessarily a potential danger. For in the interior the missionary had no physical force with which to effect his revolutionary social programme, but sought to carry out his enterprise under the patronage of the chiefs. He could in fact be a great political asset for chiefs who looked upon him as the political emissary of the Lagos Government or of the peripatetic consul on the coast, as a link between them and these local British officials.

1 J. F. A. Ajayi, op. cit.
2 One notable exception is R. Oliver, *The Missionary Factor in East Africa*, London, 1952.

It was quite logical that the political status of the missionary increased the more the chiefs depended on him. It was also natural that the influence of the chiefs began to decrease in the eyes of both the missionary and his wards. This was the experience of people like Eyo Honesty II, Duke Ephraim of Duke Town and other Nigerian potentates who patronized missionary enterprise. In other words the chiefs discovered that patronage of missionary activity implied acceptance of British influence as well. Indeed wherever missionary propaganda became successful as in Abẹokuta, Bonny, Brass and Old Calabar, the chiefs noticed and regretted that they had lost considerable influence and power to missionaries and the Christian groups before the *Pax Britannica* was formally established. For the converts became more or less detribalized. This does not mean that they became rudderless individuals but rather they transferred their loyalty from the chiefs to the missionaries who, in H. H. Johnston's words, became 'exceedingly patriotic' and began to display a great deal of 'the British bunting'.[1] Missionary propaganda was one of the potent factors in the expansion of British influence in many parts of Africa and many missionaries and administrators recognized this fact. It is not surprising that, having observed the role of many of his colleagues in the spread of British influence among the Ibibio, a Primitive Methodist missionary, in his private papers, discerned truth in and recorded the following humorous statement ascribed to a schoolboy in England,

> Africa is a British Colony. For this England is much indebted to her missionaries. When the missionary arrives in a hitherto unknown part, he calls all the natives to him. When they have gathered around him, he makes them kneel down and close their eyes. This done, he hoists the British flag and proclaims the country British territory.[2]

It is important to emphasize that in the interior of Yorubaland, for instance, missionaries occupied a very difficult position; they found themselves poised between two loyalties—loyalty to the chiefs and loyalty to the Lagos Government on the coast. Missionaries had to be dutiful and faithful to the chiefs, whose goodwill must be courted for permission to establish stations, move from place to place and evangelize. They had to bribe the chiefs with appropriate European articles; when political or economic advice was sought it must be unhesitatingly given: when the chiefs wanted to communi-

1 H. H. Johnston: 'Are our Foreign Missions a success?', *Contemporary Review*, November 1887.
2 M.M.A., Robert Fairley's private papers in West Africa Box 5.

cate among themselves or with the Lagos Government the missionaries must become their secretaries.

So long as there was peace in the interior, missionaries preferred to work within tribal politics. This was advantageous to them in many ways. Their role as advisers to the chiefs enhanced their prestige considerably. Many of them felt that, should European administration supersede indigenous authorities, not only would they lose their position as counsellors to the chiefs, but the unedifying manifestations of European civilization, such as drunkenness and moral laxity, which they had begun to deplore, would follow European administration.

There were occasions when tribal politics were a source of anxiety to missionaries, European and African. Nor could cordial relations subsist between the chiefs and the missionaries all the time. For one thing, as a rule, the chiefs remained attached to the traditional religion from which they got political influence and deplored any spectacular success of the missionaries among their subjects. However, the greatest cause of strained relations between chiefs and missionaries was the irritating behaviour of the Lagos Government, to which the missionaries might not necessarily subscribe. A classical example was the aggressive policy of Glover towards the Ẹgba and Ijẹbu between 1865 and 1872. The missionaries in the interior protested bitterly against this policy and their agitation influenced the decision of the Colonial Office to recall him.

Nevertheless denunciation of the doings of the Lagos administration by the missionaries did not help the latter's cause. The chief could not be persuaded to believe that the religious teachers, their erstwhile friends, did not approve of the aggressive policy of the white man in Lagos. All white men were believed to be birds of the same feather, and traders, consuls and missionaries had been seen flocking together in Badagry, Lagos and Abẹokuta. The result was that the chiefs began to read political intentions into the activities of the missionaries, whose religious and social non-conformity only helped to deepen the chiefs' suspicion of missionary activity.

Once suspicion had been engendered, the chiefs began to look with disfavour on the mediation of the missionaries between themselves and the Lagos Government, which had hitherto been appreciated. It was natural, that, in this atmosphere of suspicion in which the missionaries worked, they should seek security by establishing contact with the Lagos Government, and render to it loyal services when this was asked for. For the missionaries found out that, although the Lagos Government was not really in a position to intervene on their behalf in any quarrels between themselves and the chiefs, neither the latter nor the people were aware of this. In fact they believed the white man was capable of anything, was 'Ekeji Olorun'[1] (Second to God) and could not be molested with impunity. Missionaries drew a great deal from the store of Government prestige for their personal safety. They could not be sold into slavery or sacrificed to the tribal gods.

Indeed, long before the 'scramble', missionaries were playing more than a passive role in the extension of British influence in Nigeria. They furnished the British Government, through the local officials, with geographical and strategical data about Yorubaland, the Niger and the Benue, which found their way to the War Office and were used for military intelligence.[2] The journals of anglicized African missionaries like Bishop Samuel Ajayi Crowther, Charles Phillips and Samuel Johnson, are more imperialist in tone than the official dispatches of the Lagos Government and of the consular authority. A missionary expressed in 1889 a sentiment echoed by others when, after reviewing the unstable political situation in Yorubaland, he said what an 'unspeakable mercy it would be if some benevolent civilized power should interpose. I have good reason for saying that such intervention would be welcomed by the poor, harassed, impoverished people as a blessing from Heaven.'[3] On the Niger, no consul before 1882 was as importunate as Bishop Crowther in urging that the Lokoja Consulate be re-established and that the Niger chiefs should be forced by the British Government to accept treaties by which peace, a rarity then, would prevail and British subjects be protected. In Old Calabar the Presbyterian missionaries were constantly critical of the lack of formal and effective administration in the Niger Delta.

What now constitutes Nigeria was looked upon by all British missionaries as Britain's 'informal' empire, or, as the influential organ of the C.M.S., by far the most important of the Christian Missions in Nigeria, put it, the 'unquestioned spheres of English national influence'.[4] For, their patriotism apart, they could not conceive of their enterprise flourishing under any other flag than the British, and missionary journals of this period breathed anti-French and anti-

1 *Church Missionary Intelligencer*, 1893, p. 360.
2 C.O. 806/141, 'Lagos: Information respecting Colony: Memorandum by Mr. [Rev.] Faulkner', with a map. F.O. 84/2019, 'Military Notes on the countries of West Africa visited by Major Macdonald July–November 1889' by Mockler-Ferryman. The information was provided by African missionaries and agents of the Royal Niger Company. These educated Africans, he said, 'would be invaluable for intelligence work'.
3 M.M.A., Halligey to Osborne, 15 Apr. 1889. See also ibid., Milum to Kilner, 31 Dec. 1880, C.M.S. G3/A2/01, Wood to Secretaries, 14 Dec. 1881.
4 *Church Missionary Intelligencer*, 1888, p. 542.

German feelings.[1] These feelings were shared by educated Africans even on the Niger, where they hated the Royal Niger Company. In spite of the generosity of the French Niger trading companies, they became anti-French when the latter sought to annex Onitsha and Brass. In Yorubaland the French influence disseminated by the priests of the Society of African Missions of Lyons was neutralized by the British influence of the educated Africans and British missionaries.

No territory offered missionary propaganda a greater opportunity for the extension of British influence than Yorubaland in the last quarter of the nineteenth century. For in this period there appeared a new factor in the power politics of this sectionally-ridden, warring people, who, divided into tribal groups, could not resolve their problems on their own, and therefore longed for the intervention, as peacemakers, of a completely external influence. This was the feeling of the majority of the people and chiefs in Abẹokuta and Ibadan when, in June 1877, the eternal enmity between the Ẹgba and Ibadan triggered off what was to be the longest war of attrition in Yorubaland, the Sixteen Years' War.

The bewilderingly complex diplomacy of Yoruba power politics and the civil war are outside the scope of this study. But it is essential to emphasize that the proliferation of the Ẹgba–Ibadan raids from 1878 onwards was intimately connected with the establishment of the C.M.S. Ondo Mission in 1875. Then the problems created by the foundation of the Ondo Mission reveal clearly how the missionaries, and not the administrators or the traders, were the torch-bearers of British influence until the Ijẹbu Expedition of 1892.

The Ondo Mission was in a sense the creation of the Lagos Government. Both the Ondo and the missionaries liked to emphasize this fact. It was Governor J. H. Glover who succeeded in 1872 in opening up an eastern route to Ibadan through Ondo, as a convenient alternative to Ẹgba and Ijẹbu roads which were often closed or opened at will by the two states. Glover had invited the C.M.S. to establish themselves in Ondo, after he had restored the solidarity of the unfortunate Ondo under Osemawe, their king.[2] The Governor assured the Ondo of the support of the Lagos Government, and warned the Ifẹ at Oke Igbo to stop harassing the Ondo upon whom they had brought disaster for over thirty years.

The eastern route, as it was called, was not used until the foundation of the Ondo Mission. At the outbreak of the civil war the

1 Ibid. pp. 541–2, also February issue 1889. *Unwana Efik* No. 2, Vol. III, Feb. 1889, a newspaper published by the U.P.M. at Old Calabar.
2 C.M.S. G3/A2/o3, Wood to Lang, 28 Oct. 1885.

political, military and economic history of Yorubaland became largely dependent on this route. Perhaps the most important consequence of the utilization of this route was the opportunity it provided for fulfilment of the political aspirations of educated liberated Ijẹshas, who in 1876 formed the Ijẹsha Association, the nucleus of the *Ekitiparapọ*, the Ekiti Confederation that declared war against Ibadan in 1878. It is interesting to note that it began as a politico-Christian group, holding weekly prayer meetings and praying that, as the

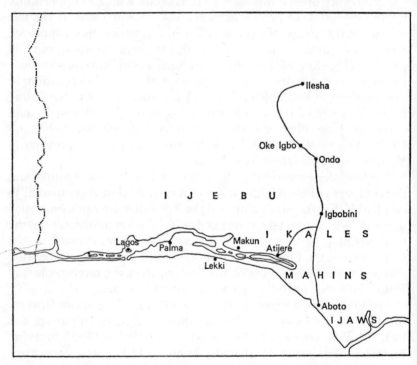

The Eastern Lagoons and the Eastern Route

correspondent of the *African Times* put it, 'God may bring about in due time events which may ameliorate the condition of their country, the leading one of which was the sending of Christian missionaries into the Ijesha country'.[1] The anxiety of this Association for the reopening of missionary work in their territory was primarily political, to provide a means for stirring up rebellion against the imperial yoke of Ibadan. Both the Ibadan authorities and the C.M.S. missionary, Hinderer, had discerned their political objective, and the former

1 *African Times*, 1 Feb. 1877.

discouraged all attempt to reopen the Mission station at Ilesha.[1] But Ibadan could check their so-called zeal for missionary enterprise only so long as there was no alternative route to the Ijesha country. This alternative was provided by the new eastern route opened up by missionary propaganda. With the support of Charles Phillips,[2] leader of the Ondo Mission, not only was a commercial link established between Lagos and the interior by the Ijesha Association and other educated Africans, but many members of the Association moved to Itebu and Ayesan, two strategic points on the route, as traders and farmers with the primary aim of transmitting ammunition to the *Ekitiparapo*, whom they incited to rebel against Ibadan in 1878.

The missionaries and educated Africans regarded themselves as representatives of British Christian civilization, and expected Britain, as represented by the Lagos administration, to fulfil its secular obligation to them by offering them protection. The secular arm was needed to overawe the congeries of small tribal groups of Makun (Ijebu), Mahin, Ijaw and Ikale, whose political and economic world was upset suddenly by the use of this route by missionaries, educated Africans and caravans from the interior. Particularly incensed were the Ijebu who, apart from their fanatical reactionary traditionalism, had been taught to look at the invasion of Yorubaland, especially the occupation of Lagos, as the handiwork of missionaries. Once let in the missionary or his minions, the educated Africans, so it seemed to the Ijebu, and all traditional social laws and institutions would break down, and as a matter of course sovereignty would disappear before British customs, institutions, and rule. This was why the Awujale, the paramount king of all Ijebu, sent messages from time to time to the Ondo, Ijaw, Egba and Ibadan, urging them to drive away the supposed greatest enemies of Yorubaland, the missionaries and their followers, from the country.[3] As will become clear later in this chapter, this was a policy and conviction from which the Ijebu never wavered until missionaries helped in bringing about the expedition

1 Ibid., also 1 May and 1 Aug. 1877. CA2/049 (a), Hinderer to Wright, 15 Dec. 1874. A.P.S., T. Lloyd Harrison to Fox Bourne, 27 Jan. 1892. Harrison gives a full account of the Ijesha Association comprising Ijesha and Ekiti. 'This Association has ever had its hands full in the pacification of Ekiti countries till the end.' The *Ekitiparapo* was founded in 1881.

2 Charles Phillips, born in Sierra Leone in 1847, was for many years a catechist in Abeokuta, Ijaye and Lagos. He was transferred to Ondo in 1877, where he remained until his death in 1906, being made Assistant Bishop of Western Equatorial Africa in 1894.

3 C.M.S. CA2/04, Phillips to Maser, 26 Sept. 1878, *The Phillips Papers* in the National Archives, Ibadan.

against them in 1892, and turned them into the most zealous Christians in Nigeria throughout the remainder of our period. Then there were the ferocious Mahin, their eastern neighbours. Cursed by lack of solid land on which to farm, and wedged between the Makun on the west and the Ijaw on the east, they took to raiding. Hitherto they had done some trade with Benin and Lagos, but the emergence of the Ẹpẹ, Kosọkọ's desperadoes, in the west, and the ascendancy of the Ijaws in the east, dealt their legitimate trade a heavy blow.

The answer of the Ijẹbu and the Mahin to the violent intrusion into their world of missionary propaganda was to commit outrage upon outrage on all the users of this new long-distance route. The lagoon disturbances, as the official dispatches described them, became a problem to the Lagos Government, which was expected by the missionaries to punish severely these small tribal groups who dared to hinder the penetration of British influence into the interior. This remained the attitude of missionaries until the establishment of British administration in the last decade of the century. In one of his many entreaties to the Lagos Government, Phillips said,

> I might not write at this length to your Excellency if I am not actuated by some jealousy for the ascendancy of the influence of the Lagos Government in this part of the country; for I am persuaded that it is only under its benign influence that the work of the C.M.S. which I have in hand and at heart, can prosper in Ikale, and Ondo countries, and that slavery, the curse of the country, can be discouraged.[1]

However, Lagos was not in a position to offer the firm political support the missionaries desired; never in the history of Lagos had the administration been so weak as it was from 1875 to 1891. In these years Lagos was in the doldrums. The administration simply had neither the means nor the will to assert any authority outside the island of Lagos. The incorporation of Lagos Colony to the administration of Gold Coast from 1874 to 1886 made swift action on any matter impossible, as the administrator in Lagos had to receive orders from the Governor in Accra. Then there was the perennial dread of the financial implications of a forward policy. There was also a personal aspect. Alfred Moloney, administrator and governor of the island almost continuously from 1877 to 1889, was a man determined on a pacific policy.[2] Primarily interested in botany and agriculture, the cornerstone of his policy was avoidance of political

1 C.M.S. G3/A2/o1, Phillips to Moloney, 29 Aug. 1881.
2 A. B. Aderibigbe, 'The Expansion of the Lagos Protectorate 1861–1900', Ph.D., p. 82.

differences with the various African states at all cost. He questioned the propriety of missionary propaganda disturbing the *status quo* on the eastern lagoons and paid deferences to the wishes of the various tribal groups, particularly those of the Awujalẹ.

Thus the period 1875 to 1891, when Christian missions were seeking to expand and needed most protection from the secular arm, coincided with the time when the administration withdrew to the shell of Lagos island, so to speak, and was least able to encourage their enterprise. The correspondence exchanged between the Rev. J. A. Maser, the local European secretary of the C.M.S. and Moloney (not sent to the Colonial Office, which certainly would not have condoned Moloney's views) showed clearly the utter powerlessness of the secular arm.[1] In one of his letters Maser reminded Moloney of his imperial duty thus,

> I sincerely hope that the Government will see their way clear to put a stop to robbery and murder on the lagoon, which has now been committed twice, not even twenty miles distance from the settlement (Lagos) which, is, if I remember correctly, the zone allowed by the English Government within which the administration may bring crime to its due punishment.[2]

Moloney's reaction was to confess the weakness of the administration. He pointed out that no protection could be offered to any users of the eastern route, whether missionaries or traders. He advised the missionaries to obey the Awujalẹ's order that they should abandon the route, that is, close up their enterprise! Moloney did not, however, represent the views of the Colonial Office, which could not be indifferent to the importunity of Salisbury Square that the administration should establish law and order in these regions and thereby make the atmosphere congenial to missionary activity. In 1880 a steamer, *Gertrude*, was built to patrol the lagoons and Igbogun island was occupied to check the Makun. The lagoon disturbances remained, however, because the Mahin could not be pacified by the administration. The whole problem was ultimately solved by the missionaries who cooperated with the Ijẹsha Association in their settlements at Itebu and Ayesan. At first the Mahin were pacified with gifts, but in 1883 the Association employed physical force successfully against the Mahin and asserted their right to use the eastern route unmolested.[3]

The lagoon disturbances were in point of fact the maritime side

1 Cf. numerous letters in C.M.S. CA2/04.
2 Ibid. Maser to Moloney, 2 Oct. 1878. Also same to same, 23 Nov. 1878.
3 C.M.S. G3/A2/03, Phillips to Maser, 29 Nov. 1883.

of the ubiquitous civil war, and revealed the fundamental problems of the extension of British influence in Yorubaland by Christian missions until the Ijẹbu Expedition. As has been noted already, since the power of the Lagos Government was legally and in practice circumscribed, missionaries along the eastern route had to shift for themselves. Naturally they had to turn into politicians and to develop the most intimate relationship with the Mahin, Ondo and Ijẹsha rulers. They settled disputes between the Ondo and Mahin, between the Ondo and Ijẹsha, and between the Ondo and Ikalẹ. But while operating within the politics of these tribal groups, they still claimed and paraded British citizenship. This gave them a certain measure of political status in the eyes of the chiefs. It only needed a period of distress to increase their political stature further.

It has to be emphasized that by 1877 the African missionaries in Yorubaland had reconciled themselves to the circumstances of Yoruba politics. As shown in the first chapter, their dual capacity was highly appreciated by the chiefs. In their dual capacity, wittingly and unwittingly, they prepared the way for the British occupation and the traders, without the use of machine guns, except in the Ijẹbu country. It was done in a very unostentatious but effectual way. This unostentatiousness explains why the historian of the spread of British rule in Yorubaland could not accord the missionary factor its due significance. The dual capacity of missionaries promoted some measure of understanding, and encouraged mutual confidence, which promoted peaceful relationship. It predisposed the chiefs for the acceptance of the British Raj.

This quiet preparation of the way for British occupation was most effective after 1877, when all important rulers of the country, except the Ẹgba and Ijẹbu, for reasons that will be examined later, yearned for deliverers to save the country from complete ruination. For before the outbreak of the civil war the goodwill of the chiefs was not automatic or cheaply bought. But the chiefs' position in 1877 was quite different from that of the Ijaye war, already noted. The Sixteen Years' War was on a much larger scale. Politically, diplomatically and militarily, there was something of a stalemate by 1881. It would have been an admission of weakness and a loss of prestige for any of the Kiriji camps, the Ibadan and *Ekitiparapọ*, to solicit, at least openly, the intervention of a peacemaker, but such an intervention, or rather interposition, was needed, because both sides were tired of the war. Militarily the balance was virtually equally drawn between the two, while economically the country was being ruined. Neither the attempted intervention of the Sultan of Sokoto nor that of the Alafin of Ọyọ, the titular head of the Yoruba country, was acceptable, because neither of them was a disinterested party. The Sultan of Sokoto was both the political and spiritual overlord of Iḷọrin, which had declared war on Ibadan in 1879, partly in sympathy with the aspirations of the Ekiti for independence, and partly to revive old scores with a power that had stemmed the tide of the *jihad* in the forties. The Alafin, Adeyẹmi I, was wily, and played one party against the other, particularly against Ibadan, in an attempt to regain a prestige and power already irretrievably lost.

This was the stalemate of Yoruba politics which could be healed only by a completely neutral outside influence. The missionaries were found to be the best medium for fulfilling this role. African missionaries, such as Daniel Olubi in Ibadan and Samuel Johnson of Ọyọ, had no inhibitions that could make the Ibadan camp doubt the genuineness and disinterestedness of their guidance. Olubi was an Ẹgba, whilst Johnson, though of Ọyọ origin, grew up in Ibadan. But they had never, nor could they have, interfered in the politics of the military state of Ibadan. No people could have been as qualified for forging connecting links with the Lagos Government, for cultivating goodwill, solving difficulties and giving proper advice. They knew the intricacy of Yoruba politics and the unwritten laws of conduct towards the chiefs to whom they gave respect, while the chiefs in turn respected their mysterious knowledge of the white man's way. In like manner Charles Phillips, an Ẹgba, had been extremely influential with the Ondo, mediating between them and their neighbours, whether Ijẹsha or Ikalẹ. He too became a channel of communication between the *Ekitiparapọ* and the Lagos Government.

An individual acceptable to both camps was the Reverend J. B. Wood, the Yorkshire-born C.M.S. missionary, whose political stature in Yorubaland reached an incredible level between 1881 and 1885. The anti-white feelings of 1861 to 1875 among the chiefs subsided in face of a suicidal civil war. Posted to Abẹokuta in 1857, he remained there until the *ifọle* of 1867, an event which seems to have left him with the deep conviction that, in the circumstances of Yorubaland, the missionary could make headway only by becoming part of its politics. Appointed Superintendent of the C.M.S. interior mission in 1883, he identified himself with Ẹgba politics until his death in 1897. His proclivity for things political was bewildering. This is clear from his papers, which are indispensable to an understanding of Ẹgba and Yoruba politics from 1877 to 1892. So great wàs his interest in Yoruba politics that he refused to be transferred to Sierra Leone, where he was offered the highly remunerative post of the Colonial Chaplaincy. Nor, to the chagrin of the C.M.S., was he attracted by

39

repeated offers of the proposed episcopate for Yorubaland, which would have turned him into a full-time ecclesiastical administrator.[1] A fluent Yoruba speaker and author of some works on Yoruba grammar and literature, he also wrote the useful history of Lagos up to 1861, the first work of its kind.[2] Constantly he appealed to Salisbury Square to persuade the British Government to intervene in the civil war. According to him not less than 161 towns and villages had been destroyed in the internecine warfare in Yorubaland since the disintegration of the old Ọyọ empire.[3] His influence over Ogundipẹ, the uncrowned king of the Ẹgba (more of him later) until his death in 1887, and the latter's faith that Wood could settle the civil war; the belief of the Alafin that Wood could be the saviour of Yorubaland; the incredible prostration before him of Ogedemgbe, the generalissimo of the *Ekitiparapọ*, imploring him to use his supposed influence to put an end to the war, and the conviction of the exiled Awujalẹ in 1886 that, if Wood wished, he could restore him to his throne[4]—all show the extremities into which all heads of Yorubaland were driven, their yearning for British influence and the importance attached to missionaries in the solution of the political problem of the territory. In fact so great was Wood's influence that, had he had just 100 soldiers, what he called the 'material force', the war would have come to an end in 1885.

The preparation of the minds of the two camps for reception of British rule from 1881 to 1886 must not be underestimated. Hence when the Lagos Government felt that it would be safe to interpose between the two camps at Kiriji, and that its interposition would be appreciated and its prestige unstained, it did the best possible thing in selecting both Samuel Johnson and Charles Phillips to carry out the diplomatic negotiations and settle the terms agreeable to both camps without loss of prestige by either. All that the Lagos Government did was to provide the 'material force' that stood between the two camps until they dispersed. Under the leadership of these two African missionaries, representatives of the two camps went down to Lagos and signed the so-called treaties of protection and commerce which, as Dr. Aderibigbe shows,[5] were in principle the same thing. Various states in the interior promised that they would accept British protection and would have nothing to do with any other foreign

1   C.M.S. G3/A2/09, Ernest Fry, 'The Late J. B. Wood', June 1897.
2   Manuscript is in C.M.S. CA2/096; it was published in 1878.
3   N. A. Ibadan Wood's papers in C.M.S. (Y) 4/1, File 8.
4   C.M.S. G3/A2/02, Alafin to Wood, 15 Oct. 1881. G3/A2/03, Chief Ogedemgbe to Wood, 19 Jan. 1865; ibid. Wood to Lang, 27 Apr. 1885.
5   A. B. Aderibigbe, op. cit., p. 139.

power. The ease with which these treaties were obtained, and the way in which independence in foreign affairs was bartered away, is surprising to the historian of the expansion of the Lagos Protectorate.[1] Except for the Ifẹ Treaty, all the treaties of friendship and commerce were the handiwork of both Phillips and Johnson.

But what mattered to the combatants was the goodwill established between them and the Lagos Government, and not the treaties. British sovereignty was already assumed and accepted as a matter of course. As the patriotic French missionaries of the Society of African Missions (hereafter S.M.A.) noted, whatever power put an end to the civil war would occupy the territory.[2] The combatants had been so driven to extremities in 1883 that the *Ekitiparapọ* camp was ready to accept the French if France would intervene, just as the Alafin was prepared to have the French if they would help him solve his political problems[3]—by helping to roll back the *jihad* which had established Ilọrin's authority in his province of Iseyin, and by bringing back the over-mighty state of Ibadan to submission. Hence by putting an end to the stalemate in the Yoruba country, Britain, through the Protestant missions, bestowed the greatest blessing upon the chiefs. This was how the rulers saw the efforts of the missionaries and the Peace Treaty of 1886. In fact it was assumed that the presence of the British Raj was indispensable to the carrying out of the terms of the treaty and the prevention of a recurrence of the war. Transmitting the wishes of the *Ekitiparapọ* chiefs to the Lagos Government in 1888, Charles Phillips declared, 'The only hope of the country is Your Excellency. All eyes are turned to you in this matter (of peace). No written advices, counsels, or remonstrances can prevent the impending calamity of a general war.'[4]

In fact many educated Africans had begun by 1886 to notice the obvious logical outcome of the missionaries' efforts to put an end to the civil war. Hitherto they had applauded the altruism of these missionaries and had pressed the Government to lend positive support to their peace efforts.[5] Now when prospects of peace were near, they no longer desired peace, suspecting that British intervention and cessation of the war would eventually lead to the annexation of the

1 Ibid. pp. 145–6.
2 *Les Missions Catholiques*, 1884, p. 569.
3 Ibid. p. 582. S.M.A., Father Holley, 'Account of Journey through Yorubaland' in J. B. Chausse File, 1883–85.
4 C.O. 147/66, Phillips to Moloney, 3 Sept. 1888, enclosure 1 in No. 317.
5 P.P. (LXI), 'Correspondence respecting the war between Native Tribes in the interior and the negotiations for peace conducted by the Government of Lagos', 1887, p. 10. Foremost was James Johnson. Others were I. H. Willoughby, H. Robin and ex-king Dosunmu.

country.[1] Unlike the less sophisticated and largely illiterate Christian converts of the Niger Delta, who demanded annexation of their respective states, the educated Africans in Lagos and Abẹokuta were illogically seeking to make a distinction between British protection and effacement of the sovereignty of the independent states in the interior. It did not occur to them that invocation of the former by themselves must logically lead ultimately, though gradually, to supersession of native rule in the interior. Already articulating nationalist sentiment, they were one-sided in their notions of the purpose of the British presence in Nigeria. In their view Britain was in Nigeria to establish law and order, but she should not wield political control; she should seek to revolutionize the economy of the country by scientific farming and trade, but this must be done in the interest of Nigerians and not of her nationals; British administration in Lagos was welcome, but should be staffed by themselves and not by white men; revenue should be deployed on education, and not on prisons or elegant quarters for British officials. In the same manner they could not see the incongruity on the one hand of their desire to have the sovereignty of the interior states preserved and on the other of their own urging that British intervention was indispensable for the peace of the country.

It is indeed astonishing that the scales were not removed from their eyes until the era of the 'scramble' began. It is even more astonishing that even in these years educated Africans did not perceive that the inevitable occupation of Yorubaland by Britain was not just the result of the efforts of the missionaries to put an end to the civil war, but was the logical consequence of missionary propaganda of which they themselves were a part. It was not until the turn of the century that the process of the white man's intrusion into the country was examined closely. By this time the prestige of the European missionaries had fallen and the zeal of the educated Africans towards missionary propaganda had greatly diminished. They then observed, though they could not explain adequately, that there was a necessary connection between missionary enterprise and British imperialism; that missionaries prepared the way for the trader and administrator. This is the explanation for the extraordinary but belated virulence of the Lagos Press against missionary propaganda in the last twenty years of the period of this study. Ironically it was left to the die-hard and conservative, but nevertheless perspicacious, Ijẹbu to analyse correctly the process of British occupation of Yorubaland.

In 1886, then, some educated Africans attempted to persuade the

1   Ibid. Report of Mission by Rev. C. Phillips; among opponents were now J. H. Haastrup, and in 1892 James Johnson.

42

combatants not to agree to any peace terms. Like the educated Africans themselves until now, what these patriots were advocating was beyond the understanding of the chiefs, who were tired of the war and perceived no signs that the Lagos Government and missionaries had any design on their country.[1] Rather they were profuse in gratitude to missionaries whose names, they said, would be enshrined in the history of their country. Bishop Phillips was looked upon as their deliverer by the *Ekitiparapọ* who obtained independence through his efforts. In fact churches for Christian worship were already erected in their camp, and practically all towns and villages in the Ekiti country offered land and gave a hero's welcome to missionaries who entered their territory after the war. In Ibadan too, where most of the chiefs were Muslims, Olubi's prestige reached its peak after the peace treaties of 1886 and 1893. For the first time chiefs handed over their children, and not slaves as heretofore, to him for education, and no measure of the Lagos Government's was ever acceded to until after consultation with him.[2]

Indeed, chiefs in the Ekiti country continued to show gratitude to missionaries for a long time. The latter were the first intruders into their villages and towns and were regarded as part of the Lagos administration. The white man's religion came to be associated with peace, and it was because of this belief that missionary enterprise was zealously patronized by the chiefs. Moreover the latter found the missionaries extremely helpful in the last decade of the century, when they were used as intermediaries between themselves and the administrators, the Travelling Commissioners as they were styled. The administrators were ignorant of indigenous customs and behaviour, which they would have violated to the exasperation of the chiefs, but for the missionaries, who explained these to the administrators and calmed the chiefs when they were broken. The Phillips Papers[3] make it abundantly clear that both the administrators and the chiefs were most grateful to the mission agents for this role, which gradually acclimatized the Ekiti chiefs to the machinery of British administration. In fact the assimilation of most of the Yoruba country into the Lagos administration was gradually and almost imperceptibly carried out, extending over a period of nearly thirty years, and it was never complete. Legally it was not until 1911 that Ibadan's attenuated independence was ended; the Ẹgba retained theirs until 1914.

The chief effect of Yoruba acceptance of missionaries, and the

1   C.M.S. G3/A2/04, Wood to Lang, 19 Aug. 1885.
2   C.M.S. *Annual Letters*, 1895, p. 269; 1898, p. 110.
3   Cf. also C.M.S. G3/A2/09, 'Account of work in the Ondo Mission 29 June 1898', by Bishop Phillips.

consequent automatic acceptance of British influence, was that they were thereby saved from the fire and sword which from the last decade of the nineteenth century onwards the British brought upon the heads of Nigerian peoples who refused intrusion of missionaries or traders or administrators. The only people in Yorubaland who tasted the British fire and sword were the anti-missionary Ijẹbu. It was because of the existence of British influence in all of Yorubaland that between 1892 and 1914 the Lagos Government showed no eagerness to establish direct and elaborate administration in the interior to the degree the Niger Coast Protectorate was compelled to do. Northern Nigeria and Eastern Nigeria, where, partly because of the suspicion entertained towards the missionary intruders, missionaries were not allowed to establish themselves beyond the coast and the Niger river, British influence and sovereignty were forced on the peoples by maxims and seven pounders.

But two tribal groups, the Ẹgba and Ijẹbu, did not share the gratitude which the chiefs further inland were expressing to the missionaries at the making of peace in 1886. For one thing they were the least affected by the war. Since 1879 the Ẹgba were more or less militarily out of the war, while in Ijẹbu the majority of the people were against the war from the beginning. In 1883 they overthrew their king for dragging them into the war, and then made peace with Ibadan. By 1886 both the Ẹgba and Ijẹbu found British influence as represented by the Protestant missions distasteful; they became intensely anti-British and really desired to have the French in preference to the British. From 1880 onwards the Ẹgba authorities began to patronize the French Catholic priests of the S.M.A. in order to counteract the British political influence of the Protestant Christian party. But they found the latter too formidable, and accepted the rise of the Christian party into power as a *fait accompli* in 1891. The hatred of the Ijẹbu for the missionaries steadily deepened, until after the expedition against them.

Although out of a probable population of 40,000 the Christians did not number more than 6,000 at the most, yet they constituted a most formidable group in Abẹokuta. By 1886 they were an *imperium in imperio*. Circumstances and events of Ẹgba politics were in their favour. They lived together in specified quarters and were united. On the other hand, in the absence of any pressing external danger, after the British Government had warned off Dahomey for the last time in 1876, the Ẹgba chiefs were hopelessly divided. From 1869 onwards the titular head king, the Alake, exercised no authority beyond the Ake quarters. So much had the Alake been bereft of power that, it is said, that Oluwaji, the fourth Alake, who was elected in February 1885, was visited only twice by his chiefs in his four years of so-called reign.[1] The three chiefs who reduced the king to a mere cypher were the Onlado, head of the *Ogboni*, the civil rulers, Ogundipẹ, the head of the *Olorogun*, the war chiefs and the Magaji, another war chief. But the war chiefs and the civil rulers were themselves not agreed.

The Christians were very fortunate in the protection offered them by Ogundipẹ, whose name runs through the journals of all missionaries in Yorubaland during his lifetime.[2] Although the atomization of political authority made one-man rule impossible, he was the uncrowned king of the Ẹgba from 1867 to 1887. As a French priest observed at Abẹokuta in 1880, 'A vrai dire, le seul dictateur d'Abẹokuta est Ogudipe'. Reported to have been offered the kingship, and to have rejected it, he styled himself 'Alatishe', that is, 'one who puts things right'. Dreaded as a plague, steeped in juju and believed to be allied to the ghosts, he became, ironically, the greatest patron of the white man's religion and adherents. But why did this greatest of Ẹgba military chiefs assume this position? A remarkably shrewd man, he looked upon Ẹgba politics and security in terms of the secular arm, which the white man's people, the *Saros*, had invoked from time to time against Dahomey, and without which, he judged, the state would fall into parts. While deploring the assertiveness of the Christian party, he felt that no sacrifice was too great for protecting the Christians to whom the Ẹgba should be eternally grateful. In 1867 he stopped the *ifọle* by sending his staff, the symbol of his authority, at the presence of which the looters ceased their activity. As a sign of respect for Christians, he would not work at his smithy on Sundays. Although he wanted the independence of the state preserved, he was more friendly with the missionaries and more accommodating to the Lagos Government than the other chiefs. As long as he lived, a pro-French inclination by the Ẹgba authorities was impossible.

Indeed to be against missionary propaganda was also to be against Ogundipẹ. This was the greatest mistake of G. W. Johnson, nicknamed 'Reversible Johnson', whose achievements in Ẹgba politics should not be unduly emphasized. Though Christian-born in Sierra Leone in 1828, and though he received his early education in a Wesleyan school, Johnson had lost all respect for Christianity by 1865

1 C.O. 147/66, enclosure 3 in Moloney to Knutsford, 9 May 1888.
2 Excellent biographical sketches of Ogundipẹ are to be found in M. Holley: *Voyage à Abeokuta*, Lyon 1881, pp. 23–31, and in *Lagos Times*, 10 May 1882. From these and other mission sources I draw much of what follows.

when he settled in Abẹokuta. He was believed by many missionaries to be the fomenter of the *ifọle*. He was never on good terms with Ogundipẹ, who foiled his schemes, and he was expelled from Abẹokuta four times between 1869 and 1892. From 1869 onwards his attempt to weld the Ẹgba into unity under an all-powerful Alake was foiled by the Christian party led by the influential Henry Robbin, a strong C.M.S. layman and the richest African trader in Abẹokuta in his days.[1] In 1869 Johnson favoured Oyekan as Alake-elect, a man who had boasted that if he came into power he would complete the *ifọle*. The Christian party backed the candidature of his less qualified nephew, Ademọla, and won. Having learned his lesson, when in 1877 the Alake throne became vacant, Oyekan canvassed for the support of the Christian party, whose interest he promised to respect if he was crowned as king.[2] This was why in 1881, during his reign, 'Reversible Johnson' drew up a constitution that formally recognized Christianity and the right of Christians to participate in the administration of the country.[3] Immediately afterwards when Johnson drew up a tariff scheme which discriminated against Christians the latter did not find it difficult to incite the chiefs and people of Owu quarters to beat him publicly.

Ogundipẹ found in Wood the man after his heart. They became intimate friends. In the chaotic political situation in Abẹokuta, the Christian community found it easy to come into prominence under Wood's leadership. Wood himself boasted once that he was indispensable to the wellbeing of the Ẹgba; that the political decline of the Ẹgba between 1867 and 1883, years when he was in Lagos, was attributed by the Ẹgba to his absence.[4] There must be some substance in his claim. When he died in 1897, never was a funeral so largely attended by the Ẹgba from the districts including both Muslims and 'pagans'. King Gbadebọ, Alake from 1898 to 1920, testified that of all the missionaries to the Ẹgba it was Wood's name that 'will never die'.[5] He is said to have been initiated into the *Ogboni* cult. It is clear from his papers that he was consulted by the triumvirate on all important matters of state, particularly Anglo-Ẹgba relations, and it was he who drafted the Ẹgba dispatches of 1886 to the Lagos Govern-

1 Herskovits, op. cit., p. 341.
2 C.M.S. CA2/056, James Johnson to Wright, January 1879.
3 *Egba Documents 1865–1934* in University of Ibadan Library.
4 C.M.S. G3/A2/01, Wood to Hutchinson, undated and entitled 'Visit to Abeokuta'. He visited Abẹokuta in 1880. 'My absence they (the Ẹgba) regarded as an omen that boded ill for the town'; cf. also G3/A2/03, Wood to Lang, 18 Jan. 1884. In same to same, 22 July 1885, the new king, Oluwaji, asked Wood to be his adviser.
5 C.M.S. Minute Book, entry for 14 June 1904.

ment by which the diplomatic relations which had been broken off in 1880 were resumed.

The Christians set up in 1881 a Court of Redemption, which disbursed funds for redeeming slaves according to the traditional custom; a Divorce Court was established in 1886 under the chairmanship of Wood, the court granting divorce to C.M.S. Christians instead of the native courts.[1] Incidentally the assertiveness of the Christians was in proportion to their military strength. From 1874 they became the real defenders of the state, whether against the Dahomian incursions or against Ibadan, under the leadership of John Owolatan, alias Okenla, the only chief of Abẹokuta who became a true Christian. He founded the Christian village of Shuren.

The assertiveness of the Christian party increased between 1883 and 1891 to the consternation of the Ẹgba authorities. Nothing showed the decadence of Ẹgba authority in these years more than the rise of the Christian party into power. In 1883 the Christian party, with Wood as chairman, had founded 'the Abẹokuta Patriotic Association'.[2] This society looked upon Abẹokuta's destiny as depending upon the Christians, and Wood urged them to constitute themselves as 'public opinion'. In January 1888 an observer commented that if the Christians united, 'they would revolutionize Abẹokuta; they have an indefinite power',[3] a view shared by Bishop Ingham of Sierra Leone, of whose diocese Yorubaland was a part. The chiefs did not like the way the Christians were using their 'indefinite power'. They seemed to be co-operating with the Lagos Government against what they, the chiefs, considered Ẹgba interests. The Christians were held as being responsible for the escape of their slaves to the Lagos sanctuary. For in 1879 the C.M.S. Parent Committee had caused its resolutions on slavery to be distributed among the Christians in Abẹokuta. To the chiefs this was represented as a calculated attempt by the Lagos Government to force them to give up a most important factor in the social and economic structure of society.

Moreover, to the chiefs, the Christian party constituted a danger to the security of the state by their supposed *rapprochement* with the hostile power of Dahomey. This charge, levelled at the Christian party from 1887 to 1891, was not without reasons, and yet the authorities had no power to deal with the Christians. The celebrated Halligey incident might be cited here. In 1887 J. T. Halligey, the new Chairman of the Wesleyan Mission, wishing to take the opportunity of the 1886 Treaty, set out from Lagos with missionaries for new stations in Isẹyin, Ibadan and Ogbomọshọ. He arrived in

1 C.M.S. G3/A2/07, Wood to Baylis, 1 June 1893.
2 *Lagos Observer*, 13 Mar. 1884.   3 Ibid. 21 and 28 Jan. 1888.

Abeokuta in March. He was, however, indiscreet in the choice of his carriers, for among them were some Dahomians. The Ẹgba intelligence officers had forewarned the authorities of this before Halligey and his party arrived in the town. As a missionary who had been many times in Dahomey, where the Wesleyan Mission had many stations, the Ẹgba took him for the white man, who, they said, had been at Ketu, a big Yoruba town destroyed by Dahomey the previous year. The Ẹgba alleged that he was the person who had taught the Dahomians military science, and many averred that they had seen him firing canons at Ketu. The African missionary, W. George, was also described as the black captain who, they alleged, had led the Dahomian troops. What could have brought these two people to Abẹokuta except to survey the vulnerability of the Ẹgba, they asked. In the heyday of Ẹgba power the Dahomians would have been summarily killed and the missionaries, who harboured them, expelled. Unlike Glover's annexation of Ebute Metta, sixty miles away, which provided the occasion for the *ifọle*, the supposed plot of the missionaries to overthrow the state was a much greater danger, involving the security of the state. And yet, at the intervention of Wood and the appearance of Ogundipẹ's well-known staff, the Dahomian porters who had been put in chains were released and no threat was issued to the Christians. Furthermore the Ẹgba authorities apologized to Halligey for the hostility against him and invited him to come back and resume his journey to the interior.[1] In spite of the humiliation suffered by the Ẹgba authorities the reaction of the African missionary was to urge the Wesleyan Missionary Society in London to appeal to the British Government to punish the Ẹgba who needed 'the interference of civilized nation, not only to protect the interest of British subjects but a proper system of government'.[2]

This was a congenial soil for a successful dissemination of French influence, for which the French Catholic priests of the S.M.A. were eminently fitted. On arrival at Abẹokuta in 1880, they found many of the chiefs already regretting the incompleteness of the *ifọle*. As mentioned already, the C.M.S. resolutions on slavery were causing a great deal of excitement. Furthermore, as a proof of the design of the Lagos Government on Ẹgba territory, so it seemed to the Ẹgba, the Lagos Government sent Tickel, the Commissioner for Badagry Division, to Abẹokuta. They would not let him into the town because it was felt he was coming on a political mission. Their fear seemed justified when Faulkner, a European missionary, established a close contact

1   M.M.A., Halligey to Moloney, 19 Mar. 1887. C.M.S. G3/A2/04, Wood to Hamilton, 6 Mar. 1887.
2   M.M.A., W. B. George to General Secretaries, 21 Mar. 1887.

with the forbidden Lagos Government official. In fact Tickel was sent by the Lagos Government to discuss possible Ẹgba efforts in putting an end to the civil war. The Tickel mission and the slavery issue also formed a part of the flag affair brought about by G. W. Johnson. For the latter, in one of his futile attempts to create Ẹgba unity, had ordered a flag for the Ẹgba nation. It contained the names of the Ẹgba kingdoms but had in the middle the insignia of the crown of Queen Victoria.[1]

Fathers Holley and Chausse at once disclaimed political interests, and were therefore allowed by Ogundipẹ to establish themselves in Abẹokuta, against the wishes of G. W. Johnson and the Protestant party. Henceforth the priests succeeded with the chiefs in proportion to the degree of annoyance caused by the Protestant party. Indeed the Catholics had every advantage on their side. Their religion seemed similar to indigenous religion. The Cross, the medals and their images looked like similar symbols of indigenous worship. Particularly attractive was infant baptism, which was looked upon as *fetiche de blance*, a rock of defence for their children. Hence chiefs handed over their children for education, and thousands of infant and adult baptisms were recorded within five years.[2] Socially, too, Roman Catholicism was more tolerant than Protestantism. For slavery was at first regarded as conducive to the growth of Roman Catholicism. In Africa, as earlier in South America, Roman Catholic missionaries adopted the practice of redeeming slaves and settling them into Christian villages. Moreover the impecunious priests identified themselves more than the Protestants with the people. They ministered to the body by attending to the sick and working among lepers.

It is against this background that the Viard affair of 1888 should be understood. The Ẹgba thought that the French would be more accommodating than the British, and that they had everything to gain by allowing in French influence to destroy what the Ẹgba regarded as pernicious British influence of the Protestant party. For a long time, the priests claimed, the Onlado had been French at heart[3] but the influence of Wood and the Protestant party over the Magaji and Ogundeyi, another powerful chief, was decisive until Ogundipẹ's death in 1887. The French priests had prepared the way very well when Viard, an impecunious Frenchman, arrived in Lagos in March 1888. It is worth mentioning here that Viard was an official of one

1 M. Holley, op. cit., pp. 20–3.
2 S.M.A., Father Chausse to ?, 23 Nov. 1888 in 'Documents pour Biographie P. Holley'.
3 Ibid. *Chausse File*, 1885–90, François to Père Superior, 10 July 1890.

49

of the French companies on the Niger and had sought to promote French imperialism there. Secretly he was scheming with the French priests in Lagos and Abẹokuta to have the Ẹgba sign a Protectorate treaty which the priests alleged the chiefs had asked for.[1] Viard was not a commissioned agent of the French Government, although he claimed he was. Viard and the priests wished to present the French Government with a draft treaty—which they imagined that Paris could not refuse to ratify—securing for France the western half of Yorubaland stretching from Ẹgba country, through Ọyọ, towards Bussa on the Niger. Already the Alafin and the Awujalẹ were won over to the French side by the priests. The latter were already smarting under the humiliation of the French surrender to Goldie on the Lower Niger.[2]

From Porto Novo, which was already French, Viard went to Ilaro, an Ẹgbado town subject to Ogundeyi, the Jagunna of Abẹokuta. Here Viard left with the chiefs a paper they did not understand, a Protectorate Treaty, to which they put their hand.[3] Then the chiefs gave him messengers who led him to Ogundeyi's house where he stayed for a few days before removing to the Catholic Mission. A treaty was actually signed, according to which the French were to give the triumvirate £3,000, build a railway to connect Porto Novo, Ilaro and Abẹokuta, and were to recognize domestic slavery. In return the Ẹgba were to come under a French Protectorate. The priests and chiefs also agreed that the Protestant party should be expelled and their churches confiscated.[4] Thus the Uganda situation was nearly re-enacted.

Wood, the watchdog of British influence, launched a countermove. The Protestants were organized to prevail on Ogundeyi not to sign the treaty, and so strong was the pressure that the chiefs denied that they had signed it.[5] The fact that the chiefs could be questioned and made to deny acts of foreign policy showed the degree of their weakness and the strength of the Protestant party. The latter had one other asset; they were well-armed, while the chiefs suffered from the embargo on ammunition placed upon them by the Lagos Government. Neither the Lagos Government nor the Lagos Ẹgba were aware of Viard's doings in Abẹokuta until Wood went down to Lagos and gave all the information to Moloney, himself a devout Catholic. Wood also mobilized the Lagos Ẹgba against the chiefs so that, whenever they wanted to cede their territory to any outside power,

1   *Les Missions Catholiques*, 1891, p. 342.
2   C.M.S. G3/A2/05, I. D. Fairley to Wood, 3 Sept. 1888.
3   Ibid. Wood to R. Lang, 23 Apr. 1888.
4   Ibid. Same to same, 15 May 1888.   5   Ibid. Same to same, 23 Apr. 1888.

that power should be Britain.[1] The C.M.S. sent a strong memorial to the British Government and withdrew the fresh minutes on slavery intended for distribution in Abęokuta.

Had Wood and the Protestant party not raised the alarm, which caused the British Government to establish contact immediately with Paris before Viard could present his treaty, the French Government would have ratified the Viard treaty. This was the view of the French priests. Wood's alertness, and the public opinion he mobilized, caused the British to settle the western frontier of Nigeria with the French in a treaty signed on 10 August 1889. Well might the French priests become disillusioned by France's failure to ratify the treaty. The French Government, they said, had been beguiled by the excitement stirred up by the 'heretics'. In fact so strong was the Protestant party that the chiefs changed face and ordered the priests to leave Abęokuta within thirteen days. Father Chausse, the local superior of the Mission, described the non-ratification of the Viard treaty by Paris as 'une sottise et une grossièreté marquante'.[2]

The Viard affair reduced considerably the power of the Ęgba authorities and reinforced the confidence of the Protestant party. The authorities knew that the *ifǫle* could not be repeated. It was natural that the Protestant party seized the initiative even in purely domestic affairs. In 1890 the French dealt severe blows at Dahomey in Porto Novo. The defeated Dahomians fell upon Itibǫ, a Yoruba town in the west, and thus set all the Yoruba along the western frontier on the move. Among these were the Ibęrękodos who, though the traditional enemies of the Ęgba, had no alternative refuge than Abęokuta. Naturally, the Ęgba regarded them as their prey. Two of the triumvirate, the Jagunna and the Magaji, who began to raid the refugees, did not consider Wood's reaction. These chiefs suffered the humiliation of being sharply reprimanded by this white political master who instructed them to stop their atrocities at once if they wanted any place in heaven.[3]

Fearing that Wood might bring the wrath of the Lagos Government upon them, the Ęgba, for the first time in their history, were guided by Christian humanitarianism. They made a stringent law that the refugees, who soon numbered over 8,000, should not be plundered or enslaved. Anyone who broke this law would be killed and his property confiscated. Furthermore the chiefs made contributions in money to meet the immediate necessities of the refugees and

1 Ibid. Same to same, 23 Apr. 1888.
2 S.M.A. Private File of J. B. Chausse. Chausse to Trappiste (his brother), 29 Dec. 1888.
3 C.M.S. G3/A2/o6, Wood to R. Lang, 11 June 1890.

gave them land and houses. In the same manner, the Eruwas, their northern neighbours, were given the same terms of treatment.[1] Not content with obedience to his bidding by the chiefs, Wood organized a Protestant Refugee Relief Committee, and saw no point in informing the Ẹgba authorities of it. The Committee was to see that the laws passed by the authorities were carried out to the letter, and appealed to Lagos for funds and clothing. Over £600 was subscribed and the Lagos Government sent a case of medicines.

The authorities were exasperated by this winning of the initiative by the Protestant community. Moreover they learned that the Lagos Government was playing host to Dahomian messengers. The chiefs unanimously swung to the French side. The French Government renewed contact with the Ẹgba authorities on attractive terms. Through the Resident in Porto Novo, the French asked the Ẹgba to send 2,000 troops to Porto Novo to be equipped and trained by the French and to join the French army in marching to Abomey, Dahomey's capital.[2] No greater sop could have been offered to the Ẹgba; they would participate in the destruction of their greatest foreign enemies. The Ẹgba concluded that once more the French were proving to be their best friends and the British their enemy. But the chiefs could only act clandestinely in face of the Protestant party. Moreover the latter accused the French priests of being responsible for the onslaught on Ẹgba farms by Dahomey. So great was anti-British feeling among the Ẹgba that, as Wood painfully observed, 'one might live in this town for years and not hear even an allusion to what England had done for the Ẹgbas in the years gone by'.[3]

With the hope of the advantages that would come to them if they were under French protection, the chiefs made the last attempt to get rid of British influence by literally 'begging' the Protestants, three times in 1891, to leave the town. In January they felt they had had enough of Wood. They charged him with being a British 'Ajẹlẹ';[4] that he was now the law-maker for the Ẹgba, and that he no longer had any regard for the authorities. Wood marshalled his defence in classical Yoruba. Christianity and British influence, he lectured the Ẹgba authorities, had come to stay in Abẹokuta; he reminded them

1 Ibid.
2 S.M.A., Franoçis to Père Superior, 2 July 1890, quoting in full letter of M. Ballot, French Resident in Porto Novo to the Onilado and chiefs.
3 N.A. Ibadan C.M.S. (Y) 2/2, script by Wood dated January, 1893.
4 A man placed by the conqueror in a conquered town as the representative of the conquering power to watch its adherents and see that they do not suffer any damage; something like a colonial governor. In other words Wood was Britain's representative in Abẹokuta and behaved as if Abẹokuta was already conquered by the British.

that the British Government had done incalculable good for the Ẹgba and deplored their pro-French inclination; Britain, he said rightly, had prevented the Ẹgba from being gobbled up by the Dahomians, had introduced the cultivation of cotton and brought to them a prosperity that was the envy of their neighbours; the authorities were ingrates. The Christians, he continued, were entitled to have a say in the administration of the town, and as most of them were offspring of the Ẹgba, they could not leave Abẹokuta; he would not leave, nor would the other missionaries;[1] and he challenged the authorities to employ force against them. Of course the authorities knew that the challenge was not Wood's but the Lagos Government's. They could not pick it up. It is small wonder that the stupefied authorities begged G. W. Johnson to return to Abẹokuta to restore the lost unity and waning authority of the Ẹgba.[2]

Clandestinely the chiefs strengthened their links with the French Government through the French priests. Some volunteers accepted the French invitation to Porto Novo, in order to have a share in the destruction of Dahomey. The authorities were united in sentiment for coming under the French Protectorate, in protest against the British Government for whom they nursed the deepest bitterness. Father François wrote the following to M. Ballot, the French Resident in Porto Novo, in February 1891, on behalf of the Ẹgba authorities,

Onilado me charge d'écrire en France pour supplier les Français d'établir le commerce entre Porto Novo et Abẹokuta. Les Ẹgbas ne veulent plus avoir aucune relation avec les Anglais. Ils ont l'intention, dès qu'ils pourront se procurer du sel et de la poudre de P. Novo, de fermer les chemins de Lagos à tous les commerçants. Ils prient les Français d'établir des comptoirs à Okeodan; si les Anglais veulent mettre une douane à Agilete, les Ẹgbas les chasseront en leur disant qu' ils ont depuis longtemps donné leur pays aux Français et que les Anglais n'ont pas le droit de reprendre.[3]

Nevertheless, on the surface, the chiefs dared not oppose the Protestants, whose political assertiveness was accepted with intense bitterness. The Protestants armed for resistance against any attacks. By June 1891 the chiefs' surrender was complete, probably because no answer came to their request to France to establish a Protectorate in Ẹgbaland. The Nlado wrote to Wood, 'You are bearing the burden

1 Cf. copy in Ẹgba Archives, Ake Palace, Abẹokuta.
2 Ẹgba Archives, G. W. Johnson to Alake, 12 Jan. 1892.
3 S.M.A., François to Superior, 12 Feb. 1891.

of our town that it may be at rest.'¹ The Jagunna wrote, 'Be assured
of this—no one will trouble you any more; for I regard you as
entirely an Ẹgba, we understand you and you understand us. It is
true you are a whiteman, but you have the mind of Ẹgbas.'² When
in February 1892 the chiefs learned of the fate that would soon befall
the Ijẹbu and perhaps themselves, they looked to Wood for safety.
The triumvirate wrote to him jointly: 'Give us advice always about
all European matters, for our enlightenment and to prevent us
making mistakes.'³

By 1891, therefore, the independence of the traditional authority
in Abẹokuta was already becoming a farce. The Christian group,
barely forty-five years old in Ẹgbaland, and in a way a foreign
element, had become part and parcel of Ẹgba politics and thus
prepared the way for the actual taking of the country. Indeed 1914,
which saw the cancellation of Ẹgba independence, was implicit in the
events of 1875 to 1891. Ẹgba independence was already comprom-
ised, and British influence strongly entrenched. This was why it was
so easy for Governor Carter in 1893 to sign a treaty with the Ẹgba.
Indeed Carter himself was astonished at the ease with which he
obtained it. So effete was the authority of the Ẹgba traditional rulers
that, when the British flag was unfurled in Ilaro in August 1891,
they were in a quandary and could do no more than fulminate
against the Christians, whom they held responsible for the annexation of what was indisputably Ẹgba territory. Once more the
Protestants armed for resistance, and it was left to them to draft the
letter, most conciliatory in tone, to the Lagos Government.⁴ But
although the Ẹgba were bitter about the annexation, and although
they closed their roads to Lagos and persuaded the Ijẹbu to follow
suit, Abẹokuta escaped punishment because British influence was
already strong there. It was the Ijẹbu, with whom commercial relations were good, and whose relations with Britain were more
cordial than Anglo-Ẹgba relations, who were militarily subjugated
in 1892.

It was in the logic of things that the anti-missionary state of
Ijẹbu came to be stigmatized as the veritable obstacle to *Pax Britannica* in Yorubaland. To be anti-missionary meant also to be anti-
British. This was how the Ijẹbu saw the whole affair of 1891 to 1892;
missionaries accepted responsibility for it; European merchants, who

1 C.M.S. G3/A2/06, Nlado to Wood, 22 June 1891.
2 Ibid. Jagunna to Wood (undated).
3 Ibid. Onlado, Jagunna and Magaji to Wood, 20 Feb. 1892.
4 C.M.S. G3/A2/06, Wood to Fenn, 17 Aug. 1891.

54

had no commercial grievances against the Ijẹbu, talked in terms of 'Christian England' showing 'pagan' Ijẹbu her power;[1] James Johnson, the greatest African missionary-nationalist of his day in Nigeria, wondered why the British Government became an 'iconoclast' determined 'to wipe this [fetishism] out by force'.[2] Carter justified the expedition on humanitarian grounds because the Ijẹbu 'were heathens of the most uncompromising description' who had 'refused to have missionaries in the country even of their own race'.[3]

In a sense, the Ijẹbu Expedition may be designated as the Missionary war. The Ijẹbu could not have escaped it. Although they viewed the invasion of Yorubaland in its entirety—missionary, commercial and political—with the deepest resentment, missionary propaganda was in their judgment the Sword of Damocles that hung over Ijẹbuland in particular and over Yorubaland in general. Kosọkọ of Lagos against whom, we have seen, missionaries had worked, poisoned their minds against these spiritual intruders who were capable of deposing kings and invoking against them fire and sword. Indeed the sequence of events seemed to have justified Ijẹbu apprehensions. Territorially the occupation of Lagos was followed by the annexation of the two Ijẹbu islands of Palma and Leke. Commercially, the establishment of the Ondo Mission diverted much of the interior trade with Lagos to the 'white man's road', the eastern route, thus affecting their middleman's position. Strategically, this route was employed until 1883 by their eternal foes, the Ibadan, for the importation of ammunition. Politically, said the Ijẹbu, missionary propaganda threatened their sovereignty, because of its supposed alliance with Ibadan militarism. Above all the Ijẹbu were convinced that patronage of missionary propaganda would lead to the seizure of their country as it had done in Lagos.

These are the facts to bear in mind in any analysis of the events of 1891–92 which led to the Ijẹbu expedition. From the Ijẹbu viewpoint there is little or no evidence for the commercial explanation that is usually assumed but never proved in explaining the expedition.[4] The Ijẹbu were not attacked because they were middlemen traders, for the Ijẹbu were no more middlemen traders than the Ẹgba, the Ijaw and the Efik until the turn of the century; moreover evidence shows that, just as the European traders in the Niger Delta were satisfied with the middlemen pattern of trade, even so the European traders

1 A.P.S., 'The Jebu Matters', by the Jebu Descendants.
2 Ibid. James Johnson to Fox Bourne, 9 May 1893.
3 *Report of Proceedings at a Banquet—to Sir Guilbert Carter*, 16 June 1893, Liverpool, 1893, p. 10.
4 A. B. Aderibigbe, op. cit., p. 188 f.

in Lagos were pleased with it, because there was no alternative.[1] Indeed as late as 1903 the middlemen system was more or less legalized by the Lagos Government, which allowed all the Yoruba states, except the Ijẹbu, to collect tolls, the very thing that the Ijẹbu were accused of doing in 1892, and which had always been done by every tribe in the Bights of Benin and Biafra. As will be shown presently, all evidence points to the fact that if any war was to be waged on behalf of commerce in 1892, it was the Ẹgba who ought to have been attacked.

Apart from the factors mentioned as determining the anti-missionary attitude of the Ijẹbu was their ultra-conservatism. They had every reason to be traditionalist to the core. Self-confident and prosperous, they had the unusual fortune of enjoying relative tranquillity. Their territory was saved from the devastations of the Yoruba wars, in which they participated outside their own borders. The few people who passed through Ijẹbuland bore testimony to their relative economic prosperity,[2] which depended largely on their trade in the interior and in the markets of Ejinrin, Ikorodu and Ikosi, where Lagos traders met them. They felt no need of any external influence other than trade, which was regulated in such a way that their independence would not be infringed. There was a regulation that no Ijẹbu should owe any Lagos trader any debt, lest the Lagos Government made that a pretext for invading the territory.[3] With pride they boasted to the Lagos Government about their religion, which was best for them and made them peaceable and prosperous, unlike the white man's religion which, they said, fomented war.[4] Unlike the Ẹgba, who welcomed their liberated children back to Abẹokuta, the Ijẹbu refused to allow liberated Ijẹbu to settle in the territory. The latter, who wore European clothing and had adopted a foreign language and religion, were not regarded as Ijẹbu but white men. Their settlement among them, they contended, would make the seizure of their territory easy. Missionary journals spoke of the 'stubborn dislike' of the Ijẹbu to English costumes, particularly to long trousers, shoes and socks, and to umbrellas.[5]

Many attempts were made before 1890 to introduce missionary activity into Ijẹbuland, but on every occasion events occurred that justified Ijẹbu fears. Before 1861 influential Ijẹbu, liberated Africans

1 C.O. 147/133, 'Minutes of the Evidence taken by the Commission of Trade' in March and April 1898, enclosed in Denton to Chamberlain, 4 June 1898.
2 C.M.S. CA2/o56, James Johnson to Wright, 21 June 1878. Alvan Millson, 'Yoruba', paper read to the Manchester Geographical Society, 5 June 1891, p. 5.
3 C.M.S. CA2/o56, James Johnson to Wright, 21 June 1878.
4 C.O.147/23, J. A. Payne to Glover, 27 Sept. 1871, enclosure in No. 55.
5 C.M.S. CA2/o56, James Johnson to Wright, 21 June 1878.

of royal blood, had tried to persuade the Awujalẹ, Ademiyẹwo, to allow missionaries to settle in his territory. The King consented to a visit by a missionary and in August 1861 the Reverend Thomas Champness, Chairman of the Wesleyan Mission, Turner, a close relation of the King's, and the Reverend Bickersteth, a liberated Ijẹbu, went to Ijẹbu-Ode. No time could have been more ill-chosen, for they set out on the 24 August, nearly three weeks after Dosunmu was forced to cede Lagos to the British. Champness was apparently well received, though the king protected himself by placing a number of gods between himself and the missionary. The Wesleyan Chairman expostulated on the virtues of Christianity and the greatness it would confer on the Ijẹbu country. With the spectre of the recent annexation of Lagos before him, the king tactfully warded off the missionary: 'Don't be in a hurry; we Ijẹbus never do things in a hurry; we have had our religion for a long time and we cannot give it up in a hurry but all will be right after a while.'[1]

What the Awujalẹ meant by 'all will be right after a while' was expressed in unconcealed hostility to missionary enterprise. According to Glover, the *ifọle* was engineered by the Ijẹbu, who also sent messengers to the Ibadan to do the same.[2] In 1872 they would not allow Bishop Ajayi Crowther to pass through Ijẹbu, and sent to the Ibadan to drive him back to the Niger.[3] As has been mentioned the Ijẹbu advised the Ondo and Ijaw to expel the 'white man's people' from their territory. The Awujalẹ was never reconciled to the British occupation of Lagos or to the humiliation to which Dosunmu was subjected. Time and again he urged the Lagos Government to restore the traditional ruler to his former power.[4]

The missionaries in turn became uncompromisingly hostile to Ijẹbu. This is clear from their journals and correspondence on the lagoon disturbances, in which the Makun gave much less trouble than the Mahin. Since the latter allowed a mission station at Itebu Phillips and Wood, surprisingly, excused and explained away the disturbances perpetrated by the Mahin for economic reasons. On the other hand, they spared no language to denounce the Ijẹbu in Ẹpẹ and the Awujalẹ.[5]

The Peace Treaty of 1886 worsened the relations of the Ijẹbu with

1 M.M.A., Champness to Secretaries, 7 Oct. 1861.
2 C.O. 147/14 Glover to Kennedy, 17 Jan. 1868, enclosure in Blackall to Duke of Buckingham and Chandos, 30 Jan. 1868.
3 C.M.S. CA3/04 (b), 'Report of Overland route from Lokoja to Lagos November 10 1871 to February 8 1872', by Bishop Crowther.
4 C.O. 147/23, J. A. Payne to Glover, 27 Sept. 1871, enclosure in No. 55.
5 C.M.S. G3/A2/01, Phillips to Governor, 29 Aug. 1881; Phillips to Wood, 4 Feb. 1882; Wood to Secretaries, 17 Mar. 1882.

missionaries. While the traders, all Africans, were still using the Ondo route, and while the white traders had no intention of going into the interior, the missionaries directed attention to the shorter Ijẹbu routes. To discourage this, the Ijẹbu imposed heavy exactions. In July 1889, Tunwase, the new Awujalẹ, who had ascended the throne three years before, responded favourably to the exertion of James Johnson and Otunba Payne, an Ijẹbu prince and Registrar of the Supreme Court of Lagos, and allowed an African missionary to begin work at Ijẹbu-Ode. Within two weeks of the last event European missionaries began to appear. The account of this missionary, George, and the perilous atmosphere in which he worked, is an interesting document.[1] First to appear was Thomas Harding of the C.M.S. who had just been located in Ibadan, and he brought with him Daniel Olubi, a man especially hated. After much effort to allay their fear of the ill-omen which Harding's coming was thought to presage, he was forced to pay six pounds. So inhospitable were the Ijẹbu to this missionary that they would not entertain him and would not even sell him water when he offered to pay for it.[2]

This incident should be borne in mind in order to appreciate the attitude of this missionary to the situation that arose in February 1892. He never forgot it. Nor was he the only one. The 'Joyful News', a branch of the Wesleyan Mission, allocated S. G. Pinnock and Matthews to Ibadan and Ọyọ respectively. The treatment to which they were subjected was not forgotten as late as 1917 when Pinnock put down his reminiscences.[3] In February 1890 Halligey was forced to return to Lagos, as he could not pay the fifty pounds demanded by the Ijẹbu if he wished to pass through their country. It was natural that the Ijẹbu were alarmed at this influx of European missionaries. But there was also the indiscretion of many African missionaries who added to their fears by claiming the right to use the Ijẹbu routes as representatives of the 'whiteman'.[4]

In order to ward off the danger of these Protestant missionaries, the Awujalẹ made repeated attempts between 1886 and 1890 to have the French priests of the S.M.A. established in his territory. The Alafin had spoken well of these priests whom he, the Ẹgba and the Awujalẹ, believed were preferable to the British. Time and again, the priests' records emphasized, the Ijẹbu declared that they did not want the

1 N.A. Ibadan CMS (Y) 4/1, File 10, 'The Beginning of Missionary work in Ijebu Ode 1889–1890'.
2 C.M.S. G3/A2/06, Harding to Lang, 16 Oct. 1890.
3 S. G. Pinnock: *The Romance of Missions in Nigeria*, Richmond, p. 42.
4 M.M.A., Halligey to Osborne, 7 Mar. 1889; C.M.S. G3/A2/06, Harding to Lang, 16 Oct. 1890.

British and their pathfinders, the Protestant missions. They wanted the French and Roman Catholicism.[1] It is probable that the Awujalẹ heard favourable views of the priests from the Ẹgba authorities. Hence while the Protestant missionaries were being discouraged from using the Ijẹbu route the Ijẹbu allowed the French priests to use their routes free of charge to Ọyọ.

It was during this mounting suspicion of the Protestant missionaries that Acting Governor Denton visited the Awujalẹ in April 1891. The African missionary and Tunwase were jointly accused of having sold the country to the British for £1,000.[2] There was a plot to kill the missionary who escaped at night and the invitation to the French priests was renewed. The Ijẹbu refused to discuss trade with Denton, or accept 'gifts' to which he had affixed some 'papers'. This was the 'insult' that Denton claimed had been administered to him and the British Government. Later on, it is significant to note, the *Pampas*, the commercial experts of the Ijẹbu, sent word to Denton that they were ready to discuss trade and routes with him.[3] In spite of the dubious account calculated to discredit the Ijẹbu,[4] sent to the Colonial Office, the latter was not prepared to avenge the so-called insult. A blockade might be considered, but, minuted an official, 'we don't want a little war even to clear the road'.[5] This remained the view of the Colonial Office up to the middle of March 1892.

As long as Moloney continued to administer Lagos Colony the missionaries knew that they could not plunge him into war with the

---

1 S.M.A., Chausse to Superior, 11 June, 22 July, 9 Sept., 4 Oct. and 19 Oct. 1886. He actually went to Ijẹbu-Ode and was well received.

2 N.A. Ibadan C.M.S. (Y) 4/1, File 10 cited.

3 C.O. 147/79 (private letter), Denton to Hemming, (undated).

4 Cf. the emotional detailed account by the 'Jebu Descendants' in A.P.S. papers, written by Otunba Payne, one of the people used by Carter to obtain the 'treaty': it is quite a different version. It is worth pointing out that Carter apologized to the Rev. James Johnson when the A.P.S. informed him, Carter, of the intentions of educated Africans to take legal action against him for not reporting facts correctly and for writing adversely and wrongly on James Johnson. Carter admitted that the facts in his official dispatches on the Ijẹbu Expedition were not necessarily the correct version. In fact educated Africans threatened to publish papers on the crisis that might have discredited Carter but the A.P.S. urged them not to do so since Carter had apologized. James Johnson accepted Carter's apology (not made public) but expressed regret that future historians were likely to use the official materials to his discredit, a prediction that has been fulfilled. Cf. Aderibigbe, op. cit., pp. 226–32; see also A.P.S., James Johnson to Fox Bourne, 12 Feb., 29 Aug. and 27 Dec. 1893 (apology quoted); R. B. Blaize to A.P.S., 29 Aug. 1893, forwarded money for legal action against Carter.

5 C.O. 147/80, Minute by Meade on Denton's 'ill-treatment' at Ijẹbu-Ode, Dispatch No. 202.

Ijẹbu, whom as late as 1888 he had described as 'most friendly'[1] to the Lagos Government. In fact as late as 1890 he appreciated the efforts of educated Africans led by James Johnson, who were endeavouring to enlighten the Ijẹbu on the benefit of missionary enterprise and free trade.[2] The appointment of Guilbert Thomas Carter as his successor in March 1891 was hailed by missionaries who expected a change of policy.[3] And he did not disappoint them. He had worked in various administrative capacities in West Africa since 1870 and came immediately from the Gambia. A firm believer in the forward policy, he repeatedly reiterated his view to an unyielding Colonial Office that the best way of dealing with African chiefs was to browbeat them with an escort of soldiers. He was favourably disposed to missionary enterprise, not because he was a zealous Christian himself, but because he believed, like Johnston, in their civilizing, and therefore imperial, influence. 'Missionary effort has unquestionably accomplished a good deal for Africa,'[4] wrote Carter in 1896. He was very close to missionaries, particularly to Herbert Tugwell, later Bishop, with whom he often dined.

Carter arrived in Lagos in September 1891 with the preconceived plan of smashing the Ijẹbu and Ẹgba if they continued to close their routes, in spite of a warning by the Secretary of State for the Colonies, Lord Knutsford, that he should not work for war. By January 1892, however, his hostility was concentrated on the Ijẹbu alone, although the latter did not close their routes like the Ẹgba, who fulminated that they would not open them for fifty years. Carter's hatred for the Ijẹbu stemmed from their imperviousness to British influence, as represented by missionary propaganda, their 'jujuism', slavery and addiction to human sacrifice, 'every vice a native race could have',[5] in which he believed the Ijẹbu to be pre-eminent.[6] In December 1891 when the Colonial Office reiterated emphatically that it would not sanction war, he informed missionaries that he had obtained a mandate to crush the Ijẹbu.[7] In a very bellicose speech to the Legislative Council on 27 November 1891 Carter indicated that he would not spare the sword in the cause of 'civilization'. 'I am by no means an advocate of a resort to Arms,' he said, 'but no unprejudiced mind

1   C.O. 147/63, Moloney to Holland, 21 Aug. 1888.
2   A.P.S., James Johnson to Fox Bourne, 9 May 1893.
3   C.M.S. G3/A2/06, James Vernal to Hamilton, 14 May 1891.
4   E. W. Blyden, *The Lagos Training College and Industrial Institute*, Lagos 1896, p. 5.
5   *Report of Proceedings at a Banquet . . . 1893*, p. 10.
6   C.O. 147/84, Conf. Carter to Knutsford, 18 Mar. 1892; C.O. 149/3, Minutes of Legislative Council, 14 Dec. 1891.
7   M.M.A., H. H. Richmond to Hartley, 21 Dec. 1891.

will deny that it is sometimes expedient to use it in the Interests of civilization.'[1]

In order to force the Ijẹbu to accept 'civilization' he wrote to the Awujalẹ in December to send down representatives to apologize for the 'insult' suffered by Denton and discuss routes. On 18 January 1892 the Ijẹbu sent a deputation which was given a mandate to concede the two points, apologize for the 'insult' and declare that the routes were open. The deputation was also asked to tell the Governor to bring the warring Ibadan back to Ibadan from the Offa camp. The composition of the deputation shows clearly that they were ready to discuss routes. There were four *Agurins*, four *Ogboni*, three *Pampa* and eleven *Parakoyi*, making twenty-two in all. The *Agurins* were the special and confidential advisers of the king, the *Ogboni* his principal advisers. These two classes were to satisfy the Governor on the apology issue, as the executive arm of the Ijẹbu government. The remaining fourteen members of the deputation were commercial experts. Had Carter therefore confined himself to the two issues on which he had demanded their presence an amicable settlement would have been reached. Carter assumed an unfriendly disposition from the beginning. The olive branch offered by the Ijẹbu, who presented him with ten sheep, was rejected.[2] For the occasion of receiving the deputation the Governor invited 'the principal mercantile and missionary interest of the community'[3] in Lagos. After a military parade calculated to compel the Ijẹbu to fall in line with his wishes, Carter demanded and was given apology for the 'insult'. Then, either by design or by accident, Carter gave an address the deputation did not expect. It was a bolt from the blue and constituted his entire speech. This is how he reported it to the Colonial Office:

I then proceeded to the question of the roads, briefly alluding to the past history of the question and speaking very plainly on the subject of their backwardness as compared with the neighbouring tribes. I particularly adverted to their folly in refusing to receive Missionaries in the country, and though I could not coerce them into adopting such a policy yet I strongly advised them to follow the example of those who had done so. I bade them compare the position of Lagos with that of their own country, and told them that the results which they could see with their own eyes, had not be

1 C.O. 149/3, Minutes of Legislative Council, 27 Nov. 1891.
2 J. P. Haastrup: 'Report of the Deputation of the Native Inhabitants of Lagos to Ijebu Ode', April 1892.
3 C.O. 147/84, Carter to Knutsford, 15 Jan. 1892.

[sic] achieved by the policy of isolation which they had adopted, but by liberal and advanced views, by free trade, and by the encouragement of Missionaries who established schools and endeavoured to introduce a higher standard of morality and a purer form of religion than at present existed amongst those Natives which were ignorant of the Bible.[1]

No speech could have been more shocking to the deputation. Once more the spectre of missionary propaganda, with the imagined calamities it would bring, was raised. For this they had no mandate. They became intractable, and not even at gunpoint would they touch the 'Book'—a Treaty, which, they said, was against their 'fetish'. To save face, Carter called upon two liberated Ijẹbu, Otunba Payne and Jacob Williams, a trader, to 'sign' the Treaty on their behalf, an extraordinary procedure. After this ceremony kolanut was taken, supposedly in the 'country fashion'. A copy of the 'treaty' with a gift of £20 for the king and chiefs was given to the deputation. The latter did not dare to take the 'book' to Ijẹbu. According to this so-called treaty, the Ijẹbu were to throw open all roads and rivers to all people and receive from the Lagos Government £500 annually for the loss of their tolls. It should be recalled to mind that at this time, January 1892, it was the Ẹgba, and not the Ijẹbu, who closed their routes.

The legal validity or invalidity of the 'treaty' is not relevant to this study. The point to emphasize is that the Ijẹbu saw no need for war on the two points Carter originally wanted. Since neither the trader nor the administrator had immediate interest in going into the interior, no clash arose between the traders and the Ijẹbu. The position of the missionaries was quite different. The Wesleyan missionaries, who had been attending the annual conference in Lagos, wished to take advantage of a 'treaty' which was a triumph for them over their traditional enemy. The missionaries, through a series of indiscretions, tactlessness and display of a great deal of 'the British bunting' brought about the 'breaking' of the 'treaty' in the middle of February, barely a month after it was 'signed'.

On 1 February Thomas Harding, the man who was refused water in 1890, left Lagos for Ibadan with twenty-seven carriers, landed at Itoiki, an Ijẹbu port, and left some of his loads there. According to his own account, he and his carriers were warmly received and he arranged with the king that he would send other carriers from Ibadan for his loads at Itoiki. In Ibadan he explained the 'treaty' to the Ibadan, and came to be looked upon as the saviour of Ibadan.

1   C.O. 147/84, Carter to Knutsford, 25 Jan. 1892.

The first reaction of the latter was to subject the Ijẹbu in Ibadan to indignities.[1] For the Ibadan had many grievances against the Ijẹbu. Since 1883 the Ijẹbu had been oppressing the Ibadan by various exactions, because the latter depended upon them for salt, and particularly for the supply of ammunition with which Ibadan was carrying on the war with Ilọrin at Ọffa. On Harding's evidence, the Ijẹbu exploited the extremities of the Ibadan to the full. The Ijẹbu collected tolls at the Ibadan gates leading to Ijẹbu, and bought articles at their own price. Also no judgment could be given against any Ijẹbu in Ibadan whatever his crime. This latent Ijẹbu-Ibadan animosity—which still persists—was of vital importance in determining the events leading to the Ijẹbu expedition.

The latent anti-Ijẹbu hostility explains the wild reaction of the Ibadan to the 'treaty'. On 9 February, in place of the twenty-seven carriers Harding had taken to Ibadan, the missionary sent additional Ibadan carriers and a few traders took the advantage of joining the mission labourers to use the route. On getting to Ijẹbu territory these mission labourers began to deride the Ijẹbu, declaring that the road was now the white man's and theirs, the Ibadans'. To this insult they added larceny and enslavement of Ijẹbu.[2] All this Harding did not report to the Lagos Government but he painted the Ibadan carriers as innocent and ill-used people.[3] Nor did he report the anti-Ijẹbu atrocities to the Governor. Had he reported all this to Carter, and had the Colonial Office been told all the facts, it is plain that the alleged breaking of the 'treaty' by the Ijẹbu would have been excused by a consideration of extenuating circumstances. Naturally, the Ijẹbu retaliated by beating up the wild mission labourers. The physical punishment suffered by these labourers was described in the worst possible phraseology, and an appeal was made to the Government to clear up the difficulties that had arisen. Had the 'treaty' not been made, said Harding, he would not have used the Ijẹbu route.

But even then the Ijẹbu had not broken the 'treaty', and they exercised forbearance to an astonishing degree. All that was necessary, according to the 'treaty', was for both the Lagos Government and Ijẹbu each to appoint an arbitrator to investigate the cause of the incident of 9 February. In the temporary absence of Carter at Ondo, Denton announced his intention of doing this. Before he could do so, however, the missionaries rendered any such course of action impossible. Tugwell, a highly temperamental man, who had hailed

1 C.M.S. G3/A2/06; Harding to Lang, 11 Apr. 1892; Harding to Wigram, 8 June 1892.
2 Ibid. Journal of M. D. Coker for 1892; J. P. Haastrup, op. cit.
3 C.O. 806/375, enclosure 2 in No. 39, T. Harding to Governor, 13 Feb. 1892.

the 'treaty' with extraordinary delight and had called upon Salisbury Square to send missionaries for Ijẹbuland at once, felt it his duty to go to Ijẹbu-Ode on 15 February to find out what had happened to the mission labourers. His behaviour was outrageous. On getting to the gate he would not allow the gateman to announce his coming to the Awujalẹ, a measure necessary in order that he might be well received and arrangement for his lodging made. Tugwell dashed through the gate, having pushed the gateman aside. This action, said Tugwell later, was justifiable according to the 'treaty'.[1] In Yoruba tradition Tugwell's action was a gross insult to the Awujalẹ and the Ijẹbu people. When he was led to the town, he refused to pass through the king's officials as was customary, but insisted on seeing the king directly and at once. Even then the Ijẹbu bore patiently with him. They offered to carry Harding's loads to Oru, the northern boundary of the Ijẹbu country, whence the Ibadan could take the loads from them. They also offered Tugwell passage to Ibadan if he wished. Tugwell's answer to all this generosity was to go into the streets and begin preaching.[2] It was all these acts of indiscretion that aroused the young men, who hooted him, but allowed him to escape unhurt.

Carter was the last man to miss the opportunity given by the alleged ill-treatment of missionaries by the Ijẹbu. Denton had quickly forwarded the inaccurate reports of the missionaries to the Colonial Office. On the dispatch enclosing the reports of the missionaries Lord Knutsford, who had hitherto remained unresponsive to the anti-Ẹgba wishes of the merchants championed by Hemming, a Colonial Office official, minuted, 'This affords sufficient ground for attacking the Jebus.'[3] It was not until now that Carter received a mandate to employ physical force against the Ijẹbu.

The commercial explanation that has been offered for the Ijẹbu expedition requires further modification. The Lagos Chamber of Commerce, which consisted of the main trading concerns in Lagos, did not, as a body, advocate the use of force by the Government.[4] In its correspondence with the Government it specifically asserted its faith in the sanctity of the independence of the various Yoruba states and made no complaints whatsoever against the existing trade pattern. The Chamber declared in unequivocal terms that all that its members wished the Governor to do was to undertake a goodwill

1 C.M.S. G3/A2/012, Bishop Tugwell to Baylis, 22 July 1905.
2 C.O. 806/357, enclosure in No. 151, James Johnson to A.P.S., 30 May 1893.
3 C.O. 147/84, Minute on Denton to Knutsford, 20 Feb. 1892.
4 C.O. 147/79, Lagos Chamber of Commerce to Denton, 27 Jan. 1891, enclosure 1 in Denton to Knutsford, 7 Feb. 1891.

tour of the interior which would regenerate friendliness towards the British and thereby improve the relations between those states and the Colony of Lagos. And although some of the European members, in their capacity as individuals, favoured military subjugation of the Ijẹbu by 'Christian England', it should be noted that their view was not expressed through the Chamber. This was probably due to the fact that African merchants constituted the most powerful group, numerically, in the Chamber and their disapproval of the belligerent attitude of the Lagos Government to the interior states was undisguised. Among the sixteen African members of the Chamber were C. B. Moore, an Ẹgba patriot and treasurer of the Chamber, R. B. Blaize, the founder of the *Lagos Times*, J. B. Benjamin, editor of the radical and anti-imperialist *Lagos Observer*, J. P. Haastrup, an Ijẹbu patriot, who wrote a pamphlet against the expedition, and J. S. Leigh, an Ẹgba patriot whom Carter accused of encouraging the intransigence of the Ẹgba to the Lagos Government.

It is clear from the documents that the European traders were more anxious about the Ẹgba than about the Ijẹbu routes. They had asked Carter to annex Iganmu and Ishẹri, two strategic points on the commercial route of the Ẹgba, to neutralize the closure of the Ẹgba routes. In February Denton reported that the Lagos merchants were badly hit by the closure of the Ẹgba routes,[1] and Frederick Osbourne, Secretary of the Chamber, cabled to Liverpool, 'Abẹokuta roads closed, trade stopped, see Secretary of State'.[2] Long after the Ijẹbu roads were closed, the merchants in Britain were unrelenting in their demand that the Ẹgba be forced to open their routes, the word 'Ijẹbu' hardly occurring.[3] At a meeting in Liverpool, in which representatives of Manchester, Glasgow and Liverpool, including A. L. Jones of the shipping interest, were represented, it was resolved that Abẹokuta should be annexed under the pious excuse of setting slaves free.[4] Echoing the desire of the merchants, Hemming saw Abẹokuta as the criminal who should be taught a lesson: 'It would I venture to think, be better to "take the bull by the horns" and settle the question once and for all by the subjugation of Abẹokuta. It is a nest of slave dealers and intriguers, and it would be well to break it up.'[5]

For reasons which are not clear from the records—perhaps they were inclined to the missionary view—Meade and Lord Knutsford

1 C.O. 147/84, Denton to Sir Augustus, 13 Feb. 1892.
2 Ibid. Denton to Knutsford, 16 Feb. 1892.
3 *Manchester Guardian*, 19 Feb. 1892.
4 *The Liverpool Courier*, 9 Mar. 1892.
5 C.O. 147/84, Minute paper by Hemming, 14 Mar. 1892.

considered views favourable to the missionaries. On the same dispatch from the merchants they minuted that the Egba had never acknowledged British supremacy, therefore they should be left alone to exact tolls as middlemen. They then asked Carter for trade statistics, which he did not possess. The case of the Ijębu, they contended, was different because they had broken the so-called treaty.[1] In vain did the merchants protest for more than five months after the expedition against the Ijębu that it was the Egba they had wanted crushed. As early as February, Carter had decided that the Egba would not be attacked. As has been mentioned, he knew the influence of the Protestant party there and was in communication with Wood, the dispenser of Egba security.[2] The issue that was really at stake was that British influence, in the form of missionary propaganda, was already strong in one state and completely absent from the other. The latter therefore were assumed to be at fault. Economic considerations were neither looked into nor given priority. Indeed Carter never defended his action on economic grounds but time and again posed as an apostle of humanitarianism. It is significant that he told the Liverpool Chamber of Commerce in 1893 that the real reason why the Ijębu did not want any treaty was not economic, and had nothing to do with routes *per se*, but fear of an end to slavery.[3] Carter's apologetic argument later on, to justify his decision not to attack the Egba, was that the Egba would be the only losers economically as trade would be diverted to the new routes in the Ijębu country. Carter admitted that the surrender of the Egba was only a question of time; that the Protestant party was already strong there, and that all the Egba authorities were doing was to save face.

The European missionaries accepted responsibility for the war. On the other hand African missionaries were torn between their loyalty to missionary propaganda and their African nationalist sentiments, and found it very difficult to reconcile the two. Educated Africans had no doubt that the missionaries were responsible for what they described as an '*unrighteous war*'[4] and regretted the missionaries' mood for 'bloodshed rather than conciliation'. Anti-white feelings, already exacerbated by the pro-Crowther 'rebellion' (discussed in chapter 7) were further accentuated. An American missionary reported home, 'The missionary is always blamed for troubles that

1 Ibid.
2 C.M.S. G3/A2/06, Wood to Lang, 17 June 1892; Tugwell to Fenn, 31 Aug. 1891 (showed Wood's letter to Governor); C.O. 147/84, Carter to Knutsford, 3 Feb. 1892.
3 *Report of Proceedings at a Banquet . . . 1893* cited.
4 A.P.S., 'Jebu Matters', cited.

lead to great reforms, whether social or political. While I was addressing an audience at the anniversary meetings of the native Baptist
Church week before the last, I was hissed, scoffed at and almost sworn
at.'[1] The mood and expectation of the missionaries on the eve of the
expedition was well summed up by the same missionary, C. C.
Newton:

> There is strong opposition on the part of many in Lagos to
> England's invading the interior. . . . Thousands of slaves will
> rejoice to see the Union Jack waving above their masters' heads
> and their own country proclaimed free. . . . *War is often a means of
> opening a door for the gospel to enter a country. A sword of steel often goes
> before a sword of the spirit.* The landing of troops here now may be
> part of the divine plan for answering our prayers and opening
> Ijẹbu and other interior countries to the gospel.[2]

The missionaries provided the reason why they brought about the
missionary war. They had observed that, of all the coastal tribes they
knew, the Ijẹbu were the most intelligent, the most industrious and
the shrewdest. If converted, they believed, they would become the
spearhead of missionary propaganda in the rest of the country. Their
observation was quite correct. Africans of Ijẹbu origin in the Wesleyan and C.M.S. missions were the best stock they had. There was,
for instance, James Johnson, who enjoyed the reputation of being the
best Christian in West Africa, and whose zeal for evangelization
throughout the period was unequalled. The Methodist Mission
boasted of J. P. Haastrup and Bickersteth, and there were lay leaders
like Otunba Payne and Turner. Commenting on the so-called treaty,
Tugwell wrote,

> The Ijẹbu people are said to possess many sterling qualities and
> where members of their tribe have been converted they have shown
> a missionary spirit: is it possible that this people who like Saul have
> hitherto persecuted the people of God in times past are eventually
> to preach the faith which once they destroyed. Why not? May God
> give us faith to believe it shall be so.[3]

At the end of February the Ijẹbu closed their roads and more and
more missionaries were turned back. The Wesleyan Mission agents,
who had come to Lagos for their annual conference, were stranded.
The Ijẹbu made the last bid to have missionaries expelled from the
interior. They sent to Ibadan to say that they would not supply them

1 C. C. Newton to Tupper 12 Apr. 1892, in *Foreign Mission Journal*, Vol. xxiii,
   July 1892.
2 Ibid. (italics are mine).
3 C.M.S. G3/A2/o6, Tugwell to Lang, 22 Jan. 1892.

with ammunition and salt any longer until they, the Ibadan, should have decapitated both Harding and Olubi.[1] On 12 May, soldiers composed of Hausas and troops from the Gold Coast, numbering less than 500, left Lagos and by 9 May the Ijẹbu were defeated after an unexpected stiff resistance.

During the years that followed the Ijẹbu Expedition was fraught with more consequences for the missionaries than for the traders and administrators. The Ijẹbu territory became the most important missionary field for all Christian missions, at the expense of the rest of Yorubaland. Among these conquered people they found a spontaneous response not found anywhere else in Nigeria, except in Brass from 1874 to 1886. This was due partly to the disappointment the Ijẹbu suffered from their juju. Before the expedition they were buoyed up with the hope that a most powerful deity was fighting on their side, and were reported to have sacrificed 200 men and women to propitiate it.[2] Then there was the question of the 'divine' king who was now superseded by military administrators. Until now it was commonly believed that the Awujalẹ was so sacred that to mention his name was to incur disaster. It was natural that now that maxims and seven pounders had exploded the myth of his supernatural powers, and now that the Ogboni House was destroyed, the vacuum created in the spiritual life of a deeply religious people should be filled with the religion of the conquerors. This was the explanation of the curiosity of the people to know the secret of the white man's power, which they felt was contained in his religion. By 1900 there were over 7,000 adherents in Ijẹbu territory.

The Ijẹbu expedition added a wholesome fear of the British Government to the respect which the far interior chiefs had already for it as a result of the peace efforts of the missionaries in the civil war. So fearful were the Ibadan and Ilọrin who were still fighting that they had actually started to decamp before Carter finally separated them early in 1893. In Ondo immolation and the annual human sacrifice to the *Oramafe* god came to an end immediately. British sovereignty was accepted automatically. The chiefs were henceforward afraid of all people supposed to be connected with the Lagos Government—educated Africans, missionaries, soldiers, in fact all who had some pretension to learning. Travelling Commissioners were posted in Ilesha, Ondo, Ibadan and Odo Ọtin. These formed all the administrative machinery set up by the Lagos Government in a vast territory.

But it was among the Ijẹbu and the Ẹgba that missionary propa-

1 Ibid. Harding to Lang, 11 Apr. 1892.
2 C.O. 147/85, Carter to Knutsford, 20 June 1892.

ganda produced the greatest effects. Statistically, Ijẹbu territory became the centre of missionary activity, superseding Abẹokuta in 1900. Politically the power of the Awujalẹ and chiefs was considerably reduced, and a more direct form of administration was established than at any other place in Yorubaland outside Lagos. Among the Ẹgba the political revolution, noted up to 1891, continued. The Alake and his chiefs saw that discretion was the better part of valour, and in effect gradually allowed the educated Africans to assume a preponderance out of proportion to their numerical strength. In a way they appreciated at last that the silent revolution that had occurred by their patronizing of missionary propaganda paid after all. The Ẹgba were allowed to retain a great deal of independence. It was better to be guided by their own children, educated Africans, than to be ruled directly by administrative officers, as was the case in Ijẹbuland. From 1898, when the Lagos Government created the Ẹgba United Government, Ẹgba administration came to be run on 'Christian' lines, either missionaries or ardent Christian laymen naturally taking control. In 1902 the Secretaryship of the Ẹgba United Government fell to the Reverend J. H. Samuel, better known as Adegboyega Ẹdun; C. B. Moore, son of an African minister and the wealthiest Ẹgba layman, became Treasurer whilst the highest judicial authority was held no longer by the Ogbonis or the Alake but by a Christian, J. Martin. It was a reflection of the revolution that had occurred in Abẹokuta that the Rev. D. O. Williams became the 'Prime Minister' of the Alake between 1898 and 1911.

In fact Ẹgba monarchy could not resist the onslaught of British influence, as represented by missionary propaganda. For the first time since the inception of Christianity in Ẹgbaland an Alake, Gbadebọ, attended church in 1900 at the opening of the Townsend–Wood Memorial church, and henceforward became a regular church-goer. In doing this he cast to the wind the tradition that his face must not be seen by his brother chiefs, and still less by the common people. Instead of consulting the traditional priests at times of drought or illness, the Alake supplicated to the white man's God at St Peter's, kneeling before the altar. In imitation of the British monarchy, he had a chaplain. He became patron of the African Church, and found it necessary to know the white man's country, which he visited in 1904. He was received by King Edward VII and offered the gift of a Bible. Naturally he went to Salisbury Square, was received by the Parent Committee, and expressed immense gratitude to the C.M.S. for the progress its missionaries had brought to his country. Well did he become, in the eyes of the Lagos Governors, the ideal ruler in West Africa!

Car s'il est vrai de dire que souvent le missionaire precède le
commerçant et le soldat; il faut aussi reconnaître que bien souvent
les efforts du premier resteraient sterile si Dieu dans ses aimes
providentielles, n'avait pas armé la main de l'homme de guerre.

Father Zappa,
S.A.M. missionary in Asaba

3 The Missions and 'Southern' Nigerian Politics and Society, 1875–1900

Social life, trade and politics in the Niger Delta, which towards the end of the century came to be designated as 'Southern Nigeria', were closely bound up with missionary enterprise in the last four decades of the nineteenth century. Whereas in the interior of Yorubaland more than forty years elapsed before missionary propaganda became a decisive political force, Christianity in the mangrove-ridden, easily accessible city-states of Brass, Bonny, Okrika and New Calabar, became an explosive force within five years of its establishment in Bonny in 1864, Brass in 1868, New Calabar in 1874 and Okrika in 1880. In absolute ignorance of the implications of what missionary enterprise meant politically, these city-states displayed an astonishing eagerness in their desire to have Christian missions. Unlike anywhere else in Nigeria during this period they bore half the initial expenses of mission establishment as a necessary price for the privilege of having missionaries. Their enthusiasm did not spring from desire for a new spiritual dispensation, but from the hope that their commercial positions would be improved through the education of their children. The one man who discerned from the beginning the palpable danger of Christian missions to the social and political heritage of Southern Nigeria, and who spared no efforts to destroy the new-fangled faith, was Jaja, the greatest political figure in the Bights of Benin and Biafra in the period under survey. And it is for this reason that most of this chapter deals with him.

The city-state of Bonny, which was the scene of much political disturbance in the nineteenth century,[1] came also to be the state in which missionary activity produced the greatest political and social effects. The establishment of missionary work in Old Calabar awakened the jealousy of King William Pepple, ruler of Bonny from 1835 to 1867, as early as 1848 when he approached the United Presbyterian Mission Board in Edinburgh. He and his chiefs offered to pay all educational expenses of missionary activity in their king-

[1] Fully discussed in K. O. Dike, op. cit.

dom for twenty years.[1] The king renewed the approach in 1849 and 1860, offering in the latter year an additional inducement of an annual salary of £500 for the upkeep of a missionary. It is significant to note that, apart from the alleged unhealthy climate of Bonny, the United Presbyterian Mission Board spurned Bonny's offer because the Bonny chiefs could not accept the Mission's condition that they should destroy *ikuba*,[2] the tribal temple, the grotesque but most prominent feature of Bonny, with its carefully arranged, painted and decorated bones of human enemies.

All further effort by King William Pepple to attract missionaries to his kingdom failed until, in 1864, Samuel Ajayi Crowther, the liberated Yoruba who had started the Niger Mission in 1857, accepted the king's invitation. From its inception the missionary factor was a strong element in the maelstrom of Bonny politics and was partly responsible for the Bonny civil war of 1869 to 1873. According to the Manilla Pepple faction it was not merely a war against Jaja's political ambitions but was as well a war on behalf of Christianity against the tribal religion with which the Annie Pepples, Jaja's faction, were uncompromisingly identified.[3] Also, on the evidence of Edward Fitzgerald, editor of *African Times* and the 'Representative' of the kingdom of Bonny in London, the 'real cause' of Jaja's decision to leave Bonny was his hatred for missionary propaganda.[4] Evidence shows clearly that whatever the political rivalry between the two factions before 1864, the introduction of the missionary widened the rift between them and accentuated the political tensions. It strengthened the forces with which Jaja would have to contend if he was to gain political ascendancy in Bonny. Leagued against his faction were not only the missionaries, but the pro-missionary traders and the 'converted' Manilla Pepple faction. Faced with these formidable forces Jaja should have realized that he could not achieve supremacy in Bonny politics, that he could not successfully imitate the tactics of the ex-slave Alali.[5]

For the Manilla Pepples, not yet aware of the potentially subversive effects of missionary activity on their social order, embraced Christianity, at least outwardly, with extraordinary zest between 1867 and 1870. The most enthusiastic acolyte of the missionaries was wealthy Oko Jumbo, Jaja's strongest and bitterest enemy. He was the first to learn reading and writing, took the Bible to the Qua Ibo river,

1 U.P. Minutes, 7 Nov. 1848, 6 Mar. 1849 and 2 Oct. 1860.
2 Hope Waddell: *Journals*, 26 Dec. 1849.
3 C.M.S. CA3/010 W. E. Carew, *Journals*, 15 Sept. 1869.
4 *African Times*, 29 Apr. 1873.
5 For details of ex-slave Alali's role in Bonny politics, cf. Dike, op. cit.

Bonny's chief oil market, and indicated that he would not object to Christianity spreading there.[1] He put thirteen children in the boarding school at once at a cost of £156 a year and erected the church bell at his own expense. Oko Jumbo became an ardent reformer, announced an end to twin murder in 1868 and supervised the slaughtering of the iguanas,[2] the big lizard which was the animal totem of Bonny. Within two years *ikuba* was already being neglected by the majority of the people.

But Jaja clung steadfastly to *ikuba* of which he was the high priest.[3] He had refused to sign the letter of invitation to Bishop Crowther in 1864.[4] At first he toyed with the new learning, but soon gave it up and refused to put any child in school. He was dismayed by the desertion of the temple, which he rebuilt to make it superior to the church and school building. He replaced the wooden stands with iron stanchions and covered the sides and roof with corrugated iron sheets in place of bamboo. He collected the scattered bones of war victims, carefully rearranged them and erected a new platform for new accretions.[5] Not even the serious illness that prostrated him in June 1868 could make him respond to missionary appeal. Sleeping under three chickens suspended from the roof with heads downwards, four of his lieutenants propitiated the gods by sacrificing human beings, goats and fowls. He frankly told the missionary (who warned him that it was his adherence to a 'false' faith that brought about the illness) that his, Jaja's, theology was not unsound, for he believed in the Supreme Being who ordained human destiny.[6]

It was not therefore by accident that chief priest Jaja chose a Sunday, 12 September 1869, to challenge the Manilla Pepples to begin fighting, an invitation which the latter, being 'Christians', refused until the following day.[7] It was not an accident either that Jaja's greatest grievance against his enemies was the cold-blooded murder of his women and children by the Manilla Pepples in the 'Sacred Juju Town' in the kingdom of Bonny.[8] Added to his aversion to missionary enterprise was the strong support which the missionaries naturally gave to the Manilla Pepples by offering their women and children protection in the Mission House, while Jaja's own

1 C.M.S. CA3/o10, W. E. Carew: *Journals*, 3 June 1868.
2 Ibid. 20 June 1868.
3 C.M.S. CA3/o4 (a), Bishop Crowther to Venn, 27 Feb. 1867.
4 C.M.S. CA3/o2, D. C. Crowther to Wigram, 10 May 1883.
5 C.M.S. CA3/o4 (a), Bishop Crowther to Venn, 27 Feb. 1867.
6 C.M.S. CA3/o10, W. E. Carew: *Journals*, 21 June 1868; quotes Jaja, 'true; He do anything he likes and no man fit ask Him what thing He do'.
7 F.O. 84/1308, Livingstone to Stanley, 26 Oct. 1869.
8 F.O. 84/1326, Livingstone to Clarendon, 6 June 1870.

people were slaughtered mercilessly for lack of such protection. It is nothing to wonder at then that once he escaped from Bonny he determined to exclude missionaries from his territory at all cost. Bishop Crowther, who on one occasion deliberately and publicly ridiculed Bonny's religion and *ikuba*, became the enemy of Jaja, whom he described as 'a bad man'.[1]

Although Oko Jumbo was the most important figure of the Manilla Pepples, he and all the other chiefs rallied round their anglicized king, George Pepple I, who had ascended the Bonny throne in 1867, with whom they shared the same political and religious aspirations.[2] They looked to the Consul, Charles Livingstone, brother to the famous missionary-explorer, to view Bonny politics in terms of Christianity in their contest with Jaja, a view countenanced by both the English traders and the Foreign Office.[3] To the Earl of Granville, Secretary for Foreign Affairs, and to the English public, George Pepple was a beacon of light and hope for Southern Nigeria because of his education and the cause of missions he championed. In Lord Granville's words, he was an 'intelligent and well-disposed chief',[4] while his English admirers made him a gift of a steamer in 1878.

But, although he had travelled with his brother for six years, Consul Livingstone did not, surprisingly, believe in his brother's programme of Africa's regeneration by missionary propaganda.[5] In all the disputes that arose throughout the Niger Delta between missionaries with their acolytes and the religious traditionalists, the Consul gave decision in favour of the latter. For instance in 1873 the part of Duke Town in Old Calabar known as Henshaw Town, the most responsive to missionary teaching, formed the *Young Calabar*, mentioned in Chapter One. On the surface their programme was purely social and religious. It consisted of casting off the tribal religion, *en masse* acceptance of Christianity, and adoption of European clothing. In a society like the Efik's where religion could not be separated from politics, this programme implied political independence of Duke Town. Moreover the missionaries encouraged Henshaw Town's aspirations and one of them took part in the coronation of an independent king for the 'town'. Duke Town authorities, the diehard 'pagans', sought to nullify all this by using *Egbo*, a kind of free-

1 F.O. 84/1377, Livingstone to Granville, 13 Mar. 1873.
2 F.O. 84/1356, Address presented to King George Pepple by Bonny chiefs on 21 May 1870 enclosed in enclosure 2 in Livingstone to Granville, 6 Aug. 1872.
3 F.O. 84/1326, Earl of Clarendon to Livingstone, 8 Apr. and 13 May 1870.
4 F.O. 84/1356, Granville to Livingstone, 18 Sept. 1872.
5 F.O. 84/1343, Livingstone to Vivian, 12 July 1871.

masonry with 'pagan' rituals. Livingstone reversed all that the missionaries had done, backed up Duke Town and emphasized to the Foreign Office the virtues of *Egbo*.[1] Five years later a pro-missionary consul, Hopkins, approved the programme of *Young Calabar*.

Moreover Livingstone was not impressed by the results of missionary enterprise in Bonny. In his opinion Bonny was the most intractable of all the city-states; its men were 'thorough liars' and he would rejoice at its complete destruction.[2] It is not astonishing that he was annoyed that Bonny refused to submit its dispute with New Calabar, a state about twenty-five miles north-west of Bonny, over the Obiabutu markets to the arbitration of the *Long Juju* in 1867.[3] He loved to stress Jaja's addiction to juju to explain his methods of settling the dispute between Bonny and Opobo. Hence Bonny's representatives had to take the humiliation of going to Opobo, and not vice-versa, because Jaja had made a vow to the god of the *Iguana* that he would never cross Opobo waters,[4] the very reason why he could not go to England in the crisis of 1886 to 1887; Jaja refused to be summoned to the Consul's boat for a meeting because it would take a long time to perform the necessary rituals to the gods before he could enter any boat.[5]

But, his anti-Bonny feelings apart, Livingstone could not have been unaffected by the tactics of Jaja, who, though unlettered, had plenty of common sense. He knew that he needed the Consul's help in order to break away from Bonny and so he did not fly in the Consul's face until he was securely established in Opobo. He committed himself to Livingstone whom he flattered profusely, on one occasion calling him 'my father'.[6] On the other hand George Pepple was tactless. His education was in a way an inhibition, making him presumptuous and without fear and much of the respect for the Consul displayed by the unlettered docile kings of the Niger Delta. He was imbued with the idea that ultimate power did not rest with the man on the spot but with the Foreign Office, with which he had contact through Liverpool and London, a thing reprehensible to Livingstone.[7] In fact there was acrimonious correspondence between George Pepple and Livingstone. The latter had to swallow the bitter pill of being severely reprimanded by the Foreign Office who instructed him to forward

1 F.O. 84/1377, Livingstone to Granville, 7 Jan. 1873.
2 Ibid. Livingstone to Granville, 2 and 17 Apr. 1873.
3 F.O. 84/1277, Livingstone to Stanley, 24 Dec. 1867.
4 F.O. 84/1377, Livingstone to Granville, 7 Jan. 1873.
5 F.O. 84/1326, Livingstone to Clarendon, 6 June 1870.
6 F.O. 84/1326, Jaja to Livingstone, 15 Feb. 1870, enclosed in Livingstone to Clarendon, 17 Apr. 1873.
7 F.O. 84/1377, Livingstone to Granville, 28 June 1873.

every letter by the favourite king (so that the latter's view might be known directly) and deal with him 'courteously on all occasions'.[1] Livingstone was in a great measure responsible for the successful rebellion of Jaja. He had done a great deal of harm to Bonny before the Foreign Office noticed that 'the Consul must be suffering from his head'[2] and therefore dismissed him. He refused to allow Bonny to blockade Jaja at a time it was in a position to drive victory home; he sided with the two firms of George Miller and de Cardi, who supplied arms to Jaja, against the eight English firms in Bonny, and against the explicit instructions of the Foreign Office;[3] he allowed Jaja to confiscate about £30,000 worth of oil palm in the interior markets;[4] he countenanced the erection of barricades by Jaja on the Bonny creeks that led to the oil markets, and he sought to divert what remained of Bonny's trade to New Calabar.[5] Livingstone deliberately misrepresented George Pepple I to the Foreign Office and sowed seeds of discord between the king and his chiefs when the former went to England to represent Bonny's interest to the British Government.[6] Then he drew up the famous Treaty of January 1873 which was to cause so much trouble to Britain in the eighties, giving most of the markets to Jaja and some fictitious markets to Bonny. The necessity to redress the balance which had been too much tipped in Jaja's favour was the main theme of the Niger Delta's politics until the removal of Jaja in 1887.

Consequently by 1875 Jaja was already paramount in the Niger Delta politics. Strongly entrenched in Opobo, he had put his house in order, it is said, by putting to death with the aid of juju all the heads of the Houses who had followed him to his new state.[7] Livingstone's successor, G. Hartley, found him already 'insolent',[8] having no more respect for consular authority and breaking with impunity the Treaty of 1873.[9] He was showing the European merchants that he was their master. He gave them a spot five miles away from Opobo township, taxed them as he wished and gave them stringent

1 F.O. 84/1356, Minute by Granville, 27 Sept. 1872.
2 F.O. 84/1377, Minute by Granville, 27 July 1873, on Livingstone to Granville, 10 June 1873.
3 Ibid. Livingstone to Granville, 16 June 1873.
4 F.O. 84/1343, Hopkins to Granville, 6 Nov. 1871.
5 F.O. 84/1377, Livingstone to Granville, 16 Aug. 1873.
6 F.O. 84/1326, Livingstone to Clarendon, 24 Mar. 1870.
7 F.O. 84/1343, Hopkins to Granville, 27 Nov. 1871, enclosed Oko Epelle's evidence. Epelle was a chief.
8 F.O. 84/1418, Hartley to Derby, 10 Apr. 1875.
9 Ibid. Hartley to Granville, 20 Feb. 1875; Hartley to Derby, 22 Oct. 1875.

rules that no one should stay overnight in Opobo township,[1] lest indigenous morality and social order be upset. He was already in full control of all important markets, seizing by his suitable geographical position the Qua Ibo markets which by a treaty of 2 December 1826 had pledged to sell their oil to Bonny alone. To show his complete mastery of the situation he made it clear to the European traders that he did not need their opinion or advice on anything, because he did not trust the 'soundness of their advice'.[2]

It is essential to go into some detail about the two contrasting actors in the political drama in the years under investigation—George Pepple I and Jaja—and examine their aspirations and programme for the Niger Delta which they both strove to dominate. One would not wish, Carlyle-fashion, to paint either of them as a hero, but present them as the records indicate. Both believed that they were working in the best interest of the Niger Delta peoples, the one as an unbending exponent of Christianity, the other as its relentless enemy and a diehard protagonist of indigenous religion. In the long run events showed that Pepple was more farsighted than Jaja. Aided by his education in Britain, Pepple was aware of the immense power of that country, a power which he believed would support the consuls in their pro-missionary efforts. He also believed that it would be folly to resist such a powerful force as missionary propaganda. Moreover, convinced of the material progress that missionary endeavour would bring to the Niger Delta, Pepple felt that the Delta peoples should thankfully welcome missionaries.

Jaja on the other hand did not travel outside the Niger Delta. Consequently he was ignorant of world trends and obscurantishly local in his mental horizon. Having become the most powerful ruler in the Bights of Benin and Biafra, he was ignorant of the military power of Britain. Determined on preserving indigenous religion and institutions at all costs, even when events began to show that he was resisting the irresistible, he spared no effort to oppose the Christianization of the Niger Delta.

George Pepple I had the purest royal blood in his veins, as the direct descendant of the founder and first king of Bonny kingdom 'and all its dependencies'. He had been educated in England for eight years and became a diehard convert to Christianity and European civilization, the trinity of the C's defined by him as 'that civilization, that commerce and that christianity which I should like to see diffused among my subjects'.[3] Except for polygamy and the

1 *Primitive Methodist Missionary Records*, 1892, pp. 623–6.
2 F.O. 84/1455, McKellar to Derby, 18 Jan. 1876.
3 Appendix 'K' in the *Fombo Collections* in History Department, Ibadan. Address by George Pepple to the city of London School Committee, 26 July 1878.

divine aura of his family, he saw nothing worth preserving in the customs and institutions of Bonny. He found himself more at home in Britain where he was greatly admired for his erudition and after-dinner speeches, and was once received by the Prince of Wales. The Lord Mayor of London was his 'special friend'.[1] Like Europeans who did not find the lethal climate of the Niger Delta congenial to their health, George loved to recoup his health on the seas and in Madeira,[2] thus defying the traditional Bonny custom that no king should travel beyond Bonny waters. He purged *Owu Ogbo*, a secret society, of all heathenism, reducing it to no more than a 'Play Club'.[3] He refused to take oaths or perform rites incompatible with his adopted faith. The extent of his anglicization was exemplified in his reading of *The Times* regularly, his adoption of a London-tailored suit and gumming of his moustaches to a fine point. A contemporary friend recorded that he 'smokes cigarettes, scents his handkerchiefs with the newest essence, dilates on the acting of Ellen Terry and Irving, and criticizes the comic operas of Gilbert and Sullivan'.[4]

In the view of the traditional chiefs, George's obsession with Christianity entailed grave political and social consequences for Bonny in the seventies and eighties. For he sought to replace the constitution which rested on indigenous religion, with the chiefs as partners in the government of the country, with a 'Christian' constitution in which the traditionalist chiefs would have no place. In fact he appealed to the chiefs to be modernist enough to sanction the establishment of an 'assembly' for Bonny.[5] He saw the hope of the implementation of his ideal constitution in the 'rising generation', the schoolboys, for the 'promotion of Christianity and Civilization in our benighted country'.[6] The Bonny constitution and laws, as they were when he ascended the throne in 1867, were socially and ethically unjust because of the distinctions between slaves and free-men; therefore he was determined 'to give to Bonny equal laws and a just constitution', fight for 'Truth and Right', and secure complete emancipation for the slaves.[7] He and other members of his family were not ordinary members of the Church. He was a Sunday School teacher and was appointed in 1881 to the Finance Committee of the Niger Mission. For political advice he found it more natural to

1 C.M.S. CA3/04 (b), Address to him by Bonny school-children, 1 Jan. 1879.
2 Ibid. J. Boyle to Bishop Crowther, 14 Oct. 1879.
3 *The Niger Delta Chronicle*, 1897, pp. 27–36.
4 F.O. 84/1828, Johnston to Salisbury, 24–8 Sept. 1887.
5 *Fombo Collections* Appendix 'M', letter by George Pepple to his chiefs dated 7 Dec. 1881.
6 C.M.S. CA3/04 (b), Reply to Bonny schoolboys' address, 1 Jan. 1879.
7 Ibid.

depend on the missionaries than on the 'pagan' chiefs who were, in his view, discredited by relapsing to undiluted 'paganism', refusing to be 'civilized' after 1870.

The strong opposition to the Christianizing policy of George Pepple I by his chiefs between 1870 and 1884 notwithstanding, Pepple did not see himself as an enemy of Bonny and Southern Nigeria. Like the other educated Africans of his age he believed that the political and social progress of Southern Nigeria lay in the Christianization of the territory. In 1875 he asked that nut-cracking machines be introduced into Bonny. Of all the nineteenth-century Nigerian potentates Pepple I was the only one who accepted the social and spiritual side of missionary enterprise as a thing good in itself. In this sense he was unique, and he showed himself a modernizing man who wanted to bring his people into the modern age of a new egalitarian Nigeria. Moreover George knew from the beginning what the Egba only learned by experience—that patronage of missionaries had political and economic advantages; that a people who accepted missionaries could hardly incur Britain's displeasure in the era of pacification. As will be shown presently the Bonny chiefs by 1886 had come to agree with Pepple I, that missionary enterprise could be of decisive political and economic advantage to their territory.

Jaja on the other hand rose from the lowest social levels. He was a bought slave of the Annie Pepple family of Bonny. By his industry and ability, he gradually moved up, became very wealthy, was selected head of the House that bought him, and by 1869 was aiming at the seizure of political power.[1] He was, as has been noted, traditionalist to the marrow as far as the vital institutions of the Delta society were concerned. Convinced that indigenous religion was the cement of the African society he stuck to it and was thus in Opobo both the spiritual and secular head of the state, the only monarch in the Niger Delta to combine the two posts. Jaja's attachment to juju must be seen in the context of the traditional African society. Scholars of African religion and anthropologists are agreed on the fact that religion is central to the life of the Africans. It hedged the king with divinity and awe, permeated the life of every individual from birth to the grave, subjected the lowborn to their superiors and, because of the fear it instilled, formed the basis of secular authority. Remove its religion from an African society and it was deprived of its very life; its moral and political systems collapsed at once. It is therefore clear, following this argument, that the Christian converts that renounced the tribal religion, threw away the healthy restraints of the old religion. It is true that they entered into new obligations

1 For a rather sympathetic view of Jaja's rise, see Dike, op. cit., pp. 182–202.

but these were not really binding, and held no fear to the converts as did the tribal juju. The political authority of the chiefs could be thrown to the winds with impunity. It was all this that Jaja foresaw; even in the hectic days of 1887 he told Lord Salisbury, quite frankly, 'juju is our religion and we must keep to it'.[1]

Jaja's discernment from the beginning of the dangers of missionary activity to the sovereignty of the Niger Delta potentates and the laws and customs of the Southern Nigerian peoples is significant in the history of Nigerian nationalism. It is essential to emphasize that in his perceptiveness, in the nationalist sense, he had no equal among his contemporaries in other parts of Africa. For the Awujalẹ, as already noted, while aware of the danger of the missionary, was willing to yield to the importunity of educated Africans and experimented with an African missionary before expelling him. Jaja refused to experiment in Opobo. Neither Moselekatse of Matabeleland nor Mutesa I of Buganda was gifted to see in the ostensibly friendly and altruistic missionary the harbinger of both the European exploiter and administrator until it was too late.

Unlike the Awujalẹ, Jaja was not a reactionary traditionalist willing to resist all manifestation of foreign culture. He accepted the technological side of European civilization whenever he saw that it could lead to true progress. But, even then, he did this selectively, allowing both the European and the African to jostle together rather than allowing the latter to be entirely discouraged. Hence while he disapproved of the semi-nakedness of the Delta peoples, he himself adopted something like a naval rig but wore it sparingly. He attached greater importance to the more dignifying regal dress, 'a fathom of cloth, strings of coral beads on his sinewy neck, (and) a smoking cap on his head'.[2] Well informed on European etiquette, he received his European visitors in his well decorated big banqueting hall and entertained them sumptuously on African-made plates;[3] while providing them with European cutlery which he never used, he preferred his hands in the African manner.[4] While he placed all kinds of European alcohol at the disposal of his European friends, he allowed his chiefs to taste palm-wine only, himself remaining a teetotaller because he believed that 'drink make man fool' and was unworthy of any African ruler worth his salt. Jaja with his chiefs went in for European-style houses and he boasted of his house to Lord Granville, in order 'to show you that the West Coast of Africa is not quite so

1 P.P. (C.5365), Jaja to Salisbury, 5 May 1887.
2 F.O. 84/1828, Johnston to Salisbury, 24–8 Sept. 1887.
3 Undated *Times of India* reproduced in *African Times*, 1 May 1885.
4 S. Griffiths, *Trips in the Tropics*, London 1878, pp. 97–9.

uncivilized as is generally inferred at home'.[1] His cast of mind was illustrated by the fact that he was 'fond of trade matters or the manners and customs of his people'.[2]

According to contemporary observers, Jaja's state was the best administered in the whole of West Africa.[3] In place of the social and political upheavals which honeycombed the city states of Bonny, New Calabar and Brass, where missionary enterprise was allowed in, there were perfect peace and order and commercial prosperity in Opobo. An enlightened autocrat, he saw to it that every able-bodied man was a trained soldier. By the aid of his juju, for which he was mostly dreaded, and the European weapons which he had in large quantity, including the three Gatlings of which he was mostly proud, civil strife was impossible in his dominion.[4]

In fact Jaja was a remarkably enlightened man, and he valued the educational aspect of missionary enterprise. If Christianity could have come without upsetting society, as it seemed to be doing in Bonny, he would gladly have allowed it. As he often told missionaries he wanted his subjects to 'saby book'.[5] Jaja sent one of his children, Sunday Jaja, to Glasgow for education. Indeed Jaja was able to have a school established in Opobo without any Christian spiritual activities attached to it. This he did through one Miss White, an American negress of whom he became enamoured. This lady was born of slave parents in Louisville, Kentucky, and was converted in early life at a Methodist camp meeting. After the civil war of 1861–65 she emigrated to Liberia and traded on her own account along the West African coast until Opobo struck her fancy and she settled there in 1875. Although she was poor when she reached Opobo her remarkable talents and force of character attracted Jaja's attention. She found her way into his good graces and was advanced step by step. She changed her name to Emma Jaja and married an Opoboman by the name of Johnson. Few enterprises were undertaken by Jaja without her advice being solicited. She became his private secretary and 'prime minister'. And yet she failed to convince Jaja of the spiritual advantages of Christianity. On many occasions, according to her, she tried to read the Bible to him but had to stop doing so for the King threatened to kill her. Emma Jaja's school was made up of sixty boys and girls, and according to Bryan Roe, a Wesleyan

1 F.O. 403/20, Jaja to Granville, 15 May 1883.
2 F.O. 84/1828, Johnston to Salisbury, 24–8 Sept. 1887.
3 *African Times* 1 May 1885, S. Griffiths, op. cit., pp. 97–9.
4 The author was taken round Opobo in May 1961 and saw the planning of the town which was explained by Mr E. T. M. Epelle.
5 *Primitive Methodist Missionary Records*, August 1886, Burnett's letter dated 11 May 1886.

missionary who visited the school in 1885, so well had the children been instructed that they compared very favourably with English children of the same age.[1]

It is essential to emphasize that Jaja also had commercial reasons for outlawing missionary enterprise. Nor was he alone in this, but found ardent supporters in the European traders on the Opobo river who were not supporters of Christian missions. They contrasted with the European traders in the rest of Southern Nigeria. In Brass, New Calabar, Bonny and Old Calabar, many of the traders took their religion seriously and gave financial support to Bishop Crowther's mission. The traders in Bonny were the most ardent Christians and in 1874 they erected a church, St Clements, for themselves and educated Africans. In Bonny too the Court of Equity, for many years under the chairmanship of the influential Captain R. D. Boler, used its influence against the persecution of the slave converts in the seventies and early eighties.

Yet the European traders in Bonny, as well as the traders in other parts of Southern Nigeria, looked with disfavour on any attempt by missionaries to penetrate into the interior. This was because by going into the interior Christian missions were likely to upset the *status quo* by which the European traders utilized the Delta peoples as middlemen, an absolutely satisfactory system to them until the end of the nineteenth century.[2] The missionary behind the coast was necessarily a potential danger to the interests of both the European traders and the Delta middlemen. Against the interest of the latter Christian converts were likely to become 'enlightened' and less docile, and seek to sell directly to the European traders; against the interest of the European traders the Christian converts tended to become harder bargainers, refusing the traders' price and demanding more goods for their produce. For the city-states founded and thriving on the middleman's trade the danger of missionary propaganda to their interest was real. This was why it was a law in Bonny that no one should take a stranger into the Okrika country, immediately behind Bonny; this was why the Presbyterian missionaries supported the Efik traders on the coast by refusing to allow commerce to follow them on the Cross River as they spread into the interior. For Jaja, the greatest monopolist, missionary enterprise was the greatest danger to his prosperity and prestige, while Bishop Crowther found opposition from traders to be the greatest obstacle to his design of pushing missionary frontier into the interior.[3]

1 C. R. Johnson: *Bryan Roe: A Soldier of the Cross*, London 1896, pp. 63–4.
2 C. Gertzel, 'Relations between African and European traders in the Niger Delta 1880–96', *The Journal of African History*, Vol. ii, No. 2, p. 362.
3 *African Times*, 2 Apr. 1877.

That Jaja's instinct was well founded became clear during the social and political turmoil in which Brass, New Calabar and Bonny found themselves after 1875. In Bonny Oko Jumbo and all the other chiefs, except King George, began to regret their shortsightedness in inviting and patronizing, as it seemed to them, so dangerous a creed as the white man's religion, which after 1870 began to show effects detrimental to their interests. Not only had missionary propaganda failed to vanquish Jaja in the civil war and lost their markets to him, but it began to shake the entire society to its very foundations. Their social order, as guaranteed by the House system of government and social relationships, was being upset. Their slaves, by far in the majority, were finding in Christianity a most convenient safety-valve for their cumulative grievances against the social order of House Rule. For Christianity stood for social ideals such as brotherhood, freedom, individual rights, justice and honour, which African missionaries, rather injudiciously, dinned in the ears of the slave converts. Missionary propaganda began to implant into the latter new desires, new motives and new appreciations.

It cannot be overstated that whatever the advantages of House Rule for both masters and slaves, the latter were not satisfied with their social status. There should be no illusion as to the merits and demerits of this pecular institution in the Niger Delta. Although missionary observers were liable to paint too black a picture of House Rule and did not recognize its merits, evidence of non-partisan observers shows that outside Brass, in the decades under consideration, the position of slaves under House Rule was not an enviable one.[1] As a rule the slave was badly fed and ill-used. His master had power of life and death over him. House Rule denied to the slaves many liberties which, to missionaries, 'Christians' should have, viz., liberty of speech, inheritance, marriage, action and liberty of contract. This was why the House Rule Ordinance by the Southern Nigerian administration, enacted in 1901 in the name of Indirect Rule, while removing abuses as much as possible, yet came under heavy criticism from missionaries and the Aborigines Protection Society.[2] In 1916 Lord Lugard, despite his advocacy of Indirect Rule, repealed it.

In any case the results of missionary enterprise in the Niger Delta showed clearly that slaves embraced the white man's faith as a means of escape from their degraded state. Missionary propaganda made

1 M. Kingsley: *West African Studies*, London 1899. Appendix I by Le Comte Cardi, pp. 479–80. Cardi's experience of the Delta trade was spread over a period of more than thirty years.
2 J. H. Harris: *Domestic Slavery in Southern Nigeria*, London 1912.

retention of the House system in the traditional form impossible, simply because the missionaries did not preach obedience to constituted authority at all hazards as the Church did in medieval Europe. Rather, they incited the slaves against their masters, whom they denounced from the pulpits, choosing apposite scriptural passages and comparing the slaves to David who would ultimately slay Goliath, the slave system.[1] They assumed the role of 'fathers', commiserating with the slaves in their physical sufferings, and showed solicitude which the masters could not feign. In the Church the slaves were treated on terms of equality with their king and the freeborn, while at school the children of the chiefs and slave children lived together. Christianity was proving a social leveller.

In all the states of Southern Nigeria where Christian missions operated it was only among the Efik of Old Calabar that the rebelliousness which missionary propaganda was capable of fomenting among slaves was on a relatively small scale. There were several reasons for this. As indicated in the first chapter of this book social changes, which ameliorated the condition of the slaves, were forced on the Efik rulers by the Consular authority and by the reforming zeal of Eyo Honesty II. Slaves gained freedom to embrace Christianity; they could no longer be killed at their masters' death; they could no longer be sacrificed to the gods. But although they were restive their rebellious instincts were suppressed by the all-powerful *Egbo* which forced on the slaves obedience to constituted authorities. All slaves, whether they embraced Christianity or not, were beneficiaries of the measures adopted by both Eyo Honesty II and the consular power. The effect of the measures, ironically, was that many slaves saw no intrinsic advantages in becoming Christians. Consequently their response to missionary activity, numerically, was much less than in other parts of Southern Nigeria. In places like Brass and Bonny where the *Owu Ogbo* cult was not a powerful engine of government and fear as *Egbo*, the paroxysmal political and social effects of missionary enterprise on society were glaringly manifested.

It was in Brass that political and social revolutions first occurred, in 1879. The most humane of all the rulers in the Niger Delta, Brass chiefs were more accommodating to Christianity than anywhere else. Persecution of slave converts was much milder here than in Bonny. In 1871 the religious traditionalists were already regretting their invitation to Bishop Crowther three years before. Looking for a pretext to destroy this incipient faith they ascribed the outbreak of smallpox in that year to Christianity and its adherents. Fortunately for the converts Acting Consul Hopkins, pro-missionary Chairman of

1 C.M.S. CA3/04 (b), J. Boyle to Bishop Crowther, 21 July 1879.

the Court of Equity in Brass, warned the chiefs of the backing of Consular authority for the Christians, an action commended by the Foreign Office.[1] Unlike in Bonny where the Christian converts were being chained or tortured to death, or their heads smashed with clubs by the anti-missionary chiefs, all the punishment which the Brass chiefs inflicted on the converts for the alleged responsibility for the smallpox epidemic was a fine of £70. Henceforward the chiefs conceded religious freedom to the slaves. In return for the unusually liberal gestures of the chiefs the slaves behaved themselves. According to King Ockiya, by 1874 the Christians had become the most useful and law-abiding citizens of the state.[2] They were industrious and they carried the principles of their faith to the markets where the producers found them more trustworthy than the non-converts. The state entered a prosperous era and in 1876 King Ockiya and chiefs Sambo, Spiff and Cameroons surrendered their idols, sent to Salisbury Square, and became Christians. Almost the whole of Tuwon, about 5,000 people, was converted, while in Nembe, the capital of the Brass people, thirty miles beyond the coast, the majority of the 10,000 inhabitants were converted.

The attempt of what remained of the 'pagan' party in Nembe to assert claims for the tribal religion (the python was the animal totem of Brass) after Ockiya's death in 1879, gave the signal for the seizure of power by the Christians. The African missionary in charge, Garrick, urged the slaves to take up arms.[3] As soon as the news of the peaceful *coup* reached Tuwon, chiefs Sambo, Spiff and Cameroons, themselves of slave origin, led the Christian party to putting a finishing stroke to 'paganism' there. They attacked the idol houses and the residences of the priests. All objects of worship were removed and the priests themselves became Christians. Thus in a matter of days Brass became a Christian state.

In both New Calabar and Old Calabar there were struggles between the Christian and the traditional factions. In the former, where in 1879 Christianity was only five years old and where Jaja's influence was now paramount, there occurred a fierce civil war which the chiefs, probably at Jaja's instigation, ascribed to the spiritual invasion of their country. For although the Kalabari, as New Calabar people are known, had no temple of skulls, they had a juju house into which they dumped all colourful cloths, pictures, mirrors and earthenware with patterns, all of which were regarded as 'juju'. All

1 F.O. 84/1343, Hopkins to Granville, 27 Nov. 1871.
2 C.M.S. CA3/022, W. F. John: *Journals*, 21 Sept. 1874.
3 C.M.S. CA3/04 (b), Garrick to Bishop Crowther, 29 Dec. 1879. The Christian party in Nembe had 'over 800 rifles, besides a great many badly armed'.

the chiefs took an oath to the gods to destroy completely all emblems of missionary enterprise. The African missionary was expelled and all books and Bibles were deposited in the groves.[1] Indeed so reactionary did the New Calabar chiefs become that they prepared a lotion with which they wiped the faces of their children who had been attending school, with the hope that all the supposed stuff and nonsense the children had learned from 1874 to 1879, and which was supposed to have contributed to the fierce civil war, would be washed away from their heads.[2]

In Old Calabar Consul Hopkins, a practising Christian who often preached in both Fernando Po and Old Calabar, and who would not open any session of the consular courts until missionaries had said prayers, carried out the programme of *Young Calabar*. Henshaw Town became virtually independent of 'pagan' Duke Town. It became something of a classical theocracy. The constitution by which the 'town' was to be administered henceforth stated that every inhabitant of the town must observe the sabbath strictly by doing no work at all. Anyone breaking this regulation would be fined twelve manillas for the first offence. Article V of the constitution stated, 'There shall be no worshipping of images or sacrifices made to supposed Gods, nor Devil making (connected with burial) or making offerings to the spirit of deceased persons.' The first offence carried a punishment of a fine of 120 to 300 manillas.[3]

In Bonny no easy or quick solution was possible because the forces were almost equally drawn. On the one hand were the 'pagan' masters and Jaja, on the other over a thousand slave converts (by 1880), the pro-missionary Court of Equity and the peripatetic and sickly Consul Hewett. The contest between these two forces largely makes up the history of Bonny between 1878 and 1887, and in the end the triumph of the Christian party was to pave the way for Jaja's downfall.

It is not clear how far the slaves were influenced by the events in Brass but it was after the success of the Christian party there that something like a mass movement to Christianity among the slaves in Bonny began. By 1882 over 1,000 slaves had already become Christians. They were determined to assert some independence and were strong enough to stand up to their masters. They became disobedient

1 Ibid. Carew to Bishop Crowther, 21 Dec. 1879.
2 A. B. Batubo: 'The History of Baptist Church at Buguma' (typescript in possession of the Rev. Cecil Roberson of the Southern American Baptist Mission, now in Lagos).
3 F.O. 84/1508, Agreement dated 6 Sept. 1878, enclosed in Hopkins to F.O. 28 Aug. 1878.

and ungovernable. They began by refusing to take part in the House juju by which the unity of the House was preserved; they would no longer 'chop juju' with the customers in the interior markets, a ceremony that was of vital importance in the subjection of the latter to Bonny's economic interests. On Sundays they cleaned themselves up and went into the church instead of pulling canoes to the markets. Even in the markets they built chapels and turned themselves into 'bishops', as the chiefs put it.[1] Particularly galling to the chiefs was the casting away of all wives but one by some of the slave converts as a result of missionary teaching. This created a big social problem; for the rejected women could not marry again, as intra-House marriage was taboo. This meant additional burdens to the masters on whom the rejected wives depended.

The insubordination of the converts to their masters was a serious offence in the Niger Delta society. Traditionally a slave dared not disregard the tenet of the head of the House, for he would either be killed or sold to the interior tribes as food for the gods. What was hitherto regarded as sacred and unassailable, the juju, and regarded by the chiefs as a reality, was now looked upon as an absurd superstition devised by the masters to deceive them. In a sense, then, the slave converts were asserting spiritual superiority over their masters. No amount of physical punishment including starvation, exile and scourging, was of any avail; nor did offers of higher status to slaves who returned to House juju attract them. The determination and insubordination of the converts were reinforced by the utterances in the church of Archdeacon Dandeson Crowther, the Bishop's youngest son, who resided in Bonny, which the chiefs described as 'highly seditious when taken into consideration with the wild instincts of our slaves, many of whom are unreclaimed savages'.[2] Largely through the intervention of the Consul and Court of Equity the chiefs could no longer after 1878 inflict physical punishment on the slave converts.

The chiefs were particularly incensed by the lack of sympathy for their well-founded grievances by Bishop Crowther. Himself a one-time victim of the slave trade he could hardly have been expected to have a shred of sympathy with an institution that deprived people of complete freedom. Rather than teaching them that Christianity did not preach disobedience the Bishop was forthright and tactless. He unrestrainedly defended the slaves. From 1874 onwards he became a *persona non grata* whose many summons to conferences were rejected. Reporting his last meeting with the chiefs to Salisbury Square, the Bishop revealed how he lectured the chiefs on the theology of the

1   C.M.S. G3/A3/02, D. C. Crowther to Lang, 30 June 1884.
2   Ibid. Chiefs of Bonny to T. Phillips, 12 Mar. 1883.

body and the soul and stung them with jibes which they could not be expected to forgive. The Bishop reported as follows:

As regards the complaint that they [the slaves] were reluctant to go to the market on Sunday, I told them that it was God's law which every man, master or slave is bound to obey; that though they own the slaves who must obey them, yet they own and enslave the body only, but that God claims both body and soul; that it was His will that they enslave their bodies, and demand their services during six days in the week, God demands the service of their souls on the seventh; and to convince them of the truthfulness of this, I put the question to them individually whether when God does send His messenger death to take away the soul of any of their slaves, could the owner prevent that soul from obeying the summons by the hand of death? They unanimously replied, No. I then said, well, in that case God has taken away the most important part of that slave which belongs to him, and left the body to them, the material substance which they had purchased with their money; that they were perfectly at liberty to employ it whenever they pleased, Sunday or not: they remained puzzled. I said if the dead body did not obey their orders, it should be compelled to do so by being beat [sic]; they were silent: nay, I said, you must make it obey your orders put it into the canoe, lash it to its seat, and lash the paddles into his hands and compel it to the paddle, here they saw the impossibility.[1]

Since they could no longer impose physical punishment on their slave converts the chiefs' last resort was to pass edicts against church attendance. The first of these was passed in December 1880 but in 1882 the chiefs discovered that the latter were planning to imitate the Brass *coup*. In this year the converts deliberately broke an edict of December 1881. This edict was the chiefs' answer to the independent action of the missionaries and the converts over a new iron church which they wanted to erect. According to the House system the property of every individual member of a House belonged to the Head. The slave converts therefore violated an important law by making subscriptions without prior sanction of their masters. King George himself encouraged the converts to break this law, as the treasurer collecting the subscriptions. As the chiefs rightly remarked, the action of the missionaries and their converts 'is unprecedented and calculated to sow the seeds that will precipitate a violent subversion of our domestic system'.[2]

1 C.M.S. CA3/04 (b), Report for 1874.
2 C.M.S. G3/A3/02, chiefs of Bonny to T. Phillips, 12 Mar. 1883.

In order to make the edict effective, all the chiefs, except the king, made a law that each chief should enforce the rule rigorously and be held responsible for any breach by paying a fine of nine puncheons, that is about £180. In Bonny before Christianity an edict like this would have been carried out to the letter. But although the missionaries advised the converts to obey the edict, their insubordination and zeal had passed beyond the control even of the missionaries. On Christmas Day, according to arrangement by themselves, a certain number of slaves from every House went to church, thus breaking the edict. This meant that the chiefs had to impose fines on themselves. On attempting to deal with the rebels individually all the slaves, carrying arms, presented a united front, and challenged the chiefs to punish them together. Scared by a possible rebellion the chiefs fled to the plantations and conceded liberty of worship immediately.[1] Henceforth the power of the chiefs over their slaves declined. Never henceforward could any such edict be passed in Bonny.

The liberty the chiefs were compelled to grant to the converts, whose cause was championed by the King, widened the gap between the chiefs and their King. From 1870 onwards the King was discredited in their eyes. The white man's religion had meant the surrender of their markets to Jaja, who went on prospering in his attachment to the tribal religion. Moreover George Pepple lacked the qualities which Jaja was utilizing for the progress of Opobo. George was impoverished and did not scruple to undersell his subjects in the markets.[2] Unlike Jaja who defrayed the cost of his excellent administration George used the 'comey' for himself alone; unlike Jaja who led his soldiers in the various wars that extended his empire, George could not fight, and he failed to avenge Bonny's honour when it was tarnished by New Calabar.[3] He left the opening up of the new markets to chiefs Oko Jumbo and Warribo Manilla Pepple while he demoralized the Bonny army by asking the slave converts to refuse to take the traditional juju which the chiefs believed could ensure victory in the various wars with Okrika and New Calabar for new markets. George was therefore, in their opinion, the greatest enemy of the kingdom over which he ruled. In 1878 the chiefs decided that they had had enough of him and attempted to depose him. They wished to put on the throne one of his brothers, Charles Pepple, himself a well-educated man and commander of the Bonny contingent that helped in the capture of Kumasi in the Ashanti war of 1873–74. Thanks to the timely intervention of Consul Hopkins, who was instructed by the Foreign Office to inform the

1 C.M.S. G3/A3/02, D. C. Crowther to Wigram, 17 Apr. 1883.
2 F.O. 84/1508, Hopkins to F.O., 23 Nov. 1878.   3 Ibid.

chiefs that Bonny would not receive the countenance of the British Government if George was removed, the plot came to naught.[1]

George learned nothing from the crisis that faced him but continued to champion the cause of missionary propaganda at the expense of the economic interests of the state. Since 1870 Bonny had been saved from complete economic strangulation by the opening of the Okrikan country, the Okrikans selling oil through Bonnymen to the European traders. By 1870 Bonny had become impoverished and were it not for its good harbour which made it an entrepôt for the other Delta ports, including Opobo, Bonnymen would have been reduced to 'pirates and fishermen'.[2] It was therefore in Bonny's economic interest to prevent any attempts by either traders or missionaries to penetrate the intricate creek system that led to Okrika.

For the missionaries who had collected information on the strategic importance of Okrika as the gateway to the Ibo country, which they were anxious to invade, the extension of the missionary frontier to Okrika was of supreme importance. Incidentally, for the Okrikans, veritable cannibals, missionary propaganda was the only solution to their economic and political grievances. They hoped that missionaries would 'enlighten' them so that they might rise to the economic level of the other states and deal directly with the white traders. Hence their constant appeal to the missionaries for a teacher. In 1880 they erected a church that could seat over 400 people. Bonny chiefs opposed the attempts of Archdeacon Crowther to honour Okrika's invitation. George Pepple, however, brushed aside Bonny's economic interests. In 1880 he provided the Archdeacon with a guide[3] who was clandestinely murdered by the chiefs when he returned. A Christian teacher was sent to Okrika and by 1883 Bonny's fears were already justified. Okrika became 'enlightened' to the stage of declaring the independence of Bonny and repudiating a debt of over £1,000. The Okrikans began to send their oil directly to the white traders at New Calabar. What is more, seizing its geographical advantages, Okrika wrenched the Ndele markets from Bonny.[4]

But apart from the social and economic reasons already outlined, the chiefs had political grievances as well. Archdeacon Crowther became in effect the ruler of the country as the chief confidant of the king. What is more the Church Missionary Society journals and British newspapers ascribed to George a constitutional status much higher than the Bonny constitution accorded him.[5] He was not

1 Ibid.   2 Ibid.
3 C.M.S. G3/A3/01, Archdeacon Crowther to Hutchinson, 5 July 1880.
4 C.M.S. G3/A3/02, Archdeacon Crowther to Wigram, 10 May 1883.
5 Ibid. Bishop Crowther to Lang, 6 Aug. 1884.

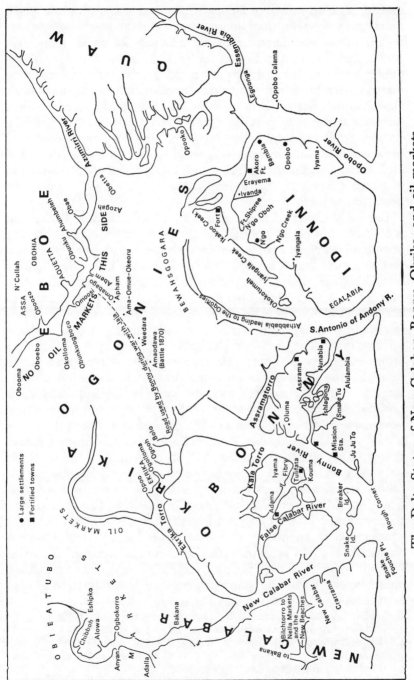

The Delta States of New Calabar, Bonny, Okrika, and oil markets

spoken of as an ordinary king, with limited authorities and chiefs much more powerful than himself because of the wealth which they possessed, but was described as the only ruler of his kingdom. Nor could they forgive the Bishop for presenting them to the British public as thieves, because they saw nothing unbecoming in removing materials of a Mission they so much hated, including the stairs to the church which one of them used for building. What incensed them most was that they were relegated to the background in the administration of their country. As they put it, 'we find schemes are concerted between these two parties (George and Archdeacon Crowther) and after being well-fitted together a meeting is called of the chiefs and just such portion of the subject is revealed to us as is considered necessary by them'.[1]

Curiously enough Bradlaugh's doings in the British Parliament reverberated in Bonny politics. For the Bonny of the eighties was not unenlightened. The people were sensitive to British press comments on them. For instance in 1878, following what the Bishop had written in a C.M.S. journal, a law was made forbidding stealing of mission property.[2] In 1882 one of Oko Jumbo's sons, Herbert, returned from Liverpool College where he had been trained for eight years. He had followed Bradlaugh's behaviour on oath-taking and found the anti-missionary feelings in Bonny a suitable opportunity to back up his father and the 'pagan' party. He urged the chiefs to consider building a jail for the missionaries for, 'one Bradlaugh, cleverer than any English Bishop or clergy has opened the eyes of England that there is no God'.[3] Archdeacon Crowther had to turn the pulpit to a political husting in order to put an end to 'Bradlaughism in Bonny'!

Jaja was not an onlooker in the political and social disturbance of Bonny,[4] although the economic ruin of the country could not have been unpleasant to him. As we have seen, in New Calabar where his influence was supreme, missionary enterprise was completely destroyed in 1879. As early as 1877 both he and Oko Jumbo had sunk their differences and pledged themselves to destroying missionary propaganda throughout the Niger Delta.[5] In 1878 Old Calabar, another citadel of Christianity, mounted guns in preparation for war which it was rumoured Jaja and Oko Jumbo were planning to wage on it.[6] Jaja's influence in Bonny was supreme from 1880 to 1884. Oko

1 Ibid. Bonny chiefs to T. Phillips, 12 Mar. 1883.
2 C.M.S. CA3/04 (b), James Boyle to Bishop Crowther, 1 Mar. 1880.
3 C.M.S. G3/A3/02, D. C. Crowther to Lang, 30 June 1884.
4 C.M.S. G3/A3/03, R. D. Boler to Hamilton, 27 Jan. 1884. G3/A3/02, George Pepple to chiefs of Bonny, 5 Feb. 1883; D. C. Crowther to Wigram, 10 May 1883; D. C. Crowther to Lang, 13 Feb. 1884.
5 *African Times*, 1 Oct. 1877.   6 Ibid. 1 Feb. 1878.

Jumbo requested his help in the solution of the problems that faced the country. Jaja made complete destruction of missionary enterprise the one condition that must be satisfied before he could come to Bonny's rescue. He ascribed Bonny's continued impoverishment to the toleration of Christianity and the abandonment of the tribal gods. If they destroyed Christianity, Jaja said, all economic ills of the state would be solved. He promised to give Bonny many markets, naming Koeffe markets, and to intervene on their behalf for the markets of Ndele and Obiabutu, of which Okrika and New Calabar respectively had deprived Bonny.[1]

Jaja's anti-missionary policy extended to Okrika. In 1883 the seizure of Ndele markets led to war with Bonny. King George of Okrika sent to Jaja for aid. Jaja informed Okrika that the true cause of the war by Bonny was continued patronage of Christianity by Okrika and not the repudiation of their debt to Bonny or the seizure of their markets.[2] If they destroyed the church and school, then, he would intervene on their behalf. Of course, the Okrikans could not do such a thing in view of the fact that, as noted, missionary propaganda was fulfilling their hopes supremely well. It had improved their prosperity and had made them independent of Bonny.

Jaja became the only hope of Bonny chiefs. In 1883 the C.M.S. sought to make Bonny its headquarters for the Niger Mission, with the hope that Bishop Crowther and European missionaries would reside there. The chiefs put the matter before Jaja who advised that the offer be rejected as it would be a prelude to the occupation of the country by Britain.[3] George, who pressed the chiefs to accept the proposal, was accused of having sold the country to Queen Victoria for £1,000.[4] The chiefs seized the occasion to ask the C.M.S. to remove all the African missionaries and replace them, as a better alternative, by European missionaries who would not interfere with their social laws and politics.

With the tempting offers by Jaja before them the chiefs deposed George Pepple and expelled Archdeacon Crowther, who removed to Brass. The immediate occasion for Pepple's removal was his claim to the manilla casks hoarded in the past by Perekule, the richest of Bonny rulers, as his personal property. The other chiefs rejected this claim and contended that this wealth belonged to the state. Warribo Manilla Pepple was made Regent.

1 C.M.S. G3/A3/03, George Pepple to Bonny chiefs, 5 Feb. 1883.
2 Ibid. James Boyle to Bishop Crowther, 2 Apr. 1884; R. D. Boler to Hamilton, 27 Jan. 1886.
3 C.M.S. G3/A3/O2, George Pepple to Bonny chiefs, 5 Feb. 1883.
4 Ibid. D. C. Crowther to Bishop Crowther, 13 Nov. 1883.

But, like the Ijẹbu, both Jaja and chiefs of Bonny were mistaken in thinking that Christianity could be destroyed in the presence of British Government representatives. In the eighties Jaja and the Bonny chiefs were running against the imperialist tide, which had been flowing since the 'scramble'. Britain had to awaken from complacency and had begun to make 'formal' her 'informal' empire of Nigeria in face of French and German aggression in the Bights of Benin and Biafra. This implied more vigorous aid to missionary enterprise. So far the help given by the Consular authority, with the approval of the Foreign Office, in Brass, Bonny and Old Calabar had rendered impossible the effacement of Christianity in these places. For, except Livingstone, no other consul had any doubt that by promoting the cause of British Christian missions they were also promoting the imperial cause. What the pro-missionary *African Times* had repeatedly emphasized, with particular reference to the Niger Delta, was now to be put into effect—that 'it is the ruling desire of the people of Great Britain that the light of the glorious Gospel of Jesus Christ shall have free course among the African populations' and that in the Niger Delta 'persecution of Christian converts will lead, sooner or later, to their (the persecutors') destruction'. Such 'ruling desire',[1] we have seen, had led to Livingstone's 'destruction'. Echoes of the prediction of Jaja's fall as a persecutor of Christianity are to be found in the Foreign Office dispatches.[2] In 1878 Consul Hopkins reminded the Foreign Office that Bonny chiefs were against George Pepple principally because of his pro-missionary views and the destruction of his influence by Livingstone's misrepresentations.[3] An official sympathized with the king's cause and minuted that the 1873 Treaty must be revised 'when a convenient opportunity offers'.[4] In this ominous statement we find the beginnings of Jaja's fall.

In fact George Pepple had never wavered in his conviction that he would ultimately triumph with the backing of Britain. He had stopped the persecution of slaves by frightening the chiefs with the threat of appeal to the Consul on behalf of the slaves for 'liberty of conscience'. Indeed in spite of his deposition George Pepple continued to reside in Bonny instead of being either killed or exiled as had been the case with many of his predecessors. Like the Ẹgba in 1891, the Bonny traditionalists were aware that to molest this

1 *African Times*, 1 Oct. 1877.
2 F.O. 84/1508, Minute dated 13 Jan. 1879 on Hopkins to F.O., 23 Nov. 1878. F.O. 84/1828, Minute by Sir T. V. Lister on Hewett to Salisbury, 20 Aug. 1887.
3 F.O. 84/1508, Hopkins to F.O., 23 Nov. 1878.
4 Ibid. Minute dated 13 Jan. 1879.

avowed friend of Britain would mean to incur the Consul's displeasure. They had to allow him to stay in Bonny and intrigue with the British and missionaries. It is not surprising that he laughed the chiefs to scorn when they deposed him, ridiculed their fighting against Christianity and pitied them for pinning so much hope in Jaja. He wrote to them,

> I must caution Oko Jumbo that he may not molest me and mine with impunity; for I shall place myself, my house, property, land chattels, and right, etc. under the protection of Her Majesty Queen Victoria of Great Britain: and Oko may keep what remains of Bonny and Bonny independence.[1]

That George was not merely boasting was soon clear to the chiefs. In 1884 they had to learn that the British Government regarded George as *de jure* king irrespective of their action and that missionary enterprise had come to stay in Bonny. In the first week of August 1883 Consul Hewett, who was now ready to begin making treaties, went to Salisbury Square and promised to do something about the political situation in Bonny.[2] Had he been on the spot, he said, George's deposition would have been impossible. In the Protectorate Treaty which Hewett had asked Bonny and other states to sign there was a religious clause by which they were to guarantee freedom of worship and protection to missionaries. Regarding Clause VII, the Religion Clause, as a razor applied to their necks, the Bonny chiefs refused to sign the treaty unless the clause was removed.[3] Knowing quite well what the gunboat was capable of doing, they were browbeaten into signing it in its entirety. Then the Consul, who had in the meeting treated George as the king, said that the treaty could not be regarded as valid until George had signed it. The Consul's action was tantamount to a political imposition. George's restoration was only a matter of time. The treaty, hailed with undisguised satisfaction by the C.M.S. and with ecstasy by Bishop Crowther, was a great humiliation to Oko Jumbo.[4] Most of the chiefs, reading the writing on the wall, deserted him and began to pay at least lip service to the religion they had so much persecuted. To mark this triumph the converts completed the destruction of the iguana; Hewett told the missionaries that the interior was now theirs for the taking.[5] Henceforward, politically, Jaja's fortunes had begun to wane.

In the middle of 1886 Hewett returned to Bonny and dealt what

1 C.M.S. G3/A3/02, George Pepple to Bonny chiefs, 5 Feb. 1883.
2 C.M.S. CA3/L2, R. Lang to Hamilton, 9 Aug. 1883.
3 C.M.S. G3/A3/03, Bishop Crowther to Lang, 6 Aug. 1884.
4 C.M.S. G3/A3/03, Bishop Crowther to Lang, 6 Aug. 1884.   5 Ibid.

remained of 'paganism' and the power of the 'pagans' a final blow. For twenty-one days he listened to the charges of the Christian party against Oko Jumbo and the 'pagan' party. Among the issues he looked into were the deposition of George, the strangling of a Christian, John Martin, on Oko Jumbo's order, the earlier prohibition against converts going to church and the question of the manilla casks left by Perekule. The last issue was summarily settled in George's favour in order to allow him to obtain financial power indispensable to successful kingship in the Delta. He could not yet be reinstated as king because he was heavily in debt and unable to satisfy his creditors, 'which is a great disgrace in these countries'.[1] Oko Jumbo and Warribo Manilla Pepple, the two inveterate enemies of both Christianity and George, were the greatest sufferers. They were fined respectively fifty and fifteen puncheons of oil and were removed from all authority for their conspiracy with Jaja to destroy Christianity.[2] Thus Hewett removed, because of their opposition to Christianity, the two men who had been the dominant figures in Bonny politics for over thirty years, the very people who had set Jaja fleeing. A council of five pro-Christian chiefs was set up with legislative and judicial powers.[3] The Consul retained control of foreign affairs and was the final court of appeal. Then Hewett told the chiefs that more independence should be given to the slaves and that the latter had the right to appeal to the Consul in case of maltreatment. The financial position of the slaves was further improved, at the expense of their masters, when he abolished 'topping'.[4] He expostulated on the virtues of free labour and advantages of abolition of slavery. He urged the chiefs to stop importing slaves from the interior and advised them to apprentice their slaves to Accra carpenters whom they were also employing to catch fish for them, and also to teach them coopering, brickmaking, painting and tailoring. This humanization of slavery and restoration of a great measure of liberty to the slaves is worth bearing in mind when contemplating the sympathetic views of later administrators like Macdonald and Moor in regard to slavery in Brass, Bonny, New Calabar and Old Calabar, places where Christian missions were successfully established.

1 F.O. 84/1749, Hewett to Rosebery, 12 July 1886.
2 C.M.S. G3/A3/03, Archdeacon Crowther to Lang, 21 July 1886.
3 Ibid.
4 F.O. 84/1749, Hewett to Rosebery, 12 July 1886. 'Topping' was a tax equal to 20 per cent which it had been the custom for the European traders to retain out of any payments for oil which free or half-free men under the protection of a chief, or slaves sold on their own account. This topping was credited to the account of the head of a House. The abolition meant that slaves would be henceforth better off economically.

Missionary enterprise was practically successful in Bonny, at least politically. Oko Jumbo immediately lifted the prohibition on the members of his House about church attendance.[1] There is no evidence that he returned to Christianity but he did become a patron of the faith he had done so much to persecute. He donated liberally to the new iron church, went to Liverpool for a surgical operation on his eyes, and bought a huge bunch of British national flags.[2] Warribo Manilla Pepple threw off 'paganism' and became an ardent supporter of the missionaries, even before the deposition of Jaja.

Logically the chiefs brought up to date the constitution of the state to reflect the changes that had been brought about by missionary enterprise. Never had missionary activity achieved such a political revolution as it did in 1886 in Bonny. George was made literally an autocrat, to wield vast powers that none of his predecessors ever wielded. Henceforward, ran the new revolutionary constitution, George was to have the 'sole and exclusive right at all times and from time to time to receive *all* revenue'; then, 'the person of the said our King George Pepple shall be ever held holy and sacred'. He was free to travel anywhere, except the Ibo markets. He was completely exempted from taking part in '*any ceremony that may be contrary to his religion*'. The chiefs swore to support the king 'substantially and heartily' in any scheme he might have for 're-opening the roads to the interior markets, so as to bring back good trade to Bonny'.[3] This was more or less a declaration of war on Jaja. Archdeacon Crowther was implored to return to Bonny,[4] where his influence was to last until his death in 1938, at the age of ninety-four. In 1888 the death-knell of indigenous religion was sounded when *ikuba* was officially destroyed. Comte de Cardi, who knew Bonny so well, wrote its epitaph: 'the "juju" house of Bonny, once the greatest showplace of the town, has now completely disappeared and its hideous contents are scattered'.[5]

Jaja could not have been happy with the dramatic turn of events in Bonny from 1884 onwards. In every direction the stars in their courses were against him. Although he could not be accused of anti-British feelings and had sent troops to help the British in the Ashanti war of 1873–74; although he loved to show the sword which the British Government presented him on the occasion and was profuse in his

1 C.M.S. G3/A3/03, 'Notes on various changes at Bonny in the three years from 1884 to 1886' by Bishop Crowther.
2 *African Times*, 1 Aug. 1885.
3 *Church Missionary Intelligencer*, 1887, pp. 499–500 (italics not mine). C.M.S. G3/A3/03, Adda Allison to Bishop Crowther, 24 Feb. 1887.
4 C.M.S. G3/A3/03, Adda Allison to D. C. Crowther, 25 Feb. 1887.
5 Comte de Cardi, op. cit., p. 514.

loyalty to Britain in his banquets to visitors, yet, he had to learn like the Ijẹbu that in the circumstances of the eighties and nineties of the last century, at least in Nigeria, loyalty to the British was not complete in the opinion of pro-Christian officials on the spot if Christianity was opposed, particularly where it suited these officials to use Christianity to obtain subjection, subjection being their goal. Right from 1870 the *African Times* had been consistently campaigning against Jaja and had declared immediately after the pro-Jaja Treaty of 1873, 'we confess that, in our indignation, we would sweep this Ja Ja [sic] and his newly established title from the face of the earth'.[1]

Between 1884 and 1887 Jaja was being hedged on all sides by missionary propaganda. New Calabar accepted the Protectorate Treaty with the Religion Clause and early in 1887 the C.M.S. reopened its station there. East of Opobo, the triumph of *Young Calabar* checked his commercial expansionism on the Qua Ibo. For Chief Henshaw looked westwards of Old Calabar to carve a commercial empire in 1879. He established a new settlement at Idua Oron, on the left bank of the Cross River estuary. From here he planned to open up trade with the Qua Ibo and so obtained the backing of Watts. Both of them went to Qua Ibo in 1880.[2] In 1882 Watts obtained the support of the Foreign Office against Jaja, and the latter's trade there was paralysed. To make their defiance complete chief Henshaw and Watts introduced Christianity among the Ibuno. In Old Calabar King Eyo Honesty VI of Creek Town was as anglicized as George Pepple, and was chairman of the Finance Committee of his church.[3]

The significance of this envelopment of Opobo by missionary propaganda lay in the fact that Jaja was thus deprived of what was probably his greatest asset in the trade and politics of the Niger Delta until now—the political and social upheavals in the various states which compelled them to concentrate all attention on their domestic problems or fight against themselves. Furthermore these political disturbances harnessed his paramountcy and provided the situation by which he intervened, and was requested to intervene, in the affairs of the other states. In his interventions Jaja was not an honest broker, but saw that it was in his interest to have the states knock their heads against one another. Now that the states agreed to live with missionary enterprise and its consequences, and were putting

1 *African Times*, 29 Apr. 1873.
2 C. Gertzel, *John Holt: A British Merchant in West Africa in the Era of Imperialism.* Oxford D.Phil. 1959, pp. 176–9.
3 U.P. Minutes, 24 Feb. 1880.

their houses in order, Jaja could have no further excuse for intervening in their affairs; his political claws were clipped, his political stature considerably reduced. In Bonny such a unity as there never had been since 1830 henceforth supervened, and all attention was concentrated on the demand for the return of their markets from Jaja. A revision of the 1873 Treaty was inevitable. There could be no doubt any longer in the minds of the chiefs that after all, King Pepple's religion promised all success for the commercial prosperity of the country, with the Consul prepared to fight for Bonny.

From 1884 onwards it should have occurred to Jaja that in his struggle against missionary enterprise he was running against the spirit of the times. Opobo itself was being threatened by the new fashion. In a sense the missionary problem was nothing new to Jaja. Missionaries had been pressing him since 1874 to allow them to establish stations in Opobo.[1] An extraordinarily astute diplomatist, he had been able to outwit them on many occasions. Knowing quite well the many favours that George Pepple was receiving from the British Government, he was not the man to throw down the gauntlet to missionaries. He welcomed them as visitors and, until 1887, never declared openly his intense aversion to their efforts. Probably because he was aware that Christian missions had a 'spheres of influence' policy and that Opobo fell within the 'spheres of influence' of the C.M.S. under Bishop Crowther, he had always told his missionary friends that he was not opposed to missionary enterprise in principle but did not want 'black' missionaries.[2] This statement, swallowed by many European missionaries, should not be taken at its face value. It was no more than a convenient statement to fob them off. For Jaja had the African 'patriot' in him.

In addition to points already made that illustrate this, one further example out of many may be offered. In 1873 both George Miller Brothers and Livingstone, his 'father', vainly persuaded him not to allow educated Africans to participate in the brisk Opobo trade.[3] Up to 1875 European merchants continued to press this demand on him. Furthermore they asked the shipping companies to refuse the oil of the educated Africans and refuse their orders from England. Jaja threatened to stop all trade at once if this discrimination against Africans was not stopped.[4] Both the traders and shipping companies had to surrender to his wish. Jaja gave the educated Africans separate quarters and many of them remained loyal to him to the

1 *Primitive Methodist Missionary Records*, January 1875, pp. 7–9.
2 Ibid. November 1875, p. 6.
3 *African Times*, 30 Nov. 1874.　　　　4 Ibid. 31 Dec. 1874.

end. It is worth noting that most of them were not of Ibo origin but came from Sierra Leone and Lagos. He gave them a monopoly of trade in manufactured articles from Lagos for sale in Opobo.[1]

While therefore Jaja hated Bishop Crowther as a man that had backed up his enemies he did not hate 'black' missionaries because they were 'black', but because of the exotic (as he conceived it) religion they were propagating, which was unsuitable to Africans. Jaja had implacable hatred for missionary propaganda whether disseminated by Africans or Europeans. There is abundant evidence to illustrate this, but one instance should suffice at this point. In 1879 the fanatically pro-missionary Consul Hopkins invited John Milum, Chairman of the Wesleyan Mission, to accompany him to the Niger to prospect for mission stations in the Nupe kingdom. He had talked to Jaja on the advisability of accepting missionaries and asked John Milum to see Jaja. Shrewd and cautious, Jaja did not tell either the Consul or the missionary that he did not need their spiritual interference, but received Milum. He entertained him in his usual lavish manner, impressed him with his charm and dignity, expressed warmly how anxious he was to receive missionaries and showed him a piece of land for a possible mission station. Jaja must however dictate the impossible terms on which a mission could be established in Opobo; he must provide the building himself and settle the details of salary and so on. He told the Wesleyan Chairman that negotiations could be completed on the latter's return from the Niger. By a stroke of good fortune for Jaja the Consul soon expired. After visiting the Nupe kingdom Milum came back in hopes, expecting that final agreement would be reached. But so far as Jaja was concerned the matter was closed and he did not really expect Milum to come back. He refused to listen to any further talk about a mission in Opobo. He told the missionary that the Consul's death had altered matters and that negotiations should be suspended indefinitely.[2] John Milum went back to England with the best views of Jaja and publicized his views to the subscribers of the mission!

Jaja feared Christianity like a plague. The trader was the friend whom he taxed and controlled, and this was legal, according to the treaty of 1873. The Consul he did not fear because he was seldom seen, having single-handed to look after the wellbeing of British subjects in a territory the size of Burma. The missionary on the other hand was a bugbear. Unlike all others he could not be controlled but sought to control African rulers in the name of a supposed spiritual

1 Ibid.
2 M.M.A. John Milum to Kilner 27 May 1879; same to same 29 Sept. 1879; John Milum to Jaja 6 Sept. 1879.

superiority and sought to disparage juju, which Jaja valued most in his life. For an autocrat whose fiat was law the domineering missionary was the greatest enemy. Worst of all he was a disturber of the society, preaching individualism in a well-knit communal society, egalitarianism among a class-ridden people where slaves and masters had their allotted place, and encouraging the low-born to rise up against their masters.

In July 1884 Consul Hewett asked Jaja to sign the Protectorate Treaty. While Jaja did not object to coming under British protection, although he demanded a guarantee that his territory would never be taken, unlike the other chiefs he was not to be easily browbeaten on the Religion Clause. Jaja told the Consul pointblank that he did not want any missionary, white or black, and that he would not sign the Treaty unless the clause was expunged.[1] But the Consul himself would not surrender to Jaja on this question. This is a vital point to bear in mind in any consideration of the attitudes of the British officials on the spot to their imperial task. It took Hewett another five months before, probably aware of the gunboat or trusting to his diplomacy that had never failed him, Jaja agreed to accept 'white' in place of 'all' missionaries. Nevertheless, in a sense, Jaja was ensnared.

For, from 1885 to 1887 the British Primitive Methodists who had settled in Fernando Po since 1869 directed their attention to Opobo. In these years not less than seven visits were made to Jaja.[2] In Fernando Po the Spanish authorities had sufficient grounds for suspecting the political danger of British Protestant missionaries working on the island. The enlightened people of Santa Isabel, the most important settlement, were ethnically connected with the Efik of Old Calabar and the liberated Africans of Sierra Leone, the Gold Coast and Lagos. Naturally, their sentiment and outlook were British; their language was the English language while the two European firms on the island were British. In order to combat the suspected pernicious influence of these unwanted missionaries all kinds of obstacles, most of them absurd, were placed in their way. Spanish Catholic priests were introduced and Catholicism declared the state religion, while gratuitous education was started by the state. Yet the anglicized inhabitants preferred to go to the Protestant church and sent their children to the fee-paying schools of the Protestants where English was taught. To the chagrin of the authorities the Mission refused to

1 F.O. 84/1749, Hewett to Rosebery, 13 July 1886. 'An objection was raised and obstinately adhered to by Jaja with respect to Article VII.'
2 M.M.A. (W. Africa Box 5) 'The Chronicles of Fernando Po Missions' by W. R. Burnett; *Primitive Methodist Mission Records*, December 1886, pp. 100–1.

withdraw in face of formidable obstacles. Nothing short of outright expulsion would compel the Mission to withdraw and from 1885 onwards the government of the island was bent on this.

Before now the Governors had been unable to expel the missionaries because the Spanish Government had been forced to proclaim freedom of worship in the days of Beecroft. But, in 1885 the Governors of Spanish Colonies were given discretionary powers on matters of education. Governor Don Jose Montes de Oca wasted no time in using the new power against the missionaries. He announced that henceforward all teaching must be done in Spanish; that only the state could give education; that the Protestants had no right to ring bells for their services or to sing at all. In September 1885 the Reverend William Welford was flung into jail, and in January 1886 banished for over four years after being heavily fined. The Mission had no more white missionaries and was left in the hands of Napoleon Barleycorn, a Bubi, who had been trained in England and Spain. Hardly had Welford left the island than the governor nailed up the church and put an end to Protestant services. Soon the native missionary was hounded into prison.[1]

It was all this that impelled the Mission to decide to remove to Opobo, only eighty miles away and the best location they could think of. To this end a *Jubilee Movement* was formed to raise funds specifically for the proposed Opobo Mission and the Reverend W. Burnett was already provisionally located there. Being Europeans they thought that it would be quite easy to found a mission in Opobo. Now that he saw the determination of the white missionaries Jaja told them pointblank that he did not want them.[2] For fourteen years then, the missionaries discovered, Jaja had been too clever for them; had been hoodwinking them. They turned to Hewett who told them that by the Protectorate Treaty of December 1884, signed by Jaja, they had a right to occupy Opobo.[3]

By 1886 therefore there were two forces of Christian missions determined on a head-on clash with Jaja, with the power of the Consul in the background. There was the Christian state of Bonny demanding a review of the 1873 Treaty; and there was the Primitive Methodist Mission desiring occupation of Opobo as a matter of right. These forces were in themselves powerful but in 1887 the man best qualified by conviction, temperament and determination to promote the

1 *Primitive Methodist Mission Records*, April 1886 pp. 29–31; Dec. 1886 pp. 104–6.
2 M.M.A. (W. Africa Box 5), Robert Fairley's Private Papers. Diary entitled 'Partly Missionary, Partly General'.
3 *Primitive Methodist Missionary Records*, Aug. 1886, letter by Burnett dated 11 May 1886.

victory of missionary propaganda became acting consul. This was H. H. Johnston.

So far as the British public was made to understand, the conflict that arose in 1886 and 1887 in the Niger Delta between Jaja and the merchants, Bonny and Johnston, was strictly a commercial one. This is the unmistakable impression given by the official records.[1] But it is essential to note that there was a religious aspect to Jaja's fall. It is significant that Dr Gertzel, having used the John Holt papers, contends that a commercial explanation of Jaja's fall is not itself convincing.[2] It would be misleading to think that the events that led to Jaja's fall dated back to only 1886 or that it was due mainly to his quarrel with a section of the British merchants. This work has shown that Jaja's fall was deeply rooted in the past, in the unresolved conflict between the missionary factor and himself as the champion of indigenous religion with commerce inextricably woven in. Hewett considered his obligations to missionary enterprise as of greater importance than those to free trade. Consequently he never enforced the free trade clause of his treaty, against which all the Delta states protested, but forced the Religion Clause on all of them. This was why he backed up the Christian party in Bonny and was unyielding in his desire to force the Religion Clause on Jaja. As Jaja himself averred many times, Hewett had special hatred for him,[3] and so far back as 1883 Hewett had recommended Jaja's removal from the Niger Delta. Largely through the opposition of the traders, who disliked his enmity to Jaja, and the lack of cooperation on the part of the naval officers, Hewett could not put his desire into action. In any case the main actors in the drama of 1886-87—Bonny, Johnston and the Primitive Methodist Mission—regarded the missionary factor as of the greatest moment.

The fundamental point is that the commercial and economic aspects of the Jaja story were by no means the sole factors explaining the situation. The whole economic tangle was woven into the religious aspect also, making Jaja not just a monopolist, but an evil and irreligious monopolist. It is clear from this work that before the commercial element appeared there were other forces already arrayed

1 For full details of the Jaja crisis from official records cf. R. Oliver: *Sir Harry Johnston and the Scramble for Africa*, London 1957, pp. 107–33. The writer wishes to make it clear that he does not reiterate the commercial and economic causes behind the Jaja affair, not because they were not of any account, but because Professor Oliver and Dr Gertzel have examined them thoroughly. What the writer proposes to contribute is an analysis which shows that this whole very complex story had a very distinct religious aspect.

2 C. Gertzel: thesis cited, pp. 266–86.

3 F.O. 403/18, Jaja to Granville, 25 Apr. 1882.

against Jaja. Whether the merchants complained or not an open clash between Jaja and Bonny and the Consul would have been very difficult to avoid. The missionary forces at work, together with the role of Johnston ready to act where Hewett had merely talked, were the real determinants of Jaja's fall in 1887.

If individuals may determine the course of history, then Acting Consul Johnston did so in 1887, and his assumption of Consular authority was a bad omen for Jaja. Although Hewett was, as noted already, a warm supporter of Christian missions, he lacked the means to exercise authority over Jaja. The latter could have no respect for a Consul who in the various disputes that arose between the other states had been constrained to request his (Jaja's) services.[1] Nothing shows more clearly the powerlessness of Hewett over Jaja than the successful refusal of the Opobo king to pay the fine of three puncheons of oil which Hewett had imposed on him in 1880.[2] It is not surprising then that Jaja, after sacrificing a human being in the usual manner before the coming of every Consul to Opobo,[3] rejected Hewett's pretensions to solving the dispute that had arisen between himself, Jaja, and the European traders. He flatly refused to pay the fines that Hewett imposed and preferred to deal directly with the Foreign Office to which he sent three of his chiefs.

Johnston was a man of different calibre. Jaja was amused at his small stature and completely misjudged the pro-missionary man who was to darken the remaining days of his life.[4] Like Hewett, but for different reasons, Johnston was not liked by the traders. They hated his intellectual aloofness. A man of varied abilities, he had been greatly interested in the ethnology of the Niger Delta. Energetic and adventurous, he possessed a constitution that defied the Niger 'fevers' that had often sent Hewett home. Johnston's interest for us lies in his views on Christian missions. Though an unbeliever he was probably the greatest supporter of the missionary cause among the empire-builders in Africa in the era of the 'scramble', and was ceaseless in advocating that they should be given all backing possible because 'they do and have done in the past an amount of good that has never been sufficiently appreciated either by the Government or the people of England'.[5] Johnston must be ranked with Sir Frederick Lugard as one of the few administrators in Nigeria who saw their task in the

1 Ibid. Jaja to Granville, 26 May 1882.
2 F.O. 403/86, enclosure 2 in Admiralty to F.O., 30 Apr. 1886.
3 *Times of India* (undated), reproduced in *African Times*, 1 Dec. 1886.
4 H. H. Johnston: *The Story of My Life*, London 1923, p. 192.
5 F.O. 84/1882, 'A Report on the British Protectorate of Oil Rivers', by H. Johnston.

country as more than the Foreign Office notion of merely looking after British commercial interests. He went further than both Beecroft and Hopkins in that he educated the Foreign Office in what Britain owed to the peoples of the Niger Delta in terms of 'moral obligations'.[1] Although a well-informed critic of Christian missions, whose dogmas he believed were beyond the comprehension of Negro 'savages', yet missionaries were for him 'the preparer of the whiteman's advent'.[2] In the Niger Delta he ranked them much higher, as 'civilizers', than the traders. Through the education they gave and the new tastes for European goods created in their wards the converts became 'civilized' and industrious and could be instructed to cultivate crops which Europe wanted. It was his conviction that missionaries should cease clinging to the coast but penetrate into the interior and produce there the social and economic results that were concomitants of their activity.

On the evidence of a naval officer in the Niger Delta at this time, it was in his vice-consular period that Johnston held the strongest views on the imperial usefulness of Christian missions.[3] It was not an accident therefore that it was in these years, 1887 to 1889, that in lectures and articles he praised the Christian missions in the Niger Delta and was the only non-missionary defender of Christian missions against their assailants in these years in Britain.[4] Johnston was forcibly struck by the imperial achievements of Christian missions in Southern Nigeria where they were successfully teaching their wards 'a desire for political incorporation with the British Empire'.[5] As a result of their teaching the Niger Delta peoples, except Opobo and Jaja's people, were the most docile and the most pro-British people he had ever seen. It was quite possible to hold such a vast territory with only 100 soldiers. He described their docility as follows:

'In spite of all temptations to belong to Other Nations' they have invariably inclined towards an English rule, even at a time when our policy was most unsympathetic and vacillating. They have been cheated by British merchants, bombarded by British captains, and fined by British consuls, and *yet* they like us, and stick by us, and are proud of being all same Ingilis man . . .[6]

It is with these views in mind that Johnston's attitude to Jaja

1 Ibid. Memorandum by same 26 July 1888.
2 H. H. Johnston: 'British Missions in Africa', *Nineteenth Century*, 1887, p. 723.
3 *West African Mail*, 29 Apr. 1904.
4 Cf. articles by Johnston cited. Johnston's article in *Fortnightly Review* (Vol. 45, 1888) was a defence of Christian missions against Canon Taylor's article, 'Our Foreign Missions a Failure' in *Fortnightly Review*, October 1887.
5 F.O. 84/1882, Memo. cited.   6 Ibid.

should be understood. Although he did not clearly say so to the Foreign Office until after Jaja's removal, when he reported how he compelled Opobo to accept missionaries, there can be no doubt that Johnston's 'war' on Jaja was mostly due to the latter's anti-missionary attitude. His friendship with George Pepple, whom with all his education he regarded as a lesser man than Jaja, cannot be explained otherwise.[1] It is significant to note that Johnston arrived in Bonny in 1886 at the very time that missionary propaganda was gaining ascendancy, and it was here that he wrote his first letter to the Foreign Office, asking for Jaja's removal, basing his judgment on facts collected from Bonny.[2] Furthermore he pleaded the cause of Bonny unblushingly during the crisis, a pleading that was echoed in Parliament with the Foreign Office giving a guarantee that Bonny would be given access to Jaja's markets.[3] In any case, to the Bonny people the matter was not merely one of trade but also one of the Christian faith, a revivification of the Bonny politics of 1864 to 1870. Johnston only came to fulfil the role they had expected Livingstone to fulfil in the civil war.

Johnston's bitterness against Jaja rose to the highest pitch when he discovered that his power rested on juju, 'the cruel and nonsensical fetish rites which formed such a serious barrier to trade'.[4] After himself experiencing bitterly the immense power of Jaja's juju on the oil producers in the interior, he compelled Jaja to send two of his big chiefs to follow him, Johnston, to Ohambele and 'break juju' in his presence, and also announce publicly that Jaja wanted the people to trade with the European traders and Bonny people. It does not appear that the juju was well 'broken' for, when put to the test, Johnston and a few merchants were forced to retreat in face of jeers and insults heaped on them by Jaja's emissaries headed by one Ekike Notsho. Johnston's head was nearly smashed.[5]

The Consul decided at first to blockade the Opobo river entirely, but gave up this idea because this would affect Bonnymen whom he encouraged to go to Jaja's markets of Uranta and Azumini.[6] He therefore issued a proclamation forbidding all trade with Opobo. In telling phrases Johnston contended that the British Government should back him up, partly because Bonny, on whose help he relied, was looking on and its loyalty would be lost if Jaja was not removed,

1 H. H. Johnston: *The Story of My Life*, p. 194.
2 F.O. 84/1750, Johnston to Salisbury, 15 Jan. 1886.
3 *African Times*, 1 Sept. 1887, quotes W. F. Lawrence M.P. asking Sir J. Fergusson on 22 Aug. 1887.
4 H. H. Johnston, *Fortnightly Review* cited, p. 486.
5 F.O. 84/1878, Johnston to Salisbury, 20 Aug. 1887.   6 Ibid.

and partly because Britain's prestige was involved. Jaja was contemplating flight into the interior where he had an arsenal and had built a house; if he were once allowed to escape, British authority and trade in the Niger Delta would come to an end, for Jaja would be able to prevent oil coming down to the coast. It was also reported that Jaja was arranging to transfer his loyalty and territory to either France or Germany if the Foreign Office did not back him, Jaja, in the crisis.[1] There can be no doubt that had Jaja managed to escape into the interior the history of south-eastern Nigeria would have been different. It is in the stultifying of such a plan of Jaja's that the action of Johnston and the Bonny Christians is of the greatest importance.

It is essential to emphasize that in the crisis of 1886 to 1887 neither the protests of the white merchants nor those of the naval officers were materially of great significance. Although the traders inundated the Foreign Office with protests and the latter was disposed to remove Jaja only the naval officers could effect their wish. Following the report by the naval officer in West Africa the Admiralty did not sympathize with either the traders or the Consul.[2] The part played by Bonny in the circumstances should not be underestimated. Johnston regarded its help as of real significance. There was an extraordinary friendship between Jaja and the naval officers in West Africa; as far back as 1876 the naval officers had been on Jaja's side even when they acknowledged that he broke the Treaty of 1873.[3] The records show that the consuls were pro-Bonny while the naval officers were pro-Opobo. This brought about an open clash between Hewett and the naval officers on many occasions.[4]

Naval officers were Jaja's regular visitors. In their view he was Britain's best friend in Southern Nigeria and 'our interests will be better served by keeping on friendly terms with him, while holding him to his Treaty obligations (1873 Treaty), than by burning his town'.[5] Johnston's allegation that it was mainly Jaja's hospitality to the officers that made them refuse to act against him is only partially true. A fact that should not be lightly regarded was the extraordinary personal charm and natural dignity which Jaja possessed, his humour and hypnotic presence, which Johnston himself could not escape and

1 F.O. 84/1828, Johnston to Salisbury, 11 Sept. 1887.
2 F.O. 403/31, Real-Admiral Salmon to Admiralty. As late as September 1887 the Admiralty informed the F.O. that 'there are other means of bringing Jaja to his Treaty obligations without having to resort to hostilities'. Cf. F.O. 403/86, F.O. to Admiralty, 6 Sept. 1887.
3 F.O. 84/1455, McKellar to Derby, 12 Feb. 1876.
4 F.O. 403/31, Hewett to Granville, 12 Feb. 1884; Rear-Admiral Salmon to Admiralty, 6 Mar. and 13 May 1876.
5 Ibid. Rear-Admiral Salmon to Admiralty, 6 Mar. 1884.

which had bewitched the missionaries. His was not the terrifying hypnotism of a monomaniac, but something natural, subtle but inescapably effective. One P. Butler of London, whose contact with Jaja was a very brief one in 1874, had the following to say of the impression that had not yet left him in 1888:

> I experienced the hospitality for which Ja ja was famous and though my acquaintance with this remarkable man was of short duration, it has left on me a lasting and agreeable impression; . . . At Ja Ja's table I have had the pleasure of meeting some British naval and colonial officers, and subsequently in various parts of the world I have met others, and all recalled with pleasure their acquaintance with one who was so interesting in character as he was picturesque and dignified in bearing. All acknowledged his remarkable ability, confessing him a man born to lead and to rule, one of nature's gentlemen, intrepid, hospitable and courteous.[1]

Except for Lord Salisbury, who was not in Britain at the time, opinion in the Foreign Office was unanimous: Jaja must be broken and Johnston supported. Sir T. Villiers Lister minuted on a dispatch by Hewett (in England then) in which the latter asked that Jaja be removed to St Helena, 'Ja Ja is a false and cruel chief under our Protectorate, who interferes with British traders and missionaries, breaks treaties and laughs at H.M.G. The cup of his iniquity is now full.'[2] When in September 1887 Johnston received a telegram, probably deliberately vaguely worded by the Foreign Office officials, approving his actions against Jaja, he believed that the backing he had asked for had been approved. He telegraphed to Captain Hand to send more gunboats in addition to H.M.S. *Goshawk* which was then lying off Opobo. The answer he received was 'Impossible',[3] although H.M.S. *Icarus* was lying idle in the Lagos Roads. Jaja commanded an army estimated at 4,000. Johnston could therefore in the circumstances rely only on Bonny. He arranged with the Bonny chiefs to block with their war canoes certain creeks at the back of Opobo, so that in case Jaja should attempt to escape into the interior his flight might be arrested.[4] On 20 September Johnston summoned Jaja to the gunboat and gave promise of a safe-conduct. Jaja was given an ultimatum, either to leave the gunboat and be treated as an enemy or to surrender and be shipped to Accra. Believing he was right and that the British Government would do him justice, Jaja chose the latter course. To add to Jaja's humiliation he was first shipped to

1 A.P.S. G.18, P. Butler's letter dated 3 May 1888.
2 F.O. 84/1828, Minute on Hewett to Salisbury, 20 Aug. 1887.
3 F.O. 403/86, Johnston to Salisbury, 24–8 Sept. 1887.   4 Ibid.

Bonny where he was transferred to a mail steamer. In Bonny Jaja's fall aroused 'almost unmeasured'[1] joy, and King George advised Johnston that Jaja must not be allowed to stay in West Africa as he could still do mischief.[2]

Acting on this advice Johnston, exaggerating, urged the Foreign Office to remove Jaja from the West African coast because of 'Ja Ja's powerful influence as a "juju" man, which extends along the West Coast of Africa from Sierra Leone to Old Calabar'.[3] It is worthy of note that in his judgment at the so-called trial in Accra Rear-Admiral Sir W. Hunt-Grubbe told Jaja that he was convicted on three charges, the first of which was that he kept 'the "juju"' on Ohambele after the Protectorate Treaty was signed.[4] Partly because of his attachment to indigenous religion, then, his 'presence in the (Opobo) river would be fatal to peace and progress'.[5]

How far Jaja saw his downfall in terms of opposition to the white man's religion is not easy to ascertain. It is probable that he understood the crisis of 1886 and 1887 in such terms, for according to his successor and son, Sunday Jaja, Jaja thought seriously on the necessity of receiving missionaries during this period.[6] This must have been after March 1887, probably after his removal, because in this month he turned down another effort of the Primitive Methodists to establish themselves in Opobo. Jaja could not have been unaffected by the fact that Bishop Crowther witnessed his being transferred from the gunboat to the mail steamer in Bonny[7] and that Archdeacon Crowther saw him in his humiliation in Accra. He decided that if allowed to return to Opobo he would receive missionaries.

The fall of Jaja did for the hinterland of the 'Oil Rivers' what the Ijẹbu Expedition did for Yorubaland. Except for the Aro-chukwu Oracle there was no longer any obstacle, as serious as Jaja, to the spread of Christianity into the interior. Johnston himself led the way. After depositing Jaja in Accra he undertook a tour of the oil markets that once belonged to Opobo and took the Archdeacon along with him. In Ohambele and Abo he asked the people to accept Christianity, while at the same time he compelled the oil producers to take oath that henceforward they would trade with Bonnymen, the slave

1 Ibid.
2 F.O. 84/1828, G. Pepple to Johnston, 21 Sept. 1887, enclosed in Johnston to Salisbury, 24–8 Sept. 1887.
3 F.O. 403/74, Johnston to Salisbury, 4 Jan. 1888.
4 Ibid. Rear-Admiral Sir W. Hunt-Grubbe to Jaja, 1 Dec. 1887, enclosed in No. 1.
5 Ibid.
6 *Primitive Methodist Missionary Records*, 1892, pp. 623–6.
7 C.M.S. G3/A3/03, Bishop Crowther to Lang, 13 Oct. 1887.

converts.[1] In Opobo he introduced the Archdeacon to the people and seized the occasion of the rudeness which 'Ja Ja's boys' had shown him to impose a fine of £64, which he promised to remit provided within six months they should have consented to the establishment of the C.M.S. in Opobo 'and shall have given to that body a gratuitous grant for the purpose of erecting schools'.[2]

It was not long before missionaries began to reap the result of Jaja's forcible exile. While he was pining away in the West Indies the Bonny converts erected chapels in his markets. By April 1891 there were already more than eighteen chapels and over 600 converts. In 1892 the Niger Delta Pastorate, which seceded from the C.M.S., came into being and took up the evangelization of the interior. Bonny entered into a new era of prosperity. From 31 August 1891 to 31 July 1892, Bonny's export amounted to £370,796 13s and it imported goods to the tune of £196,091 13s 11d.[3] The annual income of the Pastorate ranged between £1,500 and £2,000 in the first six years of its existence. The burden of evangelization was carried by the chiefs under the leadership of Warribo Manilla Pepple. The prosperity that accrued to the state was associated with the triumph of missionary propaganda. By 1906 there were over twenty-five chapels in the interior over eighty miles away from the coast.

Opobo came next in importance to Bonny. By 1890 Chief Uranta, who had been protected by Johnston in his rebellion against Jaja, had erected a chapel. The following year Opobo too began missionary activities and erected a church at Queenstown on the Opobo river. Chief Samuel Oko Epelle alone was responsible for a number of churches in the interior as far as Aba.[4] The triumph of Christianity over Jaja was a complete one. For before 1914 a member of his House, F. D. Jaja, was already an Anglican teacher and was ordained in 1931,[5] the first Opobo Anglican pastor. In February 1919 Chief Cookey Gam, Jaja's chief lieutenant and one of those sent to the Foreign Office in the 1887 crisis, became a Christian and was publicly baptized. On 4 September 1932 Jaja's grandson, Mac Pepple Jaja, the Amanyanabo of Opobo, also embraced the faith that had clouded his grandfather's last days, and was publicly baptized.[6]

The relatively easy success achieved by the Christian missions with the aid of the secular arm along the eastern coast of Southern

1 F.O. 84/1881, Johnston to Salisbury, 5 Apr. 1888. C.M.S. G3/A3/03, D. C. Crowther to Bishop Crowther, 30 Mar. 1888.
2 F.O. 84/1881, Johnston to Salisbury, 5 Apr. 1888.
3 F.O. 84/2191, Report on the 'Oil Rivers' Protectorate.
4 E. M. T. Epelle: *The Church in Opobo*, Aba, 1958, p. 11.
5 Ibid.   6 Ibid.

Nigeria was not repeated in the hinterland, which remained in the main out of bounds to missionaries, traders and administrators until the turn of the century. Penetration into the hinterland was only possible along the Niger and Cross rivers. But even along these highways the social and political situation was not conducive to the flourishing of Christianity and the imposition of British sovereignty until the beginning of the twentieth century. On the Lower Niger, where European traders and missionaries had begun operation in 1832 and 1857 respectively, conflicts between one chief and the other, between one town and the other, were rife, in the absence of a centralized authority that could weld together the independent towns of the Ijaw, Ibo and Igalla tribes. A new kind of law and order in the riverain areas began to prevail only as from 1886 when the Royal Niger Company, the trading concern that had since 1879 been directed under the grasping and ruthless energy of Taubman Goldie, obtained a Royal Charter. Until the end of the century the situation along the Cross river was less secure than on the Lower Niger. This was because, starting from Old Calabar, the ethnic groups of Efiks, Enyong, Umon and Akunakuna were monopolist in their commercial activities. One tribe along the river would not allow the other to pass through its territory for the purpose of trade. The tradition was that the Akunakuna must sell to the Umon, the Umon to the Enyong and the latter to the Efik.[1]

It is clear then that the peoples of Southern Nigeria did not hanker after the spiritual dispensation of missionaries and the political domination of the British officials. They were instinctively suspicious of all intruders—missionaries, traders and administrators—whose physical presence was in no way solicited. The inhabitants of the hinterland must have known the unpalatable consequences of the white man's activities in the coastal areas. Not only were the traditional rulers being stripped of their sovereignty by the 'intruders', but the society was being upset. With the establishment of effective consular administration in 1891 British authority in the coastal areas became supreme. Even before the formal establishment of British administration *Egbo* had been deprived of its judicial functions by the consular authority in Old Calabar,[2] while so-called Native Councils had been established in Brass, Bonny and Opobo, to the evident delight of missionaries and traders. Socially, as has been observed, slaves had been encouraged to become less submissive to their masters

---

1 For detailed analysis of the relations of the various ethnic groups along the Cross River cf. J. C. O. Anene: 'The Boundary Arrangements for Nigeria, 1884–1906', Ph.D. London 1960, Chapter III.
2 F.O. 84/2020, Annesley to Native Council of Old Calabar, 7 Jan. 1890.

and schoolboys had begun to question the traditional parental control.

The resistance of the rest of Southern Nigeria to missionaries, traders and administrators in the last decade of the nineteenth century, then, should not be ascribed, as the administrative officers and missionaries affected to believe, to the supposed barbarism of the people or their unwillingness to be 'civilized'. For these people believed not only that they were civilized but that their customs and institutions were the best for themselves. Alien customs and institutions, they thought, would bring disaster upon them. Moreover they were jealous of their political sovereignty and territorial integrity, on behalf of which they were prepared to fight. This viewpoint must be clearly borne in mind by people reading the official dispatches and missionary correspondence, in which only the European viewpoint is emphasized.

The European opinion was that there was something inherently evil in the nature of the peoples of Southern Nigeria that made it impossible for them to perceive their true interest—acceptance of the Christian faith and the political rule of the British. The unity of sentiment and action of missionaries and administrators in this respect is still to be studied in detail. But up to 1900 a favourable disposition to missionary enterprise became the undisguised policy of a set of administrators who, reflecting the religious side of Victorian England, believed that destruction of 'fetishism' was an essential part of their imperial task. In outlook, intention and action, they believed that *Pax Britannica* was in a sense also *Pax Christi*, for the moral and spiritual regeneration of the Nigerian 'pagans' lay in 'Christianity and Civilization'.

It was natural that Sir Claude Macdonald, High Commissioner of the Niger Coast Protectorate from 1891 to 1894, was not only a good sabbatarian but also a member of the Church Committee of the Presbyterian Mission in Old Calabar.[1] The Okrikans, regretting that the Protectorate authority they had been led to accept by Peter, their African pastor, meant that they could not eat their human enemies with impunity, appealed to Macdonald to remove both the church and the Christians. The High Commissioner answered them with a parade of troops which, he said, would destroy Okrika if the converts were attacked.[2]

Macdonald's attitude indicated the spirit of the administrators who destroyed the centres of pagandom in Southern Nigeria between 1892 and 1902. As Consul Annesley put it, the era of the Cross going before

1 U.P. Minutes, 30 May 1893.
2 C.M.S. Memo. of interview with F. Baylis, 2 Mar. 1893.

the Flag had passed. What was 'urgently' needed to pacify the territory was 'not the Bible but the sword'.[1] Then, 'as soon as order, peace and security exists in the Oil Rivers, then the Bible may be brought out with advantage but not before'. The missionary element was present in all the major military expeditions of the decade under consideration. Probably not unknown to Nana of Itsekiris and Overami of Benin, two consular officials on their coast, Captain Harper and Phillips, respectively, were planning to introduce missionary enterprise into their territory in 1893. Captain Harper was nephew of the Bishop of New Zealand, and Phillips son of Archdeacon of Barrow-in-Furness. Both officers 'begged . . . most earnestly' for Christian missions to begin work among the Edo and Itsekiri.[2]

In 1894 Nana, whose father had warded off Bishop Crowther in 1875, and who himself boasted to the Aborigines Protection Society that by the aid of his juju he had scared away Ijaw cannibals[3] from his territory, incurred Sir Ralph Moor's displeasure. While preparation for the bombardment of his territory was on hand, Bishop Tugwell was informed to get ready for a spiritual entry into the territory.[4] Nana was exiled to the Gold Coast but was allowed to return to Nigeria in 1906, having been chastened by experience to become a Christian. In 1897 Phillips, despite all warning, defied Benin's 'fetish', and was murdered with most of his party. For avenging the defiance of their religion the Edo had a visitation of the 'vengeful destructive and desolating sword of the British'.[5] Their independence came to an end, their *Oba* was exiled and the appeals to Christian missions were renewed. Perhaps thinking that conformity to the white man's religion might lead to restoration of the *Oba*, some members of his family joined the Anglican communion.[6]

In 1901–02 the decision arrived at by both Sir Ralph Moor, Macdonald's successor, and the Presbyterian missionaries as early as 1898, that the Aros would be 'dealt with',[7] and Christianity imposed on the Ibos, was put into effect by the Aro Expedition. Three columns of troops converged on Aro Chukwu and blew up the *Long Juju*, the citadel of Ibo religion and an integrative institution of Eastern Nigeria. In this operation the steamers of the Presbyterian Mission took an active part, while Dr Rattray, one of its medical

1   F.O. 2020, Annesley to Salisbury, 29 Oct. 1890.
2   C.M.S. G3/A3/06, J. S. Hill to Wigram, 2 Jan. 1893.
3   A.P.S., Nana to Fox Bourne, 5 Nov. 1894.
4   C.M.S. G3/A3/06, Bishop Tugwell to Baylis, 23 July 1894.
5   C.M.S. G3/A3/09, James Johnson to Baylis, 24 Sept. 1904.
6   C.M.S. G3/A3/011, James Johnson's report for 1906.
7   U.P. Minutes, 23 Mar. 1899.

missionaries, was chaplain and medical officer to the troops.[1] Immediately after the expedition a Dr T. B. Adams, an official attached to the army, began preaching, followed a few weeks later by James Johnson and at the end of the year by the intrepid 'white queen of Okoyong', Mary Slessor.

But, perhaps, of all the inhabitants in the interior of Southern Nigeria it was the western Ibo people in the hinterland of Asaba who were most affected politically and socially by the activities of missionaries. Alien penetration of the western Ibo began to be effective from 1888 when the Royal Niger Company forced the chiefs of Asaba to put an end to immolation of slaves. In fact many slaves were set free and handed over to the S.M.A. missionaries who had begun working in the Lower Niger in 1884.[2] In the hinterland it was at Issele-Uku that missionary activities began to threaten the society. For in 1893, when Egbosha, a minor, became king the female regent ruling on his behalf invited the S.M.A. to establish themselves in the town, in spite of opposition by all the other chiefs.[3] Like Eyo Honesty II of Creek Town, both king and regent turned reformers. They set free their slaves on condition that the latter rendered them services two times a week. When Egbosha came of age he refused to perform ceremonies which were incompatible with the Christian faith that he had adopted. It was not long before the slaves declared themselves absolutely free.

The consequence of all this for the society may be imagined. In order to put an end to this state of affairs a secret organization known as the *Ekumeku*,[4] was formed at Ibusa and soon spread to other parts, becoming a popular movement. In 1898 they raised the standard of revolt at Issele-Uku, Alla, Ebu, Ezi, Okpanam and Ibusa and attacked Mission establishments. Through the S.M.A. missionaries Egbosha got in contact with the Royal Niger Company, Major Festing, a devout Roman Catholic who in the previous year had participated in the expeditions against Bida and Ilọrin, led a force of well-disciplined troops officered by six Europeans and punished the *Ekumeku* in a manner similar to the punishment inflicted upon the Ijẹbu. Egbosha was confirmed on his throne at Issele-Uku. In all the towns the people were compelled to restore the Mission establishments and their chiefs offered to grant them protection henceforth. The chief of Ibusa was deposed and a Company's nominee appointed. Some troops were stationed in the interior until the end of the Com-

1 Ibid. 24 Sept. 1901.   2 S.M.A., Zappa to Superior, 4 Oct. 1888.
3 Ibid. Same to same, 26 Jan. 1888; 7 Oct. 1898.
4 For detailed information on the Ekumeku, cf. J. C. Anene: *Southern Nigeria in Transition 1885–1906*, Cambridge, 1966. pp. 240–6.

pany's rule. Many of the captives of the expedition were not released until 1900.

The series of military expeditions launched in Southern Nigeria into the first decade of the twentieth century began the halcyon days of Christian missions. Eastern Nigeria was invaded by them from all directions. The Scottish missionaries left the riverain area of the Cross River, turned left into the interior and occupied Itu and Bende in the south-east; the Niger Delta Pastorate concentrated their efforts in the Delta area; the Qua Ibo Mission, a Congregationalist organization based in Belfast, worked into the interior along the Qua Ibo river and established its headquarters at Etinam; the Primitive Methodists diffused their energy among the Ibibio and established their chief centre at Uzuakoli; the C.M.S. and the Roman Catholic Mission of the Holy Ghost Fathers made the nodal centre of Onitsha the spring-board of their penetration into the unexplored interior via Awka and Owerri. From Asaba both the C.M.S. and the S.M.A. moved ever westwards towards Benin and the Kukuruku area. A mass movement towards Christianity began.

Personally I should like to see the Missions withdraw entirely from the Northern States, for the best missionary for the present will be the high-minded clean living British Resident.

Sir Percy Girouard,
Governor of Northern Nigeria,
1907–1909

4 The Crescent and the Cross in Northern Nigeria, 1900–1914

One perennial bugbear of Christian missions in Nigeria in eth second half of the nineteenth century was Islam, the monotheistic creed believed by its adherents to have been promulgated by Allah through Mohammed, the Seal of the Prophets, in Arabia in the seventh century A.D. Antedating Christianity in Nigeria by several centuries and spread in that period largely peacefully and unobtrusively, Islam was decisively propagated by fire and sword from 1804 to 1831 in the larger part of Northern Nigeria, by *jihadists* who drew inspiration from Usuman dan Fodio, the scholar and reformer-initiator of the Fulani *jihad*. The result was the establishment of the Sokoto caliphate which embraced most of what is now Northern Nigeria. By the middle of the nineteenth century, when Christian missions revived their propaganda on the Atlantic seaboard, Islam had already assimilated the northern periphery of Yorubaland to the Sokoto caliphate and had been embraced by parts of the population of large Yoruba towns of Ogbomosho, Iwo, Iseyin, Ketu, Badagry and Lagos. On the Niger the Islamic faith had percolated as far south as Idah; the Islamic frontier had also crossed the Benue, making forays into the areas inhabited by the Idoma, the Jukun and the intractable Tiv.

Although evidence points to the fact that in Yorubaland itself the statistical progress of Islam was considerable, and occasionally alarmed missionaries,[1] it was the Sokoto caliphate on which missions fixed their eyes as the real battleground where they should enlist against the Muslims. Hence, as early as 1855, with millions of 'pagans' behind him, T. J. Bowen,[2] the pioneer missionary of the Southern American Baptist Mission, attempted to found a station in the Muslim town of Ilorin. Also regarding the evangelization of the 'pagan' Ibo inhabitants as of less urgency than that of the Muslims,

1 C.M.S. G3/A2/014, Tugwell to Baylis, 21 Feb. 1910.
2 T. J. Bowen: *Adventures and Missionary Labours 1849–1856*, Charleston, 1857, pp. 188 ff.

Samuel Ajayi Crowther was impetuous and relentless in his effort to push the missionary frontier ever northwards on the Niger. As early as 1857 he had desired the evangelization of Northern Nigeria. Tactfully and patiently and by his personal friendship with the Emirs of Nupe he was able to establish stations at Lokoja, Egga and Kipo Hill. He also succeeded in persuading the Emirs of Bida, Ilọrin and Gwandu and the Sultan of Sokoto to receive Arabic Bibles from the Church Missionary Society.[1] By 1880 both the Wesleyan and Church Missionary Societies had indicated a sanguine desire to establish stations as far north as the Chad, whilst the previous year W. Allakurah Sharpe, a Kanuri Wesleyan agent, had pleaded with the Wesleyan Mission to provide him with facilities to take the gospel to his tribe in Bornu.[2] Even as late as the nineties the American Baptist missionaries advised their Foreign Mission Board that white missionaries should vacate the south for the north completely, in the hope that the Royal Niger Company would offer them protection.[3]

Why, it should be asked, were the Christian missions so attracted to Northern Nigeria? Why, also, were they sanguine about the ease of converting the peoples of this vast territory, one third of the size of India? Some part of the answer is to be found in the fact that Northern Nigeria was part of the large belt of open grassland and semi-desert between latitudes 9 and 12 degrees north, running from the Atlantic in the west to the Red Sea in the east, which came to catch the attention of Christian Missions in a special way since the death of the missionary-disposed General Gordon in Khartoum and the establishment of the Mahdist regime there. Anti-Islamic feelings were aroused among the Christian missions in Britain and in the United States when the Mahdi and his successor, the Khalifa, won more and more successes. The long imprisonment of the French Catholic priests by the Khalifa, the retreat of Emin Pasha before his victorious force and the abandonment of Emin Pasha's province, all inflamed Christian ardour. Christian missions looked forward to the day when Christian England would avenge Gordon's death and destroy the Islamic theocracy in the Eastern Sudan.[4] While the British occupation of Uganda after 1890 was a guarantee that the Khalifa could not extend the Crescent's frontier southwards there was the fear that the deluge of Mahdism might sweep westwards and envelop what was known as the Central Sudan, roughly the present Northern Nigeria. Moreover, just as the Sudan belt was one of the

1 C.M.S. CA3/04 (b), Annual Report for 1873 by Bishop Crowther.
2 M.M.A., W. A. Sharpe to John Milum, 8 Sept. 1879.
3 *The Foreign Mission Journal*, July 1893, p. 355.
4 *Contemporary Review*, April 1885, pp. 562–78; Apr. 1888, pp. 537–59.

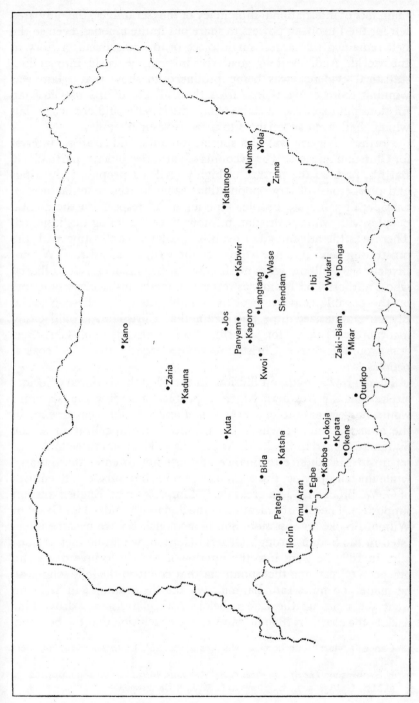

Northern Nigeria: Principal Mission Stations

main foci of international diplomacy of the 'scramble', the only area left for the European powers to share out in the nineties, even so the belt remained the largest single piece of unevangelized territory in the world. And, as if to goad the missionary world into action, statistical evidence was being produced to show that Islam was winning more converts in Africa than all the efforts of Christian missions put together,[1] a claim which the latter would not accept but which challenged subscribers to increase their liberality.

Northern Nigeria was of a special romantic and strategic interest for Christian missions. The accounts of various explorers, particularly Barth's, painted the picture of highly civilized peoples, industrious and prosperous; of large populations eager for the manufactures of Europe; of a literate people, superior in all respects to the coastal peoples with whom Christian missions were becoming disillusioned. There was the advantage of healthy highlands contrasting with the prostrating coastal areas. Moreover the writings of Edward Wilmot Blyden, the well-known pan-Africanist negro missionary of Liberia, whose authority on Islam was respected, made missionaries sanguine on the possible conversion of the inhabitants of Northern Nigeria. Blyden emphasized time and again that Christianity could easily incorporate Islam, for Muslims were already half-Christians and would embrace Christianity more eagerly than the coastal peoples.[2]

There grew a myth, an illusion, in the Church Missionary Society circles that the Northern Nigerian peoples, including the Muslims, would be very easy to convert. This illusion would seem to explain the amazing interest which the prospect of evangelization of the Sudan awakened in England. As early as 1886 a committee had been set up in Manchester to finance any attempt to enter the Sudan,[3] while the self-denying, transparently genuine but quixotic adventures of G. W. Brooke made a great deal of impression on English mission supporters. The Christianization of the Sudan was indeed for Graham Wilmot Brooke an obsession. Son of a colonel, Brooke became interested in the Sudan through General Gordon, whom he met personally. In 1884 he went into the interior of Algeria to investigate the prospects of reaching the Sudan via that country; the following year he made 500 miles into Bambuk via the Senegambia; in 1887 he went 500 miles up the Congo before African resistance drove him back to the coast. In 1889 he came to the conclusion that the best and

1 Canon Taylor: 'Our Foreign Missions a Failure', *Contemporary Review*, Oct. 1887.
2 E. W. Blyden: *The African Problem and other Discourses*, London 1890, pp. 102–3.
3 C.M.S. G3/A3/05, L. K. Shaw to C.M.S., 5 Dec. 1892.

only way to reach the Sudan and evangelize its peoples was via the Niger from the Niger Delta. When in that year he decided to undertake his enterprise under the auspices of the Church Missionary Society, eleven missionaries, graduates from Cambridge and Oxford, were ready to go with him, while other mission fields were crying for labourers. The missionaries, called the Sudan Party, expected very quick results, for Brooke had calculated that within six months much of Northern Nigeria would be converted.[1] No such large band of missionaries had been dispatched to a single mission field at one time as the Sudan Party; no set of missionaries had been given greater publicity; no Exeter Hall meeting had been more largely attended than the one in which the missionaries were dispatched; no missionaries had excited so much hope as the Sudan Party. And yet, surprisingly, their resounding failure, rather than being acknowledged, evoked sympathy and increased the illusions. In January 1890, three months before the missionaries set out for Lokoja, Brooke began a series of cheap but informative *Sudan Leaflets*, sold at a penny, and enjoying a wide circulation.

In contrast to the unbridled optimism and illusion of the Church Missionary Society and the Sudan Party was the hostile reaction of Northern Nigerians to white people in general—all of whom they regarded as 'Christians'. As early as the twenties of the nineteenth century the Kanawa were reported as being apprehensive of white 'strangers'.[2] Both Mohammed Bello, one of the sons of Usuman dan Fodio, who succeeded his father as Sultan of Sokoto, and the Shehu of Bornu had at the same time believed that intrusion of white people into Northern Nigeria should be discouraged if the territory was not to be assimilated into the British Empire as India had been.[3] The records also show that the Muslims had implacable contempt for *kafiris*, as they termed the 'unbelievers'. Many Muslims believed that 'Christians' did not have the features of human beings, whilst others felt that infidels were cowards who could not fight successfully against the true believers.[4] Of particular interest is the religious interpretation some of the rulers in Northern Nigeria gave to the Greek War of Independence against Turkey, the French invasion and occupation of Algeria, the Russo-Turkish war of the seventies and the Arabi

1 BMSS F5/3, Brooke to Father, 29 May 1888.
2 Denham, Clapperton and Oudney: *Narrative of Travels and Discoveries in Northern and Central Africa in the years 1822, 1823 and 1824*, London 1826, pp. 42, 47, 48, and 49.
3 Ibid.
4 H. Clapperton: *Journal of a Second Expedition into the Interior of Africa*, London 1829, p. 161.

Pasha 'rebellion' of 1881–82 in Egypt.[1] In all these events they manifested solidarity of feelings with their North African and Turkish co-religionists.

The experience of the Sudan Party in Lokoja cannot be surprising in the light of the mood of Northern Nigerian Muslims specified above. Hardly had the Party arrived in Lokoja than the missionaries discovered that they did not have the supposed magic wand with which to turn the Muslims into Christian crusaders. In fact the methods they had hoped would achieve the expected miracle had the opposite effects. By wearing Muslim clothing, turban and shoes, the ordinary Muslim was elated that they, the missionaries, were at last taking the first step towards becoming Muslims.[2] The Emirs regarded them as political spies and sent their own spies to survey the military strength of the Niger Company at Lokoja. Moreover, the Anglo-French and Anglo-German Treaties of that year, published in Cairo and Tunis, were being circulated in Northern Nigeria.[3] By the former, many of the Emirs and *malams* should have noted with consternation the pretentious claims of the British to owning the Sokoto caliphate. In fact many Emirs were reported as mobilizing their forces to attack the Niger Company at Lokoja. Not a single convert was made. One by one the Sudan Party fell off, either by resigning or by being invalided home or by dying. Not even Brooke's apparently invincible idealism could withstand the reality of facts. As he saw his vision collapse like a house of cards his letters conveyed gloomier and gloomier forebodings. Early in 1892 he wrote, 'the long gathering political troubles seem coming to a head, and I greatly fear that we may be on the verge of a general Muhammedan rising'.[4]

The unmitigated failure of the Sudan Party did not quench the ardour of people who had been led to believe that the Hausas would be the most excellent material for mass conversion to Christianity. In 1893 three Canadians and Americans went into Northern Nigeria with Kano as their goal. After suffering much privation two of them died at Girku, a town about forty miles from Zaria, while Bingham, destined to be the head of the Sudan Interior Mission until his death in 1942, was lucky to return to America.[5] Then there was the pathetic attempt of two young Englishmen from Bolton, Edward White and Thomas Holt. Both had been to North Africa, had learned

1 *Les Missions Catholiques*, 1884, p. 537. Sultan Bello asked Clapperton whether any other Christian power, apart from the British, was helping the Greeks in their revolt against Turkey. He also alluded to European bombardment of Algiers (1815).
2 *Sudan Leaflet* No. 9.   3 *Sudan Leaflet* No. 12.
4 C.M.S. G3/A3/05, Brooke to Hamilton, 5 Jan. 1892.
5 J. H. Hunter: *A Flame of Fire*, Slough 1961, pp. 58–60.

some Arabic and Hausa, and had attempted unsuccessfully to reach Northern Nigeria from Tripoli. In 1893 they found their way to the Niger Delta, but like the apostles, had neither purse nor stores, hoping that traders would help them. Both succumbed to the Niger 'fever'.[1]

The Sudan Party left a legacy significant for the pacification of Northern Nigeria by disseminating anti-Fulani feelings, holding up to the British public the Fulani as religious impostors whom the Hausa would be happy to have removed. Clearly, they did not perceive the non-racial nature of the so-called Fulani *Jihad*, that there was considerable support for the holy war among devout Hausa. They did not also discern the fact that the distinction they were trying to make between the Hausa and Fulani elements of the population of Northern Nigeria was largely hypothetical. For the Fulani, who preponderated in the *jihad*, were the town-dwellers, and not the non-mixing Bororos, who had become a Hausa-speaking people, had intermarried with the Hausa and were participating fully in the commercial life of the cities. The Sudan Party missionaries were certainly mistaken in identifying the Fulani with genuine Islam and describing the Hausa as nominal Muslims, for Islam preceded the Fulani to Nigeria. Nevertheless in their letters the missionaries talked of the Fulani as being anti-British, implying that it was the chivalrous task of Britain to destroy them, and they extolled the qualities of the Hausa. The first issue of the *Sudan Leaflets*, written before the missionaries came to know the Fulani, contained the following ominous words:

> Though the military skill of the fierce Fulani conquerors has reduced the Hausas to the position of a subject people, yet they are probably the best race in Africa. Every traveller who has met with them has written of them with enthusiasm, and their capacity for good seems very great. In intelligence they seem in no way inferior to the Europeans, and though brave enough when occasion requires, they seem peaceably disposed, their requirement and courtesy of manner being attractive. Unlike the Fulani they seem to have no ferocious fanaticism, and the tenets of Islam are followed in a very lax manner, and almost entirely discarded when they are away from the surveillance of their conquerors.[2]

Views like these were expressed in the writing and speeches of George Goldie,[3] but it was the Hausa Association, formed in late

1 C.M.S. G3/A3/o5, Dobinson to Baylis, 28 Feb. 1893.
2 *Sudan Leaflet* No. 1, January 1890.
3 G. T. Goldie: 'The Future of Nigeria', *The Independent*, 5 May 1899.

1891 ostensibly for the study of the Hausa Language, which clearly
called upon Britain to destroy the Fulani 'impostors' in order that
the supposed thirst of the Hausa for Christianity might be assuaged.
This Association was formed in memory of J. A. Robinson, Brooke's
chief companion, who died in August 1891, but had started to translate portions of the Bible into Hausa before his death. But the
Association did not conceal its proselytizing aims. The Presidents of
the C.M.S. and the Wesleyan Missionary Society were among the
officers of the Association and its General Executive was dominated
by Church dignitaries.[1] Nor was the Chairman, Goldie, unwilling to
see the Association carry out missionary activities. Rather he encouraged it towards this end. The threefold objects of the Association, he declared, were to enable Englishmen to study Hausa, to
broadcast among the Hausa copies of translated works, including the
gospels and to establish, possibly in Liverpool, a college where the
Hausa would study English, and Englishmen Hausa.[2] And to show
that he was serious about the 'sword of steel' going before the 'sword
of the spirit', he settled over 100 slaves, who had escaped as a result
of the Nupe war of 1897, in a territory given by the Niger Company,
called Victoria, and allowed missionaries to turn them into Christians.[3] For Canon Robinson, brother of J. A. Robinson and 'Professor' of Hausa in Cambridge, the Association was a proselytizing
agency. The Bible was to be translated into Hausa and a Missionary
College established in Kano.[4]

When Canon Robinson went to Northern Nigeria in 1894, he and
Bishop Tugwell arranged that within six months the latter would
join him in Kano. With the encouragement of Flint,[5] the Agent-
General of the Niger Company, the C.M.S. had made all preparation
when suddenly two of Robinson's party took ill and he was forced to
leave Kano after three months. On returning to England Robinson
had a special interview with the Parent Committee in November
1895. He gave a most favourable view of the readiness of the Hausa
to receive Christian teachers; in Kano the Emir had met him at the
gates with gifts; the most learned malams were put at his disposal and
the latter were, of their own volition, anxious to translate the Bible
which, they said, the people would most gratefully buy. There were
no Koranic schools in Northern Nigeria, he said, except in Kano

1   H. C. Robinson: *Hausaland*, London 1896, pp. 286–7.
2   *The Journal of Commerce* (Liverpool), 14 July 1894.
3   C.M.S. G3/A3/07, L. Nott: *Journals*, March 1897.
4   C.M.S. G3/A3/07, 'The Hausa Association occasional paper No. XIII',
    March 1898.
5   C.M.S. G3/A3/06, Tugwell to Baylis, 5 Oct. 1894.

where there were from thirty to forty. The country, he went on, was only '*nominally mohammedan*' and the fierce bigotry of the Eastern Sudan was completely absent. Only one third of the entire population was Muslim but nine-tenths of these knew nothing about their religion. There were very few mosques in the territory, one in Kano and one in Sokoto. He was fully convinced that there would be '*no opposition*' to Christianity for at any rate some years; even the malam in Kano, one of the best educated men, had no copy of the Koran. The C.M.S. should first occupy Keffi and then Kano, where a school should be established.[1]

Of course, Robinson oversimplified and grossly underrated both the extent and intensity of Islam in Northern Nigeria at the end of the nineteenth century. By fire and sword much of the territory had already been Islamized for over sixty years, and excepting the myriads of fierce tribes in the hilly belt south of the Bauchi plateau and Adamawa hills, the peoples of Northern Nigeria were under Muslim rulers appointed from Sokoto. When the British began to pacify the territory the spiritual eminence of Sokoto was acknowledged throughout the territory, though there were strains and stresses in the political relations of some of the Emirs and Sokoto. The strength of Islam in the nineties is clear from Dr Flint's book. In 1892 Yola refused to have any relations with the Niger Company until the latter assured the Emir that missionaries would not be introduced into his territory, while the war against Ilọrin and Bida evoked the religious susceptibilities of the Emirs.[2] The historical and literary records which Professor Charles Smith of Ahmadu Bello University, Zaria, has compiled show clearly that the Islam of Northern Nigeria was of high quality and the Maliki law in operation throughout the courts.

By 1897 the Church Missionary Society with many of its missionaries had begun to look forward to a military subjugation of Northern Nigeria, which event they hoped would, as in Southern Nigeria, open the door to the Christianization of Northern Nigeria. The expectation of the C.M.S. was quite legitimate for, as analysed so far, the 'sword of steel' and the 'sword of the spirit' had been going together in the experience of recalcitrant Nigerian peoples who attempted to prevent intrusion of either the missionary or the administrator into their areas. In Northern Nigeria the C.M.S. expected that the British bayonet would remove the Fulani 'impostors', the main obstacle, as it seemed to missionaries, to the evangelization of the territory. It is

1 Ibid. Memo. of interview with Group III, 15 Nov. 1895.
2 J. E. Flint: *Goldie and the Making of Nigeria*, London 1960, pp. 178 and 296.

not surprising then that the Society interpreted the military expeditions against Ilọrin and Bida as the beginning of the fulfilment of their hopes. In ecstatic mood the Society likened the Bida war to the Battle of Plassey. The 'Hausa race' which was 'being mulcted' by the Fulani impostors, it declared, would soon be liberated and slavery given a mortal blow, and it went on, 'Fulah oppression is now to be superseded by the direct exercise of British authority'.[1] No one rejoiced as much as Bishop Tugwell of the Ijẹbu Expedition who held an imperialistic view of his post. British rule was the only panacea for the political and social evils which, he observed, engulfed Nigeria. For him the welfare of all Nigeria was the joint responsibility of both missionaries and the officials. This was his conception of 'true empire building'.[2] According to his observation the inhabitants of some parts of Northern Nigeria had before 1896 been eager for 'the presence of Europeans' in their midst to guarantee peace, good order and prosperous trade.[3] Keffi had issued a 'clear and emphatic' summons to missionaries to establish themselves there in 1896. In his usual sensational manner he announced to the British public, through *The Times*, that the victory over Bida and Ilọrin was not for commerce alone but that by it Britain assumed a religious commitment also. His moving appeal was rewarded with the substantial 'advance fund' of over £2,000.[4]

With the road now opening, so the C.M.S. thought, preparations were being made for the spiritual intrusion into Northern Nigeria. In 1898 a number of missionaries were sent to Tripoli to study the Hausa language. Tripoli was chosen because there was some Hausa settlement there, and it was frequently visited by Hausa pilgrims, who, due to the unsettled state of the Eastern Sudan, used the Tripoli route on their way to Alexandria and Jedda.[5] The C.M.S. had decided that the missionaries should spend at least two years here, but hardly had they been there for a year than Dr Walter Miller, destined to be the best known white man in Northern Nigeria until his death in 1952, pressed the Society to allow them to move to the field of their labour at once. Miller's anxiety was awakened by political reasons. He had been spending his time on collecting political information from the Hausa pilgrims and on impressing upon them the blessings that would fall to them if they accepted British rule. Miller's patriotic feelings arose out of the 'feverish energy' and

1 *Church Missionary Intelligencer*, 1897, p. 355.
2 C.M.S. G3/A3/010, Tugwell to Nott, 19 Dec. 1905.
3 C.M.S. G3/A3/07, Tugwell to Baylis, April 1896.
4 *Lagos Weekly Record*, 29 Jan. 1898.
5 C.M.S. G3/A3/08, A. E. Richardson to Baylis, 7 May 1899.

'extraordinary activity of the French'[1] in the areas bordering the Hausa country. Between 1898 and 1900 French military expeditions against the Senusi *tariqa* were many, and no less than three state-sponsored political expeditions were dispatched to the Lake Chad area.[2] For a fanatic like Miller who believed that no other power but the British could rule the Hausa well, no greater peril than the French hung over the Hausa people. But his patriotism apart, the Hausa pilgrims spoke of the earnestness of their countrymen to receive them. Miller wrote:

> The people who for years past have been practically ignorant of the English, who they are, etc. are beginning now to know, and there is, so we are told by all malams who come here, a universal belief in the Soudan that the Power, prophesied in their sacred books, which is to conquer and rule the Soudan is to be the English and that it will now be very soon. Those who have been here and met Christian English and have had their ideas altered have gone back with quite new thoughts and say they believe we shall be gladly welcomed.[3]

Miller emphasized that Northern Nigeria was already British in sentiment, but the Government should take 'some more energetic steps ... to make what is only a name reality'. Born in 1872 in Devonshire into a Puritan family Miller was already as a child uncompromisingly anti-Islamic and anti-Turk and had wished he were in Armenia in 1896 to avenge the Armenian massacres.[4] His interest in the evangelization of Hausaland dated back to 1893. In Tripoli, even before he knew the Fulani, he had believed that they were the worst oppressors and the largest slave-raiders in the world, a conviction which neither old age nor fifty-two years' sojourn in Northern Nigeria made him modify. His anti-Fulani feelings rose to fever height as the pilgrims related to him the oppression in the Fulani empire. Miller burst out, 'the slavery of Socoto [sic] and raiding in all the 7 big Hausa states is terrible and will have to be put down'.[5]

Miller expressed the universal sentiment of all Christian missions, particularly that of the C.M.S. In the special 'Hausa Number' of the *Niger and Yoruba Notes* (published in London) the Society declared,

1 C.M.S. G3/A3/08, Miller to Baylis, 11 June 1899.
2 E. E. Evans-Pritchard: *The Sanusi of Cyrenaica*, O.U.P. 1949, Chapter 1. *Church Missionary Intelligencer*, March 1900, pp. 202-4.
3 C.M.S. G3/A3/08, Miller to Baylis, 11 June 1899.
4 W. Miller: *An Autobiography*, Zaria, 1953 p. 1.
5 C.M.S. G3/A3/08, Miller to Baylis, 11 June 1899.

obviously distorting the prophecy Usuman dan Fodio had made early in the century:

> The end is drawing near. The kings of Hausa cities are renouncing their religious allegiance to the Sultan of Sokoto. The people prophesy the advent of the whiteman with the Christian religion, which all the world will accept for a short space of forty months. . . . The sacred writings of the Hausas predict the second coming of Christ as the victorious leader of a great army. Next year (1900) is marked out as the time. So it comes to pass that the whole Hausa world is waiting for Christ. Now, we believe that Christ will appear in Hausaland next year, not as the people expect Him however. He will appear, not as a true Moslem, the son of a false faith, but as the crucified one, the Son of God.[1]

The bellicose mood and unbounded optimism of the C.M.S. and the missionaries who left England in December 1899 should be seen in the context of the assumption of the administration of the territory by Britain and the appointment of Lugard as the High Commissioner. For Bishop Tugwell all had gone very well since 1898 when he had moved among the military officers in Jebba. He had asked that a chaplain be provided for the new administration, and many of the military officers had invited him to accompany them in their reconnoitrings.[2] The pioneers, consisting of the Bishop, Miller, Burgin, Ryder and Richardson, all university graduates, had no cause whatsoever to entertain any fear from Lugard, a man who was already admired by Bishop Tugwell for his brilliant career in Uganda.[3] The Bishop and Lugard had met on the Niger in 1894 when the latter was making his famous race to Nikki.[4] Moreover, although Lugard was not a Christian or a churchman, he fitted well into Tugwell's conception of 'true empire building'. According to Tugwell, had Lugard not demanded the co-operation of the C.M.S. missionaries and their converts against anti-British French Catholic priests and their followers in the crisis that faced both Lugard and the Protestants in Uganda in 1890?[5] Had he not also, like Carter and Johnston, admired the civilizing task of Christian missions in his book on East Africa?[6] Above all, had not the new Administrator of Northern Nigeria cast his lot with the Bishop in the latter's anti-liquor mania and duel with the anti-missionary Mary Kingsley?[7]

The point has to be emphasized here that contrary to a general

---

1 January 1900.   2 C.M.S. G3/A3/08, Tugwell to Baylis, 19 Oct. 1898.
3 C.M.S. G3/A3/06, Tugwell to Baylis, 4 Sept. 1894.   4 Ibid.   5 Ibid.
6 F. D. Lugard: *The Rise of Our East African Empire*, London 1893, pp. 69–71.
7 F. D. Lugard, 'Liquor Traffic in Africa', *The Nineteenth Century*, Vol. XLII, 1897.

impression created by books written by his lieutenants,[1] an impression endorsed by many scholars,[2] Lugard was in no way opposed to missionary enterprise either by conviction or policy. In fact, as will be clear presently, no one could have been more generous, so tolerant and so helpful as Lugard was, to Christians missions from 1900 to 1906, and this in the most difficult phase of the pacification of Northern Nigeria. Had he desired in 1899 Lugard could have with justification prohibited missionary enterprise in the Muslim areas in view of the religious susceptibilities of the Emirs of which he was already aware. He ought to have known that an administration which was just feeling its way in an Islamic state should not run the risk of exciting the ill-feelings of Emirs who had indicated that they feared that the British were contemplating forcible interference with their religion. It required no special imagination for Lugard to know that missionaries would be regarded by the Emirs as political emissaries in disguise, the advance-guard of forcible imposition of British 'Christian' rule. Lugard may also not have been unaware that Lord Cromer had refused Christian missions permission to occupy Khartoum after the destruction of Mahdism in 1898. Had Lugard looked upon Christian missions from the point of view of what would be safe for his new administration in 1899 and afterwards, he would have discouraged missionary enterprise entirely as the East India Company did in the eighteenth century.

But Lugard did not do this. In August 1899 both Bishop Tugwell and himself had an official meeting in London at which the intentions of the C.M.S. were clearly stated.[3] Goldie's encouragement had been secured, the Bishop said, and the Society wanted the full co-operation of the administration, for which they did not want to create any political problems. Lugard gave approval to the enterprise, whose object was Kano, but advised that the missionaries should not go beyond areas where the Government would be able to afford them protection. What Lugard wanted then was that effective occupation and missionary enterprise should go *pari passu*. The political implications of any precipitate action on the part of the missionaries could indeed be very serious for the administration. In his book on East Africa Lugard had pointed out that European occupation of African territories was successful principally because of the prestige Africans attached to the white man,[4] his supposed supernatural powers and

1 C. W. Orr: *The Making of Northern Nigeria*, 1911; C. L. Temple: *Native Races and Their Rulers*, Cape Town, 1918.
2 J. F. Ajayi: op. cit., p. 627.
3 C.M.S. G3/A3/08, Copy of Lugard to C.O., 17 Aug. 1899.
4 F. D. Lugard, op. cit., pp. 73–4.

the death he had at his disposal for any community that should attempt to kill him. In the political situation of Northern Nigeria the possibility of the missionaries being murdered could not be ruled out. There were, for example, the wild cannibal tribes of the hill belt, who were dreaded by the caravans. Then, Muslim susceptibilities might be aroused with French military pressure on the Senusi towards the Nigerian frontier. In fact anti-white feelings were already being disseminated by the Brotherhood as far south as Lokoja.[1] Should a missionary therefore be killed the administration would be duty-bound to avenge the white man's prestige, a thing Lugard wished to avoid, particularly when there was no adequate force to do so. All this was elementary common sense, and it was lack of this common sense on the part of the pioneer missionaries that brought about the divergence between Lugard and the missionaries and a redefinition of the relationship between Government and missions.

But missionaries, particularly the missionaries we are dealing with, could not be bound by such logic and realism for which Lugard stood. Their cause was one of militant idealism before which all argumentation and rationalization must fall, particularly when Britain's imperial sword could, so they believed, sweep off the anti-British Fulani 'usurpers' from the face of the earth. Not even the fact that 'invincible' Britain was facing a stiff opposition from the Boers in South Africa and was asking for the military succour of other members of the Empire could affect their conviction that a complete military subjugation of Northern Nigeria was not only desirable but feasible.

Right from the landing of the missionaries on the coast of West Africa their journey received great publicity. At Axim on the Gold Coast they were warmly received by Casely-Hayford, the West African nationalist, and the Hausa settlement there.[2] The usual assurance that they would be enthusiastically welcomed was given, but they did not understand the serious joke that each would be given many wives. The presence with them of Druna, a Hausa boy who was with Gordon at the latter's death in Khartoum, the sensational reception given them in Lagos, the spontaneous voluntary service as carriers by many of the conquered Ijẹbu, the delight of seeing the human product of missionary enterprise in the neatly dressed anglicized students of the Training Institute at Ọyọ—all these were sufficient to excite immeasurable hopes and induce forgetfulness of the undertaking given to Lugard in August.

As they reached Ilọrin, the first Muslim town in Northern Nigeria

1 C.M.S. G3/A3/08, Hill to Baylis, 9 Aug. 1900.
2 C.M.S. G3/A9/01, Richardson to Baylis, 1 Jan. 1900.

by their route, they were already thinking about the masses who would benefit a great deal from the impending pacification of the territory. Miller noted in his diary: 'the people here seem quite confident that the English have come to stay ... the Bishop is particularly struck with the change in the country and in the attitude of the people, and looks forward to a very speedy deliverance for these poor, deluded, down-trodden, oppressed people'.[1] In Jebba, the headquarters of the new administration, Lugard and the military officers reinforced their confidence by the warm reception given them. Lugard dined with the Bishop and Miller and spoke 'very strongly' on the liquor traffic which, he said, would be prohibited throughout the Protectorate. As the Bishop delightedly wrote, quoting Lugard (and so pleased that he could not care for punctuation) to possess 'cheap noxious spirits' would be penal. 'The man found in possession of such spirit not only suffers the loss of such property but is liable to prosecution for being in possession. This is most satisfactory.'[2] Services were held for the officials, Lugard attending.

Lugard informed the missionaries that the road would be safe to Daba only, a small town about 100 miles from Bida. From here Bishop Tugwell was to get in contact with Colonel Morland, who was only two days ahead and who would be able to inform the missionaries how far it would be safe for them to go. But the rousing welcome accorded them everywhere by the common people—such people usually responsive to missionary appeal—was so impressive that the missionaries felt that they could go anywhere. In their progress the missionaries explained to the people the purpose of British occupation—to deliver them from the grinding yoke of their taskmasters.[3] They succeeded in creating among the masses 'a desire for the advent of the British Government'.

The point must be made that the rousing welcome given by the masses to the missionaries from Jebba to Zaria was genuine, and they expected the British Government to supersede the Fulani authority. Without the moral support of the masses the pacification of Northern Nigeria would have been different and is the best proof of the disaffection of the people with the Fulani regime. Up to Zaria, wrote the Bishop, 'we have been welcome everywhere by the people; we have been laden with presents, sheep, corn, fowls, yams, cooked food for the men (carriers), honey etc. have been presented to us in every town ... British influence is evidently welcomed by the poorer

1 Ibid. 'Diary of the Hausa Party' by Miller, dated 16 Mar. 1900.
2 C.M.S. G3/A9/o1, Tugwell to Baylis, 19 Feb. 1900.
3 Ibid. Tugwell, Miller and Burgin to Lugard, 14 Feb. 1901.

people'.[1] Even so feared a man as the Nagwamanchi of the Sudan, the slave-raiding Emir of Kontagora, gave instruction throughout his territory that no one must offer opposition to the white men, but begged the missionaries to sell him cartridges.[2]

The political situation in Zaria was such that the coming of white men was a godsend to the Emir. He had incurred the displeasure of the Sultan of Sokoto and would either have been deposed or overthrown by the Sokoto faction in the town.[3] The advance of British officers up the Kaduna River gave him undisguised satisfaction. He provided accommodation for the missionaries and did not wish them to leave the town. The political ends for which he wanted the missionaries was secured. Miller advised him that his security on the throne depended on his welcoming the British, and influenced the letter which the Emir sent to Lugard asking for British protection.[4] This political achievement for the embarrassed administration which had been compelled to halt its advance and send troops to Ashanti and Aro-Chukwu was significant in many ways. It made a common front by Zaria and Kontagora impossible, and thus rendered possible the dramatic capture of the Emir of Kontagora by Captain Abadie. It rolled back the frontier of Fulani opposition to British invasion by over 100 miles, to Kano and Sokoto. Then it produced a moral effect on the masses to whom the Emir of Kontagora was a terror. This was an imperial task which neither Abadie nor Lugard could forget and explains why in 1904 the C.M.S. was allowed to establish in the heart of the highly Islamized Zaria city, an establishment without precedent in Muslim territories.

Had the missionaries stopped in Zaria, the fortune of missionary enterprise would have been different. Lugard's *pari passu* plan would have been carried out, at least in some measure. For the fact must be emphasized that although the Fulani rulers looked upon the purpose of British occupation as one of proselytization—and Lugard himself gave this impression in his first letter to Sokoto[5]—there is no evidence that the masses were prepared to resist British occupation on behalf of their religion. Contrary to what Lugard and his successors used to aver, no pledge was ever given to the Emirs that missionary enterprise would be prohibited from their territories. Lugard was the last man to give such a pledge. The so-called pledge given was that the Government would not interfere with Muslim religion,

1 Ibid. Tugwell to Baylis, 11 Mar. 1900.
2 Ibid. Richardson to Baylis (undated).
3 W. Miller: *The Reflections of a Pioneer*, London 1936, pp. 72–3, gives reason.
4 C.M.S. G3/A9/01, Miller to Baylis, 18 Feb. 1902.
5 In Arabic translated and in exhibition at N.A. Kaduna.

which was quite a different thing. Lugard himself acknowledged later on that no promise to keep Christian missions out of Muslim areas was ever given to the Sultan and the Emirs.[1]

In point of fact, often unknown to the administration, Miller preached openly in most of the large cities of the territory between 1900 and 1912.[2] The Emir of Katsina reiterated his desire to have missionaries from time to time and invited Malam Fati, an educated Christian convert, to his palace, introducing him to the malams whom he invited to listen to the Christian teacher's preaching.[3] Indeed had the common man had any religious fear of the white invaders of their territory it is doubtful whether the small forces of the Government would have been able to pacify Northern Nigeria. If permitted, missionary propaganda would not have appealed to the majority of the Muslims, whose contempt for Christians and white men was unconcealed. 'Ah, *before* you were a heathen: *now* you are a man,'[4] said Kwassau, the Zaria Emir whom the missionaries had helped, when Miller wore a Muslim costume.

For Christianity has never converted Islam. The intractableness of Muslims was already demonstrated not only in Bida and Lokoja but in the Yoruba towns. In the Zaria district not up to twenty converts were made by the C.M.S. missionaries between 1900 and 1914. What obtained in other parts of the Muslim world obtained in Northern Nigeria also. Muslims were already fossilized in their faith and were prepared to give protection to the 'people of the Book' as the Koran enjoined. A disillusioned Miller noticed the futility of converting the Muslims with their 'hide-bound minds', and looked forward only to the 'unsophisticated pagans' to 'revolutionize this Colony of Nigeria'.[5] On the evidence of the fanatically pro-Islamic and pro-Fulani Resident, Major Burdon, there was not 'the slightest fanaticism against Christians in the bulk of the Mohammedan population out here'.[6] Indeed the Emirs assured C. L. Temple, the fanatical worshipper of Indirect Rule,[7] that they entertained no fear for their subjects from the dogmas of the Christian faith; what they dreaded like the plague were the political and social implications of missionary propaganda.[8] That the Emirs were correct in their surmise of the political danger of missionary activity to their position will be

1 C.M.S. G3/09/03, Memo. of interview with Lugard, 25 July 1912.
2 C.M.S. G3/A2/015, Memo. on Government Restrictions in Northern Nigeria by Miller, 1914.
3 Ibid.   4 C.M.S. G3/A9/01, Richardson to Baylis, 29 July 1900.
5 W. Miller: *An Autobiography*, p. 24.
6 N.A. Ibadan CSO 1/27, Vol. 2, Burdon to Lugard, 7 Apr. 1902.
7 M. Perham: *Lugard, The Years of Authority*, London 1960, pp. 474 and 476.
8 C. L. Temple, op. cit., p. 215.

treated in detail in the next chapter, but even in Zaria by July 1900 Kwassau had already begun to have second thoughts about the wisdom of his friendliness towards the missionaries. They soon made it clear to him that they were his masters and could not recognize his authority over many of his subjects in certain respects. It was not long before the administrative officials informed him that the Zaria province belonged to the 'Queen of England' and that he must protect the missionaries. The latter had already threatened to bring about his overthrow if he did not stop slave-raiding, 'extortion and oppression'.[1] Girku, hitherto loyal to him, became intransigent and defied his authority with the backing of the missionaries and Lugard. So exasperated did Kwassau become that, having failed to persuade them to leave his territory, he secretly caused their huts in Girku to be burned down.

Whatever anti-missionary sentiment may therefore be found in Lugard's official dispatches in 1900 and after, and his attempt to restrict their activities, sprang from the injudicious zeal of the missionaries—outrunning all discretion, tact and common sense—which made them carry their march to Kano. The Emir of Zaria's intelligence that Kano would not receive them well, their awareness of the injunction by the Sultan of Turkey to the Emirs to oppose the British, and the cold reception they received on the way would not break their determination. It is significant that later both the Bishop and Miller accepted that their going on to Kano was a colossal blunder.[2]

In Kano the missionaries were guided in a two-mile procession to a small incommodious room in a hot climate. They were put under the special care of the *Maaje*, the third man in the state, and his steward, Kurege. For carrying their liberality too far the former was later fined 400,000 cowries or £10 and the latter executed publicly.[3] The missionaries were treated in the most contemptuous manner. The day after their arrival they were led to the Emir at Faniso, six miles outside the walls of the city. The view entertained of the missionaries was clear from the instruction given them by their guides on how to behave before the Emir. They must remove their shoes and stockings; they must not stand in his presence; they must not look on the face of the Emir but hold their head on the floor. In the 'Judgment Hall' they were arraigned before the Emir, the Bishop and his lieutenants looking like rats before a ferocious mastiff. Bishop Tugwell was

1 C.M.S. G3/A9/01, Miller and others to Emir of Zaria, 10 July 1900; Tugwell's diary, entry for 19 July 1900.
2 C.M.S. G3/A9/01, Miller to Baylis, 1 Apr. 1901.
3 Ibid. Richardson to Baylis, 26 July 1900.

hushed up in his attempt to plead for Christianity and the missionaries were told that the Koran had everything they desired to have. A peremptory order was given that they should leave the city within three days.[1]

The missionaries were very fortunate to escape being murdered in their attempt to go to Khartoum before Omdurman. In fact perhaps never in their lives were they so near to death as they were when they arrived in Kano. There was a heated discussion for over three hours between the Emir, Aliyu 'the Great', and about forty of his lieutenants. The Emir was rather inclined to kill the missionaries, as the majority of the chiefs wished. But the Waziri put his foot down that the missionaries should not be molested. What made wiser counsel prevail in the Emir's court was the military subjugation of Zinder, a neighbouring town, by the French after the killing there of two Frenchmen. If the Kanawa killed the missionaries, the argument went, they would suffer the same fate.

Naturally Lugard was white with rage when he learned of the blows which had been so decidedly administered to the white man's prestige.[2] Moreover rumours that the missionaries had been murdered were carried as far down as Lokoja. What was more, the missionaries gave no information of the affair to the High Commissioner, who had to learn painfully from the British press the accounts of the events that had transpired in Kano. The humiliation administered to the white man's prestige, which Lugard emphasized throughout his life as the guarantor of the white man's security in Africa,[3] must be seen as the origin of the Kano Expedition. Any compromise or diplomatic relationship with Kano was henceforth out of the question. As in the Ijẹbu Expedition, the maxims and seven pounders must follow the missionary's trail.

It is essential to note that from the documentary evidence in their possession the Church Missionary Society could not have expected the Cross to vanquish the Crescent by the ordinary processes of evangelization. The friendly disposition of some Emirs to Bishop Ajayi Crowther notwithstanding his African staff made no headway in their attempt to convert the Muslims of the Nupe kingdom. As early as 1881 Archdeacon Henry Johnson of Ilọrin ancestry had warned the Society emphatically in a report on the spot on the futility of working among the Muslims. 'There are no more fanatical or bigoted people anywhere than in this part of the world,' he wrote, 'the rulers of the country know nothing of that compromise called religious toleration, but take their stand on the precise dogmatic

1   Ibid.   2   C.M.S. G3/A9/01, Lugard to Tugwell, 1 Nov. 1900.
3   F. D. Lugard: *The Dual Mandate*, 1929, p. 589.

teachings of the Koran.'[1] In 1888 the S.M.A. priests, who had arrived in Lokoja four years before, wound up and retired to the Ibo south, having failed to soften the prejudices of the Muslim population towards them. Even in 1899 and 1900 many unheeded voices in the C.M.S. circle in Nigeria warned on the futility of the intrusion of the Cross into Islamic Northern Nigeria.

The triumph of the Cross over the Crescent envisaged by the missionaries, then, was that which could be brought about only by the forcible removal of the Fulani rulers by the British and the reinstatement of the traditional Habe rulers. Once this was done, so the missionaries believed, Islam would be scorched out of existence and the supposedly well-disposed Hausa would embrace Christianity. They lost no time in lecturing Lugard that Christianity was the 'just right, the common right of all mankind'[2] that must not be denied to the Hausa. On the other hand they spared no language to describe the Fulani 'robbers and oppressors' who had by their *jihad* established the 'most iniquitous government', a 'hopelessly perjured and putridly rotten'[3] administration in Northern Nigeria.

With all this at the back of their minds, and in the spirit of the amity that had prevailed between missionaries and administrators in Nigeria so far, the missionaries lost no time in asking the secular arm to unsheath the sword on behalf of the Cross against the Crescent. The Fulani, the Church Missionary Society declared, had inflicted an 'insult' on the British Empire by the treatment they had given to the missionaries and they should therefore be 'dealt with'.[4]

But in Northern Nigeria the missionaries were denied the success they had hitherto enjoyed. The peculiar situation of Northern Nigeria —its tremendous size, the unifying effects of Islam, the absence of horrible barbarities like twin-murder, trial by ordeal, human sacrifice, and the impressive literacy that existed—made impossible the co-operation of Government and missions that characterized the military expeditions of Southern Nigeria. Moreover, whatever his personal predilection for Christianity as the best agency for the elevation of Africans, Lugard had to be realistic; he did not wish to antagonize the Emirs further by putting before them the bugbear of Christianity; his human and financial resources were extremely limited and patently inadequate; he had to acknowledge the fact that whatever the imperfections of the Islamic administration of the

1 C.M.S. G3/A3/01, 'Report on the upper Niger Mission for 1881', by Archdeacon Henry Johnson.
2 C.M.S. G3/A9/01, Miller, Tugwell and Burgin to Lugard, 14 Feb. 1901.
3 Ibid. Miller to Baylis, 18 Feb. 1902.
4 *The Daily News*, 22 Jan. 1903.

Sokoto caliphate it had excellent features that should commend it to any administrator; he began to observe that all that was needed was to gradually check the excesses of the Fulani rulers. In his capacity as an administrator Lugard could no longer afford to be as idealistic as the missionaries. The implication of this for the missionaries was that the administration henceforth could not back the Cross against the Crescent at all hazards, and wherever they could create difficulties for the administration their activities had to be restrained. The consequence of this was that in many areas the Crescent became stronger and stronger in the absence of any competition from missionaries and in the atmosphere of the law and order created by the Pax Britannica.

But in 1900 other forces were working against the Cross in Northern Nigeria. Undoubtedly with the political troubles which the missionaries had created in his mind the Foreign Secretary, Lord Salisbury, gave his memorable 'missionaries are not popular' speech in Exeter Hall on 19 June 1900, deprecating the fact that Christian missions were directly or indirectly responsible for many of the military expeditions that were taking place in many parts of Africa. He made specific reference to attempts to convert Muslims. Although the speech was given to the Wesleyan Missionary Society it was undoubtedly intended for Salisbury Square. 'You will not convert them' [Muslims], Lord Salisbury said, 'I do not say you will never do so— God knows that that is far from our fears. But dealing with the event of the moment, I think that your chances of the conversion of them as proved by our experience are infinitely small, and the danger of creating great perils and producing great convulsions, and it may be bloodshed which shall be a serious and permanent obstacle to that Christian religion which we desire above all things to preach, is a danger that you must bear in mind.'[1]

Moreover the British merchants with an interest in Northern Nigeria adopted a very hostile attitude to the Cross in Northern Nigeria. As they had always done throughout the nineteenth century, fluctuating as their interest demanded in their pro-military or anti-military attitude, the traders in West Africa generally had every cause to deplore any form of military expedition in 1900 in any part of West Africa. This was because by then all the West African Governments subsisted entirely on duties levied on imports. Every military expedition extended the administration farther into the interior and was a temptation for the administration to increase duties and impose fresh ones. For, as will be clear from a later chapter, no administrator before 1914 dared essay direct taxation.

1 The Times Weekly Edition, 22 June 1900.

The merchants and missionaries were then in opposite camps in their attitude to military expeditions. The unity of sentiments of both in the removal of Jaja and the Ijẹbu Expedition had disappeared. But the traders also hated the missionaries for the latter's unrelenting strong agitation against the liquor traffic which provided the governors with a most convenient opportunity for raising duties. The views of the traders about the 'high cost' of the administration, the latter's attempt to regulate trade, opposition to the political implications of missionary proselytization, and bitterness over the series of military expeditions that marked the years 1900 to 1908 in Southern and Northern Nigeria, are to be found in the letters of John Holt of Liverpool, and two newspapers that became the official organs of the traders. By coincidence, in the month of May 1900 when the missionaries were being bullied in Kano, a monthly (later weekly) journal, called *West Africa* came into being. It was followed three years later by the more radical, fiercely anti-missionary *West African Mail* (later *African Mail*), which like *West Africa* also surveyed the commercial situation of West Africa but was particularly the official organ of the British Cotton Growing Association.

The news of Bishop Tugwell leading a missionary party to Northern Nigeria was disturbing to John Holt, head of a commercial concern that developed from humble beginnings to a big firm in Nigeria. In 1899, that is when the missionary party was about to leave England, he, as well as the Lagos Press, was getting apprehensive of the probable political consequences of the missionaries' adventure. He wrote to De Ville, later E. D. Morel, thus:

> He (Bishop Tugwell) has work enough in all conscience nearer the coast, and there is a danger in sending such a man amongst people who are extremists as big as he and quite as mad, but in opposition to him. Such a man as this is likely to breed trouble . . . we may have another little war as a consequence of his probably unwelcome visit.[1]

And his anxieties increased with the anti-Fulani propaganda of the Church Missionary Society and the continued toleration of the missionaries in Zaria district by Lugard. In fact the military officers were helping in the erection of houses in Girku. Holt burst out, 'Get that Bishop Tugwell out of the Niger if you can. Fancy Lugard and he setting Nigeria [as Northern Nigeria was then called] in a blaze to introduce the Anglo-Christian Church.'[2]

Indeed the first editorial of *West Africa* was on the political impli-

1 M.P., John Holt to De Ville, 15 Dec. 1899.
2 Ibid. John Holt to De Ville, 21 Aug. 1900.

cations of missionary enterprise in Northern Nigeria, a defence of the Fulani and a plea to Lugard to administer the territory through these very people the Anglican Press was advocating should be removed. The paper said:

> No fitter people to govern through could be found than the Fulani; the prosperity of the Sokoto Empire—a prosperity unrivalled in Mohammedan Africa—is the palpable evidence of their statesman-like qualities. There has been much talk of 'breaking the power' of the Fulani—for which read the mowing down of thousands by Maxim fire—as a preliminary to civilizing them. . . . *Festina lente* should be General Lugard's motto, and patience the cornerstone of his policy.[1]

The failure of the missionaries to establish themselves in Kano was hailed 'with undisguised satisfaction', for 'England does not want a great religious war on her hands in West Africa to add to her other troubles in that region of the globe'.[2]

The traders saw in Northern Nigeria a great commercial inheritance. Nothing could, in their view, be more insane than any military expedition that would alienate peoples naturally disposed to welcome traders. Trade, the merchants argued henceforth, through Mary Kingsley and others, was the only reason for Britain's presence in West Africa and the administration must seek first and foremost its interest. All wars that arose, they contended, were either of the creation of the missionaries or of the military governors and the medal-hunting officials. They noticed that the various military expeditions were justified by the administrators in Southern Nigeria on philanthropic grounds. This was the alliance between the Bible and the Sword, in Holt's words, 'conversion by force'.[3]

But the opposition of traders to missionary propaganda was not confined to the continued belligerency of the missionaries. It raised wider issues. For the first time in Nigeria both administrators and merchants began to speak on behalf of Nigerian peoples, exclusively of the missionaries; they began to consider what the moral obligations of the administration ought to be. Until now the questions of the moral and social regeneration of the Nigerian peoples was assumed to be the prerogative of the missionaries, though in close alliance with, and in a sense a part of the Government. Both merchants and Government began to talk of 'Indirect Rule', a system of rule to which they said they were adhering but to which they supposed missionary enterprise was antagonistic.

1 *West Africa* (published in London), May 1900, p. 5.
2 Ibid. 20 Apr. 1901.   3   M.P., John Holt to Morel, 4 Aug. 1904.

The attack of the traders on Lugard, himself believed to be the apostle of Indirect Rule, raises the whole question of the system of administration *vis-à-vis* missionary enterprise. As the latter stood for Christian absolutes—absolute justice, absolute form of approach to God, absolute morality and so on—which sought ideally a complete effacement of the customs and institutions of the society, particularly the Islamic society's, Indirect Rule in this book must be understood in the rigid form as interpreted by Lugard's successors. It implied sanctification of indigenous customs and institutions that were not repugnant to humanity and insulation of the indigenous society as far as possible against all external forces—commercial, political and above all spiritual. It implied a complete proscription of missionary propaganda not only in Muslim areas but among the 'pagans' as well whenever possible.

Measured by this yardstick Lugard was not an Indirect Ruler, and it is essential to examine more closely his views and policy on missionary enterprise *vis-à-vis* the system of administration that has been ascribed to him. In theory, Lugard declared, missionary propaganda was of considerable value to the administrator.[1] The Christian was as a rule more loyal to the British Raj than the Muslim, who could not be weaned from his contempt for the 'infidel'. 'A Government therefore, from a purely political point of view, sees the spread of Islam with misgiving.'[2] As an administrator who genuinely sought to promote the welfare of the people he ruled, perhaps more than any other administrator in Nigeria before and after 1919, he would like them to be Christians because Christian missions taught 'a higher form of Civilization'[3] than Islam. Consequently he was prepared to compromise with the Christian missions on education. Himself a convinced believer that moral instruction was an essential ingredient of true education he sought to make it compulsory and sometimes equated it with Christian instruction. This was why he was prepared in 1906 to have the C.M.S. inaugurate an education scheme in Zaria for the whole Protectorate, a scheme which was on the verge of being put into effect when he resigned.[4] It is essential to note that the object of the scheme, as the C.M.S. made it clear to him, was that it should be a proselytizing instrument while at the same time giving the children of the Emirs the literacy which Lugard wanted.

Highly appreciative of Miller's depth of knowledge of the Hausa language and people and his passion for Britain's imperial destiny in

1 C.M.S. G3/A9/01, Miller to Baylis, 1 Apr. 1901.
2 N.A. Kaduna 1270/1906, Lugard to John Bailey, 15 June 1906.
3 Ibid.
4 C.M.S. G3/A9/01, Miller to Baylis, 26 Sept. 1906.

Northern Nigeria, Lugard developed a strange intimacy with Miller. He sought Miller's advice on all important issues of administration between 1900 and 1906[1] and depended on his political intelligence, whether on the feelings of the people towards the Government, or on the Arabs in Kano importing arms from North Africa and strengthening the intractableness of Kano,[2] or on French doings around the Nigerian frontier.[3] Lugard made it clear that he was prepared to allow Miller to go anywhere in the Muslim provinces and preach openly and that if missionaries of Miller's stamp could be obtained the Government would impose no restrictions whatsoever on Christian missions in the Muslim provinces.[4] In fact Lugard offered Miller the high office of a Resident on very liberal terms. Miller could use his position as Resident of a whole province for evangelistic purposes after official hours.[5] When it is remembered that 'Indirect Rule', as far as toleration or prohibition of missionary enterprise was concerned, came to mean the wish of the Resident, the advantages that the C.M.S. would have had would have been considerable. But the Society prevented Miller from accepting the post.

Nevertheless, in the circumstances of Northern Nigeria during his first tenure of office, Lugard had to impose restrictions on missionaries in predominantly Muslim areas. He had rationalized principles on mission establishments in Muslim areas. The administration would not impose Christianity on the Muslims; missionaries would not be allowed to operate in Muslim areas, except on expressed voluntary invitation to missionaries by the rulers of such areas; if missionaries were allowed to establish themselves in Islamic emirates the rulers would believe that the Christian teachers were a part of the British administration, and should missionary propaganda provoke disorder and the lives of the missionaries should be threatened, the administration would have to punish the assailants for the sake of the white man's prestige. Such an untoward event would cost the administration a great deal in terms of money and reputation. In any case, contended Lugard, why should missionaries wish to convert a people who would not be converted? Why should they not concentrate their efforts on the teeming population of 'pagans' in the territory?[6]

Even then, in spite of the indiscretion of the Kano affair, Christian missions had all they could effectively have during Lugard's first

1 Ibid. Same to same, 24 Nov. 1901.
2 N.A. Kaduna. Two undated letters (1902) in G.O.K. 1/1.
3 C.M.S. G3/A9/01, Lugard to Miller, 15 July 1901.
4 Ibid. Same to same, 12 Apr. 1901; also Miller to Baylis, 1 Apr. 1901.
5 Ibid. Miller to Baylis, 7 May and 5 Sept. 1902.
6 C.M.S. G3/A9/01, Memo. of interview with Lugard, 23 July 1906.

administration. In 1899 the Toronto Industrial Mission were allowed to occupy Pategi, a Muslim town on the Niger. In 1902 the same Mission and the C.M.S. were allowed into Bida with the full co-operation of the Resident and the Emir. The C.M.S. station was by the Emir's desire close to the palace and the Emir provided the ridiculously cheap labour with which the buildings were erected, the Emir and the chiefs gratefully sending their children to school.[1] In 1904, as noted, the C.M.S. were permitted to establish a station in the heart of Zaria city, whilst the Cambridge University Mission Party, an Anglican mission which later became the Sudan United Mission, began work in Wase, a Muslim town in the Nassarawa province. In 1905 the Mennonite Brethren of the U.S.A. were allowed to open a station in Ilọrin. The year 1905 was one of lost opportunities for the C.M.S. They were invited by the Emirs of Kontagora and Katsina to begin work in those places, whilst Lugard also granted permission in respect of Kano.[2] It was the Church Missionary Society that did not occupy these places on the alleged grounds that they had no men to send to those places.[3] By the time they wanted to seize the opportunity the man who had granted it was already away in Hong Kong, and a king that knew not Joseph had come to the throne.

In fact the group of Residents led by Major Burdon noted the pro-missionary tendency of their overlord. Burdon disagreed with the pro-Christian attitude of Lugard from the beginning and attributed the mounting estrangement between the administration and the Sultan of Sokoto to the proselytizing impression which his chief was still giving to the Sultan. He even went to the extent of asking Lugard to acknowledge the submission which Islam enjoins on all Christians and pledge the administration's religious submission to the Sultan of Sokoto. If this was done, contended Burdon, the pacification of Northern Nigeria would be peaceful and the Sultan would use his spiritual authority in favour of the political submission of all the other Emirs to the administration.[4]

Since Lugard's first letter in which he claimed he was representative of the 'Most Christian Nation'[5] in the world left no doubt upon the Sultan's mind that British occupation was one of Christian proselytism he had treated Lugard with impolite disdain, refusing his letters. In order to appease the Sultan the High Commissioner asked him to choose successors to the vacant thrones of Kontagora

1   C.M.S. G3/A3/09, Alvarez to Baylis, 10 Aug. 1904.
2   Ibid. Miller to Baylis, 9 Mar. 1905.
3   Ibid. Same to same, 4 Sept. 1905.
4   N.A. Ibadan CSO 1/27 Vol. 2, Burdon to Lugard, 7 Apr. 1902.
5   N.A. Kaduna, in exhibition.

and Bida after the subjugation of those places. Lugard's gestures were of no avail. The excellent opportunity for successful appeasement was provided, in Burdon's view, by the capture of the Emir's son, the dreaded Emir of Kontagora, who had literally rendered desolate a wide area by his indiscriminate slave-raiding. Burdon appealed to Lugard to surrender the Emir to his father for trial instead of the new British administration trying him. On Lugard's contending that the Sultan had not 'begged' for surrender of his son Burdon warned:

It must be remembered that the Sarakin Sokoto is also Sarakin Musulumi. He is the religious as well as the temporal head of all this land. Can he be expected that he should, in his own and subjects' estimation, demean himself to 'beg' a Christian? This is a vital point. He will of course some day have to acknowledge the superiority of the Christian but in the way such acknowledgement is forced on him depends the question of bitterness or loyalty from the Mohammedan subjects.[1]

Lugard was not the man to stoop to such a degrading suggestion that he, a 'Christian', should 'beg' the Sultan, and he loathed the equation of the Muslim Fulani and Christian British as partners in the evangelization of the 'pagans', a conception which Burdon reported was held by the Bida malams. Lugard retorted, 'As to the Fulani classing themselves with us against the heathens (as co-evangelists) which you seem to endorse I trust that as long as I am here, the British will never lend themselves to such a classification.'[2]

This was sufficient lesson for Burdon, while the other Residents, who did not have the boldness to make anti-missionary suggestion to Lugard, learned their lesson from the peculiar relationship subsisting between Miller and their overlord. Every one of them had to pass through Miller's language teaching and they sought to befriend him.[3] Both the Residents of Bida and Zaria showed unusual eagerness in introducing the C.M.S. to the Emirs of both towns. In 1905 Major Sharpe, the Resident in Kontagora was importunate in his appeal to Miller to begin work in Kontagora.[4] Appreciating the fact that Lugard was not an Indirect Ruler, Salisbury Square expressed gratitude to him in a resolution in 1906. F. Baylis, Secretary of the Society, wrote to Lugard:

The Committee felt that by your resignation they are losing a

1 N.A. Ibadan, CSO 1/27, Vol. 2, Burdon to Lugard, 7 Apr. 1902.
2 Ibid. Lugard's Memo. to above, 17 Apr. 1902.
3 C.M.S. G3/A9/01, Miller to Baylis, 11 Apr. 1905.
4 Ibid. Same to same, 9 Mar. 1905.

friend in the Field upon whose kindly considerations and fair-minded treatment they have been always able to rely . . . they have desired me to express to your Excellency their grateful recognition of the sympathy and help extended by you to the Society and its missionaries when most needful and valuable.[1]

Lugard's pro-missionary policy was possible because, as his biographer makes clear, he was hardworking, vigilant and autocratic, and was able to subject his lieutenants to his will and policy from 1900 to 1906.[2]

One remarkable feature about the invasion of Northern Nigeria by both missionaries and Government in 1900 is that they both discussed formally what they considered the best interest of the Northern Nigerian peoples. The missionaries had a political blue-print for the country, which Lugard accepted in principle, though not in practice. The missionaries' political and social programme for Northern Nigeria, found in their letters, was well summed up in the correspondence between Miller and Lugard in 1903. In principle they did not differ in what they believed would be an ideal administration for Northern Nigeria. In practical terms, however, their views were irreconcilable. Miller was an idealist and an inexperienced young man; Lugard was a realist with a brilliant career behind him; the one was an extremist exponent of a Christian theocracy for Northern Nigeria, which he thought was possible, the other a shrewd master of the art of the attainable.

Briefly stated, Miller's political programme was this.[3] The territory must be ruled '*directly*' by British officials. He observed that 'the main mass of the people expected a complete deliverance on the arrival of the British Government and have been correspondingly disappointed'. This was because the Fulani spiritual and political 'tyrants' were retained as rulers by Government whereas 'for sheer cruelty, lack of justice, honour, pity of truth, I think the Fillani [*sic*] exceeds those of other nations'. The old Habe dynasty whom the Fulani had supplanted should be restored. The retention of the 'tyrants' was a gross betrayal of the people whose goodwill had made British occupation possible. It was injustice that the British Government should be strengthening a regime which, according to his calculation, would have been overthrown by the oppressed masses in ten years at the most.[4] Moreover it would be decidedly in Britain's

1 L.P., Baylis to Lugard, 11 Oct. 1906.
2 M. Perham: op. cit., pp. 182–3.
3 C.M.S. G3/A9/01, Miller to Lugard, 29 July 1903 (all italics are Miller's).
4 W. R. Miller: 'Northern Nigeria. Two Outlooks', *Church Missionary Review*, July 1909, p. 394.

interest to effect a 'total removal of the Fillani regime', for 'the Fillani *is not, will not be* and *cannot* ever be loyal to the British Government'.[1]

The whole Islamic education in Northern Nigeria was 'useless and rotten'. 'Liberal education' by Christian missions must be provided and the apathy of the people to education and learning removed by exempting from taxes all who gave up their children for education. It was a pity that there was no idea in the people that one day they would be self-governing, but 'apathetically they have taken for granted that all the clerks, interpreters, etc. must come from Sierra Leone and Yoruba'. 'The dense ignorance which breeds disloyalty will only break down in this country through two means, Christianity and education.' He considered that Lugard's anti-slavery measure did not go far enough. What was wanted was not a mere palliative but a root and branch eradication of this most important institution, a measure that would have had grave social and economic consequences. No amount of talking, Miller said, could make the people understand the simplest laws of hygiene. Sanitation would be achieved if the head of each house that disobeyed rules of cleanliness was either well-flogged or heavily fined, whilst taxation should fall on polygamists only. Then, he rounded up with a conviction he never abandoned until his death, 'I humbly recommend to Your Excellency that the great hope for this country is the spread of Christianity in it, not a spurious whiteman's wash of a Christian cant and phrases, but a genuine heart change followed by a change of life and mind.'

Lugard's answer is significant both for the light it throws on his supposed policy of Indirect Rule and the understanding of his liberality to Christian missions. Lugard did not doubt the veracity and desirability of all that Miller had said, although he wished Miller had been more restrained in his anti-Fulani feelings. He pointed out that the British Government had no alternative to ruling through the Fulani because the political staff

> is wholly inadequate to conduct the administration in detail . . . if we had unlimited money so that we had no need to raise taxes and could flood the country with European officials no doubt we could do much in a short time, but as it is we have not got the money and we have also to train the officials and they have got to learn everything connected with the native customs and language before our rule can be efficient so far as it goes. I know no royal road to accomplish this; it can only be done by patience and hard work.[2]

1 C.M.S. G3/A9/01, Miller to Lugard, 29 July 1903.
2 C.M.S. G3/A9/01, 'Lugard's Memo. on Dr Miller's paper', 9 Aug. 1903.

The assumption of the administration of Northern Nigeria by Sir Percy Girouard in 1907 marked the beginnings of the concept and implementation of Indirect Rule as an inexorable and immutable principle of administration. Correspondingly it marked the beginnings of prohibition of missionary enterprise from the predominantly Muslim areas, and when possible, from 'pagan' areas also. Never would the C.M.S. recover the opportunities of 1905. As he told Lugard, Girouard found a rather 'Direct' system of government on his arrival in the territory and decided to change this for the 'Indirect' system at once.[1] He conferred more authority on the Emirs, made proficiency in Hausa the sole condition for promotion of officers, rather than academic qualification and seniority in service upon which promotion under Lugard had depended. He gave more autonomy to the Residents by whose views he was henceforth guided. Primarily interested in railway building on which he was an expert, this French Canadian (who had supervised the building of the Nile railway that led to the reconquest of the Eastern Sudan in 1898) nursed the bitterest hatred for missionary propaganda in a Muslim territory. Although a Roman Catholic and an iron disciplinarian where moral issues were concerned, he had the worst views of the results of missionary propaganda. A journey through the south filled him with disgust because of the 'extraordinary condition of contact' between the administrative officers and the minions of Christian missions, the 'half-civilized ruled',[2] as he called them. No wonder he was horrified at the spectacle of Christian missions operating in Northern Nigeria under the supervision of Miller and Bishop Tugwell who were, in his judgment, respectively the embodiment of 'fanaticism' and 'tactlessness'.[3]

The education scheme which the Church Missionary Society had hoped to put through had to come to an end under Girouard's governorship. Rather than allow Christian missions to spoil the Northerners as they had done the Southerners he drew up an education system based upon Islam. Exerting pressure, through the Colonial Office, Salisbury Square pushed him into declaring early his attitude to missionary enterprise by their demand for permission to enter Kano. Unlike Lugard, Girouard asked the sulking Residents for their views and based his memorandum on their replies.[4] What the Residents would say was a foregone conclusion. There was complete unanimity in their opposition to missionary activity which, they said, was a menace to the peace and good government of the country.

1   L.P., Girouard to Lugard, 28 Apr. 1909.
2   Ibid. 25 Jan. 1908.   3   Ibid.
4   N.A. Ibadan CSO 1/27, Vol. 7, Girouard to C.O., 31 Oct. 1907.

It is significant that Captain Orr who had himself, in deference to Lugard, instructed the Emir of Zaria to accept the C.M.S. into the heart of the city, expressed the desire that the station be removed outside the town, while at the same time remarking that although the Mission was spiritually a failure yet, from the point of view of the administration, it had some temporal success.[1] The chief significance of the views expressed by the Residents, and endorsed by the Governor, lay in the fact that Mahdism became the phantom which the administration henceforth employed to counteract the influence of Salisbury Square with the Colonial Office. Cromer's policy banning Christian missions from the Eastern Sudan in 1904, circulated by Girouard to the Residents, was adopted as ideal for Northern Nigeria. Indeed, in matters of finance, education and jurisprudence Egypt and North Africa provided the model for the administration. Burdon became a regular worshipper in the mosque on Fridays while Temple, well versed in Hausa and Arabic, and other officials preferred to spend their leave in Tripoli or Morocco or Cairo.[2]

Between 1907 and 1914 the C.M.S. persistently pressed the Colonial Office to allow permission to establish themselves in Kano where the London and Kano Company had set up in 1907. The Society's agitation led to the orders by which the Company was asked to withdraw from the city[3] and to founding the *Sabongari* system for aliens, a common feature of the Muslim towns in the North to this day. It was believed that the educated Africans from the coast whose clerical services were necessary to the Government and European and African traders from the coast should have the minimum contact with the real Northerners as they, the aliens, were a solvent to the customs and institutions of the indigenous people.[4] Girouard's attitude to Christian missions was well expressed in his private correspondence with Lugard when the latter was in Hong Kong. In 1908 he wrote: 'Personally I should like to see the Missions withdraw entirely from the Northern States, for the best missionary for the present will be the high-minded, clean living British Resident.' For him 'it is a sad fact that the Missions as constituted, are not of the slightest assistance in administering the country: on the contrary a constant source of worry. They say that their religion and commonsense bear no relation to each other.'[5]

1 Ibid. Quoted in above.
2 L.P., Girouard to Lugard, 28 Apr. 1909. C.M.S. G3/09/03, Alvarez to Manley (undated), 1912. G3/A9/02, Miller to Baylis, 5 Feb. 1908.
3 C.M.S. G3/A2/013, Alvarez to Baylis, 20 May 1911.
4 C.M.S. G3/A9/03, Miller to Alvarez, 31 May 1911.
5 L.P., Girouard to Lugard, 25 Jan. 1908.

Girouard's spectre of Mahdism and tenderness for Islam could at times border on the ridiculous. Although the Maharajahs and Nawabs of India and the Sultan of Zanzibar had never evinced any spiritual qualms about a Christian Order such as the C.M.G., but like the present Emirs of Northern Nigeria, had been gratified by such conferment, Girouard gasped at the suggestion that both the Sultan of Sokoto and Emir of Gwandu should be given 'Christian Orders' for their loyalty to the Government during the Satiru Revolt of 1906. 'It is a pity there is no star they could be made proud possessors of,'[1] he regretted. Then in 1907, although Anglicans do not practise baptism by immersion, both Bishop Tugwell and Miller deliberately scandalized Girouard by baptizing an elderly malam convert in the river outside Zaria city. While the huge Muslim crowd that watched the ceremony looked upon it as a delightful amusement for jest at the evening fireside conversation, Girouard's excitement could not have failed to amuse Lugard in Hong Kong. It was, he said, the greatest imaginable act of thoughtlessness on the part of the missionaries 'for our difficulties'. His reaction is best presented in his own words:

I immediately notified Miller that any such ceremonies must take place within the missionary precincts, and informed Lord Elgin of the occurrence of this most unfortunate blunder. Miller glories in it, and is, I fear, going to raise Exeter Hall. Lord Elgin cabled asking me not to leave the country unless I was satisfied the incident would lead to no political trouble. This I was able to re-assure him on, but the baptism was only possible by the power of our bayonets, and Mohammedan bayonets at that.[2]

Whilst Girouard was infecting the Colonial Office with his fantasy, the most influential administrative official, C. L. Temple, who became the real ruler of the territory from 1910 to 1912 under the nominal governorship of the sickly Sir Hesketh Bell, was already manifesting his opposition to the missionaries on cultural grounds. In fact he was the originator and designer of the *sabongaris*.[3] His views were extraordinarily extreme in their adoration of indigenous institutions. It was his conviction that the underlying policy of Indirect Rule was 'to assist the native to develop that civilization which he can himself evolve',[4] and he eulogized the capabilities and qualities of the Fulani. What he called 'mistaken philanthropy' was European civilization in its entirety, the introduction of which would logically lead to 'Direct Rule'. This, he said, would in turn lead to 'the over-

1 Ibid.   2 Ibid.
3 C.M.S. G3/A2/013, Alvarez to Baylis, 20 May 1911.
4 C. L. Temple, op. cit., p. 30.

148

throw and abolition of native institutions by a misguided paternal government'.[1] All symbols and representatives of European civilization, whether a shirt or the railway, the educated African, the trader, the missionary, or the Resident himself, constituted a veritable danger to the sacred institutions of the indigenous society. But the greatest menace was the missionary and he must be given no quarter. The effects which his views already had by 1911 were illustrated in the paper which Bell read before the Royal African Society in which the following statement occurred:

> So far, the fundamental principles of our administration in Northern Nigeria have rested on a policy of guiding and improving Native Rule in such a manner as to interfere as little as possible with the traditions and customs of the people. We want no violent changes, no transmogrification of the dignified and courteous Moslem into a trousered burlesque with a veneer of European Civilization. We do not want to replace a patriarchal and venerable system of government by a discontented and irresponsible democracy of semi-educated politicians.[2]

Bell's claim, with its implications for missionary propaganda, was not an empty one. He believed that Christian missions introduced venereal diseases to Uganda. Under his administration Christian missions were excluded from 'pagan' areas whenever possible. For instance there was the case of the Maguzawa, the numerous Hausa 'pagans' in the Kano province whom the Fulani could not subdue even in the heyday of the *jihad*. Consequently they were left alone to continue their rituals and religion by the Emirs of Zaria and Kano. In 1912 these Maguzawa were anxious to have missionaries but the administration refused to allow missionaries to work among them partly because, it argued, Christian teaching would make the Maguzawa disloyal to the Muslim rulers under whom they were now put, and partly because the missionaries would not be able to resist the temptation of preaching to Muslims who might come to them.[3] When Dr Krusius of the Sudan Interior Mission went out to those people to collect information on their customs and folklore he was allowed to do so only on the condition that he would not attempt to convert them.

Or consider the reactionary attitude of the administration to the interesting movement of the *ansa*, a group of people named after one malam, Ibrahim, who had been executed in public in Kano about

1 Ibid. p. 33.
2 *Journal of African Society*, July 1911, p. 391.
3 C.M.S. G3/A2/015, Miller to Manley, 5 May 1913.

the beginning of the nineteenth century.[1] Ibrahim was said to have been to Cairo where he came across a copy of Arabic New Testament and read of Jesus. He became convinced of His second coming and informed the Emir of Kano of it. Part of his teaching however was that at a near future Christians would conquer Northern Nigeria. In a Muslim state this was certainly an anti-state and heretical doctrine, potentially dangerous to the security of the state when his doctrine began to gain adherents. He was therefore executed in the market. But before his death he urged his followers to flee and wait for the second coming which he identified with European seizure of Northern Nigeria. His followers fled to the outskirts of Kano province, one of them founding the kingdom of Ningi, the local history of which this writer obtained at Ningi in his tour of April 1961. In 1913 many of the descendants of the followers of this executed malam came to believe that the British were the predicted conquerors and that the missionaries were the preachers of the faith Ibrahim had spoken about. Having got in contact with missionaries in Zaria the latter decided that they should all be settled in a separate settlement, a Christian village. The administration refused to grant permission until the second period of Lugard's administration when the *ansa* settled in the Christian village of Gimi. Well did the impetuous and fanatical Miller feel that the Hausa fell on evil days after the resignation of Lugard and that after 1906 the administration of Northern Nigeria 'is despotic, anti-Christian, cruel and wicked'.[2]

When Lugard returned to Nigeria in 1912, he could not revert to his pro-missionary policy of 1900 to 1906. As his biographer recounts, the situation that he met in Northern Nigeria was one in which Residents were in full control of the day-to-day administration and he could not wield the absolute authority he was used to in the opening years of the century.[3] His influence in the Colonial Office was in some ways weaker than that of Temple. Lugard had to be guided by the views of the Residents henceforth. But his views on Christian Missions did not change. He wished to invite Bishop Tugwell to the grand durbar in Kano in 1912, and he made possible the establishment of the Christian village of Gimi. But the C.M.S. had to wait until 1924 before they were allowed into the Sabongari of Kano. Indirect Rule was becoming ossified and immaculate.

We may close this chapter with an examination of the validity of many of the reasons alleged by the Indirect Rulers of Northern

1 Ibid. Jones to Manley, 14 Oct. 1913. Miller to friends 13 May 1914. W. Miller: *An Autobiography*, pp. 51–4; W. Miller: *Reflection*, pp. 106–7.
2 C.M.S. G3/A2/015, Miller to Manley, 5 May 1913.
3 M. Perham: op. cit., p. 604, pp. 471–5.

Nigeria for their anti-missionary policy. In the judgment of the missionaries the chief reason why most of the Residents proscribed missionary propaganda in their areas of jurisdiction was the latter's fear that missionaries would not condone many of their actions. A close study of the documents substantiates this opinion in many respects. Indirect Rulers had much to hide from the gaze of the British public, through probable revelations by the missionaries to the British press. Many of the Residents were overbearing in their attitude to the natives and condoned many acts of oppression by the chiefs and Emirs. The officials were, in a missionary observer's view, 'brave English officers, genial, goodnatured, but utterly ungodly, all living loose lives, *all* having women brought to them wherever they are'.[1] Missionaries also felt that in the pacification of the territory much bloodshed that could have been avoided, the report of which never reached the Colonial Office, occurred.[2] In places where missionaries were allowed to establish themselves many people who could not obtain redress for wrongs from Residents flocked to missionaries for 'advice'.

One excuse of the Indirect Rulers for their anti-missionary tendencies was fear of anti-missionary risings by the Muslim population. There is no evidence from the records to show that such a tendency ever arose. In fact in times of tension such as during the Satiru Revolt of 1906 and the outbreak of the First World War the areas in which missions operated were the most demonstrably loyal to the British administration in Northern Nigeria.[3] It has also been established by Muslim scholars that Mahdism was not the consequence of British or missionary intrusion into Northern Nigeria, but that it had been a considerable force, anti-Sokoto in tendency, since the nineteenth century.[4] Mahdism *per se*, therefore, had nothing to do with missionary propaganda, contrary to the impression the Indirect Rulers gave in the official dispatches.

It is clear from the records that after 1906 the Northern Nigerian administration no longer wanted and regretted the conversion of any Muslim or even 'pagan' to Christianity. It was no longer a matter of the so-called pledges, or expediency or safety but a deliberately anti-missionary and anti-Christian policy. The attitude of the administration was not one of neutrality in religion which would give

1   C.M.S. G3/A9/01, Miller to Baylis, 5 Sept. 1902.
2   C.M.S. G3/A9/02, Miller to Baylis, 8 June 1908.
3   C.M.S. G3/A9/02, Miller to Baylis, 5 Feb. 1908.
4   Saburi Biobaku and Muhammad Al-Hajj, 'The Sudanese Mahdiyya and the Niger-Chad Region', given to the author by Mr El Masri of the Department of Islamic and Arabic studies, Ibadan University.

Muslims and Christian teachers equal freedom for competition. Islam was good, and indigenous religion was all right, but not Christianity. Unlike Southern Nigeria, the people were not allowed a choice of their own but the officials assumed that the people did not need Christianity.

The consequences of the prohibition of Christian missions from the larger part of Northern Nigeria are not easy to ascertain. But two generalizations may be safely hazarded. There is no evidence to show that outside the 'pagan' areas, the people would have been willing to receive western education, the aspect of missionary propaganda which hastened the political and social sophistication and 'enlightenment' of Southern Nigeria, and the lack of which accentuated the 'backwardness' of the Northern territory. As Miller who knew the people well said, the people were as a general rule apathetic to western forms of education. This writer noted the same apathy to western forms of education in the bulk of the population during his extensive tour of Northern Nigeria in April 1961, even when such education, divorced of Christian content, is supplied by Muslim Native Authorities.

Politically, the prohibition of missionaries in Muslim areas gave unrestricted power to both the Emir and the Resident. Thus the poor, often oppressed, people could not enjoy the political services of missionaries as tribunes of the oppressed. In Zaria, where Miller's vigilance was unrelaxed, cases of oppression, most gruesome to relate, were too many. Miller's political services to the oppressed led to the removal of two Emirs in 1909 and 1918.[1]

1   W. R. Miller: *Reflections* . . . , pp. 126–7.

The words written concerning the Roman Legions and their work of preparation for the advancement of the kingdom of Christ fits more appropriately the present condition of affairs in Nigeria. By a few slight alterations and the changing of names it might be said that The Rise of the British Empire secures to the nations a social order and political unity which consolidates and protects the growth of the new faith.

The Rev. G. T. Basden,
C.M.S. missionary in the
Niger Mission

5 The Missions and 'Indirect Rule' in Southern Nigeria, 1900-1914

It is clear from the preceding chapter that the anti-missionary policy of the Indirect Rulers of Northern Nigeria was not determined entirely by fear of Muslim fanaticism. Indeed, in a sense, the Indirect Rulers merely reflected an attitude characteristic of a large number of administrative officers in 'pagan' Southern Nigeria—cold indifference, or outright hostility—to missionary enterprise. But since in the south none of the governors in the years under survey established, in any formal or elaborate manner, any system of administration that may be strictly described as 'Indirect Rule', there was no question of the British administration proscribing missionary activity anywhere in the territory. Nevertheless the tension that developed between the two related groups of intruders, missionaries and administrators, deserves attention because by it the reaction of the Southern Nigerian peoples to them can be clearly analysed.

But it is essential to examine first the pattern of response of the major ethnic groups of the territory to missionary appeal. In Yorubaland, on the whole, the *Pax Britannica* ushered in the halcyon days of Christian missions. On many occasions the administration gave the missionaries, particularly the C.M.S. missionaries, direct support. For instance when in 1900 the Ọni of Ifẹ, the spiritual head of the Yoruba, declared opposition against the establishment of mission stations at Modakẹkẹ and Ile-Ifẹ and in the process caused the catechist in Modakẹkẹ, Kayọde, to be assaulted, he did not realize that sovereignty in spiritual matters no longer rested with him. For Charles Phillips and Thomas Harding reported him to his new political boss, Captain Fuller, Resident in Ibadan. The messengers who had been used by the Ọni against the Christians were dismissed from government service and the Ọni himself was warned that he could continue to persecute his Christian subjects only at the risk of his throne. Little wonder that the Ọni changed his attitude at once, ordered his chiefs to help in the construction of a church and henceforward became 'an active friend'[1] of the Church Missionary Society agents. Also when in the same year the Townsend-Wood Memorial Church, towards the building of which the Lagos Government had contributed, was opened, Governor Macgregor of Lagos ordered a special train to convey high Government officials and others to Abẹokuta.[2] Of course the Alake knew the meaning of the Governor's presence there. For the first time in Ẹgba history the Alake went to church and henceforth, as mentioned earlier, became a Christian.

In the period under consideration it was the conquered Ijẹbu who responded most enthusiastically to missionary enterprise in the Yoruba country, their zest comparing with that of similarly conquered Ibo of Eastern Nigeria. The phenomenal Ijẹbu response was due partly to the financial exertions of liberated Ijẹbu in Lagos who, like their Ẹgba counterparts, had long desired the Christianization of their country but had been prevented from realizing it by the hostility of the Awujalẹ. There was also the fact that practically all important missionary bodies in Yorubaland concentrated their resources, in terms of man-power and finance, on the Ijẹbu. The Lagos Church Mission of the Lagos Native Pastorate and the Wesleyans moved in in 1892, immediately after the expedition, and were followed in 1895 by the Baptists and subsequently by the Society of African Missions and the Bethel African Church. No part of the territory was left untouched by missionaries and Ijẹbu converts who turned themselves into unsalaried evangelists. Another major factor that hastened the statistical success of Christianity among the Ijẹbu was the educational side of missionary propaganda in an age of clerks when expanding British administration and trading companies needed educated people to man their establishments.

In Ondo district large numbers of people became Christians partly because missionaries were associated with the restoration of peace and national rehabilitation of the Ondo. Christianity was also associated in this area with the wealth brought to the people by timber concessions and the growth of cocoa. As in many parts of the Yoruba country it was becoming fashionable to be described as a Christian.

Next to Ijẹbuland it was the north-east of Yorubaland, in the Ekiti country, that Christian missions recorded the greatest success. This was partly due to the gratitude which the Ekiti felt they owed the missionaries and the Lagos Government for the peace and independence brought to their country for the first time in a hundred years.

1 C.M.S. G3/A2/010, 'Account of work in the Ondo Mission District from December 1899 to March 1900', by Bishop Phillips.
2 *Lagos Weekly Record*, 10 Feb. 1900.

African missionaries who went round the territory, which was being thrown open to the outside world for the first time, were welcomed by the chiefs and kings as Government officers. As in the Ijẹbu country the evangelization of Ekitiland in the early years was the handiwork of ex-slaves. By 1895 they had introduced Christianity into more than ten towns and villages. The achievement of these Ekiti ex-slaves was much less than that of the liberated Ijẹbu, because the latter, by their contact with Sierra Leone and Lagos, shared the prosperity of Lagos and the educational facilities of the Christian missions. Therefore they had the money and the men to deploy for the evangelization of their country. The Ekiti ex-slaves on the other hand were a different breed. They were captives of the Yoruba wars sold into Iwo or Ibadan or Abẹokuta. In their captivity they had become converted to Christianity, had witnessed the material wealth and educational advantages that had accompanied missionary enterprise in those places and had a burning desire to see similar material and social advantages in their country. Two examples of these barely literate ex-slave torchbearers of Christianity in their fatherland may be cited. There was Ifamubọni, later named Babamubọni, a native of Iyin near Ado who was captured by the Ibadan in 1874. He was purchased by the Reverend Daniel Olubi who kept him as a slave for fifteen years at the end of which he redeemed himself. From his master he learned about the new faith which he took to his country in 1894. Then there was Samuel Lasẹinde, a native of Ora. He and members of his family were captured by the same Ibadan and he was sold first to Iwo, then to Ibadan and then to a *Shango* worshipper in Abẹokuta. In 1893 a missionary was able to obtain money from a philanthropist in England to redeem him and he was apprenticed to the Reverend James Okusẹinde of Ibadan until he could read the New Testament. He returned to Ora as a farmer and an evangelist.

Another major ethnic group among whom missionaries had phenomenal success were the Ibo. Theirs was a society much less open than Yorubaland to direct outside influences like Islam and Christianity until the beginning of this century, when a series of military expeditions threw open their village communities. The impact of external influence on them was sudden and terrific. The administrator and missionary intruded into the community about the same time. There was no question of the people accepting the one and rejecting the other. In Ibo thinking both intruders were relatives who had much in common, leading the same sort of strange life, erecting the same forms of building, educating them on new forms of economy and expostulating to them on the virtues of learning. In their patronage of the Christian Church the Ibo manifested a characteristic that they have not lost ever since—that of zealous patronage of any institution that possessed the magic of success, in this case the magic wand of education in the hands of the Christian Church.

The Edo presented a contrast to the Yoruba and Ibo in their apathy to the Christian religion. This was partly because neither of the two factors that easily facilitated the Christianization of the two major ethnic groups already mentioned was available at the time of the Benin Expedition of 1897. Unlike in Ijẹbuland there was no group of liberated Edo in Lagos who could become torchbearers of Christianity in the former Benin Empire. Then there was also the fact that Christian missions were latecomers to Benin, and even when they came, they came with inadequate resources. In spite of repeated appeals to the Church Missionary Society and the Society of African Missions by administrative officers after the expedition[1] the former did not go there until 1902, the latter until 1903. In fact in 1902 when Bishop James Johnson went to Benin he did so without the encouragement of the Church Missionary Society, who refused to erect any building in Benin on the assumption that Benin had little future.[2] With the little resources at his disposal James Johnson brought Benin into the Niger Delta Pastorate as an outpost of the Delta Church. As for the Society of African Missions the large number of priests were deployed in Abẹokuta, Ibadan, Ọyọ, Oshogbo and the Ijẹbu areas.

The result of the relative neglect of the Benin division by Christian missions was that the administration, quite unusually, started to build schools in Benin City and Sapele. Naturally these schools, to which the chiefs were encouraged to send their children, were secular institutions. Above all the Benin district seemed unfortunate in most of its administrative officers, who were undisguisedly indifferent to missionary propaganda. For instance in 1902 the British administration made it difficult for James Johnson to obtain land for mission establishment. In 1904 the Commissioner in Benin, whose house was near to the church which the immigrant Yoruba traders and clerks had built, found the zest of the Christians over their bell inconvenient. Throughout the day, and far into the night, they rang their bell for meetings at intervals for an inordinate length of time. The Commissioner's appeal for moderation of their zeal having failed, he seized the bell and locked it up in a store for over three months. Arraigned

1 C.M.S. G3/A3/07, Hamlyn to Baylis, 18 Nov. 1897; S.M.A., Scherrer to Père Superior, 2 Oct. 1899.
2 C.M.S. G3/A2/012, Tugwell to Baylis, 6 Jan. 1904.

158

before the so-called Native Council over which he himself presided, the Commissioner fined the pastor a nominal fee of one shilling and the church and land became Government property.[1]

The indifference of many of the administrative officers in Benin division to Christianity was by no means unique. For the remarkable mass movement towards Christianity in Southern Nigeria in the period under survey notwithstanding, there were a number of factors vitiating the unity of sentiment and action of the Bible and the sword in the territory in the first decade of the twentieth century. One factor was the fact that most of the administrative officers, fresh recruits from Britain, represented the growing indifference to religion which was noticeable in an increasing number of Britons in the last years of Victoria's reign. Moreover the concept of the mosaic British Empire, in which the loyalties of non-Christian peoples of Asia and Africa to the Imperial Crown were being impressively demonstrated, implied a new outlook on the non-Christian religions—one of toleration. In Southern Nigeria a new note on indigenous religion began to come into the dispatches.[2] For the first time the idea that the Christian religion was not necessarily a desideratum of loyalty to the administration; that 'pagans' and Muslims could be safely governed without converting them to Christianity; that in most cases they were more docile and more governable citizens than the presumptuous converts, began to gain ground. To a certain extent this was a matter of experience, but to a far greater extent, perhaps, the change in attitude to indigenous religion was due to the ideas of Mary Kingsley, which were well known to many of the officials. Following her steps some of them made very useful sociological studies widely published by the *West African Mail*, Morel's paper, which made the missionaries of Southern Nigeria a special target. Carried to an extreme the defence of indigenous religion could lead to outright anti-Christian propaganda. An official worth mentioning is Major A. G. Leonard[3] who spent over ten years in the administration of Southern Nigeria. By allowing Christianity into Nigeria, declared Leonard, the British 'have strayed like lost sheep. . . . In this way we have subverted the entire order of natural routine and evolution into a revolution of blind emotions. Thus it is that we have treated the natives as savages incapable of good until converted into Christians.'[4]

The indifference of the new generation of officials in the interior of Southern Nigeria to Christianity was proverbial. Games were played

1 C.M.S. G3/A3/010, James Johnson to Baylis, 21 July 1905.
2 C.O. 147/155, Macgregor to Chamberlain, 26 May 1901.
3 He wrote a useful book, *The Lower Niger and its Tribes*, London 1906.
4 *West African Mail*, 28 Mar. 1907.

on Sundays, church attendance was neglected and official transactions were discharged on the holy day. Of the many incidents in mission records, the Kent incident, which came to the notice of the Aborigines Protection Society and the British public, may be cited.[1] One Sunday in 1910 Dr Hugh Kent, an official travelling through the Ijẹbu territory dispatched his men, Government servants, to impress Christians worshipping in two villages, Imuku and Isire, to carry his loads. The two churches were broken up and when the two agents conducting the services complained to Kent of his servants' behaviour they too were forced to become his carriers. At the protest of Bishop Oluwọle and the Lagos Press, and before the Church Missionary Society could stir up public opinion in England about Christians oppressed by Christian officials in a British Protectorate, Egerton, the Governor of Southern Nigeria from 1903 to 1911, ordered an immediate Commission of Enquiry. After the report, never published, Kent was 'invalided' to England at once—that is, his appointment was terminated.[2]

Even in Lagos the new tendency was clearly marked. It was calculated that of all the officials in Lagos in 1909 only the Chief Justice was a regular church-goer, while not more than thirty of the remaining 400 Europeans in the Colony attended any church at all.[3] It is not surprising then that when in the following year Egerton made an attempt to build a colonial church to correct what he described as the 'religious carelessness' of the Europeans, John Holt was amused and commented:

> The Church will no doubt be built in the aristocratic official quarter; the parson will be an official with up to date high class views on public worship and the worshippers will be at their chapels outside it if they are religiousmen, and if not, they will be anywhere but in that Church. I fear, as for the officials for the most part will attend officially no doubt, and with all the greater alacrity if there could be arranged a nice Church duty allowance out of the public revenue.[4]

Reports from the Ibo country bore testimony to the indifference of the administrative officers to Christianity, and their love for travelling and recruiting porters and labourers on Sundays. In Brass the Reverend Henry Proctor of the Church Missionary Society became so exasperated one Sunday in 1902 that he had to admonish the High Commissioner, Sir Ralph Moor, for holding political meetings with

1 A.P.S., Sapara Williams to J. H. Harris, 2 May 1910.
2 Ibid. Same to same, 21 Mar. 1910.   3   *The Nigerian Chronicle*, 9 Apr. 1909.
4 M.P., Holt to Morel, 8 Oct. 1909.

the chiefs on the holy day. To the missionary's consternation many of the converts had chosen to obey man rather than God by responding to the High Commissioner's summons:

> It is with great pain and sorrow that I learned yesterday, you had called a business on the Sabbath Day [wrote Proctor], and so prevented many who would have done so, from attending God's house. You are the Representative of a professedly Christian country, under a King, who has so lately and publicly owned God. Should you then in your public capacity so act, wounding the conscience of our fellow African subjects. . . . We as missionaries, are doing our best to train them to be true Christians, and as such, loyal subjects of our King.[1]

Probably to prevent his being dragged into an unpleasant relationship with the Colonial Office, through the dreaded propaganda machinery of the Church Missionary Society, Sir Ralph Moor felt constrained to mollify the enraged missionary. He defended himself by saying that he had come to Brass primarily to do 'God's work', and that he had discussed mainly infantile mortality which, 'from a purely Christian point of view is one of great importance'.[2]

As might be expected it was in Yorubaland that the relations between missionaries and administrators became most strained. This was because the political implications of missionary propaganda could not remain the same at the establishment of British administration and penetration of the hinterland by aggressive European trading effort. Political authority which, as noted in Chapter 2, had been wielded by the chiefs with the missionaries as counsellors, had to pass on to the new political masters, the administrators. This development implied a readjustment, if not a whole recasting, of the political relationship between missionaries and chiefs. In effect the chiefs were compelled to transfer their allegiance, however unwillingly, to the administrators, upon whose goodwill their security on the throne depended. Missionaries' political influence with the chiefs virtually came to an end, but this did not mean the end of missionaries as a political factor. For missionaries became a political danger or embarrassment to both the administrators and chiefs, through the championship of the cause of their acolytes, usually the lowest classes in the community.

The alliance between missionaries and their converts became 'a source of increasing difficulty'[3] to the administration in Yorubaland.

1 C.M.S. G3/A3/09, Henry Proctor to Moor, 3 Nov. 1902.
2 Ibid. Moor to Proctor, 3 Nov. 1902.
3 M.P., Morel to Archbishop of Canterbury, 19 Oct. 1911.

For the mass movement which Christian missions reported to their subscribers did not include the chiefs, who had every reason to deplore the effects of missionary teaching on the masses. With the majority of the converts Christianity was a political deliverer. It is essential to note that while there was happiness and contentment to a considerable degree in the traditional society there were certain aspects of tribal government and laws, which the common people did not like, but which they had to submit to because of tribal sanctions imposed by indigenous religion, customs, chiefs and 'public opinion'. For the traditional society was by no means egalitarian, and acts of oppression of the common people by chiefs and the privileged few, such as exactions of produce and travesties of justice, did occur, although the extent varied from locality to locality. Any attempt to claim for the tribal society all that was pleasant for the common people would be a romantic rather than an objective analysis of the state of things. This was why, given a situation where the unpleasant aspects of tribal life and government could be safely cast away, a large number of the common people rushed at the white man's faith, hoping that sympathy for their cumulative grievances, and protection, would be secured.

But the converts usually claimed more than protection from acts of oppression by their chiefs. Their notion of Christianity was that it conferred many positive advantages as well, absolving them from the legitimate tribal functions such as clearing of roads. The converts became, as it were, a caste of their own, refusing to acknowledge the authority of the chiefs to whom they considered themselves superior. Consequently they looked to their pastors to protect them against the consequences of the breaking of their own tribal laws, a protection the missionary was only too eager to give by appealing to the administrator against the alleged, usually exaggerated, acts of oppression of the chiefs, who, the missionary always said, were motivated by religious persecution. What is more, looking upon themselves and their converts as part of the administration that must foster the cause of Christianity the missionaries expected the officials to give judgment in favour of their neophytes as a matter of course.[1] In other words Christian converts wished to stand outside the obligations of the indigenous society and claimed that they should be treated administratively on a different footing.

This was why there were so many localized upheavals in the Ijębu territory, but particularly in the Ekiti country. With the handful of officials which the Lagos Government could afford in the interior

1 C.M.S. G3/A2/014, Bishop Oluwọle to Tugwell, 5 Sept. 1911; Mackay to Baylis, 10 Oct. 1911.

there was only one Travelling Commissioner, stationed in Ilesha, for so extensive a territory. Virtually in every village some people professed to embrace the new faith and Christian Missions were compelled to put half-educated men, some without any kind of formal education, in control of the village church-school. In effect the pastor became the most influential man in the village, as the administrator, whose agent the pastor was believed to be, always had more than enough to occupy him at the headquarters, and therefore hardly made any appearance in the village. And whenever he went on tour he confirmed the impression already held of the oneness of the administration and the Church by putting up in the Mission house, invariably the best in the village. The importance of the village pastor-teacher to the villagers as their pride can only be appreciated by anyone who even today visits villages in out-of-the-way places throughout Nigeria.

It was natural that as time went on the arrogance of the converts in the villages should lead to open clashes with the so-called pagans for whom the tribal religion was strong. Such people, mostly the older people of forty and above, saw their world collapsing before their eyes. Moreover the ridiculing of the tribal religion by the young, impertinent, hitherto loyal and respectful tribesmen was more than the elders could bear, and they could not resist the impulse to attack the apostates. In some places the chiefs and religious traditionalists accepted the situation with sullen resignation. In others like Ushi, Ise, Oke-mesi and Ora there was a trial of strength between the two religious factions, with the Governors of Lagos drawn in and echoes of the 'persecutions' in the British press, with anti-Government comments in the Church press and on the English pulpits.

It is difficult to know on what faction to fix the blame for the various 'risings' that honeycombed both the Ijẹbu and Ekiti territories during the period. There were occasions when the traditionalists were the aggressors. In many cases the chiefs put their authority to the test by deliberately fixing Sundays for communal labour, whilst the tribal priests, with the same object in view, requested the so-called Christians to remove their caps as a token of respect for the *egungun* masqueraders who paraded the town during the annual festivals. Naturally, as 'Christians', the converts could not avoid disobeying the chiefs and showing disrespect to tradition. They claimed immunity from these customary modes of paying respect to chiefs and elders on religious grounds, but the latter gave a completely political interpretation of the convert's disobedience. On the other hand there was a strong feeling among the so-called Christians that whatever the chiefs and 'pagans' did against them was done against the British

163

Government as well. They could not overcome the idea that somehow, being Christians, they belonged to the white man's Government more than the 'pagans' did.

In the circumstances the administration had to consider what was in its best interests. The chiefs and religious traditionalists could not be antagonized because they were the traditional guarantors of law and order, and in the absence of large numbers of administrators and soldiers that could enforce a particular religion on the people the administration had to play the role of peace-makers. Often, too, the administration found it expedient to remove ringleaders of the Christian groups who threatened the peace of the entire community by their outrageous behaviour in the name of Christianity. A concrete example of the behaviour of converts and the measures the administration was compelled to adopt was the doings of the Christians at Ora. It will be recalled that Samuel Laseinde was redeemed by a missionary in Abeokuta in 1893 and was in 1896 sent back to his home town. He soon arrogated to himself a position higher than that of the king of the town. When building his church he deliberately chose a spot between two groves which the traditionalists believed were the sustainers of the peace and prosperity of the town. During the *egungun* festival, instead of avoiding the masqueraders the Christians, who had refused to take part, jested at the votaries. What is more, rather than cultivate subsistence crops like corn and yam, upon which the community lived and maintained economic independence, the Christians began to plant alien inedible crops like cocoa and coffee, the value of which could not be appreciated by the people. Moreover the planting of these alien crops involved the pulling up of the highly prized kola-nut trees, which the chiefs had planted. Converts did not ask the chiefs to allot land for cultivation, as was the tradition, but chose land as they wanted. Matters came to a head when Laseinde disturbed the festivals of the 'pagans' and announced to all the people to look on him as the head of the town.[1]

For years Laseinde had been able to browbeat the chiefs into silence and submission, threatening to report them to the white man in Oshogbo, the Reverend Mackay. So long as Dr Pickles, a missionary-disposed man, was in charge of the district the aggrieved king and people could do nothing. As early as 1903 when Thomas Harding, the missionary in Ibadan, went to Ora, the king had appealed to him in vain to remove Laseinde from the town. In 1907 Pickles was succeeded by Captain Elgee, a decidedly anti-missionary man. Elgee gave a peremptory order that the church should be destroyed and the Christians, one-twelfth of the population, were

1 C.M.S. G3/A2/012, Meville Jones and Harding to Egerton, 9 Aug. 1906.

164

expelled from the town. In the so-called Illa Native Divisional Council in which Elgee presided, Laṣẹinde was sentenced to six months' imprisonment. He was also dragged to Ibadan with a rope on his neck.[1]

Although Captain Elgee went too far for Egerton, and after a very sharp reprimand the Governor humiliated him by asking him to re-settle the Ora Christians in their town, cause a new church to be built and proclaim freedom of worship, all pressure by missionaries to have Laṣẹinde released from prison was of no avail. Ignoring the measure of success their pressure on Egerton had achieved, the missionaries were not pleased and threatened to appeal to the Colonial Office.[2] In their view, Captain Elgee, 'the Representative of a Christian country', had committed a crime against the Empire. 'It is a very grievous shame,' commented the secretary of the Yoruba Mission, 'The Governor believes Captain Elgee; Captain Elgee believes the heathen chiefs, and the word of the missionary and the Christians count for nothing.'[3]

It was incidents like the Laṣẹinde affair that drove many of the administrators in Southern Nigeria to defend their stand on the grounds that their administration was that of 'Indirect Rule'. Compared with the Indirect Rule of Northern Nigeria after 1906, the Indirect Rule claim of the southern administrators was no more than a farce. So long as it meant anything at all, it meant ruling by the officials through the chiefs to the extent that the administration could not, for lack of means and men, directly supervise the day-to-day government of the different localities. This lack of personnel, rather than conviction, expediency, rather than principle, compelled the administration to pay lip service to 'Indirect Rule'. In many cases the administrators and missionaries had to take opposite sides about the ethical issues that arose over the so-called Indirect Rule. As the tribunes of the oppressed, missionaries, who were greater in number than the administrators, were always keen to point out to the wearied and overworked officials the various acts of oppression transpiring in the territory. This unsolicited incessant vigilance of the missionaries and their ethical interpretation of events in the various parts of the country, made the missionaries a complete nuisance to the administrators. Locally, that is in Nigeria, their view was that all acts of oppression by the chiefs could not be suppressed at once; that some of their persisting wickedness must be winked at by the administrators and that this was the inevitable price for the inadequacy of personnel to rule as directly as the missionaries wished. When

1 Ibid.   2 Ibid. Meville Jones to Baylis, 25 Oct. 1906.
3 Ibid. Same to same, 8 Nov. 1906.

presenting issues of contention between themselves and the missionaries to the Colonial Office, and not all were reported, the administrators dared not use such arguments. They invariably gave accounts favourable to themselves, misrepresented the facts and described the missionaries as meddlesome and political agitators.

Take for instance the Atundaolu case that was not reported to the Colonial Office. The Reverend H. Atundaolu was, like Laseinde, a captive of the Yoruba civil war who rose to become a full minister of the Wesleyan Mission in Ilesha, his home town. Seeing the political usefulness of African pastors like Olubi and Okuseinde in Ibadan and D. O. Williams to the Egba Government, Atundaolu suggested to Major Tucker, the Travelling Commissioner for the Ekiti country, the advisability of having a Native Council in Ilesha also. As the originator and one whose educational qualifications could be useful to the Council, which was duly constituted in 1899, Tucker put Atundaolu on the Council and even paid him handsomely for his services.[1] Atundaolu saw the new administrative measure in terms of Christian ethics and British law of justice. He had arrayed against him however the Qwa, the paramount chief of the Ijeshas, and the chiefs whose idea of justice and treatment of the common people was quite different from that of an anglicized African. Atundaolu deplored the corruption, bribery and extortions of the chiefs and went to the extent of admonishing the king for inflicting physical injuries on his wives. For the Lagos Government on the other hand, Atundaolu was a potential danger because he was disseminating ill-feeling against the chiefs by publicizing their misdeeds. Ethically Governor Macgregor did not deny that Atundaolu was right.[2] Administratively, that is in the 'Indirect Rule' fashion of Southern Nigeria, he constituted a danger that could lead to rebellion of the people against their traditional rulers. Luckily for the Governor, the Wesleyan Mission always liked to avoid political troubles. Oliver Griffin, the Chairman of the Mission in Yorubaland, dismissed Atundaolu from the Mission. While feelings against the rulers were rising the Governor visited Ilesha, removed Atundaolu from the Council and supported the king who wreaked vengeance on his enemy by banishing him from Ilesha.

The most celebrated case was the one that involved the Reverend S. G. Pinnock of the Southern American Baptist Mission in Qyǫ. British by birth, he had gone out in 1890 as a Wesleyan of the Joyful

1 M.M.A., *Minutes of Conference*, 1900.
2 M.M.A., Atundaolu to Findlay, 11 Apr. 1901. Atundaolu quotes Macgregor as minuting in the Council Book in Ilesha on 6 Feb. 1901 that Atundaolu was 'actuated by the least of motives, humanity and justice'.

News connection but soon became converted to the Baptist doctrine of immersion. Since 1892 he had been in Ọyọ, knew the language very well and was the honorary secretary of the Alafin in all communications between Ọyọ and the Lagos Government.[1] His relationship with the Alafin and the chiefs had to undergo a change after the events of 1895 which led to the bombardment of the Alafin's palace and some part of the town by Captain Bower. Although he and the other missionaries were not the cause of the bombardment and in fact did all they could to prevent it, the Alafin and his chiefs could not believe that Pinnock was not privy to the exemplary punishment which the usually wild and uncontrollable Hausa soldiers, officered by British personnel, inflicted on them. For his house at Oke Ishokun was the garrison of the troops and the source of the deadly shells which burned about one-fifth of the town and sent part of the population to flight. A further proof of Pinnock's complicity in their punishment, it seemed to the chiefs, was the gathering at his house of over one thousand of their slaves, and his working hand in hand with the soldiers to break off the chains and set free their human property.

After the bombardment the Alafin was further humiliated by the location in his town of a new political master, a British Commissioner. Now that his relations with the Alafin became strained Pinnock found new allies in the people who, sure of obtaining protection against whatever injustices were committed against them by the chiefs, embraced the Christian faith for political reasons. Pinnock championed the cause of the oppressed with a zeal and a frequency that exasperated the Commissioners. What is more, the latter could hardly fail to take action in the cases brought to their notice. For the Commissioners he became a complete nuisance and they accused him of interfering in politics.[2] Pinnock defended himself from the viewpoint of Christian ethics, that the drawing of the administrators' attention to proven cases of oppression could not be interpreted as interference in politics. What in effect the administrators were telling Pinnock, in a language he did not understand, was that he was behaving contrary to the principle of 'Indirect Rule'. All along Pinnock had to be tolerated by the administration and a series of unwelcome investigations conducted. Not a single case was ever found to be different from its presentation by the missionary.

The long postponed open breach between Pinnock and Commissioner Ross, a soldier, occurred in 1909. The case of a man called Ojo who was being oppressed by the Alafin provided the occasion which

1 Roberson Collection, S. G. Pinnock, 'Stories of Missionary Experience in Africa' in undated *Kind Words* magazine.
2 C.M.S. G3/A2/013, M. Jones to Baylis, 26 July 1909.

both Ross and Egerton had been waiting for. Although the case was proved in Pinnock's favour, as usual, the administration was determined on a showdown. Spies were sent into Pinnock's church to record his sermons and on one occasion his allusion to his struggle with the Alafin in which he used unbecoming language was recorded and reported to the Commissioner.[1] Since the Lagos Government could not eject Pinnock directly they found a convenient weapon in 'Indirect Rule'. On instruction from Lagos, Ross informed the Alafin that he could eject the missionary from his domain if he considered the missionary's presence detrimental to his government. Of course by the Treaty which the British had signed with Ọyọ in 1893 the Alafin did not possess such power. But this was not an occasion for legal niceties. Ross told the British missionaries not to give any support to Pinnock,[2] who had renounced his British nationality for an American one. The British missionaries reported the drama of the ejection fully to Salisbury Square, but not to the Colonial Office, which never had knowledge of the true story. The official records presented Pinnock as more of a bookseller than a missionary and a political agitator,[3] views that cannot be sustained by the records that have survived. The Alafin was ordered to remove the missionary by force, an instruction carried out in a manner that aroused the sympathy of the Lagos press and which put the Lagos Government in a very bad light.[4] The correspondence that went on between the Commissioner and the Alafin and between the Alafin and Pinnock, which left no doubt that the Alafin had acted throughout on the instruction of the Commissioner, was published by the Lagos press. Pinnock appealed against his ejection but lost the appeal on the grounds that by his championship of the cause of the oppressed he had committed 'treason' against the Alafin,[5] that is against the sort of 'Indirect Rule' in Southern Nigeria.

Not all tensions between Government and missions were due to the behaviour of Christian converts to their traditional rulers. There were times when missionaries acted as tribunes of the oppressed and watchdogs of the true interests of the natives in the face of specific measures of the British administration. The events which occurred in Ibadan early in this century provide an excellent example. The

1 Roberson Collection, Pinnock to Willingham, 24 Mar. 1913.
2 C.M.S. G3/A2/013, M. Jones to F. Baylis, 26 July 1909.
3 C.O. 520/79, Minute by C. Strachey dated 24 July 1909 on Egerton to Earl of Crew 1909, Egerton to Antrobus 4 July 1909 and Egerton to Earl of Crewe 19 June 1909 with enclosure.
4 *The Lagos Weekly Record*, 19 June and 17 July 1909.
5 Roberson Collection: 'Brief résumé of the case with the Alafin Re. S. G. Pinnock (V) Oyesile and others'.

Ibadan chiefs, traditional warmongers, having been deprived by the British administration of their habitual slave-raiding and tribute collection in their former empire, Governor Macgregor proposed measures which, among other things, were aimed at turning the chiefs into salaried officials.[1] He set up a Council in which the Baḷẹ, given the unusual title of Bashọrun,[2] wielded a preponderance traditionally unknown. The governor proposed to the Bashọrun-in-Council that a tax of five shillings a year should be levied on the enterprising people, mainly Christians, who had cultivated rubber in a particular forest. Furthermore the Bashọrun-in-Council were also persuaded to accept a surveyor and have all 'strangers' survey their land at prices that would have brought a lot of revenue to the Council. In the meantime the chiefs, who had learned to be circumspect about any proposal from the Lagos Government, refused to accept the proposal until after due consultation with the African and European missionaries. For the land survey proposal was a direct violation of the guarantee which Acting Governor Denton had given to the chiefs in 1894 that no incursion would ever be made on their system of land tenure. And at the back of the administration's mind was the desire of two unnamed commercial firms who wished to obtain land in the city on terms which were anything but traditional.[3]

At the Council meeting where the survey proposal was introduced in the form of a resolution only the Bashọrun supported it, whilst the other chiefs registered their disapproval by their weighty silence, even in the presence of the Resident, Captain Fuller.[4] One or two things should be noted about Macgregor's proposal. In the first instance the Bashọrun, who approved of such a proposal against the expressed wish of the other chiefs, could not have done so with impunity in the traditional setting. He would have been sent parrot's eggs and asked to 'go to sleep', that is commit suicide. Then, no Yoruba in pre-Colonial Africa sold land even to members of another tribe. The English idea of freehold or copyhold did not exist. Land could only be given out to all people to live on, or cultivate or use for a specific purpose. Once the land belonging to the community, for whom the chiefs were no more than trustees, ceased to be used for the purpose for which it was given it reverted to the community.

Macgregor was therefore aiming a terrible blow at the whole concept of landownership in Yorubaland when he claimed that the

1 C.O. 147/155, Macgregor to Chamberlain, 26 May 1901.
2 C.M.S. G3/A2/09, Harding to Baylis, 1 Aug. 1899.
3 C.M.S. G3/A2/010, Macgregor to Tugwell, 28 May 1901.
4 Ibid. Harding to Baylis, 16 May 1901.

Bashọrun was the 'owner of the land'[1] and asked the latter to charge 'the modest rental of 5s. a year' on each plot of land developed by the enterprising Christians for the cultivation of rubber. Then there was also the fact that the Bashọrun was not to use the 'modest rental' for the administration of Ibadan, nor did he share it with the other chiefs. He regarded it as his personal money.[2]

When the Bashọrun-in-Council 'approved' of the survey proposal, the chiefs' concept of the term 'strangers' was meant to fit the enterprising section of the community, that is, the Christians, who had the best houses, with windows, doors and corrugated iron roofs. These converts were themselves natives of Ibadan! Captain Fuller on the other hand was led to defining the term as meaning all Yoruba inhabitants who had not settled in the town for more than ten years. At the public meeting which Captain Fuller was compelled to summon to clear up the confusion about what 'strangers' meant, feelings rose to fever height, and had it not been for a fortuitous tornado that dispersed the crowd, riot would have broken out.[3] At this meeting it was the missionaries, led by Thomas Harding, who by their questions opened the eyes of the people to see what was in the offing. As the embittered Macgregor put it to Harding, 'after each one of your questions was put to the meeting the tension and excitement of the people present rose like mercury in a thermometer put into heated water'.[4] What the governor did not understand was that both the thermometer and heated water had been there and that the missionaries only took the temperature.

The British administration had to abandon the survey scheme, with its implication of direct taxation and the bolstering up of the authority of puppet chiefs in a manner other than traditional. The most important result for all Yorubaland was that it was a warning to the administration that the alien English system of land tenure should not be introduced as yet in the interior, a plan Macgregor seems to have conceived.[5] In the usual manner the behaviour of the missionaries in enlightening the Ibadan people about the grave implications of the land survey proposal of the administration was interpreted as an unwarranted meddling in local politics.

Such strains and stresses in Government–mission relations as have been analysed with respect to Yorubaland were reduced to the barest minimum in Iboland. The records show nothing of disputes over issues similar to those in Yorubaland. Several factors were responsible for this contrasting situation. In the first place, since missionaries did

1   Ibid. Macgregor to Tugwell, 28 May 1901.   2   Ibid.
3   Ibid.   4   Ibid. Macgregor to Harding, 12 July 1901.
5   C.O. 147/155, Macgregor to Chamberlain, 26 May 1901.

not precede administrators into the interior there was no pre-colonial relationship between missionaries and traditional rulers, as in Yorubaland. Consequently missionaries made a distinction between their role in the community and that of administrators, conceding law-making and exercise of authority over the traditional rulers to the administration.[1] Moreover in the absence of traditional rulers of the status of Yoruba *Obas* among the Ibo the head of the Ibo village could not override majority opinion in the village which, as a rule, was in favour of inviting missionaries in a bid to have the village children inducted into the mystery of reading and writing. In Yorubaland where the *Oba* was held as being divine, a spiritual as well as a political functionary, he could turn back missionaries without consultation with his subjects. Above all, in a community like the Ibo's, where village rivalled village, many village authorities themselves took the initiative in inviting Christian teachers into their villages and towns. On the whole, although they did not approve of many doings of the administration, the missionaries in Iboland, particularly the British, believed that the administration must not be embarrassed and that it was doing a lot to improve and elevate the people.[2]

The man who viewed with horror the political consequences of missionary propaganda and who regarded the missionaries as the greatest enemy of 'Indirect Rule' was E. D. Morel, the naturalized British citizen on whom Mary Kingsley's mantle fell. With an astonishing zeal he directed his powerful pen against missionaries. All administrators who had grievances against them thanked him, among them Girouard and Hesketh Bell of Northern Nigeria, the real Indirect Rulers, and Walter Egerton who found the anti-liquor agitation of the Church Missionary Society too extreme.[3] A peculiar kind of imperialist, no one advocated and publicized the principle of Indirect Rule as much as he did through his popular *West African Mail*, which he boasted every important administrative officer in Northern Nigeria patronized.[4] His exposition of Indirect Rule sprang from his conviction that British interest in West Africa was principally commercial. Both he and the traders were apparently unaware that credit for the absence of any military expedition at this time was to a large extent due to the missionaries. And in his view the rapid economic transformation that was going on, particularly in Yorubaland, was due to British administration. To say or do anything to

1 C.M.S. G3/A3/012, Basden to Baylis, 3 Dec. 1910.
2 C.M.S. G3/A3/010, Tugwell to Nott, 9 Dec. 1905.
3 M.P., Egerton to Morel, 1 Oct. 1911; 25 Sept. 1911; Hesketh Bell to Morel, 3 Oct. 1911.
4 M.P., Morel to Egerton, 25 Oct. 1911.

discredit such an admirable administration was for him a crime; to be antagonistic to the chiefs through whom the administrative officers professed to maintain law and order was for Morel unpardonable folly. Order could only subsist by the administrators upholding the authority of the chiefs at all hazards. He visualized the administration of Southern Nigeria as a delicate hierarchy, with the family at the base respecting the head of the family, the family heads owing allegiance to the village heads, the latter to the 'paramount' chiefs and these in turn paying respect to the British Raj. Lecturing the Archbishop of Canterbury, who asked him to explain why he had been so bitterly 'levelling' his 'lance' at missionaries in Southern Nigeria, he drew up his hierarchical pattern and said, 'If any one of these links are destroyed, the whole chain snaps; anarchy takes the place of order, and the British power must eventually be used to put down that anarchy with a strong hand, and that means dead men's bones, to begin with and worse to follow.'[1]

But how far were the charges levelled by Morel against Christian missions correct? How far did missionary enterprise constitute a danger to the form of Indirect Rule in Southern Nigeria? Did the actions of the administration show that it pursued a policy of Indirect Rule? Morel's allegation that the converts refused to recognize the authority of the chiefs could only apply to the newly opened territories of Ijẹbu and Ekiti where Christianity was new. There can be no doubt that in all places where missionaries were well established the position of chiefs was not what it used to be in the eyes of the converts. But this was also true, though perhaps to a lesser extent, of non-converts who in many places saw chiefs being deposed by the administration. Converts tended to be pushful and assertive, particularly if they were well-educated. But it would not be correct to say that educated Africans did not recognize the authority of the chiefs. If missionary enterprise *per se* logically led converts to be disloyal to their chiefs, then the greatest upheavals ought to have occurred in places like Ibadan, Abẹokuta and Ogbomọshọ where in 1914 Christian missions had been established for over fifty years. But this was not so. After the initial tension in relations between the chiefs and converts, noted in Chapter 1, and particularly at the establishment of the *Pax Britannica*, the chiefs and educated Africans had a sense of identity of interests. The chiefs in the old mission stations thankfully looked to prominent Christians for advice and help. Hence in Abẹokuta, Ibadan and Ilesha the chiefs solicited the guidance of their educated children in their relationship with the administration.

1 M.P., Morel to Archbishop of Canterbury, 19 Oct. 1911.

Missionary enterprise was not a particular danger to the counter-feit form of Indirect Rule of Southern Nigeria to the extent that people like Morel imagined. In fact Egerton privately advised Morel that the latter went too far in his analysis of the danger of missionary enterprise to the administration. All that the latter wanted was that the missionaries should teach their neophytes to hold themselves 'lowly and reverently towards their betters'.[1] In only a few districts Christians would be objected to by the chiefs even if they would carry out tribal rules and customs, and generally speaking, there was no question of any official restraining Christian missions in their activity as in Northern Nigeria. Indeed where Christian missions had been established for a long time, as for example at Abẹokuta, the Government valued their efforts. Hence in all Yorubaland it was the most Christian state of Ẹgba that was allowed to be independent until 1914. In fact the greater the Christian influence in a state the more reluctant the Government was to assume full control. Ibadan was left legally and practically in a great measure independent until 1911, while the Ijẹbu state, which was forced to receive the Bible, was the most 'directly' administered part of Yorubaland. The Awujalẹ was no more than a cipher and, against his own wish, Macgregor forced him to accept Christians into his Council.[2] Although, according to Macgregor, religious conflicts between 'pagans' and Christians were the greatest problem of the administration in Ijẹbu territory,[3] yet no complaints were ever made to the Colonial Office about missionary enterprise there constituting a danger to Indirect Rule. For there were officials to deal with the problem on the spot, in most cases in favour of the Christians.[4]

In the meantime the real potential threat to the permanence of British rule in Nigeria had appeared. Mission-trained Nigerians had begun to ventilate nationalist ideas; they had begun to criticize the way and manner in which the British established sovereignty over their country, and in which that sovereignty was being exercised. The nationalist movement had been born.

1 M.P., Egerton to Morel, 26 Nov. 1911.
2 C.O. 147/155, Macgregor to Chamberlain, 4 Apr. 1901.
3 C.O. 147/160, same to same, 6 Jan. 1902.
4 Ibid.

When we look for no *manifesto* from Salisbury Square, when we expect no packet of resolutions from Exeter Hall, when no bench of foreign Bishops, no conclave of Cardinals, 'lord over' Christian Africa, when the Captain of Salvation, Jesus Christ Himself, leads the Ethiopian host, and our Christianity ceases to be London-ward and New York-ward but Heaven-ward, then will there be an end to Privy Councils, Governors, Colonels, Annexations, Displacements, Partitions, Cessions and Coercions. Telegraph wires will be put to better uses and even Downing Street [will] be absent in the political vocabulary of the West African Native.

Mọjọla Agbebi, 1892

6 The Rise of Ethiopianism, 1875-1890

Ironically the Christian missions who heralded British rule in Nigeria also began the process of its termination. For the Church became the cradle of Nigerian nationalism,[1] the only forum of nationalist expression until the beginnings of the Nigerian-owned press after 1879, and the main focus of nationalist energies until after 1914. This is the point missed by scholars who have investigated the constitutional development of, and the nationalist movement in, Nigeria.[2] They tend to write off, so to speak, the pre-1914 period as of little constitutional and nationalist significance. Even Professor Coleman who cast a cursory glance at the contribution of Christian missions to Nigerian nationalism came to the astonishing conclusion that there was no 'causal relationships . . . between Christian missionary activity and the rise of nationalism'.[3]

1 The terms.'Nigerian' and 'nationalism' are used in this work rather loosely but not inappropriately. Although there was no Nigeria administratively until 1914, nevertheless the idea of the territorial boundaries of the future Nigeria was vaguely visualized by 1898 when a railway to Kano was being advocated in the newspapers. The 'nationalists', while cosmopolitan in their outlook, concentrated their efforts on events in what became Nigeria. On this basis they are better regarded as 'Nigerian' nationalists rather than as 'African' or 'Negro' nationalists. They were aware that they had differences with the Africans in the Gold Coast and Sierra Leone, hence the agitation for separation of the Lagos Colony from the Gold Coast Colony which came into effect in 1886. Although the 'nationalists' were mainly educated Africans with origins in Yorubaland, they spoke on behalf of the peoples of Nigeria; they opposed the removal of Jaja and the military expeditions against the Aro, the Munchi and the Fulani.

2 Joan Wheare: *The Nigerian Legislative Council*, London 1949, starts from 1914 and completely ignores the Legislative Council from 1886 to 1914 whose minutes are in the C.O. 149 series at the P.R.O. Kalu Ezera: *Constitutional Development in Nigeria*, O.U.P. 1960, also starts from 1914, completely oblivious of the vigorous press of 1880 to 1914. J. S. Coleman: *Background to Nigerian Nationalism*, California 1958, examines the pre-1914 period as mere introduction and asserts that nationalism did not really begin until after 1918; describes pre-1914 nationalism as one of 'Protest Movements', that is to say, nationalism before 1914 was negative.

3 J. S. Coleman, op. cit., p. 96.

The 'causal relationships . . . between Christian missionary activity and the rise of nationalism', which eluded Coleman, are glaringly manifest in mission archives and official records. There was hardly any strand of the nationalist movement in Nigeria between 1922 and 1960, the period that is much better known, the origins of which cannot be traced to missionary activity. Take first the exposition of the ideology of Nigerian nationality which, as Ajayi has clearly shown,[1] began with missionaries and their African minions in the nineteenth century. Consider also the cultural nationalism that pervaded the thinking of Esien Esien Ukpabio, the first Efik convert and pastor, in the book which he wrote before his death in 1902,[2] and the defence of their customs and institutions by the first Ibo pastors of the Church Missionary Society against the Europeanizing zeal of the European missionaries, in 1914.[3] The advocacy of a parliamentary system of government for the Republic of Nigeria was made not only by educated Africans in the nineteenth century, but also, as the minutes of the Legislative Council show, all the members of the Council from 1886 to 1914 were either African ministers or ardent Churchmen, and they looked upon the legislative body as the precursor of the modern House of Representatives of Nigeria. It is also a fact that in any computation of the part played by the press in the fomenting and dissemination of nationalism, much credit must be given to the Christian Church and educated Christianized Nigerians. It was not an accident that it was Dr Dikko, a Christian trained as a medical doctor in Birmingham by Dr Walter Miller and his friends, who conceived the strongest political party in Northern Nigeria known as the Northern Peoples' Congress.[4]

The point to bear in mind is that the first generation of educated Nigerians were pre-eminently equipped for a nationalist task by their learning and the circumstances of their age. Unrestricted access to the Bible, with its notions of equality, justice and non-racialism, provided the early converts with a valid weapon which they were not reluctant to employ against the missionaries who brushed these ideals aside in Church administration and in their relations with the converts. By their study of the classics, which many of the Protestant missions encouraged, and the history of the struggle of colonial peoples against their imperial masters, many of the early nationalists

1   J. F. A. Ajayi: 'Nineteenth Century Origins of Nigerian Nationalism', *Journal of the Historical Society of Nigeria*, Vol. 1, No. 4, December 1959.
2   Esere: *As seen Through African Eyes*, 1916.
3   *The Church and Native Customs*, C.M.S. Press, Lagos 1914.
4   Alhaji Sir Ahmadu Bello: *My Life*, Cambridge 1962, p. 85. The Northern Peoples Congress was at first 'a purely cultural Society'.

—all of them Church leaders—believed they had heroes worthy of emulation. By their knowledge of European customs and their own the early nationalists had the opportunity to compare the two and pronounce in favour of specific traditional customs and institutions, the usefulness and non-heathenish nature of which they could appreciate.

But before examining the brand of Nigerian nationalism expressed through the Church it is essential to define 'Ethiopianism', in the Nigerian context, for the early nationalists in the period covered by this book looked upon themselves as 'Ethiopians'. In the growing literature of African nationalism 'Ethiopianism' is one of the terms employed in describing African nationalism expressed through the medium of the Church.[1] It derives from Psalm 68 : 31, 'Ethiopia shall stretch forth her hands to God'. In Nigeria, indeed in West Africa, Ethiopianism acquired quite a different meaning from that prevalent in South and Central African settings which have been studied by scholars like Sundkler, Shepperson and Price. In these territories Ethiopianism has been fundamentally racial, arising out of the colour-bar policy of the white rulers in those places. Moreover the Christian missions in these territories did not raise up early enough an African agency which would have introduced African leadership into Church life. Consequently Africans did not find in the missions freedom and scope to express their own personality. Therefore, they seceded and founded their own churches. Thus secession became a necessary ingredient of Ethiopianism in these territories. Furthermore the racial policy of the white rulers drove these 'separatist' churches into becoming media for anti-government movements, and oftentimes for explosive subterranean organizations.

In West Africa also, Ethiopianism became fundamentally racial, but in a peculiar way. It never became anti-government, and although it was anti-white it was not on the same scale as in Central and South Africa. In West Africa there was neither white settlement nor the kind of economic exploitation which took place in Central and South Africa. Moreover missions raised up early enough an African agency and missionaries' wards found sufficient scope within the missions to express their natural desire for responsibility and

1   The best work from the point of view of the historian is Shepperson and Price, *Independent African*, Edinburgh 1958. From the point of view of the theologian cf. B. G. M. Sundkler: *Bantu Prophets in South Africa*, London 1948. Other important works are T. Hodgkin: *Nationalism in Colonial Africa*, London 1956, pp. 93–144; D. B. Kimble: *A Political History of Ghana*, O.U.P. 1963; J. S. Coleman: op. cit.; F. B. Welbourn: *East African Rebels*, S.C.M. 1961; C. O. Baeta: *Prophetism in Ghana*, S.C.M. 1962; G. Shepperson: 'Ethiopianism and African Nationalism', *Phylon* 1953.

leadership. 'Ethiopianism' came to be identified with Africa and 'Ethiopians' with the Negro race. It was also associated with the eventual conversion of Africa to Christianity and implied, ideally, the establishment of a Christian theocracy, to embrace the entire continent of Africa. The C.M.S. Grammar School in Sierra Leone called its magazine *The Ethiopian*, while in Nigeria the Ethiopian slogan, 'Africa for the Africans', was already in currency in the sixties.[1]

Conceived in the Biblical sense the term 'Ethiopia' came to have a deep sentimental connotation; it whipped up Negro racialism and became the beacon of hope and promise which educated Africans believed would be fulfilled at some future date. They looked forward to the day when Africa would become the cynosure of the world and the Negro race the model for other races. Like Garvey after the First World War, they eulogized and romanticized the achievements of the Negro race to show that the scriptural prophecy would be fulfilled and that 'the latter day glory of the Negro Race will ... exceed the former'.[2] In practical terms Ethiopianism expressed in terms of racial antagonism between the white missionaries and their wards represented the African struggle for power and position in Church government. It also had a parallel in the struggle by Africans for the higher positions in the civil service, and it awakened the dream of a nation-state to be controlled ultimately by Africans. In some cases the racial antagonism in the Church led to the foundation of 'African' Churches, but secession was not a necessary ingredient of Nigerian Ethiopianism. Consequently a large number of the educated Africans —the Ethiopians—stayed in the missions and contested, not unsuccessfully, for the higher positions in Church government to an extent without parallel in other mission fields.

It was natural that before 1914 the Church was the centre of the social, spiritual and political aspirations of educated Africans and illiterate converts. The Church meant more to them than the administration and commerce. Consequently they subscribed liberally to maintain their pastors and teachers, erected churches and financed the education of their children, at a time when they resisted taxation by the secular administration. Their deep attachment to the Church did not lie solely on the fact that the missionaries evinced interests in their welfare and showed an altruism in a way the trader and administrator did not. The point must be emphasized here that for the Lagos inhabitants the administration was, until the turn of the century, a remote establishment whose legislations hardly affected their

1 C.M.S. CA3/04 (a), Bishop Crowther's charge, Onitsha, 13 Sept. 1869. C.O. 147/4, Freeman to Newcastle, 31 Dec. 1863.
2 C.M.S. CA1/0123, James Johnson to M. Taylor and others, 19 Apr. 1873.

lives. Compared to the missionaries the administrators were detached, officious and formal in their dealings with their 'subjects'. Moreover the educated Africans had no political grievance against the Lagos Government, whose presence they welcomed because it guaranteed law and order and made possible their existence in Lagos, where they were not more than a quarter of the population.

On the other hand, as products of missionary propaganda, the most intimate relationship developed between the educated Africans and the European missionaries. Through the Church they became whatever they were, whether traders or teachers, clerks or catechists. In other words, the Church made it possible for them to fulfil their whole being, and by its involuntary monopoly of education held the destiny of their children in its hands. But from the seventies onwards missionary enterprise acquired a special significance and came to be zealously patronized and appreciated because of its political usefulness. It provided the training ground for apprenticeship in the management of their own affairs. For the missionary teaching of equality and brotherhood of all men before God which had been implanted in them came to have its logical effect. They became self-conscious and began to nurse the ambition for self-expression and self-government, a corollary to the theory of equality. The education they had received began to develop in them critical faculties, and familiarized them with the machinery of British parliamentary democracy which all the Protestant missions were compelled to establish as the financial burden devolved on the Africans themselves.

Educated Africans, in our period, accepted Christianity wholeheartedly and emphasized it apparently to the exclusion of purely political matters, not because they were not patriots, nor because they had no political vision of an independent nation. On the contrary they were intensely patriotic and believed that they were paving the way for the creation of the Nigerian nation by patronizing Christianity. But political independence, the vision of which they had, must be shelved because it could not come until Christianity was fully established and they, educated Africans, were in complete control of it; once independence in the management of Church affairs was secured, political independence would logically and automatically follow like cause and effect. In their thinking they associated the Christian faith with the civilization and emergence of nation-states in contemporary Europe. It was an article of their faith that, as the Efik nationalist put it, 'the same Gospel which accounts for the growth and supremacy of Europe will not fail to do the same thing similar for our beloved country'.[1]

1 Esere, op. cit., p. 14.

Christianity had another political appeal to the educated Africans. It promised to foment a common consciousness which would pave the way for a nation-state and thus reduce to a minimum all other sectional loyalties such as the many incipient tribal groups they were divided into in this period demanded.[1] The 'Ethiopians' were not just the parochial tribalists they were thought to be by contemporaries. The location of agents in the different parts of the country, irrespective of their tribal origins, helped many of the African missionaries to evolve a cosmopolitan attitude. Moreover a sense of oneness used to prevail among the educated Africans whenever any section of the Nigerian community suffered or was threatened by the administrators or European missionaries. James Johnson of Ijẹbu and Ijẹsha parentage worked among the Ibo, Ijẹbu, Ijaw, Edo and Itsekiri, while Mọjọla Agbebi of Ekiti stock did his most useful work as leader of the Native Baptist Church in the Niger Delta, among the Ijaw. The special deputation to Ijẹbu-Ode of April 1892, which attempted to prevent the Ijẹbu Expedition, was financed by R. B. Blaize and J. S. Leigh, Ẹgba. The Niger chiefs and converts who rallied round the African missionaries in the pro-Crowther 'rebellion' against the Church Missionary Society in 1892, which will be analysed in the next chapter, looked upon their missionaries as fellow Africans and not as Yoruba or Sierra Leonians.

If any individual is to be credited with originating Nigerian nationalism, ideologically, then that individual is unquestionably the Reverend Henry Venn, Prebendary of St Paul's London, and for thirty years, 1842 to 1872, the Secretary of the Church Missionary Society. Singlehanded and deliberately, he urged Africans to be prepared to assume the leadership of their countries. Why and how he became the spokesman of the Africans he answers in a letter of September 1871. His love for Africans, he said, began about 1800, at the age of four, at Clapham Common, where he was a playmate to African children brought up by Governor Zachary Macaulay of Sierra Leone.[2] He grew up in the environment of the Clapham Sect and was an evangelical of the deepest hue. His cast of mind is illustrated by the fact that among his correspondents were William Wilberforce, the liberator of the Negroes, and Lord Shaftesbury, the great nineteenth-century reformer.[3]

In missionary history Venn's name is celebrated in the principles of Church government contained in his minutes of 1851, 1856 and

1 C.M.S. CA2/056 James Johnson to Wright 2 Aug. 1876. There were for example 'Lagos Yoruba Association', 'Ijẹbu Society' and 'Ijẹsha Company'.
2 C.M.S. CA1/L8, Henry Venn to I. B. Pinney of New York, 22 Sept. 1871.
3 *The Venn Papers*, C.M.S. Archives C. 35.

1861.[1] These principles involved an evolutionary process, in three stages, by which churches in Africa and Asia would become indigenous. Gradually the converts in these territories were to be encouraged to assume the pecuniary burden of their ministers; when the churches in a district could do this they should combine into a 'Native Pastorate'. Side by side with the assumption of the finances by the churches the missionaries should raise up African pastors who should take charge of these churches. Once the European missionary had set the churches on their feet his work was done, for he was not to be a pastor. He should move on to a virgin field, the 'regions beyond', and repeat the process all over again. The churches were to rule themselves through various Councils and Committees, composed of the European Bishop, European and African missionaries and laymen. The process was not to be hastened but gradual and the Pastorate must continue to receive diminishing annual grants from the Parent Committee. So long as the latter continued to bear any financial responsibility so long must the administration of the Pastorate be controlled by it through the European missionaries on the spot. The ideal and aim was however the creation of a full African Episcopate in which all European control would come to an end, as far as the personnel was concerned. This was his 'euthanasia' of missions, his 'self-supporting, self-governing and self-extending' Church.

For Henry Venn his scheme was primarily a missionary and spiritual system designed to relieve the C.M.S. of providing funds for further evangelization and also to make Christianity indigenous in Africa. But for the educated Africans the scheme was attractive more for political than for other ends. It contained the principle of national independence in Church government, a principle that could be logically employed for indigenization of Christianity and declaration of political independence. African missionaries found in it beckoning opportunities for the expenditure of their energies. They could graduate from schoolmaster to catechist, then to priest and archdeacon, if they had sufficient ability; even the episcopate was not beyond their reach. The laymen, too, had sufficient scope for their abilities in the Parochial Board, the Patronage Board, the School Board, the Church Committee and the Church Council. Speaking for the Africans on their view of the Native Pastorate James Johnson said,

> We continually cherish the remembrance of the days of former native independence and glory. . . . But we see nothing around us

1   W. Knight: *Memoir of Henry Venn*, London 1882, Appendix c, pp. 412–37.

which we can call our own in the true sense of the term; nothing that shows an independent native capacity excepting this infant Native Pastorate institution. For this reason and the conviction that we have that it is capable of being made a mighty instrument to develop the principles which create and strengthen a nation we cleave to it.[1]

The political significance of the Venn scheme was clearly grasped by the educated Africans in West Africa, most of whom owed their position directly to him. As Salisbury Square was to discover in the seventies, the evolutionary aspect of the Venn scheme was not satisfactory to the educated Africans in Lagos. They conceived it in revolutionary terms to throw off the C.M.S. and to exclude completely, and at once, Europeans from the Lagos Church. It is essential to note that according to Venn's scheme Lagos Church was not yet ripe for the beginnings of a Native Pastorate when he left office in 1872. In Sierra Leone, where the Church was over forty years older than in Lagos, beginnings were made in 1861. However Venn could not have done a greater service to the educated Africans when in 1864 he brushed aside his own principles of evolutionary process of Church government, spread over a long time, and made Samuel Ajayi Crowther, an ex-slave, Bishop of the Niger Mission which was then barely seven years old. This unique experiment, never attempted anywhere else, made Ajayi Crowther a romantic figure, the symbol of the Negro race, its ability to evangelize and its capability to rule.

But Venn was also important for Africans in other ways. In minutes and instructions to missionaries he urged them not to be reckless iconoclasts but to respect African customs and institutions that could not be regarded as unchristian.[2] There were 'racial peculiarities', including slavery, he said, that must be recognized. African chiefs, he went on, were by nature friendly, and so missionaries should not make themselves imperialist agents but work in harmony with them. They should be prepared for national awakening as a matter of course as Africans 'excel in writing sensational statements, as they become our rivals in the pulpit and on the platform'.[3] In 1865 Venn wrote a pamphlet for the guidance of the Ord Commission sent to West Africa to study the position and policy of the British Government in that territory.[4] He criticized British policy in unequivocal language. British policy as hitherto pursued,

1   C.O. 267/317, James Johnson to Hennessy, 6 Dec. 1872.
2   W. Knight, op. cit., pp. 165–8.   3   Ibid. p. 167.
4   Henry Venn, *Notices of the British Colonies on the West Coast of Africa*, London 1865.

he said, had not been conducive to the true interests of the Africans; the regeneration of Africa could best be achieved by a trained African agency which should be products of medical and other technical colleges to be built in West Africa. Educated Africans would help their peoples in cash crop economy which would raise the standard of living of the people. European officials in West Africa were not only expensive but they kept on dying; all posts could be more efficiently and more cheaply occupied by educated Africans, and he pointed to the success that was attending the utilization of African agency in the Church and the signal success of the few Government appointments. There is nothing to wonder at therefore when in 1872 Edward Blyden declared that the hopes of Africans would suffer an eclipse whenever Venn was removed from Salisbury Square. He wrote, 'I trust that God may spare your *life* and strength, especially for this African work. Dark will be the day for Africa when the active influence of Henry Venn is removed from the African Church—the Chariot of our Israel and the horseman thereof.'[1]

Venn's policy did not arouse the sympathy of the European missionaries in West Africa. They saw nothing worth preserving in African customs and institutions outside the languages. This is the explanation for the painful absence of much material in their letters that would have been of immense value to anthropologists. They regarded the converts and their subordinate African staff as 'infants' reclaimed only recently from superstition and barbarism. Their attitude was mainly paternalistic; they looked upon themselves as 'Tutors and Governors'[2] and behaved as 'little local popes'.[3] This attitude was indeed consonant with the condition of the Church in Yorubaland up to 1870 because all the financial burden of the mission was borne by the C.M.S., while until 1874 all the five Anglican churches in Lagos were directly in the pastoral charge of white missionaries. In Sierra Leone the creation of the Native Pastorate in 1861 unleashed for over sixteen years a great deal of bitter acrimony between the white and African missionaries with James Johnson and Benjamin Tregaskis, Chairman of the Wesleyan Mission, as the African defender and European attacker respectively.[4] The C.M.S. missionaries said that Venn was 'mad' and reported to the then Governor that Venn was trifling with a most dangerous experiment.[5] In Lagos the attitude of the white missionaries to the educated

1   C.M.S. CA1/047, Blyden to Venn, 6 Apr. 1872.
2   C.M.S. G3/A2/012, quoted by Bishop Tugwell in a charge, 17 July 1906.
3   *African Times*, 1 Apr. 1878.
4   C. Fyfe: *A History of Sierra Leone*, O.U.P. 1962, p. 398.
5   M.M.A. (S. Leone Box), Tregaskis to Secretaries, 15 June 1868.

Africans, nearly all of whom were offspring of liberated Africans, and the resentment of the latter to this attitude was expressed by Archdeacon Johnson as follows:

> You in England cannot fancy how some of those who come here inflated with the idea that they are the 'dominant race', do treat with something like contempt the natives of the country. The truth is that they regard us this day in pretty much the same light as our forefathers were, who were rescued from the ironpangs of slavery by the philanthropists of a former generation. We are not oversensitive, but at the same time we are not unduly pachydermatous. ... But does anyone think we have no feelings at all, or no rights which are to be respected? ... Having educated us, you will not allow us to think and speak and act like men.[1]

In 1872 and 1873 the European missionaries suddenly found, to their dismay, that their supposed 'infants' were not 'unduly pachydermatous'. In the former year the Africans of all denominations went above their heads by asking Salisbury Square to allocate Henry Johnson to the Grammar School with the hope that he would be made the principal at some future date. Governor Glover joined the Africans in making this demand.[2] The following year they had the extreme pain of seeing Pope Hennessy, 'that storming petrel among Colonial Governors',[3] succeeding Glover. John Pope Hennessy was an Irishman who, having championed in Parliament his oppressed people's cause, was for two decades, as governor of successive colonies, to champion the causes of those of his subjects he deemed oppressed. His popularity, arising out of his courting of the Africans in Sierra Leone, preceded him to Lagos and he was enthusiastically welcomed. Characteristically he sought to remove the grievances which the policy of his predecessor had created for the Ẹgba and Ijẹbu. He promised that he would return to them all their slaves who had escaped to Lagos and also Ebute Metta, Leke and Palma, territories belonging to these tribal groups.[4] Although his stay in Lagos was brief, and to the disappointment of the educated Africans he was taken to the Bahamas, his policy drove a wedge between the leading educated Africans like Captain J. P. L. Davies, a naval officer and wealthy trader, Otunba Payne and Charles Foresythe, a postmaster who rose to become secretary of the Legislative Council, who agreed with him and the European missionaries who viewed his transfer as a

1   C.M.S. G3/A2/01, Henry Johnson to Hutchinson, 31 Mar. 1881.
2   C.M.S. CA2/03 (c), Glover etc. to C.M.S., 14 Mar. 1872.
3   *Church Missionary Intelligencer*, 1887, p. 650.
4   C.M.S. CA2/03 (b), Nicholson to Secretaries, 6 July 1872.

happy riddance. Hennessy nominated J. P. L. Davies to the Legislative Council of the West African Colonies, the first Nigerian to be so appointed.

It was this occasion of mounting racial animus that Charles Foresythe and Otunba Payne, respectively churchwardens of Breadfruit Church and Christchurch, seized to launch the first supra-tribal organization, with political sentiments, in Nigeria. This was the 'Society for the Promotion of Religion and Education in Lagos'.[1] The educated Africans were not happy about the education policy of the C.M.S. which, they said, was unprogressive and deliberately made so in order that a Native Pastorate might not be created in Lagos. It was estimated that the C.M.S. was spending £310 per annum on maintaining its establishment in Lagos. Therefore they decided to contribute £500 a year for the maintenance of all the churches and schools in Lagos. All the African subordinates supported the scheme and at the inaugural meeting over £98 was collected. The aim, they said, was to force the C.M.S. out of Lagos. The new Society was 'a thing ordained of God and a beginning of African Church Missionary Society'. When the European missionaries got wind of this movement which they described as 'very formidable',[2] they suspected that it was a conspiracy to drive them out of Lagos. The constitution of the Society confirmed their suspicion, for Clause 13 stated that it would manage its own funds instead of being remitted to Salisbury Square as the normal procedure was. Already Venn's scheme was found inadequate. The political situation pointed in the same direction of conspiracy to drive all white men out of Lagos. This arose out of the non-fulfilment of Hennessy's promises by Blackall, his successor. The two tribal groups, as mentioned in Chapter 1, planned a *coup* with Dosunmu.

The European missionaries spared no effort to nip this incipient nationalist movement in the bud. They threatened to dismiss the clerical subordinates if they did not abandon the movement while they sought to prevent concerted effort by appealing to each Church to act independently through themselves for any improvements they wanted in education.[3] Although the opposition of the white missionaries weakened the movement in the sense that the independence it was after was no longer attainable, yet it did not fizzle out as the white missionaries expected. In fact it resulted in the transfer to Lagos in 1874 of James Johnson, the man after the heart of the

1 C.M.S. CA2/011, various papers of this Society and minutes of the meeting of 3 September 1873; J. P. L. Davies was President and C. Foresythe, Secretary.
2 C.M.S. CA2/03 (b), Maser to Hutchinson, 19 Sept. 1873.
3 Ibid. Same to same, 18 Sept. and 1 Oct. 1873.

nationalists of our period. The C.M.S. was alarmed at the nationalist movement that sought a complete exclusion of Europeans. The only course open was to conciliate the nationalists with the more moderate Venn's scheme, the dangerous Sierra Leone experiment. To this end James Johnson was transferred to guide the nationalists' 'newly developed energies upon the lines and principles of the existing machinery of the Sierra Leone Church *rather than of launching out into some new untried system*'.[1]

The advent of James Johnson in Nigeria was more than an ordinary event. Henceforth the nationalist movement revolved round him and he deserves a close attention. He was born in Sierra Leone about 1838 of Ijẹbu and Ijẹsha parentage. Educated at the Freetown Grammar School and Fourah Bay College, he tutored in the latter from 1860 to 1863. He became the spokesman for the Native Pastorate of Sierra Leone against the opposition of Europeans and was influential in pressing for the affiliation of Fourah Bay College to Durham University. His correspondence with the ultramontane Pope Hennessy, in which both idealized the Negro race and lambasted missionaries as representatives of 'mistaken benevolence' whose contact with coastal Africans was injurious,[2] and his championship of the cause of the Native Pastorate made him unpopular with the white missionaries. The evangelization of Africa by Africans was for him an obsession, based on the belief that the reason for Islam's success lay in its use of African personnel and its retention of vital African customs and institutions. James Johnson found extremely distasteful the idea that Africans were organically inferior to Europeans proclaimed by anti-Negro figures like Burton, Winwood Reade and Hutchinson. He believed that given equal chances Africans were as capable as other beings. Instead of Europeans, he would rather have Negroes from the New World to occupy mission and Government posts in West Africa.[3]

Unlike his classmate, Dr J. B. Horton, the Ibo-born military surgeon who drew up a distinctly political programme for the nationalists and chiefs on the Gold Coast in the sixties and seventies of the nineteenth century,[4] James Johnson had no political programme divorced from Christianity for Nigeria. The conviction that Christianity and African nationalism were interdependent, and that the former should provide the superstructure for the latter, dominated his thinking throughout his life. So pious was he that he enjoyed the

1 C.M.S. CA2/L4, Hutchinson to James Johnson, 26 Feb. 1874 (italics are mine).
2 Published in *The Negro* (S. Leone), 1 Jan. 1873.
3 C.O. 806/46, James Johnson to C.O., 21 Jan. 1874.
4 D. Kimble, op. cit., 243 ff.

unique reputation of being the most genuine Christian in West Africa. For the Sierra Leonians he was 'Wonderful Johnson', for Nigerians 'Holy Johnson' and for Salisbury Square the 'Pope' of Nigeria.[1] His idea of the inseparableness of African nationalism and Christianity he carved into his motto 'God and my country' which was boldly inscribed on his writing sheets to Salisbury Square. The Native Pastorate, which was for him 'the Cause of God and the Cause of the Negro Race',[2] was only a half-measure. Native Pastorates were to combine and be transformed into an 'Independent African Church' which would wipe off sectarianism, embrace all African Christians 'and make of them all one African whole'.[3] This was to be Pan-Africanism *par excellence* and the 'means for the development of a future African existence'.[4] The African Church was to be manned at all levels by Africans because European missionaries could not identify themselves with African racial ambitions and idiosyncrasies; indeed their continued dominance would stunt the full development of Africans, eroding such qualities as 'the superior physique, the manly independence, the courage and bravery, the daring and self-reliance, and the readiness to face difficulties' which Africans who had not come in contact with Europeans were supposed to possess.[5]

It was logical that he considered that his visualized African Church should ultimately evolve a distinctly African Christianity which would incorporate some parts of indigenous religion which bore resemblance to Christianity, adopt the vernacular languages, have its own hymns and liturgy, for the Church of England '*is not our own*'.[6] Once the African Church was established then a 'Christian nation' would emerge. James Johnson was silent over the machinery and processes that would effect a complete establishment of his visualized Christian state, although he suggested that the stages in the achievement of this goal would include the backing of the Native Pastorate by the local British Government, the making of Christianity the state religion and the promotion of Africans in the Civil Service according to a code of Christian ethics.[7]

In fact nationalism was for James Johnson spiritual, and pervaded all things. For example he mourned in 1887 at the Indian and Colonial Exhibition in London because the West African exhibits

1 C.M.S. CA1/L11, Lang to Ingham, 29 July 1887.
2 C.M.S. CA1/0123, James Johnson to Taylor and others, 19 Apr. 1873.
3 Ibid.   4 Ibid. James Johnson to Sawyerr and others, April 1873.
5 C.O. 267/369, James Johnson to C.O., 26 July 1887.
6 C.M.S. CA1/025e, Cheetham to Wright, 1 Feb. 1873, quotes Johnson's article in *The Negro*, 15 Jan. 1873.
7 C.O. 267/369, James Johnson to C.O., 26 July 1887.

were the poorest, and unrepresentative of African genius;[1] because Africans should cultivate 'mainly independence' the converts must strain their purse to maintain not only their clergy but also African missionaries as well; because the British occupied African soil in Sierra Leone and Lagos and consequently seized political control from the indigenous rulers he grumbled, and while appreciating the benefits of British rule, preached the sanctity of independent African states, even when they were guilty of acts he would not approve of morally. African institutions were good and therefore he defended monarchy, the African middlemen's trade, African names and clothing. As he aged his nationalist feelings removed the supposed evils of institutions like polygamy and slavery, which his puritanical outlook had earlier made him condemn in severe language. As early as 1887 he had asked the Colonial Office to grant the elective principle to educated Africans in appointments to the Legislative Councils of West Africa. The oppressed Africans in the Congo and Fernando Po drew his attention while he wished Africans were recruited by the British to fight against the Boers in the South African war.[2]

Fearless and fanatically opinionated, he expounded his religionationalist principles to the exasperation of administrators and European missionaries. Governor Moloney likened him in 1876 to Gordon of Jamaica;[3] Macdonald was apprehensive of his influence and pleaded with Salisbury Square not to transfer him to the Niger Coast Protectorate[4] while, for Carter, he was a 'mischievous patriot'[5] whom he had been only too glad to remove from the Legislative Council, of which Johnson was a member from 1886 to 1894, because James Johnson had assailed him publicly (as Edmund Burke had fallen on Warren Hastings) over the Ijẹbu Expedition.

James Johnson was a constant source of embarrassment to Salisbury Square and a veritable thorn in the side of the European missionaries in Nigeria. For Salisbury Square he was a unique Christian and missionary who should not be dispensed with. He was 'a very remarkable man, peculiarly qualified in many respects to help forward the Native Church far above and beyond his fellows in the Yoruba Church, a man of great spiritual strength and vigour, as well as of mental and intellectual capacity, of courage and decision'.[6] On the other hand there was the nationalist James Johnson whose writings and utterances whipped up a great deal of anti-European

1 Ibid.   2 C.M.S. G3/A3/09, James Johnson to Baylis, 24 Sept. 1904.
3 C.M.S. G3/A2/01, James Johnson to Hutchinson, June 1881.
4 C.M.S. G3/A3/06, Memo. of interview, 2 Mar. 1893.
5 C.O. 147/95, Carter to Ripon, 19 June 1894.
6 CA1/L11, Lang to Ingham, 29 July 1887.

feelings both in Sierra Leone and in Nigeria. In 1873 and 1887 the C.M.S. summoned him to London, hoping to blunt the edge of his nationalist feelings by direct talk with the Parent Committee. While all the European missionaries believed that he possessed qualities for holding the highest ecclesiastical appointment, they were apprehensive of the use he would make of such an appointment. Not without some grounds, they feared that he would employ such a position to promote his nationalist aims by discarding Anglican forms of worship and repudiate the authority of the Society. Some even suggested that he would admit polygamists, Muslims and Roman Catholics into his Church.[1] James Johnson's heterodoxy therefore provided an additional reason for the persistent opposition of the European missionaries to the attempts by the Church Missionary Society to make him Bishop or make him a member of the Finance Committee, the executive of the Mission's administration in Lagos. In 1887 when the Society felt it in its interest to appoint a Bishop for Yorubaland the proposal had to be shelved because no European could be appointed, in the Society's thinking then, so long as James Johnson was alive. Little wonder that a C.M.S. secretary wished James Johnson were not born.[2]

This was the man with whom the white missionaries in Lagos had to deal as from 1874. His fame, already known to the Lagos leaders of the 'Society for the Promotion of Religion and Education in Lagos', made them accept his leadership and guidance. They communicated to Salisbury Square to this effect.[3] The European missionary in Breadfruit Church, Valentine Faulkner, made way for Johnson. Breadfruit Church was the wealthiest and most important church in Lagos. Naturally the white missionaries were alarmed at their displacement by Africans and the handing of positions of responsibility to the converts. Adolphus Mann, the local secretary of the Society who was expected to put through the Native Pastorate scheme in 1875, protested to Salisbury Square:

The native mind wants a guide, a stimulus, a superintendence, and this is the very thing you go about to take away from them through the NATIVE CHURCH. There will be no more the wholesome influence of the whiteman's energy ... the absolute independence

1 C.M.S. G3/A2/02, A. Mann to Secretaries, 16 June 1882; Maser to Lang, 17 Nov. 1882.
2 C.M.S. CA1/L11, Lang to Ingham, 29 July 1887. For a detailed treatment of this pioneer of nationalism in Nigeria cf. author's two articles on his place in Nigerian history in Vol. 2, No. 4, and Vol. 3, No. 1, of *Journal of the Historical Society of Nigeria*.
3 C.M.S. CA2/033, J. P. L. Davies to Hutchinson, 3 Aug. 1874.

of the Native I dread. .... When I am no admirer of Native independence I am so from the best of feelings for the African man: that he may be largely profited, far more than time allowed—by a wise presidency of the whiteman.[1]

The disaster predicted by the white missionaries for the Native Pastorate never occurred although it was launched in the midst of economic depression. Rather it grew stronger and stronger, to the consternation of the white missionaries. Consisting of only one church in 1875 it took in another in 1878. In 1881 James Johnson took Breadfruit Church into it while in 1889 all the churches in Lagos but one had been absorbed by the Pastorate and, to the astonishment of the C.M.S., other churches were demanded. In 1882 it became a missionary body with its own stations outside Lagos.

The creation of the Native Pastorate widened the rift in the social relationship of the white and black missionaries. In the School Board and Church Committee, where the two races were represented, bitter words were often exchanged and relationships became purely official.[2] Ousted from power which they had hitherto wielded alone, the European missionaries dreaded the directions in which the Pastorate was moving. In an effort to make it indigenous ex-king Dosunmu and his White-cap chiefs were drawn to the Breadfruit Church by James Johnson, while they in turn gave a piece of land for church building. The Prayer Book was revised to exclude prayers for the Queen and prayers for the native kings substituted. The annual reports made by James Johnson, its secretary, echoed his ideas of what the Pastorate should be. But what incensed the white missionaries most were his speeches and writings, his 'vituberations [sic]', at the anniversaries of the Pastorate and in the newspapers.[3] Too frequently he drew attention to the signal success of the African Methodist Church, founded in 1821, to which he was born, from which the Pastorate should draw inspiration. Although there was a European Bishop who supervised the Pastorate, James Johnson looked upon him as one welcomed only as a matter of 'courtesy'.[4] Referring to a speech by him in 1876 Maser, a European missionary, said, 'It grated my ears, which are, I confess, always revolting, when the tune "Africa for the Africans" is struck.'[5] The fear that the Pastorate would secede was aroused when James Johnson demanded that all Church property, formerly registered in the name of the

1 C.M.S. CA2/03 (d), Mann to Wright, 24 Feb. 1875.
2 C.M.S. G3/A2/01, Cheetham to Wigram, 3 Mar. 1881.
3 Ibid. Mann to the secretaries, 16 Nov. 1881. *Lagos Times*, 15 June 1882.
4 C.O. 149/3, Legislative Council Minutes, 30 Oct. 1890.
5 C.M.S. CA2/03 (d), A. Maser to Wright, 9 June 1876.

C.M.S., be transferred to the Pastorate. Knowing quite well that the African Churches in Sierra Leone broke away from the Wesleyan Missionary Society because of the latter's legal negligence of their property the C.M.S. refused to entertain the idea. In the judgment of the white missionaries on the spot, were it not that the property had been registered in the name of the Church Missionary Society the Native Pastorate would have seceded from the Society long before 1891.[1] As will be analysed in the next chapter, the independent Niger Delta Pastorate was able to repudiate the authority of the C.M.S. because of the land system prevailing there. In 1881 James Johnson was openly accused of being 'anti-white'. His reply was that he was not anti-white but a nationalist:

> With the missionaries of the present day an independent thought in an African and a clear enunciation of his convictions are a great crime. He has no right to them: he must always see with other people's eyes and swear by other people's opinions: he must not manifest any patriotic sentiments; he must denude himself of manhood and of every vestige of racial feeling and fling away his individuality and distinctiveness to make peaceable existence with them possible and secure favourable recommendations to the Society.[2]

The establishment of the Native Pastorate in Lagos marked the beginnings of Nigeria towards independence, under the leadership of educated Africans. It began the displacement of white rulers by Nigerians in an institution that was to mean much to the Nigerian peoples. Through administrative experience in the Church Nigerians were preparing themselves for self-rule in the state as well. Indeed the European missionaries were aware of the political implication of assumption of authority in the Church by their wards as much as the Africans themselves. The C.M.S. Church in Lagos became a hotbed of 'contest between the whiteman and the blackman'. By 'heaping authorities' on Africans in the Church, observed a missionary, the C.M.S. was also preparing them for political independence.[3] A. Mann warned Salisbury Square: 'The Committee have done their best, to bring about a root of Revolting Spirit in the Church. The cry "the native, the native", is simply the worst you can do to them. They cannot bear it. This Spirit of Revolt against the white element is in the Church and will it not go over to politics?'[4]

1 C.M.S. G3/A2/03, Cheetham to Lang, 6 Feb. 1884.
2 C.M.S. G3/A2/01, James Johnson to Hutchinson, June 1881.
3 Ibid. A. Mann to secretaries (undated).
4 Ibid. A. Mann to Lang, 9 Mar. 1882.

But although struggle for power in the Church between Africans and Europeans was most prominent in the C.M.S., African desire to minimize and then ultimately exclude European control from Church administration was not confined to that mission. Reading the writing on the wall the other Protestant missions followed the example of the C.M.S. The Wesleyan Mission was fortunate in its Chairman, John Milum, who conceded to the Lagos Circuit, created in 1878, all authority in the management of its affairs, including the payment of the salaries of pastors and teachers. Self-government was virtually complete by 1880.[1] Indeed at the annual synod conference the Chairman of the Mission ceased to wield executive authority. Discipline of African agents and other matters that affected them became the joint responsibility of all ordained agents, European and African, and decisions were determined by majority vote. From 1885 onwards the Africans were in the majority and there were many instances when they compelled the European agents to accept decisions that the latter would not have approved of.

Among the Efik, about 400 miles from Lagos, the Presbyterian missionaries of Scotland began to devolve power on their converts in a way and at a pace not yet done in Kaffraria, Jamaica and India, the Mission's other fields. As the Board in Edinburgh commented, the missionaries in Old Calabar devolved authority and responsibility on the Efik in a manner that marked 'a new era in the history of our missionary enterprise'.[2] Not only were the Efik allowed to elect elders and deacons but in 1880 a Finance Committee, composed of the converts was set up under the chairmanship of King Eyo VI. The Committee was to control all finances, which were to be spent locally and not remitted to the Board in Edinburgh as was hitherto the practice. It is difficult to ascertain how far the missionaries were prompted to do this by their liberal paternalism and the astonishingly absolute absence of distrust of African capability which is clear from their letters, and how far the events in Lagos influenced them. The first convert of the Mission, the Reverend Esien Esien Ukpabio, and the Reverend Asuqua Ekanem, the two ordained African missionaries, were put in charge of Adiobo and Ikonetu respectively, without the supervision of European missionaries. These African missionaries and King Eyo Honesty VI were also appointed members of the Mission Committee,[3] the executive of the Mission in Old Calabar, at the time the white missionaries in Lagos objected to the appointment of James Johnson to the Finance Committee. The trust of the Africans by the Presbyterian missionaries was quite exceptional in

1 M.M.A., Report for 1879 by John Milum.
2 U.P. Minutes, 24 Feb. 1880.   3 U.P. Minutes, 24 Feb. 1885.

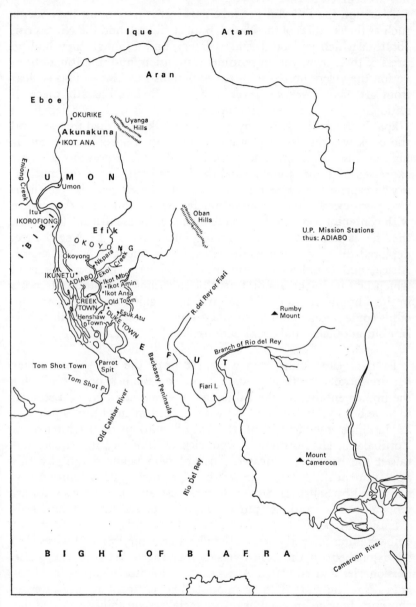

United Presbyterian Map of Old Calabar

Nigeria in the period under survey, and explains why secession has never occurred in that Mission.

Although the Efik did not take part in the nationalist movements such as the creation of the Native Baptist Church and the Niger crisis (both of which will be discussed later), and although they had no press of their own, yet, in sentiment, in vision, and in critical observation they were united with the nationalists in Lagos. This is clear from *As Seen Through African Eyes*, the first full-length piece of nationalist literature in Nigeria which was written by Esien Esien Ukpabio under the pseudonym of Esere. Ukpabio died in 1902 and the book was published posthumously, with a possible addition by his son, also a pastor. The book is a vigorous exposition of views expressed by James Johnson and the Lagos Press. It praised missionary enterprise as a whole but recognized that there were bad missionaries; criticized administrative officials who dealt with the people with contempt, refuted the idea of incapability of Africans to govern themselves and the alleged organic inferiority of the Negro race, deplored discrimination against Negroes in the U.S.A. and South Africa, and visualized an independent Nigeria, the beginnings of which he saw in the appointment of Nigerians to subordinate posts in the administration of the country. It is significant that, like many of his contemporaries in Yorubaland, he did not express Efik tribalism but adopted a universal outlook.

In the years under review, apart from the all-African Niger Mission headed by Bishop Ajayi Crowther, the best opportunity for the implementation of the Ethiopian programme in Nigeria seemed to have been provided in 1876 by the appointment of James Johnson as the Superintendent of all the C.M.S. stations in the interior of Yorubaland. His instructions were clearly Ethiopian in content and raised the hopes of educated Africans who believed that by this appointment the Negro race was being exalted. James Johnson was instructed by Salisbury Square to supervise all the Society's stations, reopen the old stations, pursue a policy of self-support and self-extension by persuading the converts to bear their own burden and embark on an extensive educational programme.[1] Since two works[2] have touched on the controversies that raged between the white missionaries and educated Africans over Johnson's doings in Abẹokuta—how he started to promote self-government in the interior churches, how he imposed heavy financial responsibility on the Ẹgba

1 C.M.S. CA2/o56, J. Johnson to Wright, 2 Aug. 1879.
2 J.F.A. Ajayi, op. cit., Chapter 7; A. Ajayi: 'A History of the Yoruba Mission (C.M.S.) 1843–80', M.A. (Bristol), April 1959, pp. 336 ff.

and Ibadan converts in order that they might become independent, how the Society's minutes on slavery, which he faithfully wished to see implemented according to instructions from Salisbury Square, provided the excuse for his removal in 1880—we should be content here with an examination of the new facts which have come to light.[1] Evidence suggests that the alleged causes of Johnson's removal from the interior were no more than excuses; that the local European missionaries deliberately worked against Johnson by inciting the Egba against him, and that the Church Missionary Society had planned his removal or supersession as early as March 1878, that is, before any trouble arose in Abeokuta.

The success that was attending Johnson's work in the interior increased the apprehensions of the European missionaries about his intentions there. He threw himself into his work with extraordinary vigour. He toured extensively, chose sites for new stations on the caravan routes, requested that agents be sent to the Ijebu territory, calmed the fears of the traditional rulers that the British in Lagos had an eye on their sovereignty, increased class dues in Ibadan, and set up in that town a body similar to Calvin's Presbytery in Geneva. But it was Abeokuta, the citadel of Christianity in the interior of West Africa in the pre-colonial era, that occupied most of his attention. Johnson believed that he was absolutely independent of the Finance Committee of the European missionaries in Lagos and began to encourage a self-support programme that aroused the misgivings of the white missionaries.[2] The latter became convinced that Johnson would before long make himself a Bishop and throw off all connections with the C.M.S. For by raising class dues among the Egba by 650 per cent Johnson more than doubled the revenue of the Abeokuta church in 1878 and he began to save a great part of the money against the rainy day, when he expected that the Society would withdraw all financial assistance to the church. Moreover he ceased to receive money from the Society for teachers' salaries and he began to expostulate to the Egba on the virtues of independence. So terrified did Maser, the local secretary of the C.M.S., become that he took the extraordinary step of saying to the Egba that the C.M.S. did not want them to become self-supporting.[3] He also wished that the Egba had stoned Johnson to death because of the 'spiritual tyranny' he had inflicted on them.[4]

The only tenable explanation that can be offered for Johnson's

1 Cf. papers on the crisis in C.M.S. CA2/011.
2 C.M.S. G3/A2/02, James Johnson to E. D. Wickham (undated).
3 C.M.S. CA2/056, H. Robbin to James Johnson, 12 Sept. 1879.
4 C.M.S. CA2/03 (d), Maser to Secretary, 3 July 1879.

removal from the interior, in the light of the documents, is that by 1880 the Church Missionary Society had come to share the conviction of their missionaries that a 'blackman' ought not to have been offered such an important post. Bishop Cheetham, who visited Abẹokuta in 1879, testified to Johnson's industry and his success in the interior, adding that Johnson 'is acknowledged by the other agents as their head'.[1] Nevertheless the Bishop felt that Johnson should be removed because 'I think to the great mass of the people he is only a black man'.[2]

In fact hardly had James Johnson been in the interior than his removal or supersession was seriously discussed by Salisbury Square. J. B. Wood was itching to go into the interior and the Society planned to send two other European missionaries into the interior by the end of 1878. In a confidential letter to Bishop Cheetham, H. Wright, the Society's Secretary, emphasized the importance of the Yoruba Mission in the Society's estimation and pleaded that a European missionary should reside in Lagos, 'a man of energy and warm missionary spirit who will superintend the work—visiting the interior from time to time infusing his own spirit into the agents of the mission'.[3] Wright suggested that the Bishop himself take up this work, reside in Lagos for at least six months in the year, assume the secretaryship of the Mission and take up the charge of Breadfruit Church, which was under another educated African, Henry Johnson. If this plan did not commend itself to the Bishop then, 'I think we ought at once to look out for a good man who might be put forward as Bishop for the Yoruba and adjacent countries'.

Johnson's removal from the interior was regarded as an affront to the Negro race by the leading educated Africans in Lagos and Abẹokuta such as I. H. Willoughby, R. B. Blaize and Henry Robbin. In Abẹokuta G. W. Johnson sided with James Johnson and made an effort to prevent white missionaries from operating in Abẹokuta.[4] James Johnson however was not prepared to give the signal for revolt against the Church Missionary Society. His confidence in the Society that it would carry out the Ethiopian programme was still very strong. The Society sympathized with him, reassured him of its confidence in him and put him in charge of Breadfruit Church again.

In the same year that James Johnson was recalled from the interior an ardent Churchman, R. B. Blaize of Ọyọ and Abẹokuta parentage, began the first Nigerian-owned newspaper when he launched the

1 C.M.S. CA1/25 (e), Cheetham to Wright, 16 May 1879.   2 Ibid.
3 C.M.S. CA1/22, H. Wright to Cheetham, 23 Mar. 1878.
4 C.M.S. G3/A2/01, Wood to Wright, 28 Apr. 1880.

Lagos Times.[1] Two years later the more radical *Lagos Observer* appeared under the editorship of J. B. Benjamin, an African business-man; in 1883 appeared *The Eagle and Lagos Critic* under the editorship of O. E. Macaulay, a member of the Crowther family, and in 1887 *The Mirror* under one P. Adolphus Marke. As would be expected nationalist feelings became more and more intense with the emer-gence of these media of propaganda. They were all committed to the furtherance of the cause of missionary enterprise, but in favour of the Africans. For the first time Africans of all denominations could speak with one voice and with effect. The policies of the various missions came under fire and the behaviour of the individual white missionary came under review. European missionaries did not look at the advent of these newspapers with favour.[2] They were henceforward pushed on to the defensive.

For the first time the necessity for the establishment of an African Church was expressed. All people who had grievances against the exotic kind of Christianity; polygamists who were denied the privilege of the Sacrament and positions in the Church began to urge the advisability of an African Church through the newspapers. In 1881 the first pamphlet calling for the establishment of such a Church was published by a dismissed Negro missionary formerly in the employ of the Southern American Baptist Mission. This pamphlet, *Hamites General Economy*, was addressed to the churches in the interior of Yorubaland where British laws and social ideas were not yet preva-lent. The writer invited the African clergy and Christian laity together to establish a Church for themselves on their own national lines in which both polygamy and slavery should be fully tolerated and never permitted to be a barrier to any of the privileges of full communion.[3] He was in fact echoing the growing desire that practical Christianity was not inconsistent with these two institutions; that these were among the social customs, the national habitudes that Christianity was not expected to disturb wherever it found them to exist; that men were free, left free by God and the controlling force of circumstances to harmonize their institutions with the Christianity of the Bible. There was also a growing idea among the laity that the Congrega-tionalist system of government, which left all control to the members of the Church, should be adopted, for they saw that the control the African clergy were fighting for in the Henry Venn scheme gave

1 There was a newspaper, *Anglo-African*, from 1863 to 1865, but it was owned by a West Indian by the name of Campbell.
2 C.M.S. G3/A2/01, Wood to Wright, 30 July 1880; Mann to Secretaries, 16 June 1882.
3 Ibid. James Johnson to Lang, 9 Mar. 1882, summarizes the content.

too much authority to the clergy. A layman wrote in February 1886:

> The time is unmistakably come when Christians in these parts, especially those of the Episcopal Church should have a deeper insight of the state of things concerning Church matters, than has hitherto been evinced, and endeavour to find out by feeling the way carefully, whether it is feasible to organize an African Church under the system adopted by the Congregationalists; ... coming events cast their shadows before ... and point to the future with an unerring finger that a revolution must sooner occur in the Episcopal Church. ... We cry aloud complainingly, and echo reverberates the sound, and a voice in reply comes to us ringing the word in our ears SECESSION! SECESSION!! SECESSION!!![1]

It was this seething nationalist ferment that made possible the foundation of the Native Baptist Church in April 1888, the first 'African' Church in Nigeria. Secession, declared the leaders of the Church, was not in their thinking because of their poor financial position.[2] They were pushed into secession by the cumulative anti-white feelings which had been gathering strength since the seventies. It is significant that the Reverend W. J. David, the missionary whose behaviour sparked off the 'revolt', made a point of this.[3]

Founded in 1845 on pro-slavery policy the Southern American Baptist Mission which arrived in Yorubaland in 1850 was behind both the Church Missionary Society and the Wesleyan Mission chiefly because it did not promote African agency. Although largely through the effects of the civil war of 1861 to 1865, the Mission had no white missionary in Yorubaland between 1869 and 1874, the Baptist cause was sustained by Negroes like J. C. Vaughn and the Hardens and Moses Ladẹjọ Stone, a native of Ogbomọshọ and one-time houseboy of one of the early missionaries in Ijaye. In 1875 the Home Mission was able to dispatch the Rev. W. J. David from Mississippi. Although in his journals he described with relish how he whipped the labourers in Abẹokuta with effect in the building of the Church there in 1876,[4] David must not be written off as an anti-Negro. In fact before his coming to Nigeria he kindled the enthusiasm of the Negroes in America for missionary enterprise by working

1 *Lagos Observer*, 6 Feb. 1886.
2 *Lagos Weekly Record*, 4 Mar. 1893. Account by S. M. Harden, one of the secessionists.
3 Roberson Collection, W. J. David to Tupper, 25 July 1888.
4 Ibid. *Journals of W. J. David 1874–1884*, July 1876.

among them.[1] Moreover in Nigeria he spoke in favour of the educated Africans against their exclusion from the Niger trade[2] and had a realistic and practical approach to polygamy. It is recorded that under him polygamists were baptized in Abẹokuta in 1883.[3] Then, he was the first missionary in the Mission to see the necessity for the establishment of a Training Institution for the raising up of a trained African agency.[4]

Nevertheless, like most of his contemporaries, David believed that Africans must be put into their proper place, 'under the superintendence of *white man*'.[5] It is not surprising therefore that he found extremely distasteful Moses Ladejọ Stone's ambition for higher education in America. Particularly galling was Stone's frequent assertion, like James Johnson, that the frequent deaths of the white missionaries and endless invalidings were Providence's warning that Nigeria was not the place for white people, and that Baptist work must be left completely in the hands of Africans. In order to achieve this end he appealed from time to time to be sent with others to America for adequate training.[6] Although he had no formal education he was ordained in 1880, the first in the Mission.

The occasion that brought about secession was David's summary termination of Stone's appointment over the question of his salary of 25s a month which Stone found inadequate. Had he been in any other mission he would have been earning not less than £5 a month. In order to make ends meet he began to borrow money from a Negro member of his church, J. C. Vaughn, and later began trading. David ordered him to stop trading, but refused to increase his salary. David justified his action on the grounds that it was the Mission that was paying Stone's salary. This was however unconstitutional, according to Baptist doctrine. He could dismiss Stone only after consultation with and consent of the majority of the members of the church. It is not surprising that David found the questioning of his authority unpalatable. J. C. Vaughn and S. M. Harden, who had experienced the inconveniences of negrophobia in America, led the opposition against what they considered a transplantation of the racial discrimination of that country to Nigeria.[7] The nationalists from the other denominations fell on David, who reported home that the whole

1 *Foreign Mission Journal*, Nov. 1874. Article by David, dated 27 Aug. 1874.
2 *Lagos Observer*, 26 May 1888.
3 *Lagos Times*, 26 Sept. 1883.
4 *Foreign Mission Journal*, January 1881.
5 Ibid.
6 Roberson Collection, M. L. Stone to Dr Tupper, 6 June 1888, 1 and 30 May 1895.
7 Roberson Collection, David to Dr Tupper, 18 Oct. 1888.

affair was brought about by 'racial prejudice'.[1] The result was that the majority of the members of the church seceded and established the Native Baptist Church while the Mission was reduced to a membership of eight! The schism was echoed in Ogbomoshọ in the interior. Nationalists contributed money and offered to teach and preach in the new church. When the permanent church was erected in 1893 the bottle deposited in the cornerstone contained, among other things, copies of the *Lagos Weekly Record*, the *Mirror*, *Payne's Lagos Almanac* and an account of the events leading to the formation of the church.[2]

The blow administered to the American Baptist Mission by the awakening national consciousness proved a resounding one from which it did not fully recover until after the First World War. For among those who broke away from David's church was D. B. Vincent, later known as Mọjọla Agbebi, whose nationalist spirit was already discernible in his various writings. Only in the previous year he had published an elegy on Henry Robbin of Abẹokuta, a fanatical admirer of James Johnson, entitled the *Ides of March* for which Alfred Moloney, then Governor of Lagos, sanctioned a gratuity from the public funds. In 1889 he published a pamphlet entitled *Africa and the Gospel* in which he called for creation of African Churches. 'To render Christianity indigenous to Africa,' declared Vincent, 'it must be watered by native hands, pruned with the native hatchet, and tended with native earth. . . . It is a curse if we intend for ever to hold at the apron strings of foreign teachers, doing the baby for aye.' At one time or another editor of every newspaper that appeared in Nigeria from 1880 to 1914, he ranks next to James Johnson both in the evangelization of Nigeria and in the articulation of nationalist feelings; his missionary zeal extended to the Niger Delta, the Cameroons and Ekitiland. Of particular importance was his effort to make the Native Baptist Church indigenous by infusing into his converts 'individuality of Race, congregational independence, self-support and self-government . . . the retention of Native names, native dress, healthful Native customs and habits, and the use of the native language in worship'.[3] Statistically the Native Baptist Church extended so much that by 1914 its adherents and churches more than doubled those of the American Baptist Mission. It was therefore

1 Ibid. Same to same, 25 July 1888. For a full account of the Native Baptist Church, cf. J. B. Webster, *The African Churches among the Yoruba 1888–1922*, O.U.P. 1964, a study which, however, ignores completely the nationalist aspect.
2 *Lagos Weekly Record*, 25 Feb. 1893.
3 *The Wasp*, 7 Apr. 1900.

natural that when the two bodies decided to co-operate in 1914 by forming the Baptist Yoruba Association the American missionaries, who now numbered thirteen, having learned what one of them described as a 'severe lesson',[1] chose Agbebi as the first President, a precedent without parallel in the history of Nigeria.[2]

A few general observations should be made about the causes and characteristics of the breakaway Churches in Nigeria, the so-called African Churches, in view of popular misconceptions entertained about them. It is commonplace to assert that these Churches came into being because the founders were looking for an opportunity to give leave to supposed sensual gratifications of polygamy. In fact the founding of the major African Churches from 1888 to 1914 had nothing whatsoever to do with the institution of polygamy. The founding of the Native Baptist Church, which has been analysed above, reveals the commonplace fallacy. As for the United Native African Church, which came into existence in 1891, it is now known that William Emmanuel Cole, the retired postmaster who was the architect of the Church, remained until his death a monogamist.[3] In the same manner polygamy was not an issue in the events which led the majority of the members of Breadfruit Church to leave the Church and found the Bethel African Church in 1901. The motives of the founders and the issues that brought about the creation of these Churches should be clearly separated from the motives and policies of the people who as time went on controlled these Churches. In the context of the Christian Church in Nigeria polygamy *per se* need not have caused any schism. This was because the majority of polygamists, on whom all Christian missions depended for financial support, elected to stay with the alien Churches that had prestige. Moreover they were given some status in the C.M.S. and Wesleyan Churches and there were instances when they were offered positions of responsibility in the Church. Even in the Southern American Baptist Mission the missionaries discovered that it would not be expedient to use the 'big stick'[4] against people who commanded respect in society. If polygamy *per se* tended at any time to occasion a schism in Yorubaland it was in the eighties when the institution was most seriously discussed by the affected educated Africans, who hoped that the Lambeth Conference of 1888 would understand the

1 *Lagos Standard*, 22 Jan. 1902, Pinnock's letter dated 9 Jan. 1902.
2 *The Yoruba Association Year Book for 1915*, Lagos 1915, pp. 20–5 for Agbebi's speech.
3 Cf. Obituary in *Lagos Weekly Record*, 12 Dec. 1891.
4 Roberson Collection, Pinnock to Dr Ray, 1 Aug. 1922.

institution in the context of African society. When the Conference pronounced against it the matter was dropped. Many reconciled themselves to the Lambeth decision by pretending to be mono-gamists while in practice leading the life of polygamists. Polygamy should be seen as the effect rather than the cause of the establishment of the African Churches. It was after their creation that some of them, like the United Native African Church and the Bethel African Church, in an effort to make Christianity indigenous, accepted poly-gamy as a respectable institution. But even then not all of them countenanced it for their clergy, whilst others like the Native Baptist Church actually proscribed it for the laity as well.

The rise of the African Churches, then, must be looked for in other causes. Resentment at the unscriptural and racist behaviour of white missionaries was undoubtedly one factor. Then there was the convic-tion held by many educated Africans that no aliens—however well intentioned—could make institutionalized Christianity flourish in Africa as a permanent establishment. In a community like that of late nineteenth-century Lagos, where a sense of history was growing, many educated Africans believed that there was a logically necessary connection between the permanence or ephemerality of institution-alized Christianity in the African environment and the degree of indigenization attained by the propagators of the Christian faith.[1] By indigenization, of course, they had in mind acculturation and the agency employed in the spread of the gospel. To them Christianity remained in Egypt, in spite of the onslaught of Islam, because it wore an Egyptian complexion, and Ethiopia had become a Christian state because the Ethiopian Church belonged peculiarly to its environment and had an unmistakable mark of Ethiopian nationality and distinctiveness. Another fact to which adequate attention has not been paid by Church historians was the resentment of the laity at the authoritarian tendency of the clergy, the desire of the leading members of a Church to have an administration in which the majority voice, that is the laity, would prevail. This was a very strong element in the Bethel secession of 1901 from the Breadfruit Church.

Some final remarks should be made about the pacific nature of Nigerian Ethiopianism, which contrasted in many ways with the different violent brands of the Ethiopianism of South Africa, Central Africa and the Congo. Whereas in the latter places Ethiopianism became a bugbear to colonial administrations, Nigerian Ethiopian-ism could not have assumed a distinctly political antagonism against

1 C.M.S. G3/A3/06, Memorandum presented to Archbishop of Canterbury through J. S. Hill by Payne and others, 7 Oct. 1892. E. W. Blyden: *Christianity, Islam and the Negro Race*, London 1887, pp. 184–9, 190–5.

the British administration. This was partly because, as mentioned earlier, the first generation of nationalists found in the missions ample scope for the expenditure of their energies, in the sharing of control of the churches with their European mentors. In most cases, in fact, the local church was virtually independent, with little or no control from European supervisors, with the approval of the latter and without resentment of European presence in the church and in the country. In other words the churches were something of a safety-valve for the awakening national consciousness, for the desire of Nigerian converts to manage their own affairs in the institution to which they had become most closely associated and thereby demonstrate their ability to rule, to evangelize and to administer. Since none of the early nationalists desired immediate political independence from a British rule—which still had to create the kind of Nigeria they, the educated Africans, could control—the politically inclined converts looked upon the churches for administrative and political apprenticeship. There is substance in Booker T. Washington's statement, in another circumstance, that 'there is no other place in which the Negro race can to better advantage begin to learn the lessons of self-direction and self-control than in the Negro Church'.[1]

In fact, unlike in East, Central and South Africa, British imperialism was welcomed by the Nigerian Ethiopians as something not quite an evil, but in several ways a positive good for the country. They could not have failed to perceive that the British introduced a new kind of order, welding several states into one, a measure which was preparing the way for their eventual control of Nigeria. Moreover they were aware that compared to Spanish rule in Fernando Po and German rule in the Cameroons, Leopold's rule in the Congo and the colonial regime in South Africa, British administration was humane, salutary and in many ways conduced to the true interest of the Nigerian peoples.[2] This is the explanation for the profusion of praises of the British administration in Nigeria by many of the Ethiopians. Bamidele Ọmọniyi, an ardent supporter of Ethiopianism, did nothing unusual when he dedicated his *A Defence of the Ethiopian Movement* to the British Parliament and declared on British rule in Nigeria,[3] 'We Africans have no complaint whatever against the British nation or British rule, but on the contrary we have every reason to be thankful that it has been our good fortune—a great part of us—to be placed under the British nation ... it is the source and fountain of true liberty and political progress in the world.'

1 B. T. Washington: *The Story of the Negro*, New York 1909, Vol. ii, p. 335.
2 C.M.S. G3/A3/09, James Johnson to Baylis, 24 Sept. 1904.
3 Published in Edinburgh in 1908, p. 93.

The African mind has been for some time much under the influence of what may be called the 'spirit of the age'. The Australians have a cry, 'Australia for the Australians'. The Africans have a cry 'Africa for the Africans'. It is a very weak and feeble imitation, but nevertheless it is a rallying point, around which every patriot is bound to come, whatever the immediate cause of the cry. From his past experience the African agitator is in the habit of looking to the Church for a more immediate advance in his social position and political power. The character of this movement therefore ought in my opinion to be looked upon as largely patriotic and political, and to this fact it owes much of its existence. It is on account of this race feeling the seed of discord has fallen into a prepared and congenial soil.

J. S. Hill

on the Ethiopian movement in Nigeria
during the Crowther crisis

7 The Successes and Failures of Ethiopianism, 1890–1914

The successful inauguration of the Native Baptist Church indicated the possibilities within the reach of the Ethiopians. Circumstances in the last years of the century induced a proliferation of African Churches. Never before had the Nigerian peoples been confronted with so menacing a European overlordship in Church and state as in these years. These were the years of military expeditions, of multiplication and extension of European commercial firms who elbowed out the African businessmen, of extension of British administration into the interior, and of the implementation of the concept, held by Europeans, of European racial superiority over Africans. The racial concept, by no means new, intruded into the Christian Church and unleashed on many occasions racial antagonism between the European missionaries on the one hand and the Ethiopians on the other. The high water of this racial animus occurred between 1890 and 1894, during the Niger crisis. By 1914 the racial tension in the Christian missions had been largely resolved by the establishment of more African Churches by incensed Ethiopians. The nationalists then began to organize distinctly political movements to obtain redress for the irritating and unpalatable measures of the British administration.

It is not surprising that the greatest nationalist feeling before 1914 surrounded the unpleasant events which marked the last years of Bishop Ajayi Crowther's life. This was so because Bishop Crowther had become in a sense the symbol of African nationalism. Until 1878 he wielded vast powers which no Bishop anywhere else in the world wielded, for he was not only the occupier of the highest ecclesiastical position but was as well the sole administrator of the Niger Mission, recruiting his agents, keeping all accounts of the Mission and deploying as he liked the resources of the Niger Bishopric's Fund which his admirers in England and Canada replenished from time to time. With the success that attended the Mission, to an extent that excited the admiration of people outside the C.M.S.,[1] Crowther showed that the African could both evangelize and administer as effectively as white men. When in 1890 it was clear to all the world that he was already deposed ignominiously from his pedestal of authority by European missionaries, all nationalist forces at work rallied round him and he himself 'rebelled', turned and died a nationalist.

But until 1891 Bishop Crowther never approved of the 'Africa for the Africans' nationalism of James Johnson and his followers. In fact he declared that so far as his own missionary enterprise was concerned the slogan was nonsense, and that 'our own wisdom would be to cry to those Christian nations which have been so long labouring for our conversion to redouble their Christian efforts'.[2] Hence he made no effort to adopt the Venn scheme of a Native Pastorate in the Niger Mission, much less of conceiving such a scheme in political terms like James Johnson. Until 1878 no Church offerings were collected in the Niger Mission and no attempt was made to prepare the Ibo and Ijaw—the major tribes among whom the Mission was operating—for leadership in Church life. Bishop Crowther was more accommodating to European civilization than people like James Johnson and Mọjọla Agbebi, and saw no conflict in Nigeria's interest in the penetration of the country by it, but rather hoped that the country would derive cultural, social and above all, religious advantages from it. Always wearing English clothes, he refused to allow the vernacular to be taught in the Niger Mission. As late as 1890 he emphasized that the medium of teaching throughout the Mission would be English.[3] He ridiculed as 'quixotic' the attempt of some European missionaries who sought to convert people by identifying themselves with their culture in dress, in food and in lodging. Unlike James Johnson he had no intention of studying African institutions and religion with the hope of understanding them and grafting Christianity on their healthy parts. Rather, he had the worst epithets for these institutions and the Delta peoples.[4] He pronounced irrationally on polygamy and thus misled the Lambeth Conference of 1888 on the real position of polygamy in African society.[5]

1 H. Bindloss: *In the Niger Country*, London 1898, pp. 286–7. A. A. Burdo: *A Voyage Up the Niger and Benue*, London 1880, p. 116. A. F. Mockler-Ferryman: *Up the Niger*, London 1892, p. 260 n.
2 C.M.S. CA3/04 (a), Charge delivered at Lokoja, 13 June 1869.
3 C.M.S. G3/A3/05, F.C. Minutes, August 1890 in Onitsha.
4 C.M.S. CA3/04 (a), 'Notices of the Delta', 29 July 1861; 'Brief Statements, exhibiting the habits and ideas of the Bight of Biafra', 31 Mar. 1875.
5 C.M.S. G3/A3/03, 'Notes on the life of Polygamy in West Africa', 1 Jan. 1887. He was chairman of the committee on polygamy at the Lambeth Conference of 1888.

This is not to say that Bishop Crowther had no African nationalist instincts in him. He would have been less than human if he had been completely Europeanized. In principle he was in no way against evangelization of Africa by African agency; in fact he welcomed it, lauded it as ideal and resented the introduction of white missionaries into his Mission in the seventies and eighties. Bishop Crowther, it must be emphasized, could not be as emotionally nationalist as James Johnson and Mọjọla Agbebi, who were not liberated slaves as he was. Moreover he was aware of the fact that he was an experimental Bishop and it would reflect badly on the Negro Race if he misused his position to encourage anti-white Ethiopian feelings. Then, he was more realistic than the Ethiopians, knowing quite well that the resources of Nigerians for the evangelization of their country were inadequate to meet the rising needs of evangelization, and European help could not be discarded. It is clear, then, that unless his lifework was about to be completely destroyed Bishop Crowther would not subscribe to the Ethiopian movement. Nor did Bishop Crowther advocate a wholesale destruction of African customs and institutions but warned his lieutenants against indiscriminate attacks on institutions and amusements that were not antagonistic to Christianity.[1] He was content to leave the *Owu Ogbo* club unmolested once assurance was given that it was reformed. It is worth noting that he did not celebrate a single marriage in his fifty years of missionary activity on the Niger because the English system of marriage, as embodied in the Anglican regulations, was unacceptable to the Niger Delta peoples.

However, in the eighties, two forces were conspiring to make Bishop Crowther reconsider his attitude to Salisbury Square and drove him to 'revolt' against it in 1891. The first was the introduction of white missionaries to the purely African Mission, now that the Niger no longer meant death to Europeans. Then there was the universal disparagement and intense hatred of the Negro race of which he was the greatest victim because of his high position. The man who began the policy of injecting European missionaries into the Niger was Edward Hutchinson, with whom the Bishop clashed over the anti-educated-African policy of the Royal Niger Company. By 1879 Hutchinson had become convinced that all talk of the treachery of the African tropical climate was rubbish and he urged white missionaries to be ready to go to areas hitherto feared on account of their deadliness.[2] In 1878 he got the chance of introducing a European into the Niger Mission when, upon Bishop Crowther's

1   C.M.S. CA3/04 (a), Charge delivered at Onitsha, 13 Oct. 1874.
2   E. Hutchinson: *The Lost Continent: its Rediscovery and Recovery*, London 1879, pp. 58–60.

demand, the steamer *Henry Venn* was given to the Bishop by his admirers in England for his missionary purpose.[1] Crowther's idea was that this steamer would be placed in the hands of an African merchant who had great knowledge of shipping and who had been associated with the Niger since 1841. In this way the steamer would be able to pay its way in a matter of five years, according to his judgment, while at the same time fulfilling missionary needs. But Hutchinson appointed a layman, J. H. Ashcroft and one James Kirk, in charge of the steamer.

No choice could have been more unfortunate. Moreover, Hutchinson asked Ashcroft to take over the 'temporalities' of the Mission, including all estimates for the Mission. Ashcroft deprived the Bishop of the use of the steamer on occasions when he needed them for episcopal visits and traded extensively with it. He and James Kirk assumed control of all the agents, some of whom were dismissed without prior notification of the Bishop. Henceforth, announced Ashcroft to the Bishop, the latter's authority was limited to the spiritual sphere of the Mission alone.[2] Although the Bishop protested to Hutchinson the latter did not reprove Ashcroft for his insolence and his assumption of the powers that had hitherto been wielded by the Bishop. Hutchinson's letters to the Bishop became decidedly disrespectful.[3] In 1879 he encouraged Ashcroft to prospect for a sanatorium in the Cameroons and to explore the Benue River for possible sites for occupation by white missionaries. In his long report Ashcroft emphasized the healthiness of the Benue region and named hills after European missionaries who had never been to the Niger, one after Hutchinson himself. He stressed the eagerness of the Benue peoples to have white missionaries, the word 'white' occurring more than fifty-two times.[4] In his ceaseless pleadings for European missionaries Ashcroft wrote on one occasion, 'I feel it is a most difficult subject at present this *purely native mission*, but I feel more and more convinced that it will have to be a mixed Mission and that Europeans must lead if there is to be any genuine substantial Christianity in the Niger.'[5] In the same year Hutchinson pointed out the uniqueness of the Bishop's unmitigated authority and therefore appointed a Finance Committee to be the local executive as in the Yoruba Mission, with a European majority.

In 1880 Hutchinson decided to appoint a Commission of Inquiry

1 C.M.S. CA3/L2, Lang to E. T. Phillips, 26 Jan. 1883. Said the steamer was 'to a great extent a personal gift from those who were interested in him (Bishop Crowther) and his Mission'. This was never mentioned to the Bishop.
2 For details of Ashcroft's doings cf. J. F. Ajayi, op. cit., pp. 566–70.
3 C.M.S. CA3/L1, Hutchinson to Bishop Crowther, 4 July 1879 in particular.
4 Cf. Report in C.M.S. CA3/05.   5 Ibid. Ashcroft to Hutchinson, 5 Jan. 1880.

into the Niger Mission, following bad reports which European merchants, who were displacing Africans on the Niger, were alleged to be spreading. In the C.M.S. Archives there is only one piece of evidence of such a report and it dates back to 1875. It is significant that Hutchinson on investigation discovered that the report was malicious and completely false.[1] Nevertheless in 1880 he appointed J. B. Wood to report on the Mission. Wood happened to go at a time when the Bishop's wife was mortally ill in Lagos. However, having confidence in his work, the Bishop instructed all the agents to give Wood all help. Taking evidence mainly from Ashcroft, Wood produced a report which, he said, he had hoped would never have seen the light of day.[2] Had he known the Bishop would be allowed to see it, it would have been quite a different report. The Wood Report was so damaging that Hutchinson remarked that the first reaction of anyone who read it would be 'to sit down in despair and pronounce the Mission an entire failure'. The Bishop's reaction was that Wood had made up his mind to 'smash up' his Mission. The Church Missionary Society would not act on the Report until Wood could prove his allegations and show how he had come about his evidence. A deputation under the leadership of the pro-African J. B. Whiting was sent to meet Bishop Crowther, Henry Johnson and Wood at Madeira. Evidence shows that Wood deliberately absented himself from the Conference. Bishop Crowther was able to prove that much of the report was premeditated and untrue. As the merits of the Wood Report have been treated in another work[3] we should be satisfied here with looking at the consequences as far as white-African feelings were concerned. The Church Missionary Society noted that 'in several instances the reports circulated respecting the Native agents had been shown to be unfounded and in some others much exaggerated'.[4] Ashcroft and James Kirk were dismissed for their 'unChristian' high-handedness in their treatment of the Africans. Wood was reproved for the way he had collected his evidence and when he protested that the rejection of his Report amounted to a vote of no confidence in himself and all the white missionaries he was reminded that no one who read the report would escape the conclusion that he had made up his mind to 'smash up' the Niger Mission and he and his European colleagues were abjured to work with the Society for the same cause, 'Africa for the Africans'.[5]

1 C.M.S. CA3/L1, Hutchinson to Bishop Crowther, 26 Apr. 1878.
2 C.M.S. G3/A2/01, Wood to Secretaries, 27 Sept. 1881.
3 J. F. Ajayi, op. cit., pp. 572–6.
4 C.M.S. CA3/L1, Lang to Bishop Crowther, 30 Dec. 1881.
5 Ibid. Lang to Wood, 11 Nov. 1881.

Probably because of the defeat of his object Hutchinson resigned shortly after the Madeira Conference. The European missionaries protested at the apparent victory of the Africans over Ashcroft, Kirk and Wood, and referred the Society to the jubilation of the Ethiopians in the Lagos press that 'most of the reports fell to the ground'.[1] Closely studied however the resolutions of the Madeira Conference were in principle not a success for the Ethiopians but a big victory for the Europeans. Wood's main suggestion, that white missionaries should be introduced into the Mission, was upheld. It was decided that a European General Secretary should be appointed for the Mission, ostensibly to promote good relations between the African agents and the European traders. This remained a mere pious declaration. In the Instructions given to the first General Secretary, E. T. Phillips, in 1882, this resolution was completely absent. He was informed that henceforth he was to represent Salisbury Square in the Mission and that part of his duty was to make from time to time 'confidential communications'[2] to the Parent Committee. The Bishop's authority was already gone; no more credence was placed on anything he forwarded to the Society and the C.M.S. admitted in 1891 that they never bothered to look at his suggestions.[3] In 1883 the Bishop was instructed not to spend any longer from the Niger Bishopric's Fund for territorial extension of his Mission because it was 'English' money.[4]

Bishop Crowther's inevitable fall was hastened by the implacable hatred for educated Africans and Christian converts developing in British thought during the period under survey. Although it was not new in the eighties, never had it been so universal among all classes of Europeans. In the sixties anti-missionary and anti-Christianity explorers and administrators like Burton, Winwood Reade and T. J. Hutchinson had castigated the educated Africans and the Negro race without much effect. For the African viewpoint was stoutly defended by the African Aid Society founded by Lord Alfred Churchill in 1860, by Henry Venn and by the Church Missionary Society.[5] The whole tendency in the Government and Protestant missions in West Africa then was to utilize African agency. The opposite views were, however, revived towards the end of the century by notable figures like Joseph Thomson, the explorer, Consul H. H.

1   Ibid. Same to same, 17 Mar. 1881.
2   C.M.S. CA3/L2, Instructions to E. T. Phillips, 16 May 1882.
3   C.M.S. CA2/L6, Open letter to C.M.S. Christians in West Africa, 4 Nov. 1891.
4   C.M.S. CA3/L2, The Secretaries to Bishop Crowther, 18 July 1883.
5   C. Fyfe, op. cit., p. 335. *Church Missionary Intelligencer*, July 1865, attacked Burton and Winwood Reade; also February 1869, pp. 53–7, refuting the theory of organic inferiority of the Negroes.

Johnston, Jaja's deposer, and Miss Mary Kingsley, perhaps the first anthropologically-minded British explorer in West Africa. The universal view, recorded a lady missionary to Salisbury Square in 1889, was that the Negroes were 'altogether depraved, a different creation from ourselves, an intermediate stage between men and brutes—without souls and incapable of being raised'.[1]

Consul Johnston is of particular interest because, as has been noted earlier, his pro-missionary views were most vigorously expressed when he was administering the Niger Delta and he based his views on his observations on the spot. Johnston was bewildered to discover that the zealous Christian converts of Brass felt no twinges of conscience when in 1885 they ate their human enemies, and that all the punishment Archdeacon Crowther prescribed to the cannibals was deprivation of the Holy Sacrament for some time.[2] Indeed Bishop Crowther went out of his way to defend, though not to justify, the cannibalistic orgies of the Christians.[3] From the eighties onwards Christian missions began to be dissatisfied with the quality of their converts. Their distrust of their converts was not entirely without foundation. For instance nationalist and Christian leaders like Captain J. P. L. Davies and Charles Foresythe were involved in charges of forgery and the latter was committed to prison.[4] Then there was the notorious Onitsha incident in which two African agents of the Mission committed a most wicked act of murder, an event which was remarked upon in the British Parliament. Johnston summed up the current belief among all classes of Europeans when he declared that 'all the drunkards, liars, rogues and unclean livers' of West Africa were Christian adherents. Throughout West Africa, he observed further, there could not be found twenty genuine Christians. Directing his denunciations at the Niger Mission agents, whom he described as 'a bad ally' to European missionaries, he went on:

> I regret to say that with a few—very rare—exceptions, those African pastors, teachers and catechists whom I have met have been all, more or less, bad men. They attempted to veil an unbridled immorality with an unblushing hypocrisy and a profane display of 'mouth' religion which to an honest mind was even more disgusting than the immorality itself. While it was also evident that the spirit of sturdy manliness which was present in

1 C.M.S. G3/A2/05, Higgins to Lang, 15 Apr. 1889.
2 H. H. Johnston: 'British Missions in Africa', *Nineteenth Century*, 1887, pp. 708–24.
3 C.M.S. G3/A3/02, Bishop Crowther to Wright, 12 Aug. 1885.
4 C.M.S. G3/A2/01, Wood to Hutchinson, 26 June 1880.

their savage forefathers found no place in their false cowardly natures.[1]

In the circumstances it cannot be surprising that the ability of Africans to rule came to be questioned. In the Native Pastorate of Lagos the hand of the clock could not be turned back. Although the white missionaries' hatred for it did not subside they found solace in the façt that a European Bishop continued to supervise the Pastorate, however much James Johnson disliked it. Furthermore they refused to evacuate Lagos, as the Pastorate demanded, but retained Christchurch in the pastoral care of Europeans. The situation in the Niger Mission was quite different. As has been mentioned, Bishop Crowther did not promote self-support until the crisis of 1891–92, although some of the Delta Christians were probably the richest in Nigeria at that time. By 1891 not a single agent was being maintained without funds from the C.M.S. Then, except for one Onitsha boy, Isaac Mba, no local people were among the African agents in the Mission. They all came from Sierra Leone although most of them were of Yoruba stock. As the C.M.S. rightly said, they were in the Niger territory 'foreign Africans',[2] and such people could not make the Church indigenous to the soil. It was a valid point made against the Bishop by Salisbury Square.

It is essential to say a few things about the Crowther administration. There can be no doubt that his administration could have been more efficient had the Bishop resided in his diocese. But he did not, and this must be reckoned as his one major fault. It was a strange spectacle. He lived in Lagos, over 200 miles away from the nearest Mission station, for nine months of the year, and performed his episcopal visits for three months or less. Moreover as he had to depend in most cases on the traders for conveyance his visits to many stations were very casual. This was a tempting situation for the agents who were left mostly to themselves. Although the Bishop had two able lieutenants in Archdeacons Henry Johnson and Dandeson Crowther who shared the territory for administrative purposes in 1879, there was much that required the Bishop's physical presence. Above all the Bishop was too fatherly and too tender in his dealings with his agents; he cautioned them when they made mistakes and would not resort to dismissal unless he had concrete proof that a particular agent was guilty of alleged serious offences. Once proved however he never hesitated to dismiss such an agent. But there were cases when his

1 H. H. Johnson: 'British Missions in Africa', *Nineteenth Century*. 1887, pp. 708–24
2 C.M.S., Africa Secretary, Wigram to Editor of *Lagos Times*, 28 Oct. 1881, in C.M.S. CA2/L5.

judgment was tempered with mercy and he re-employed bad agents. Straightforward and transparently guileless, he believed everything that his African agents reported to him, and while he could produce no absolute certainty that agents accused of particular crimes did not commit the alleged offences, he always stood by his agents unless the charges preferred against them were proved to the hilt. As he said, he would 'live or die' with his African agents, whom he judged by his own simple mind and character. No one can dispute that the Bishop made many unfortunate appointments, but even in Yorubaland the European missionaries made such appointments. Probably the best description of Bishop Crowther and his administration is the opinion recorded by G. W. Brooke in his private journals: 'He is a charming old man, really guileless and humble, I like him more each time I see him; but he certainly does not seem called of God to be an overseer. His nature is too mild and easy for him to come to a Church with a rod.'[1]

Between 1887 and 1890 there arrived in the Niger Mission European missionaries who were determined to put into effect the growing idea of the 'dominant race' and dislodge the Bishop from his nominal episcopate. They were in the main young, industrious, over-zealous and visionary Englishmen, mainly from Cambridge University, who were tainted with the quixotic idealism of the Student Volunteer Movement, seeking to evangelize the whole world in a generation. Their ideas of evangelization were radical and wild and provoked the laughter of people so varied as Sir T. V. Lister of the Foreign Office, Mockler-Ferryman, an Army officer, Dr R. N. Cust the distinguished linguist, and the Reverend John Milum,[2] for over ten years Chairman of the Wesleyan Mission in Yorubaland. Even before they did any work in Nigeria they condemned the methods of all Christian Missions in Africa. Professedly dedicated to evangelize the Muslims of the Sudan, they announced that they would adopt Muslim dress, food and lodging. Of the whole lot of these missionaries two who have been mentioned before are worthy of notice. There was J. A. Robinson, the General Secretary of the Mission from 1887 to 1890. He represented the new type of missionary who was well educated and contemptuous of the relative academic insufficiency of the African agents in the Mission. Himself a Cambridge M.A. with a First in Theology, he had been for two years principal of a college in Germany. He had the worst view of the Negro race. In

1 BMSS F4/7, *Journals*, 21 Apr. 1889.
2 C.M.S. G3/A3/05, R. N. Cust to Lang, Feb. 1891; Milum to Cust, 21 Jan. 1891; account of interview with Sir T. V. Lister at F.O., 12 Feb. 1891; Mockler-Ferryman, op. cit., p. 58.

1887 he declared to the C.M.S. that it was wasted effort to evangelize the Muslims and that the Niger Mission should not extend beyond Onitsha. He advised Salisbury Square to ask Bishop Crowther to retire honourably before the latter discovered that 'the structure which he had spent so many years in erecting was being demolished before his eyes during his own *nominal* Episcopate'.[1] When in 1889 he learned that the Muslims north of Lokoja would be evangelized by white missionaries only, he gave himself up for the new Mission. It is said that he enjoyed selecting anti-Negro choruses.[2] In a sweeping sentence in one of his numerous memoranda of discredit of Bishop Crowther and his Mission he declared, 'The Negro Race shows almost no signs of "ruling" power. This is true in Sierra Leone, Liberia, West Indies and equally on the Niger.'[3]

The second chief character was Graham Wilmot Brooke, a Don Quixote in every sense of the word. As mentioned earlier, obsessed with the idea of converting the whole Sudan to Christianity, he attempted to reach there from many points until in 1888 he came to the conclusion that the Niger was the only route open to him. Brooke's journals and letters are replete with his spiritual contemplations and unbounded hopes to turn the Sudanese dervishes to Christian crusaders. A genuine Christian, he loathed the sophistication and easy life of England. Something of a puritan, he was extremely able, highly devoted and prepared to die a martyr. With a person of his spiritual outlook it is not surprising that he came to have fanatical hatred for educated Africans, particularly the Sierra Leonians, whose pretensions, hypocrisy and dissoluteness filled him with disgust. He considered that James Johnson was the only genuine Christian in West Africa. In unmeasured language he burst out when he saw that the Niger Mission was being worked by Sierra Leonians. The Niger Mission, he said, was 'a den of thieves', and he went on, 'the lying and robbery going out there is shameful'.[4] Sierra Leone people were 'swarms of ragamuffins' and their Mission a 'charnel house'.[5]

The distinctly white staffed Sudan Mission was carved out of the Niger Mission under the joint leadership of Brooke and Robinson. All African agents but two were transferred to the reduced Niger Mission. For some unknown reason Brooke and Robinson were made members of the Finance Committee of the amputated Niger Mission,

1   Ibid. Robinson to Lang, 14 Feb. 1891.
2   Ibid. D. C. Crowther to Lang, 6 Jan. 1891.
3   C.M.S. G3/A3/04, Memo. dated 20 June 1889.
4   BMSS F5, Brooke to his father, 24 Feb. 1889.
5   Ibid. F4/7, *Journals*, 1 and 3 Apr. 1889.

and F. N. Eden, another European, the Secretary. Meanwhile between March and August they set themselves on clearing the Augean stables north of Onitsha. They branded all the converts in Lokoja adulterers and harlots and dismissed them from Church membership until they confessed their iniquities one by one; the Muslims were told that the African missionaries who had been working in Lokoja were not Christians but *kafiris*, that is, infidels. Letters to this effect were sent to the Emir of Bida who resented the removal of the Reverend Paul from Kipo Hill.[1] They urged the Muslims and converts who wanted to be received back to the Church to come forward and prefer charges against their former teachers.[2] What they set out to do, and ultimately did, was well summed up by Brooke:

> We came out here hoping to carry on and expand the work of twenty years in the place, and now after two months we are driven to admit that there is no hope of success until we have first taken down the whole of the past work so that not one stone remains upon another. I mean that the pastors, except at Gbebe, must be changed, the message preached must be changed, the time, mode and place of worship must be changed, the school children must be changed and the course in the school must be changed.[3]

Having completed what amounted to a complete effacement of the erstwhile Niger Mission north of Onitsha, the 'reformers' directed their zeal to the new Niger Mission. In the Finance Committee meetings of the last weeks of August 1890,[4] armed with the ill-garnered charges collected as mentioned above, they set up what amounted to an Inquisition. In these historic meetings the two races were equally represented. The Africans were represented by the Bishop, the nominal Chairman, Henry Johnson and D. C. Crowther and the Europeans by Robinson, Brooke and Eden. All that transpired in the meetings emanated from the 'Inquisitors', who examined in detail the unworthiness of every agent. Charges ranged from cheating to falsehood, inefficiency, slaveholding, immorality, drunkenness, actual robbery and so on. Archdeacon Crowther was himself charged with deliberate lying and robbery. Then the Bishop came under fire. Pointing at him they employed the most insulting language and called him a liar; his Mission, they said, was of the Devil because it was built with money collected from merchants engaged

1 Ibid. Letter to Emir, 24 June 1890.
2 *Sudan Leaflet* No. 6, Sept. 1890.
3 C.M.S. G3/A3/04, Brooke to General Touch, 5 June 1890.
4 Cf. Minutes in C.M.S. G3/A3/05.

in the liquor trade. The old Bishop was literally shaking. Archdeacon Crowther and the Reverend Charles Paul, who had been serving the Mission for thirty-five years, were 'suspended' by F. N. Eden, who ecclesiastically did not have the power to do so. So completely was the Bishop bereft of power. The proposed dismissal of the other agents was expected to be ratified by Salisbury Square. The position occupied by the Bishop in the Finance Committee was described by Robinson as follows: 'To see him (the Bishop) at his age and after so long a period of earnest service for the Master, placed in the position he occupied at our last F. Committee was, I felt at the time, *a cruel, though inevitable wrong*'.[1]

Their motive for inflicting this 'cruel, though inevitable, wrong' is fortunately preserved in the papers on the Niger crisis released in 1963 by Salisbury Square. Presenting their case to the Parent Committee one of them carried the views of Burton and his school to a ridiculous conclusion. He described the Sierra Leonians as the worst species of the African races. This was because, so he contended, they were the descendants of people sold into slavery by their tribes because they were the scum of African races. It was no cause for surprise that the African missionaries in the Niger Mission were not of 'a very highly elevated stock'[2] and 'we cannot expect great abilities in the way of ruling during the second generation'. Since Bishop Crowther was one of the supposed dregs of his tribe, the logic went on, 'though humble and of unstained character, (he) had shown no sign of ability to govern, and lacked the qualifications of a bishop, who should know how to govern his own house'. Henry Venn and all responsible for making Ajayi Crowther Bishop were condemned because they 'allowed zeal to outrun discretion and sentiment to have greater weight than sober facts'. As a matter of fact the C.M.S. became so much infected with this idea that it caused the history of the Niger Mission to be rewritten. This task was given to Archdeacon Hamilton, who had been General Secretary of the Niger Mission from 1885 to 1886 and whose reports then had anticipated Robinson's. Hamilton declared that the evangelization of the Niger territory by African agency exclusively was accidental and the appointment of Ajayi Crowther unintentional and regrettable.

As the news of the proceedings of the 'Inquisition' came to be known, and particularly the ill-treatment of Bishop Crowther, national feelings ran to heights never known before in the history of West Africa. This nationalist outburst was universal. As James

1 C.M.S. G3/A3/05, Robinson to Lang, 14 Feb. 1891 (italics are mine).
2 Paper entitled 'Shall Africans be chosen *now* for the higher positions in the West African Church?'

Johnson said, it was Africa that was on trial and it behoved all Africans, whether Christian or Muslim or 'pagan', to rally round the Bishop and the agents in the Mission. Protest upon protest came to Salisbury Square on a scale never known before, all declaring that it was not the Bishop but the Negro race that was insulted. Protests came from Bonny, Brass, Lagos and Sierra Leone and they were all signed by all the editors of the Nigerian newspapers. Among the Sierra Leone signatories was Samuel Lewis, later knighted, an Aku and the most popular lawyer in West Africa.[1] The Emir of Bida reacted by asking David Mackintosh, Agent General of the Niger Company, to send away the white missionaries from his territory.[2] Feelings in the Delta were so high that the chiefs and converts swore that should either Brooke or Robinson come to their territory they would club him to death. Taking the advantage of this spontaneous outburst of nationalist feelings the African missionaries in the Delta lectured the chiefs and converts on the treatment of Negroes in America.[3]

It was in this highly charged atmosphere that Edward Wilmot Blyden came to Lagos. Already a popular figure through his numerous writings and sensational speeches, Blyden was frantically received. Dazzled by the spectacle of educated Africans living on their own soil, among uncontaminated Africans, with cultural affinity with their kith and kin in the interior, no occasion could have been more propitious for unleashing the cultural racial nationalism which he had been articulating since the sixties. In his writings Blyden had regarded the Niger Mission as the only permanent hope for Christianity in West Africa, because it was in the hands of Africans exclusively.[4] In front of Glover Hall, where he was scheduled to speak, Otunba Payne caused the following inscription to be made:

Africa's destiny lay hid in night,
God said let BLYDEN be, and all was light.[5]

In his lecture entitled, 'The Return of the Exiles', Blyden urged the timeliness of forming an African Church and appealed, 'Thinking men have come to the conclusion that the call of God has become distinct and clear that they should form an African Church and take upon themselves the responsibility not only of supporting the Gospel

1 J. D. Hargreaves: *A Life of Sir Samuel Lewis*, London 1958, pp. 19–20 for his interest in the crisis.
2 *Sudan Leaflet*, entry for 19 July 1890.
3 C.M.S. G3/A3/05, Annie Jombo to C.M.S., December 1891.
4 E. W. Blyden: *Christianity, Islam and the Negro Race*, London 1887, p. 188 n.
5 *Lagos Times*, 27 Dec. 1890.

among themselves but of extending it to the regions beyond. But they are looking to Lagos as possessing far greater advantages for indigenous and independent work at that kind.'[1]

Because of this visit to Lagos in December 1890 the formation of the Native African Church has been ascribed mainly to the influence of Blyden.[2] Evidence shows that this was not so. In fact something of a myth seems to have gathered round this prolific 'Defender of the Negro race' and 'prince of *African literati*'. Whilst he might have influenced James Johnson and Agbebi, both of whom articulated nationalist sentiments before they came in contact with him, his role in Nigerian Ethiopianism should not be put out of focus. Indeed a close study of Blyden's writings and private letters,[3] makes an assessment of his contributions to African nationalism possible.

Edward Wilmot Blyden was born in the Danish island of St Thomas, West Indies, in 1832. According to him his parents were Hausa.[4] In 1849 he won a scholarship to an American College, but because of racial discrimination in that country he could not use it, a humiliation he never seems to have forgotten. He transferred to Liberia College where he found his intellectual abilities well provided for. He distinguished himself in languages, particularly in the Classics and Arabic, the latter winning him fame among the Muslims in the interior of Sierra Leone. Rather than being an opponent of Christianity, a belief held by most European missionaries, he was himself a missionary in Liberia, in the employ of the Presbyterian Missionary Society of America. In 1871 he ran into trouble in Liberia and found his way to Salisbury Square. Henry Venn appointed him as a missionary with European scale of salary and facilities, and he was to be a member of the Missionary Conference, until now composed of only the white missionaries.[5] He was expected to render the Scriptures into many languages, particularly Fula, teach Arabic at Fourah Bay and carry missionary enterprise into the interior, 'the pit whence he was digged'. Hardly had he embarked in Liverpool than the news of his alleged immorality with President Roye's wife and his dismissal by his American Mission reached Salisbury Square, and Henry Venn, much as he loved him, had to dismiss him after two months. In his

1 Ibid.
2 J. S. Coleman, op. cit., p. 176; Webster, op. cit., pp. 65 and 66.
3 This writer read twelve works of Blyden's (cf. bibliography) apart from Miss Ruth Holden's manuscripts on Blyden which contain a lot of letters. I record my thanks to Miss Holden with whose permission I saw the manuscripts in Mr Christopher Fyfe's possession in early 1963.
4 C.M.S. CA1/L8, Venn to Hamilton and Lamb, 4 Aug. 1871, ascribed it to Blyden. Coleman however avers that Blyden was of Ibo origin.
5 Ibid.

letters to Venn Blyden upheld the principle of European agency, at a time that James Johnson denounced it. He urged that European missionaries were the best for pioneering work in the interior and for supervision of African missionaries. To withdraw Europeans 'too quickly ... will paralyse the energies of the Native Church'. He went on, 'It seems to me that it should be the work of the Europeans to go out and plant schools at important points in the interior and put efficient native teachers in them, who should be under their constant supervision. The idea just now should be not to withdraw European agency but to intensify it.'[1] And as late as 1895 Blyden rejoiced at the crushing of the Ashanti confederacy,[2] at a time when James Johnson denounced such military expeditions and destruction of the independence of African states. It appears that Blyden's views and vituperations were the outcome of his reaction to the unhappy plight in which the American negroes found themselves from 1877 onwards. Blyden's nationalist writings and articulations were not Nigerian but cosmopolitan.

The rapturous welcome given to Blyden should therefore not be unduly emphasized. On his own evidence his invitation to Lagos in December 1890 was not connected with the Niger crisis and had nothing to do with the formation of any African Church. He was invited to undertake a tour of Yorubaland as an honour for his contributions to the cause of the Negro race.[3] In fact when anti-white feelings were being exacerbated by the Niger crisis, that is before he came to Lagos, Blyden was away in America, and delivered lectures in which he again upheld the principle of European agency, commending Salisbury Square for sending educated people like Brooke and Robinson, 'men of greater spiritual insight ... heralds of Christianity ... lifting up the standard of the Cross', to Africa. He praised Brooke and Robinson whose work in the 'Nigritian countries' was 'full of interest and pregnant with promise'.[4]

Moreover, unlike the Nigerian Ethiopians, Blyden did not advocate an African Church for political purposes. He advocated an African Church principally because he believed that it was only an African Church that could stem the tide of Islam and completely destroy it. For, said Blyden, Mohammed himself had prophesied that

1 C.M.S. CA1/047, Blyden to Venn, 28 Mar. 1872; cf. also same to same, 19 Jan. and 6 Apr. 1872.
2 Blyden to Dr Thirkied, 28 Nov. 1895, quoted in J. W. Bowen, ed.: *Africa and the American Negro*, 1895.
3 Miss Ruth Holden's Manuscripts, Biography of Blyden, p. 1012, quotes letter by Blyden dated 26 May 1890; cf. also p. 1013.
4 E. W. Blyden: *The African Problem and other Discourses*, London 1890, pp. 54 and 104.

'in the last times the Ethiopians shall come and utterly demolish the temple of Mecca after which it will not be rebuilt again for ever'.[1] Then, as will be shown in the next chapter, Blyden's conception of African nationality and 'personality' was on the cultural and not the political plane. His African Church was to be purged of the formularies, creeds, theology and ceremonialism which Europe had built around the pure Christianity of the Bible.

Meanwhile all eyes were fixed on Salisbury Square. On the one hand the European missionaries would not tolerate the slightest modification of their recommendations whether in principle or in detail, and they had already tipped Eden for the post of Bishop. On the other hand the Africans were determined to have nothing less than an unreserved apology to Bishop Crowther and a Commission of Inquiry to investigate and substantiate the charges levelled against the African agents. It was a veritable confrontation of two racisms. On the whole the C.M.S. managed the whole affair in favour of the Europeans. The latter were commended for the war they were waging against 'Satan',[2] and three of them, Brooke, Battersby and Eden, had the opportunity of being listened to by the Parent Committee, while the African agents did not even know the reasons for their dismissal. In December 1890 a twenty-three-man Special Sub-committee was set up to investigate fully the whole crisis. Although the committee included African-disposed men like J. B. Whiting, Dr R. N. Cust and Sydney Gedge, their voice was drowned in the proceedings. The Sub-committee used all the unfavourable documents from the Wood Report of 1880 to the ill-garnered accusations of Robinson and Brooke.

In the circumstances the Sub-committee's Report was not astonishing.[3] It upheld all the principles that the Europeans had been fighting for since 1887, except that Bishop Crowther could not be removed. The Niger Mission, so the report said, was corrupt to the core and its redemption possible only by the introduction of white missionaries, under whom whatever African agents were retained would work; the dismissal of most of the agents was ratified while a few were put on probation for one year under white missionaries, to be ultimately dismissed if their spirituality did not improve; the tone used to the Bishop was 'unjustifiable', but no apology was given; Archdeacon Crowther was not guilty of the charges of robbery and untruthfulness, but nevertheless he was to become only the Pastor of St Stephen's in Bonny under the superintendence of a new white missionary; now that their task in the Niger Mission was completed,

1 Ibid.   2 C.M.S. CA3/L3, Lang to Robinson, 7 Nov. 1890.
3 Cf. Report in papers released in 1963.

Robinson and Brooke were to cease to be members of the Finance Committee and concentrate their efforts on their Sudan Mission. Greatly astonished at the Report, which was accepted by the Church Missionary Society in January 1891, John Milum pronounced the verdict that 'the Society is in a panic altogether unworthy of it with its past history of patient plodding in working out difficult schemes of missionary enterprise' and that: 'It must go forth that, not only have the experienced C.M.S. given up the problems of building up a Christian Church by aid of Native Agents alone, but have joined with their enemies in branding them incapable and unworthy.'[1]

The Report of the Special Sub-committee apart, the tone of the Society's journals was decidedly anti-African, whilst the letters publicly addressed to the West African Churches were not calculated to appease the Ethiopians.[2] The nationalists retaliated with effect. The *Lagos Times* printed and distributed *gratis* a pamphlet of forty-eight pages entitled *The Niger Mission Question*. The nationalists refreshed their minds with the history of the American Revolution.[3] Anti-white hysteria reached unprecedented heights as the dismissed agents filled the air with the tale of wrongs that had been inflicted on the Negro race, was further inflamed by the annexation of Ilaro in August 1891 and the impending Ijẹbu Expedition. This hysteria was well expressed by Mọjọla Agbebi in an address entitled, 'The Eve of a Crisis', delivered on 20 September 1891, in the course of which he said, 'The feathers of revolution are beating the air, and revolution is prolific of results. . . . The Car of Jehovah has unloosed itself . . . and in its onward progress through the length and breadth of this country, willing as well as unwilling men who obstruct its pathway will be reduced to atoms.'[4]

For the only time in his career James Johnson not only incited but led a revolt against the Church Missionary Society. Hitherto he had reposed absolute confidence in the Society, whom he trusted would promote his visualized African Church. Now his parsonage became the rendezvous of the nationalists like J. O. Payne and Dr O. Johnson who had long been looking up to him for leadership. James Johnson became convinced that the Delta Churches must become independent of the C.M.S. at once and repudiate European control. His attitude to the Sudan Party revealed his two sides, spiritual and political. Spiritually he had hoped that he would gain from the

1 C.M.S. G3/A3/05, John Milum to Dr Cust, 21 Jan. 1891.
2 *The Church Missionary Gleaner*, January 1891, editorial entitled 'Wheat and Tares in West Africa', likened the West African Church to the Corinthian Church denounced by Paul.
3 *Sierra Leone Weekly News*, 5 Mar. 1892.   4 Ibid.

holiness and the much-lauded methods of evangelization from which spectacular results would be achieved; the nationalist in him, however, rebelled against the trying of the new methods of evangelization in the Niger Mission, which had commanded his admiration before he came to Nigeria in 1874. As he was to do in the case of the Ijẹbu Expedition, whenever there arose a conflict in the two things to which he dedicated his life—Christianization of Africa and African nationalism, he chose the latter. When he observed that the missionaries did not prove their holiness and failed to exhibit 'the spirit of the Great Master, of the loving Jesus, the Jesus of the Bible who would not break the bruised reed nor quench the smoking flax' but went on demolishing all the achievements of a purely African agency; when he saw that the Society was using those missionaries 'practically to shelve' Bishop Crowther; when the Report of the Special Sub-committee did not reflect the 'simple justice' and 'a fair and impartial enquiry' he had asked for, his patience was exhausted and he accused Salisbury Square of 'fanning up the flame of race anti-pathies'.[1]

On 17 April, under James Johnson's leadership, the educated Africans passed two Resolutions at a meeting in Lagos, inviting Bishop Crowther to declare the Delta Churches independent. They promised to give the independent church a grant of £500 for five years, diminishing annually in proportion to the financial strength of the Delta Churches.[2] At about the same time the nationalists in Sierra Leone offered £350 annually to the proposed independent Church in the Delta.

Bishop Crowther's reaction to the help of the nationalists was crucial. Had the Bishop not accepted the offer, as James Johnson observed, the whole movement would have collapsed.[3] To the astonishment of the white missionaries and Salisbury Square, rather than spurning the aid and programme of the nationalists, the Bishop accepted them without modification. In his judgment the suggestions made to him were a product of 'mature deliberation' which the anti-African policy of the Society had engendered. Incorrectly the Bishop contended that in accepting the scheme he was doing no more than putting into effect the Henry Venn scheme and he concluded, 'the way to prove failure or success is, to make a trial for a time and watch'.[4]

1 C.M.S. (papers released in 1963), James Johnson to J. B. Whiting, 24 Sept. 1890.
2 Copy of Resolutions to C.M.S. G3/A3/05.
3 Ibid. James Johnson to Wigram, 25 Sept. 1891.
4 Ibid. Bishop Crowther to General Touch, 8 May 1891.

To the C.M.S., in casting in his lot with the nationalists Bishop Crowther added a completely new strand to his character. Hitherto he had behaved in a way that showed that he was not of the nationalist cast and Salisbury Square had been led to take his loyalty for granted.[1] From 1879 onwards he had been accommodating himself to the gradual loss of his powers, however much he did not like it, until now he was no more than 'a sort of confirming and ordaining machine'.[2] Although he passed through a mental agony that finally sent him to the grave, he refused to initiate a revolt in 1891 when he could have done so successfully. He accepted the recommendations of the Special Sub-committee and when the Niger Delta chiefs and converts were burning with rage, indicating that they would not acquiesce in the Society's verdict, the Bishop asked Salisbury Square to send a deputation to appease them.[3] Instead of utilizing the nationalist forces rallying round him the Bishop wrote pathetically to Archdeacon Crowther, his youngest son then fifty years old, in January 1891, 'Patience is a gift which the Giver of all good things has given me; it may appear that I exercised it too long, and, perhaps, to my own disadvantage, but the result of it will be that the Director of the course of Providence will never err.'[4] Bishop Crowther, it is said, was always conscious of the sense of obligation he felt he owed to the British because they rescued him from slavery, hence the instruction he gave to Archdeacon Crowther that he should never complain about any European.[5]

But it would be misunderstanding Bishop Crowther to think that he accepted the offer of the nationalists in 1891 for purely nationalist or political reasons. For him, what he valued most, the Christianization of the Niger territories, was at stake; his life work was in danger. This was touching him on his most sensitive spot; his loyalty to the Church Missionary Society must break down whenever this spot was touched. This was why he deplored the monopoly of the Niger Company; this was why he welcomed white missionaries in his Mission, provided the 'impediment will be (thus) removed from the way of the extension of the Mission';[6] this was why he disapproved of the quixotic methods of the Sudan Party and why he gave the Party a

1 *The Church Missionary Gleaner*, 1892, p. 28, described the Bishop as the Society's most docile Bishop, always putting himself 'under orders'.
2 C.M.S. G3/A3/05, Battersby to Lang, 23 Dec. 1890.
3 C.M.S. G3/A3/05, Bishop Crowther to Lang, 1 Apr. 1891.
4 *The Guardian*, 15 May 1891, article by D. C. Crowther.
5 C.M.S. G3/A3/05, D. C. Crowther to Lang, 6 Jan. 1891; on Bishop Crowther's profusion of thankfulness to his benefactors cf. *Church Missionary Intelligencer*, 1892, p. 124.
6 C.M.S. G3/A3/02, Bishop Crowther to Lang, 30 Jan. 1884.

decidedly cold reception, an event which Brooke never forgot. Now, in 1891, Brooke threatened that African missionaries would even be driven away from the truncated Niger Mission by British Baptist missionaries whom he threatened to introduce.[1]

Until it was confronted with Crowther's revolt, the Church Missionary Society treated the nationalist movement with disdain. This was because the Society knew that in spite of much talking about the advisability and urgency of the creation of an African Church there was no cohesion that could ensure a realization of such a scheme. Moreover there was the fact that hitherto the Delta Churches had been responsible for none of their agents while the Sierra Leone Native Pastorate was in such financial straits that it was not yet free from the pecuniary aid of the Society. Only the Lagos Native Pastorate was strong financially, but its surplus was limited in face of its missionary programme. Bishop Crowther however presented concrete proposals which seemed to promise immediate, if not ultimate, realization. He fixed the first of January 1892 for the formal inauguration of the Independent Delta Church and made moves to have James Johnson appointed as his suffragan, with the hope that after his death James Johnson would succeed him. Thanks to the deposition of Jaja, Bonny and Opobo entered into a new phase of prosperity. The chiefs and converts of Bonny, Okrika and New Calabar welcomed the Bishop's decision and assured him that no amount of persuasion by the C.M.S. would make them rescind their determination to implement the independence scheme, for they could not 'draw back and thereby embitter your last days by proving your life work a failure as is stated in the *Record*'.[2]

Meanwhile the nationalists could not subscribe to the empty boasting of the C.M.S. that white missionaries were indispensable to the successful evangelization of Nigeria. For the Sudan Party, the 'young purifiers', were proving a 'complete failure'.[3] These missionaries, as mentioned before, made no single convert. They did not live in native houses and when illness began to fall upon them they gave up eating African food.[4] Their medical skill not only failed to win the affection of the Muslims but the latter proved more skilful than they in the cure of local diseases.[5] One by one they dropped off either by dying or by resigning or by being invalided home. By August 1891

1 C.M.S. G3/A3/05, D. C. Crowther to Lang, 12 Feb. 1892.
2 C.M.S. G3/A3/05, Letters from Lay and clerical agents in the Delta to Bishop Crowther, 23 July 1891.
3 *Lagos Weekly Record*, 9 Jan. 1892.
4 C.M.S. G3/A3/05, J. S. Hill to Baylis, 31 Jan. 1893.
5 *Sudan Leaflet* No. 18.

only Brooke remained and the following April he too expired. Deprived of any concrete results they directed their nihilist zeal at Salisbury Square which they asked to reform itself with a 'Reform Bill'.[1] It is remarkable that they too were conscious of their failure. Robinson urged that publicity about their work should cease because their achievements so far were only '*Paper* schemes [and] not yet actualities'.[2]

A deputation was sent out consisting of the Reverend W. A. Allan and Hamilton. Both were selected because they were supposed to have tackled anti-European problems in Nigeria before. Hamilton was believed to have promoted good relationship between the two races from 1886 to 1889 when he was Archdeacon of Lagos, while Allan was supposed to have weaned Africans from desire for an African Bishop for Yorubaland in 1887 when he went out to Lagos on a supposedly evangelistic 'mission'.[3] In Sierra Leone, where the deputation arrived about the middle of December 1891, only a selected number of Anglicans were invited, but even then more than half of those invited boycotted the deputation. Of those who came many emphasized that the Delta scheme could not be shelved and that in spite of trade depression £600 was already collected, largely through the house-to-house convassing of the Hon. T. J. Sawyerr and the Honourable Samuel Lewis. Nevertheless the deputation was assured by Bishop Ingham that the poor financial state of Sierra Leone Church would soon evaporate the enthusiasm of the people, while some of the pro-C.M.S. people said that the Delta would be induced to accept the position of the Sierra Leone and Lagos Pastorates.[4] With unbridled optimism Allan and Hamilton reported that Sierra Leone was won over and that they were sure of winning Lagos also.

On reaching Lagos about Christmas the deputation's optimism cooled at once, for James Johnson's influence was supreme.[5] But no amount of persuasion would make Bishop Crowther budge, and the deputation observed that he had lost all confidence in the C.M.S. James Johnson and Otunba Payne spoke for Lagos. The former declared that it was the credit of Africa that was at stake; that an African must succeed Bishop Crowther in the event of the latter's death; that the Delta scheme was to operate at once and that the Church Missionary Society must accept responsibility for paralysing

1 C.M.S. G3/A3/05, Brooke to Lang, 23 May 1892.
2 Ibid. Robinson to Lang, 20 Feb. 1891.
3 Cf. his report submitted in April and May 1888 in C.M.S. G3/A2/05.
4 C.M.S. G3/A3/05, W. Allan to Wigram, 8 Dec. 1891.
5 Ibid. Report of the Deputation, March 1892.

the Churches in Sierra Leone and Lagos by withholding independence from them too long.[1] Payne laboured on the indignities heaped on Bishop Crowther, asked the C.M.S. to account for the casks of oil which James Ashcroft stole from the Delta churches in 1878, pointed to the 'complete failure' of the Sudan Party and urged the white missionaries to quit the Niger territory entirely and try their experiment in the Lake Chad region. Lastly he lectured Allan and Hamilton on the policy of Henry Venn and his hopes for the Africans.[2]

It was in the midst of all this excitement that Bishop Crowther expired in the last hour of 1891. Whatever hope Allan and Hamilton might have entertained of the possibility of a compromise with the Ethiopians disappeared. So far as the Africans were concerned it was the C.M.S. which in a way was responsible for the Bishop's death. A few months before, a doctor in Bonny invalided him to Lagos because he was suffering from 'the effects of a partial paralytic stroke, brought about by overwork and mental anxiety'.[3] In Lagos his funeral service was attended by a large crowd including Governor Carter, Major Macdonald of the Oil Rivers Protectorate and the Colonial Secretary. James Johnson conducted the service and delivered an oration said to be 'much too racial'.[4] It is not surprising that the West African Press demanded that no better service could be rendered to the Africans than the appointment of James Johnson as successor to Bishop Crowther.[5]

Reporting back to Salisbury Square the deputation confessed that its mission was a complete failure. The Society's hope of nipping the movement in the bud by asserting rights over land and property crashed on the land tenure system prevailing in the Niger territory. With the example in mind of de Cardi's stores which had just relapsed back to the people in his attempt to hand them over to another trader, the deputation dared not mention it.[6] Nor was Macdonald disposed to use his political power in favour of Salisbury Square. He made it clear that, so far as his new administration was concerned, white missionaries were '*of no use at all*'.[7] D. C. Crowther was adamant, beyond persuasion. He declared that the scheme was his father's last will and testament. With the hope that the movement would collapse for lack of funds the deputation recommended that the C.M.S. should show it neither 'sympathy' nor 'goodwill'.

1 Ibid. Allan to Wigram, 29 Dec. 1891.
2 Ibid. Hamilton to Lang, 29 Dec. 1891.
3 Ibid. Bishop Crowther to Lang, 10 Aug. 1891.
4 Ibid. Allan to Wigram, 1 Jan. 1892.   5 *The Weekly News*, 4 Jan. 1892.
6 C.M.S. G3/A3/05, Report of Deputation, March 1892.
7 Ibid. Ingham to Wigram, 7 Aug. 1891.

Now that the question of succession to Crowther had arisen the deputation advised the Society to make concession to the Africans by appointing an African as Assistant Bishop to a European successor. The man tipped by them was Isaac Oluwọle, a particularly docile man who met the deputation secretly and confessed to them that he was not for the nationalist movement.[1] Surprisingly, however, the C.M.S. refused to make any concession to the Africans, and in May 1892 nominated a European, the Reverend J. S. Hill, to succeed Crowther.[2]

This action on the part of Salisbury Square, neither learning nor forgetting anything, was not approved by the Archbishop of Canterbury and by some white missionaries in Nigeria. Archbishop Benson therefore refused to consecrate Hill unless two Africans were also consecrated with him as Assistant Bishops.[3] The C.M.S. had to bow to the inevitable. On 29 April 1892, the Delta Pastorate was formally established 'in humble dependence upon God', and in September the independent Pastorate asked the Archbishop to consecrate James Johnson its Bishop. In their asking for an independent African Bishop the Delta Church and the West African Press were asking for the moon, a demand that could not be satisfied in a territory just coming under British rule. Nevertheless the Archbishop went more than half way in meeting the demands of the Africans. But two 'Half Bishops', as the nationalists ridiculed the Assistant Bishops, could not make one full Bishop. In July the Archbishop sent Hill to West Africa to report on the situation there and persuade the Delta Church to give up its independence. In his report (he was not new to Nigeria)[4] Hill analysed the character of Nigerian nationalism, its Ethiopian manifestation, in this period as follows:

> The African mind has been for some time under the influence of what may be called the 'spirit of the age'. The Australians have a cry, 'Australia for the Australians'. The Africans have a cry, 'Africa for the Africans'. It is a very weak and feeble imitation, but nevertheless it is a rallying point, around which every patriot is bound to come, whatever the immediate cause of the cry. From his past experience the African agitator is in the habit of looking to the Church for a more immediate advance in his social position and political power. The character of this movement therefore ought in my opinion to be looked upon as largely patriotic and political,

1 Ibid. Allan to Wigram, 22 Dec. 1891.
2 C.M.S. CA2/L6, Lang to H. Tugwell, 27 May 1892.
3 C.M.S. G3/A3/05, Memo. of interview with Archbishop by Hill, undated.
4 J. S. Hill served at Leke from 1876–78; from 1879 to 1891 he worked in New Zealand.

and to this fact it owes much of its existence. It is on account of this race feeling the seed of discord has fallen into a prepared and congenial soil.[1]

The Hill Report is an astonishing document deliberately calculated to misinform the Archbishop. A diehard C.M.S. man, he considered his loyalty to that Society as primary, and he regretted that he had to report anything unfavourable at all about it. He used the anti-African records put at his disposal by the C.M.S. and in spite of the intentional falsifications in his Report, which will be pointed out presently, he confessed that he would not have written as 'openly' as he did had the Archbishop not known 'so much' about the situation in West Africa.[2] He reported that the nationalist movement in Nigeria expressed through the press, the leading educated Africans and 'numerously and influentially signed' petitions did not actually represent 'the voice of the people'. Because the educated Africans did not conform to English habits such as eating with their wives, they were incapable of governing themselves: and authority in their hands 'is liable to one of two dangers: either excessive severity, or that of weak indulgency'.[3] After failing to secure James Johnson's consent to be made what the latter ridiculed as 'half-bishop', Hill reported most unfavourably about him. To make either James Johnson or Archdeacon Crowther an Assistant Bishop, he said, would be a surrender to the nationalists who would be encouraged to hope that further pressure would win further concessions from the Archbishop. James Johnson, he wrote, was unpopular and unacceptable to the Lagos clergy. He was 'the ablest man ... the most crotchety, opinionated, intolerant, zealous and earnest, and powerful ... he sours as he grows old'.

After consultations with Wood, the most experienced white missionary, Hill recommended two Africans, Isaac Oluwọle, Principal of the C.M.S. Grammar School at Lagos and a holder of B.A. degree from Fourah Bay, and Charles Phillips of Ondo, who had no collegiate training. They were chosen because of their docility and submissiveness to the white missionaries. In 1887 Oluwọle had said that an African Bishop for Yorubaland was an undesirable ideal as yet, in the circumstances of the Mission and, as we have seen, he confessed secretly to Allan and Hamilton that he was not for the nationalist movement. Phillips was a firm believer in the magical effect of the white man on Africans and since 1877 he had been pleading in

1 C.M.S. G3/A3/05, J. S. Hill to Archbishop, 20 Dec. 1892.
2 Ibid. Hill to Wigram, 21 Dec. 1892.
3 Ibid. J. S. Hill to Archbishop Benson, 20 Dec. 1892.

vain that white missionaries should supersede him in Ondo or visit the Mission frequently to impress the African rulers that the Mission had the backing of the mysterious white man. Wood said of Oluwọle, 'I know that he has never been carried away by any of the "fads" which are afloat from time to time. I think he would work well, and yet not go beyond his position and thus cause friction in his relation to a superior, if he were an Assistant Bishop.' He had something of contempt for Phillips who, he said, 'would make a good, sensible travelling Bishop—a sort of "gig" Bishop'.[1]

In unmeasured terms Hill fell on the Delta Pastorate.[2] He told the Archbishop that the Pastorate did not deserve his countenance because the people connected with it were rebels not only against the C.M.S. but also against the Archbishop, and this he illustrated with the action of Archdeacon Crowther who had asked the Bishop of Liberia to ordain J. A. Pratt. Being a product of the nationalist movement, said Hill, he felt the Pastorate was in the same category as the Native Baptist Church and the United Native African Church. Then he harped on the appointment of some of the agents dismissed by the C.M.S. Hill not only failed to represent the nationalist feelings in the Delta, but actually suppressed the petition of the people to the Archbishop made through him. In their petition they made it plain that they had nothing to do with the 'half bishop' proposition, nor did they want a European Bishop for 'there are natives competent to fill with credit and honour the post now vacant'.[3] They were prepared to pay for an independent African Bishop in the person of James Johnson, who had been nominated by Bishop Crowther. For them 'to accept any other than a Native Independent Bishop in succession to him (Bishop Crowther), is tacitly to admit his work among us a failure, and this will be the greatest piece of injustice and ingratitude'. Misrepresenting the facts, Hill reported that the Delta Church would soon collapse for want of funds, therefore all the Archbishop need do was to inform them that when they became financially strong and proved themselves then he would be able to consecrate an independent African Bishop. This was all the Archbishop did.[4]

The nationalists did not respond favourably to the conciliatory gestures of the Archbishop, who in June 1893 consecretated Oluwọle

1 C.M.S. G3/A3/05, Wood to J. S. Hill, 19 Oct. 1892.
2 Ibid. Hill to Archbishop Benson, 20 Dec. 1892.
3 C.M.S. G3/A3/06, 'The Congregation and members of the Delta Pastorate Church, Bonny to Archbishop of Canterbury, 29 July 1893'; Hill left it with James Johnson who sent it to the Archbishop.
4 C.M.S. G3/A3/05, Memo. by Cantuar, 6 Mar. 1893.

and Phillips as Assistant Bishops to Bishop Hill. Nothing but the appointment of an African successor to Bishop Crowther could have satisfied them. Moreover they wanted all the white missionaries out of Lagos and the Niger Delta, 'and so, why should we any longer continue to force ourselves on an unwilling people?'[1] The nationalists could not be appeased with 'second rate' Bishops, which appointment contrasted with the behaviour of the secular establishment which knighted Samuel Lewis in 1893 and in the same year accepted Edward Blyden at the Court of St James as plenipotentiary of Liberia on equal terms with the plenipotentiaries of other countries.

Probably aware of the consequences that would follow the implementation of his proposals, which we have seen were based upon deliberate misrepresentation of facts, Hill offered to resign as Bishop but his resignation was not accepted.[2] He therefore had the fatal experience of being hoist with his own petard. In spite of the popularity of Oluwọle and Phillips that was claimed in his report, no reception was given to Hill and his party. The people were apathetic[3] and incensed to the degree of hissing them on the streets. 'The present condition of affairs is grave in the extreme,'[4] reported Tugwell. Phillips was only too glad to escape to Ondo while Oluwọle retired into Abẹokuta to breathe a happier air. Phillips and Oluwọle were labelled as traitors to the Negro race. 'How can we possibly rejoice over this event?', declared the press, 'How can we do otherwise than mourn over the whole affair and write *Ichabod* upon the portals of our houses?'[5] Hill, who boasted on arrival that he was 'as hard as nails', suddenly fell into a mental depression that sent him and his wife to the grave within hours in January 1894.

Nor were the ill wishes of the white missionaries, the C.M.S. and the Archbishop for the Delta Pastorate ever fulfilled. As Bishop Crowther's legacy the nationalists regarded its success as the 'duty and anxious care of every son of Africa', while James Johnson was determined to see that it proved 'the capability of the Negro for self-government'.[6] The outside stimulus apart, the Delta converts and the chiefs displayed a spontaneity and enthusiasm which bewildered their detractors. It is remarkable that a people who had hitherto been responsible for no single agent became self-supporting and self-governing almost immediately, and successfully defied the C.M.S.

1 C.M.S. G3/A3/06, Dobinson to Baylis, 5 Feb. 1894.
2 R. E. Faulkner: *Joseph Sydney Hill*, London 1895, p. 139.
3 Ibid. pp. 177–8.
4 C.M.S. G3/A2/07, Tugwell to Baylis, 8 Jan. 1894.
5 *Lagos Weekly Record*, 12 Aug. 1893. Ichabod son of Phinehas and grandson of Eli. It means 'Inglorious'.
6 *Lagos Echo*, 15 Jan. 1898.

and the Archbishop. The liberality in giving, and the missionary programme they assumed within seven years of their independence, belie the assertion of contemporary white missionaries that the nationalist movement of 1891–92 in the Delta was imposed upon the people by the 'Sierra Leone cabal'. In addition to their feelings already indicated may be added the fact that all the money they received from the Ethiopians in Lagos and Sierra Leone was only £200. For at the end of 1892 it became clear that the people controlled funds bigger than Sierra Leone and had a balance of £495 19s 6d, apart from the £200 grant for industrial education by the Niger Coast Protectorate. Henceforth the Delta stood financially independent, having on average £1,400 annually. The Pastorate undertook heavy building expenses, boasted of a secondary school for boys and the first Girls' Secondary School in Eastern Nigeria, apart from the missionary success noted already elsewhere.

Alongside the 'most excellent work' of the Delta Pastorate was the glaring failure of the C.M.S., both on the Niger and in its two Delta stations of Brass and Abonema. Having dismissed the African missionaries it was obvious that the Society's work would 'collapse' unless a contingent of missionaries were sent at once.[1] Since white missionaries went on dying the Society fell back on the 'Europeanized Africans' from Sierra Leone without whom 'the Niger Mission will fall to the ground'.[2] From 1897 the Society had to recruit West Indians as well. The unsatisfactory condition of the C.M.S. stations in Brass and Abonema came to the notice of the Colonial Office. These two stations would be better off, observed Sir Claude Macdonald, if the C.M.S. settled its 'dissensions' with the Delta Pastorate.[3] Two missionaries who saw the Delta Churches flourishing and the Society's stations declining also urged appeasement of the nationalists. Bishop Tugwell asked the C.M.S. to apologize publicly for the misdeeds of 1890 and the 'discourteous treatment'[4] of the late Bishop Crowther, while H. H. Dobinson asked the Society to swallow its pride and acknowledge that the nationalists had '*won the battle*'.

With their predictions falsified, Salisbury Square decided to woo the Delta Pastorate to forge some links with it. This effort was not easy and lasted five years. In this effort the nationalist element was present throughout. After a series of protracted negotiations between Bishop Tugwell and Dobinson for the C.M.S. and James Johnson,

1 C.M.S. G3/A3/05, Dobinson to Lang, 13 July 1892.
2 Ibid. Dobinson to Lang, 7 June 1894.
3 C.M.S. G3/A3/06, Macdonald to C.M.S., 10 Mar. 1894.
4 Ibid. Tugwell to Baylis, 9 Nov. 1894.

Archdeacon Crowther and James Boyle for the Africans, a constitution was finally drawn up for the Delta Pastorate in 1897.[1] Unlike the Henry Venn Pastorate of Sierra Leone the constitution was therefore not an imposed one. Moreover it guaranteed what the Africans wanted by preserving the identity of the Pastorate and by stating unequivocally that it was to work in an independent African diocese. It was quite in order that the final draft of the constitution was accepted by the Africans after legalistic scrutiny by Sir Samuel Lewis.[2] It may be stated that like the so-called African Churches, the Delta Pastorate remained Anglican in their form of worship, their liturgy, music and ceremonialism.

The acceptance of a constitution by the Delta Pastorate and the consequent forging of links with the C.M.S. did not stultify the nationalist feelings in and for the Pastorate, although it brought to an end the bitter racial acrimony. Before the Constitution was accepted the C.M.S. was made to apologize to the Africans through Archdeacon Dobinson, who openly did so in Sierra Leone in March 1896. This apology was accepted by the West African press which urged the Ethiopians to 'overlook, forgive and forget the sad and painful past'.[3] Ethiopianism continued to be expressed within the framework of the 'West African Bishoprics Fund' which was created in 1900 as a result of the financial stringency which in that year forced the Delta Church to have an Assistant Bishop in the person of James Johnson, paid by the Church Missionary Society, not as an end in itself, but as a means to achieving the establishment of a full African Episcopate.

For from 1896 onwards the Delta Pastorate was finding itself in financial straits occasioned partly by its heavy commitments but mainly by the untoward fate that befell the manilla, the currency of the Niger Delta. This was brought about by the introduction of silver coinage which devaluated the manilla by 67 per cent.[4] Reckoned in terms of manillas the liberality of the people increased. Thus the income of £1,280 0s 4d realized by the Pastorate in 1899 would have been slightly over £2,000 had it not been for the devaluation of manilla in which the converts paid their dues. In this year expenditure was £1,085 15s 5d. This means that the Pastorate did not have enough surplus to maintain an independent African Bishop. This was an occasion that Bishop Tugwell had been looking for since 1894. He exploited it to the full, to make the Delta Pastorate accept an

1 C.M.S. G3/A3/06 for copy of the constitution.
2 Ibid. Tugwell to Dr Smith of Lincoln's Inn, 3 Oct. 1895.
3 *Lagos Echo*, 25 Apr. 1896.
4 Twenty manillas were now exchanged for English 3d in place of twelve.

Assistant Bishop to be paid by the Church Missionary Society and to persuade James Johnson to accept a post that he had before rejected thrice. After a great deal of thought James Johnson accepted the position, provided that certain conditions were met.[1] He pointed out that his acceptance of the position would not mean sacrifice of his principles but become the means of achieving them. It would enable him to appeal to his friends and all West Africans to help the Delta Pastorate by contributing to a Bishop Crowther Memorial Fund which would serve as an Endowment Fund for an independent African diocese in the Delta after the sum required had been collected. He would then become an independent Bishop. He further stated that the scheme must have the consent of the C.M.S. and the Archbishop, and he was to be given a free hand to launch the campaign for the funds immediately after his consecration.[2] All these guarantees were given and the sum of £8,000 named, the offertory at his consecration providing the nucleus of the fund.

On 18 February 1900 James Johnson became the 'half bishop' of the Niger Delta Pastorate and announced his 'Niger Bishopric Fund' simultaneously. Unlike the coldness and apathy with which the consecration of Oluwọle and Phillips was met by the nationalists, James Johnson's aroused a great deal of interest and made the episcopate of enhanced value in their eyes. His consecration was seen as 'a gradual and larger fulfilment of the prophecy and promise that "Ethiopia shall soon stretch out her hands unto God" upon which they have long been accustomed, amidst distracting and depressing thought over the terrible misfortunes and disasters that have befallen and oppressed their race, to centre their interest and hopes. . . .'[3] He was presented with an address by the African Association in England consisting of Africans and West Indians. The C.M.S. was thought to have honoured the Negro race when it asked Johnson to preach the Society's Annual Sermon at St Brides on 30 April 1900, being the first non-European ever invited to do so. A few weeks later he was received by Queen Victoria.[4]

Fearing that James Johnson might realize the large sum of £8,000 for his intended independent episcopate, the C.M.S. began to equivocate after his consecration by changing the scheme to 'West African Native Bishoprics Fund', which could be interpreted elastically to convey the idea that no bishopric would be created in any part until £8,000, at least, had been collected for all potential bishoprics of West Africa. Unaware of the implications of the change

1 C.M.S. G3/A3/o8, James Johnson to Tugwell, 5 Oct. 1899.   2 Ibid.
3 C.M.S. G3/A3/o11, James Johnson to Baylis, Feb. 1902.
4 *Church Missionary Review*, 1917, p. 332.

of the title of his scheme Johnson believed that he had won for West
Africa an Independent bishopric in the Delta, which would be followed by others in West Africa. He announced that the scheme was
not an Anglican or an ecclesiastical affair 'but one connected with
African Christianity generally and as a national and racial one', to
which chiefs, 'pagans', Muslims and all Christians should subscribe.[1]
Upon the success of the scheme, he judged, much depended 'the
credit and welfare of the Negro race'. On his way back to Lagos he
touched at Sierra Leone where he was received with hysterical
demonstration of joy at Wilberforce Memorial Hall. An address was
presented to him by the meeting, chaired by Sir Samuel Lewis, while
he presented his scheme before them; he was also presented with an
address by the Sierra Leone Ijẹsha Association because he belonged
to the Ijẹsha tribal group by father connection. The Governor, Sir
Frederick Cardew, invited him to dinner and contributed £5 to the
scheme, the only European that did so in Sierra Leone. Two committees were set up to collect contributions from men and women.
Before he left Sierra Leone in November over £2,020 was collected,
one S. B. Thomas, an old classmate of James Johnson's donating
£500. Never in the history of Sierra Leone had any scheme been met
with such enthusiasm, according to Sir Samuel Lewis.[2]

James Johnson's consecration aroused the greatest excitement in
Lagos. Had he desired to do so, as the nationalists hoped, he could
have employed the excitement of 1900–01 to achieve his ambition by
declaring an independent African Church with himself as Bishop,
without the trammels of £8,000 and the Anglican Communion.
J. K. Coker and D. O. Oguntolu, future leaders and founders of the
Bethel African Church, over whom he appeared to have a bewitching
influence, were already fighting his cause. The political temper in the
Lagos of 1900 was rather high. A number of grievances against the
British administration had been building up. The series of military
expeditions in Northern and Eastern Nigeria were all being decried,
whilst the supersession of indigenous administration by an alien
British one was being denounced. Discrimination against the educated Africans by the white officials was becoming ever more
pronounced. The educated Africans had begun to regret the avidity
with which they had embraced European culture indiscriminately.
Demand for greater representation in the Legislative Council was
becoming louder and emphatic opposition had been registered
against the attempt of the administration to force water and electricity bills on a people who believed that they were being asked to

1 C.M.S. G3/A2/011, James Johnson to Baylis, Feb. 1902.
2 Ibid. James Johnson to Baylis, 3 Nov. 1900.

pay for amenities of which the white officials would be the real beneficiaries.

It was natural that in the Church people who shared Johnson's Ethiopian views should see him as their leader. Months before he arrived there in November 1900 he had become, so to speak, the idol of Lagos and when he arrived he was welcomed like a hero by the Christians, 'pagans', Muslims and chiefs of Lagos. Bishop Oluwọle discovered that he had not yet finished paying the price for his betrayal of 1894. His prestige was at its nadir, looked upon as he was as an opponent of James Johnson. The Lagos women hooted him, the Breadfruit Church dispersed on him at a service and his life was threatened. He was labelled as Aachan, who would bring disaster upon the Lagos Church and indications of secession were given by the lay leaders of the Breadfruit Church.[1]

The occasion which played into the hands of the Ethiopians was the absurd recommendation of the Church Missionary Society to the Lagos Church Committee, the executive of the Lagos Pastorate, that Bishop James Johnson should be allowed to continue the pastoral care of the Breadfruit Church, while at the same time he was the Assistant Bishop of the Delta Church.[2] The C.M.S. felt that Johnson was indispensable to Lagos. The Church Committee, headed by Oluwọle in Tugwell's absence, rejected this recommendation on the grounds that Breadfruit needed a permanent minister. The laity of the Church and those of other Anglican and non-Anglican Churches interpreted the action of the Lagos Church Committee as 'unChristian' and an anti-Johnson measure. Once again, it seemed to them, Oluwọle wanted to betray the Negro race by opposing the man who was its symbol. It was quite clear that Oluwọle wanted to get rid of a man whose prestige had overshadowed his and had made his authority not well respected by his lieutenants. The anti-Johnson suspicion was confirmed by the way James Johnson had to evacuate the Breadfruit parsonage without an alternative residence having been provided for him. The laity appealed to Bishop Tugwell who had just arrived back from his theatrical March to Kano. Tugwell decided to support Oluwọle and the Church Committee at all costs after Governor Macgregor had declared that Oluwọle, and not Johnson, was agreeable. Tempers rose on both sides. The laity demanded that its will must prevail over that of the Committee and ecclesiastics who were being paid by the laity. The spokesmen of the laity directed Bishop Tugwell's attention to parts in the Scripture

---

1 C.M.S. G3/A2/o10, Oluwọle to Baylis, 19 Sept. 1900; cf. special issue of *Lagos Standard*, 8 Nov. 1901.
2 C.M.S. G3/A2/o10, F. Baylis to N. Johnson, 10 Apr. 1900.

that condemned ecclesiastical authoritarianism, reminded him of the American Revolution and its 'No taxation without representation' slogan, and lectured him on the rudiments of British parliamentary democracy which, they contended, ought to govern the Church as well. This meant, they argued, that ecclesiastics were no more than servants of the laity, to which they should be responsible, just as members of parliament were to be responsible to their electors.[1]

J. K. Coker, Oguntolu and other leaders of the future Bethel Church were led to hope that Johnson would support them if they broke away. Indignities were heaped upon Tugwell, whose bad temper and tactlessness turned him into a scapegoat. Only Johnson could have restrained the extremism of the Ethiopians, but he refused do do so. In October 1901 two thirds of his Church broke away in sympathy with him and formed the Bethel African Church. But James Johnson disappointed them and left for the Niger Delta on episcopal visits. By refusing to make use of the Bethel African Church Johnson burned his boats. The creation of a Church that had identical objects to those he had been advocating for over a generation henceforth vitiated the chances of the success of his more imperialistic West African bishoprics scheme. If any one ever lost a chance, James Johnson lost his in October 1901.

Henceforward failure dogged every step taken by James Johnson in the pursuit of his Ethiopian scheme. He made fruitless visits to the Gold Coast, Fernando Po, Old Calabar, Duala, Benin, Ọwọ and Sabongida Ora, educating the chiefs on the virtues of an independence his fanciful Ethiopian programme would bring to them. Committees were established in Sierra Leone, Cape Coast, Accra, Bonny, Fernando Po and Old Calabar. Cape Coast showed an enthusiasm next to Sierra Leone. Considering that Johnson could still create trouble for the Pastorate if his activities in Lagos were not supervised he was not allowed to campaign for his bishoprics scheme in Lagos, Tugwell himself undertaking to do so. In an address on 21 January 1902 in Lagos Tugwell announced that he had pledged himself to help James Johnson promote the scheme for an independent bishopric such as Bishop Crowther himself had wanted.[2] There is no evidence that Tugwell collected as much as a penny for the scheme in Lagos. Having considered the moment opportune the Church Missionary Society repudiated its pledge to sanction the creation of a diocese in the Delta, even when the target sum had been collected. The editorial in the *Intelligencer* of October 1902 went on to

1 Special issue of *Lagos Standard*, 8 Nov. 1901.
2 *A charge delivered in St Paul's Church, Breadfruit Lagos, on 21st January 1902*, by H. Tugwell.

assert that the Society had nothing to do with any independent African diocese and that whatever diocese that might be created would be Anglican.

All enthusiasm for the scheme cooled at once. The subscribers had been contributing purely on 'racial grounds' for one particular bishopric in the Niger Delta.[1] Newspapers in Lagos and the Gold Coast asked why the original plan for the Delta was departed from and could see nothing 'national' in a scheme that would be connected with the Church of England. They had been led to hope that Johnson would found a truly African Church such as he had been advocating since 1872, managed and controlled by Africans and completely free from 'the leading strings of foreign supervision'.[2] The Bethel African Church promised to achieve this. The subscribers asked for a refund of their money and contributions virtually ceased. In vain did James Johnson continue to plead for the scheme until 1909 when the Archbishop imposed new conditions for the grant of his wish.[3] In theory the West African Native Bishoprics Fund scheme lasted as long as James Johnson lived. Immediately after his death in 1917 the object of the scheme was completely reversed. Assistant Bishops of all nationalities came to be financed from the funds. The West African Native Bishoprics Fund scheme became the death-knell of Nigerian Ethiopianism.

Several years before James Johnson's death Nigerian Ethiopianism was already becoming a spent force and an outmoded ideology. For the essential prerequisite for the establishment of an Ethiopian Nigerian state was patently lacking in the country in 1900—mass acceptance of Christianity by the Nigerian peoples, at the point of a British bayonet if need be. But by 1914 only a small minority of the Nigerian population desired to be Christians and only a few of the Christian converts comprehended the sublime principles of the new religion in the way the Ethiopians conceived it. Moreover, as analysed elsewhere already,[4] the British administration in Nigeria had no intention of forcing the Christian faith on the Nigerians, or of establishing a government based on purely Christian ethics and principles. Rather than working together for a Christian state in Nigeria the administration and missions drew further apart, the former adopting a decidedly *laisser-faire* policy in matters of religion.

Nigerian Ethiopianism also depended on the very brittle assumption that the white missionaries would willingly subscribe to an

1 *Lagos Standard*, 10 Dec. 1902.
2 Ibid. 17 Dec. 1902.
3 Cf. paper entitled 'West African Native Bishoprics Fund' in C.M.S. G3/A3/013.
4 Chapter 5.

ideology the purpose of which was to get rid of them and their services. But no Christian mission thought of leaving the evangelization of Nigeria to African agents alone. At their best their conception was that the Church was a universal institution and that in Nigeria, by virtue of their superior civilization and a rich heritage of Christianity, they were more qualified in several ways than the Ethiopians in the spread of the Christian faith. And knowing quite well that the *Pax Britannica* would conduce to the progress of their work they supported the establishment and consolidation of British rule, the termination of which did not enter their thinking. It was natural that the nationalist articulations of the Ethiopians in Church and state were unwelcome to them.

The inadequacy of the Church in satisfying the nationalist aspirations of the growing élite in Nigeria was perceived by a number of educated Africans. Some like Herbert Macaulay, a grandson of Bishop Crowther and in his early years a strong Churchman, made the press the medium of their nationalistic expressions. On two occasions at least Macaulay toured the interior of Yorubaland and the mid-west to educate the chiefs against the anti-liquor crusade of Christian missions and the potential threat to Nigerian land tenure by the administration.[1] In 1909 Doctors Ọbasa and Randle formed the People's Union, a political organization which had nothing whatsoever to do with religion.

But no political organizations in the form of parties had emerged as yet in 1914. Ethiopians like James Johnson and Mọjọla Agbebi remained the nationalist leaders, and they took the grievances of the Nigerian peoples to the British public through the humanitarian body of the Aborigines Protection Society, an auxiliary of which was formed in Lagos in 1910. James Johnson remained the President of this auxiliary until his death and for some time Agbebi was its Vice-President.

In the meantime the nationalists were achieving success in another sphere. They were becoming disenchanted with European culture which they had been venerating for a long time. Traditional customs and institutions came to be seen as symbols of their racial identity and African Personality. This cultural nationalist movement must now claim our attention.

1 In 1909 and 1913 respectively.

We respect and reverence the country of Wilberforce and Buxton and of most of our Missionaries, but we are not Englishmen. We are Africans, and have no wish to be other than Africans.

Lagos Times,
12 July 1882

8 Missionary Enterprise and Awakening of Nigerian Cultural Nationalism, 1875–1914

At the turn of the century several factors were already blunting the edge of nationalists' bitterness against white missionaries as far as struggle for positions in the Church were concerned. In the same manner as educated Africans engaged in trade set themselves free of commercial dependence on European firms in Lagos,[1] and professionals like Dr Johnson, Dr Randle and Herbert Macaulay, rather than accept the racial discrimination in the Civil Service, resigned and became independent, educated Africans founded their own Churches and completely excluded white control. By 1917 there were no less than fourteen such Churches in Nigeria. Then there was the fact that control of the Protestant Churches passed more and more into the hands of Africans, Europeans exercising less and less control. By 1900 Anglican, Wesleyan and Baptist Churches in Abẹokuta, Ijẹbu Ode, Agọ-Iwọye and Ibadan districts had an African majority on their councils and committees. In 1904 the first Native Pastorate was created among the Ibo, in the Onitsha district.

African control of the Churches—a phenomenon that stupefied an Afrikaner missionary observer[2]—was facilitated by the extraordinary spread of Christianity that followed the *Pax Britannica* throughout Southern Nigeria, paid for by the Nigerians themselves. Between 1892 and 1914 the number of Christians more than quadrupled in hitherto difficult grounds. The implication of this, for which the white missionaries had not bargained, was devolution of power on the converts. Although the number of European missionaries increased, their prestige among the converts was no longer what it used to be. The days of the all-powerful, paternal and patronizing missionaries were over.

Nevertheless anti-missionary attacks remained and progressively became fiercer than ever from about 1895 onwards. This is in a sense surprising, for one would expect that the establishment of

1 C.O. 147/133, enclosure in Denton to Chamberlain, 4 June 1898.
2 J. Du Plessis: *Thrice Through the Dark Continent*, London 1917, pp. 52–3.

British administration would be the target of attack. In point of fact British sovereignty, as has been observed, was accepted by educated Africans as a providential blessing, and it is essential to note that such criticisms of the administration by the local press during the period would be misleading unless the important fact is appreciated that the educated Africans saw the white man's 'invasion' of Nigeria in the spectacles of missionary enterprise. British rule and the economic exploitation of the country were not seen as isolated events, but as the effects of missionary activity. The British 'invasion' also came to be seen in terms of culture. From the nineties onwards educated Africans came to venerate their customs and institutions, and the Nigerian cultural heritage became the touchstone by which the white man's doings were assessed. Hence British administration was bad only to the extent that indigenous institutions were being tampered with. For the first time the word 'imperialism' appeared in the local press and was used in the cultural sense, and a cultural interpretation was given to the Darwinian theory.[1] Since Christian missions aimed at uprooting Nigerian customs and institutions, they were believed to have imperialist motives for so doing—to render Africans a prey to the exploitation of traders and the unpleasant aspects of the political domination of the administrators.[2] By depriving the converts of their culture all sparks of self-reliance, manly independence and independent thinking were thought to be extinguished. The converts thus found themselves in a position of servility to adjust themselves towards administrators and traders.

This was why the Lagos press declared that by the nineties missionary activity in Nigeria had become 'a grave social question'.[3] Missionaries could not escape being singled out for attack by the educated Africans. For African culture was essentially a religious culture. Its customs and behaviour were geared to religious concepts almost completely. Since missionaries were trying to convert to a new religion they could not escape condemning many practices as 'heathenish'. What else could they do but attack the traditional culture, which represented the rival religion they were trying to supplant? Moreover missionaries could not bring to Nigeria the 'pure milk of the Gospel', but like the majority of human beings, were unable to emancipate themselves from the cultural, emotional and social frame in which they were accustomed to live and express their religious life in Europe and America. They lived in an age when European civilization and Christianity were believed to 'hang

1 *Lagos Weekly Record*, 21 Jan.; 26 May 1906.
2 Ibid. 8 June 1901 and 26 Sept. 1901; *Lagos Standard*, 27 Dec. 1902.
3 *Lagos Weekly Record*, 27 Mar. 1897.

together as cause and effect, as root and branch'.[1] It was natural that they considered their theological approach, their own forms of marriage and burial, their narrow concept of family and individualism as in the main the best for the Nigerian converts as well. Until the third decade of this century, when anthropology began to come into its own, there could be no question of Christianity learning to adapt itself to Nigerian forms of expression in art, architecture and worship.

But this cause and effect theory of Christianity and European civilization was sometimes carried to ridiculous extremes by some of the missionaries who came to Nigeria in the second half of the nineteenth century. Many of them believed that converts who did not drink tea or wear European clothes could not be genuine Christians.[2] They had a ready response among the early converts who were either liberated Africans or orphans. Overwhelmed by the deepest emotions of gratitude towards those who had rescued them from a life of servitude, they were not in a position to discriminate in their appropriation of the culture of their deliverers. It was also easy to make converts, in the same manner, of children whose parents had given them for initiation into the mysteries of reading and writing. The children were taught to pray, sing psalms, wear European clothes and assume European manners. They were also taught to regard traditional customs and institutions with abhorrence. To this effect their meaningful names were described as 'heathenish' and they were given Hebrew and European ones which were meaningless to them. For adoption of European culture was an outward sign of the inward transformation from the 'pagan' to the Christian state.

As time went on the converts even carried their zeal beyond the expectation of the missionaries, for they began to nurse contempt for the vernacular in which the missionaries sought to impart the new faith to them. They were inspired to believe that the religious metamorphosis they were undergoing would leave them immeasurably high, above all non-Christians, including their conservative parents. And although the missionaries might not intend it, the children were being taught to be disrespectful to their parents in regarding them as indulging in vile and inhuman practices. The effect was to sever the children from the home, the fountain-head of their lives, and from all the instincts, moral teachings, ideas and inspirations connected with it. Consequently they became deluded with the idea that the less African they were the more Christian they became.

The extent to which some missionaries and their wards regarded

1 G. Warneck: *Modern Missions and Culture: their mutual relations* (translated by T. Smith), Gemmell, 1883, p. 6.
2 J. F. Ajayi, op. cit., p. 32.

renunciation of Nigerian customs as indispensable to conversion may be illustrated by their reaction to the proposal of the C.M.S. in 1883 about the imposition of European names on converts by missionaries. Prompted by the commission of crimes by converts bearing illustrious names like Wilberforce, Buxton and John, the C.M.S. decided in a minute that Africans should be encouraged to retain their names, provided these names had no heathenish connotation.[1] In Lagos the minute created a great deal of sensation. Among the African pastors only James Johnson took the minute seriously and although he would not change his own name he refused to baptize children with names other than African. His reaction resulted in many parents leaving the Anglican communion for the Wesleyan Church where no such heresy was in vogue. Others who deferred to his wishes threw off African names immediately after the christening ceremony and gave their children foreign names.[2] In Abẹokuta the converts protested vigorously against a measure that would reduce their new-won prestige among the 'pagans', should the minute be put into effect. Some European missionaries defended the bestowing of foreign names on converts because such names, rightly, served as protection for bearers against being enslaved or sacrificed in the interior. Others contended that African names were difficult to pronounce and that foreign names were nationally significant because they introduced unity among converts of diverse tribes and thus vitiated sectional sentiment. Adolphus Mann's indignation exceeded all others. He considered the minute outrageous and contended that the converts that renounced European names were guilty of 'Anglophobia' and 'anti-English monomania'.[3]

Belief in the identity of Christianity and European civilization was general among missionaries all over the world in the nineteenth century. This was partly due to the fact that sciences like anthropology and ethnology were confined to a few travellers and a small university circle. Moreover there was a special reason why missionaries could not have reconciled themselves to the views expounded by the Anthropological Society of London, of which distinctly anti-missionary and anti-Christian travellers and officials like Winwood Reade, Burton and Hutchinson were members. The so-called anthropologists were, like the missionaries, not interested in studying African culture for its own sake, as Mary Kingsley was to do in the last years of the century, but in being doctrinaire about the Negroes.

1 R. N. Cust: *Essay on Prevailing Methods of the Evangelisation of the Non-Christian World*, London 1894, p. 25.
2 J. O. Lucas: *History of St Paul's Breadfruit*, Lagos 1952, pp. 26–7.
3 C.M.S. G3/A2/02, Mann to Lang, 28 Sept. 1883.

Without the help of objective anthropology, therefore, nineteenth-century missionaries in Africa could not conceive that what they met on the spot was civilization of some kind; the idea of civilization as taking diverse forms was beyond their ken. Therefore missionaries could not think that Nigerians had their religions, laws, social and moral sanctions, aesthetic appreciation, insight into the meaning of life and its philosophy, types of human relationship and loyalties and reverence which were different from those of Europe and America but were evolved in and best for the Nigerian environment. Hence they did not make any conscious effort to study Nigerian customs and institutions, understand their inner meaning, the reasons for their existence and the purposes they were expected to fulfil.

But if missionaries may be excused for not being anthropologists, yet it is difficult to understand why they condemned without first understanding the cultural heritage of Nigeria they were denouncing. In fact, in spite of criticism of their denationalizing methods by African missionaries like Blyden and James Johnson, missionaries did not change their Europeanizing methods of evangelization until the last years of our period.[1] As late as 1887 anglicized Africans lamented that Nigerians were not eating with their wives,[2] a revolting thing in Yoruba society, while Brooke noted in 1889 that West African Christianity was a sham because converts were not seen going out for a walk with their wives.[3] Educated Africans had become so much enchanted by European ideas that all the delegates to the Anglican Conference in Lagos in April 1887 falsified history by declaring that polygamy was never indigenous to the Yoruba but was introduced by Muslim Fulani in the nineteenth century.

Instances were not wanting of converts educated in England who on coming back to Nigeria pretended that they did not understand the vernacular, and when spoken to, spoke through interpreters.[4] Such cases might be extreme cases but they point to the climate of thinking of educated Africans. Like the English colonists of Australasia and Canada they blithely referred to England as the 'mother country' and 'home'.[5] It was a difficult task, said one paper, to persuade an educated African that he was not a European.[6]

1   Protestant Missions met at Old Calabar in November 1911 and acknowledged their faults; cf. Minutes in C.M.S. G3/A3/012.
2   *The Church in the Yoruba Country*, Proceedings of the Diocesan Conference at Lagos, April 1887, p. 25.
3   BMSS F4/7, *Journals*, 1 Apr. 1889.
4   *Lagos Times*, 26 July 1882.
5   *Lagos Standard*, 7 and 14 July 1897. J. F. Halligey: 'The Yoruba Country, Abeokuta and Lagos', *Work and Workers* (London) 1896, p. 78.
6   *Lagos Weekly Record*.

Orishatuke Faduma, a Sierra Leonian Yoruba, addressing the congress on Africa at the Gammon Theological Seminary, Atlanta, Georgia, in 1895 defined a Christian, in the context of West Africa, sarcastically as follows: 'That which distinguishes a heathen from a Christian is not moral character or allegiance to Christ, but outward dress. The stove-pipe hat, the feathered bonnet, the high-heeled shoes, the gloved hands, and all these under the burning tropical heat, make a man a Christian gentleman.'[1]

Although it was by no means new it was not until after 1895 that change of attitude of many educated Africans to European civilization became emphatic and universal. They began to have pride in African customs and institutions and regretted the avidity with which they had accepted alien forms of culture uncritically. This pride altered their thinking; it meant the beginnings of independent thinking which made them assess and criticize more strongly than before missionary enterprise, British administration and the trading pattern of the country. This is the explanation for the radicalism of the Lagos press which by 1914 had filled missionaries with dismay[2] and Lugard with indignation.[3] European civilization, for which they held missionaries responsible, they argued, 'threatens to extinguish us as a race'.[4] 'We are Negroes first and Christians afterwards . . . the whiteman may be a model but cannot be an inspiration',[5] protested one newspaper. The point to note here is that the repudiation of European culture was quite revolutionary. For the first time they did not only think of themselves as a different people but were proud to be different from other peoples.

It is essential to examine the factors that brought about this revolution in the thinking of educated Africans and the cultural renaissance that accompanied it. Probably the greatest reason was to be found in their disappointment at being baulked of the objective that impelled them to aspire to be Europeans—to be accepted into the European community in Nigeria on the basis of perfect equality. All along this hope had been stirred up by missionary teaching of the

1 J. W. E. Bowen (ed.), op. cit., pp. 126-7.
2 M.M.A., Oliver Griffin to Brown, 28 Feb. 1910. C.M.S. G3/A2/015, Jones to Manley, 27 Jan. 1914. The anti-Government and anti-missionary tone of the Lagos press became too much for the pro-white lawyer, Kitoyi Ajasa, later knighted, that he decided to start a paper that would favour both Government and missionaries. He named it *The Pioneer* and he printed it in the C.M.S. Press. Of this Jones wrote: 'We are likely to have considerable influence in its publication. I am very thankful for this, for the press at Lagos has been mostly anti-Government, anti-missionary and almost anti-moral, and an improvement is earnestly to be desired.'
3 C.M.S. G3/A9/03, Memo. of private interview, 3 July 1914.
4 *Lagos Weekly Record*, 27 July 1895.   5 Ibid. 28 Nov. 1891.

universal brotherhood and equality of all men before God. It was the logical outcome of missionary teaching that they should expect that by acquiring the language, manners, clothing and education of Europeans they would be one with white men at social gatherings, while in both Church and Civil Service educational ability, and not colour, would determine the distribution of posts. Hence they looked upon themselves as 'British subjects'. Their experience however destroyed this illusion. European missionaries would not return visits by Henry Johnson and James Johnson, while academically inferior missionaries were placed over them. For instance James Ashcroft, whose language and spelling were notoriously defective, and James Kirk, a 'vulgar'[1] dismissed agent of an American Mission in Sierra Leone, became virtually rulers over Bishop Crowther, Henry Johnson and D. C. Crowther in the Niger Mission from 1878 to 1882.

In the Civil Service educated Africans with British degrees were placed under Europeans whose experience and educational standing did not equal theirs.[2] There was a disparity in salaries and conditions of service, a disparity that could not be justified otherwise than that it was '*owing to the colour of our skin*',[3] as the four African doctors in the Civil Service protested to the Colonial Office in 1907. In the medical profession Africans in the Civil Service wanted privileges such as recruitment of health in Britain while, like European and African missionaries, they kept horses for which they wanted allowances. Racial animus was provoked by their exclusion from the West African staff which deprived them of advantages such as quarters, gratuities on retirement and promotions. Indeed in the last decade of the century the Lagos Government made no bones about throwing Africans out of key posts in favour of Europeans.

Relations between Europeans and Africans underwent an unpleasant change. This change was summed up by a white trader who said, 'for the sake of true Imperialism the black and the white should never mix'.[4] Consequently, socially, the white dominated administration of Lagos had little contact with the people they were supposed to be administering, while in 1907 Egerton was constrained to send a circular to all officials in Southern Nigeria to treat their African subordinates in a humane manner.[5] Educated Africans who held key posts were not given quarters. Not only did Europeans refuse to be medically treated by African doctors, but the Colonial Hospital was

1 C.M.S. G3/A2/01, Henry Johnson to Hutchinson, 31 Mar. 1881.
2 *Lagos Times*, 23 May 1883; *Lagos Standard*, 18 Aug. 1897.
3 C.O. 520/50, enclosure 1 in Egerton to Elgin, 30 Dec. 1907.
4 'Great Thoughts' (undated) reproduced in *Lagos Weekly Record*, 13 Oct. 1900.
5 *Lagos Standard*, 6 Mar. 1907.

rebuilt in 1896 with separate wards for Europeans and European nurses.[1] All this was new in the social history of Lagos.

The tendency towards segregation invaded all spheres of life. From 1900 onwards the European passenger on board the steamers of Elder Dempster and Company would not speak to an educated African, whatever his status, but treat him as a 'degraded member of the society'.[2] In 1908 even the common man in Lagos had a fore-taste of 'true imperialism'. Egerton peremptorily expropriated the property and land of about 2,000 inhabitants at the Race Course for official residences and announced that henceforward 'native' build-ings must not be near to European quarters.[3]

The climax of segregation policy was reached when it invaded the Church, whose duty ought to have been 'to cement the two races together by preaching down segregation'. Both Egerton and Bishop Tugwell made all effort to create what Herbert Macaulay stigmatized as an 'OFFICIAL TEMPLE OF WHITE CHRISTIANS'.[4] And it is worth noting that this incident helped to spark off the virulence which Macaulay, a grandson to Bishop Crowther, introduced into nationalists' anti-white feelings in this period. Egerton deplored the fact that about thirty of the 400 Europeans in Lagos who were Churchmen at all had to mix with Africans. In order to correct this abnormal state of things he and Bishop Tugwell sought to convert Christchurch into a colonial church with a white colonial chaplain. If this was done, said Egerton, the 'religious carelessness' of the remaining 370 spiritually indifferent Europeans would be cured. In fact nearly half of the white community demanded the creation of a colonial, that is European church, and the ministration of a white chaplain as a condition of paying attention to religion. Aware that since the seventies it had become the policy of the Colonial Office to dis-establish such churches wherever they had been established, Egerton left no stone unturned to argue a special concession for Lagos.[5] It may be noted that as early as 1875 the Colonial Office had refused to establish a chaplaincy in Lagos, had in 1876 partially disestablished the church of Sierra Leone and had in 1896 completed its disestab-lishment after Bishop Ingham's resignation, by refusing to counten-ance a successor.

Reinforced with two numerously-signed petitions by the European

1 C.O. 147/144, Blue Book Report, enclosed in MacCallum to Chamberlain, 22 Sept. 1897.
2 C.M.S. G3/A2/013, James Johnson to Baylis, 30 Mar. 1909.
3 A.P.S., Sapara Williams to Harris, 2 May 1910.
4 Nigerian Chronicle, 8 Oct. 1909.
5 C.O. 520/79, Egerton to C.O., 25 Aug. 1909. Nigerian Chronicle, 8 Oct. 1909.

community in 1907 and 1909, Egerton, who had beaten down the opposition of educated Africans over the expropriation issue, was able to convince the Colonial Office of the necessity for 'treating the case of Lagos as a special one justifying a departure from the general policy of the Colonial Office'.[1] It is surprising that the Colonial Office did not notice that in his submissions Egerton had not cared for either veracity or logic in his contentions. For instance although there were twenty-three churches on the small island of Lagos Egerton wanted room for Europeans in only a particular church; while demanding sanction of his scheme on the grounds that the European population was increasing, he ignored the greatly improved healthiness of West Africa, and particularly the conquest of malaria which rendered possible this increase, but described the territory as the most deadly in the world; although the administration was poor when it came to increasing the paltry grant given to Christian Missions for education the wealth of Southern Nigeria was 'phenomenal' when it came to spending about £1,000 a year on the colonial chaplaincy.[2]

In order to forestall this segregationist move creeping into the Church educated Africans, led by Herbert Macaulay, led the parishioners of Christchurch into opposing Bishop Tugwell. Since the church was built with public money the indignities heaped upon the Bishop at the meeting that took place on 2 April 1909[3] were sufficient to deter both Tugwell and Egerton from their attempt to have Christchurch converted into a European church. Nevertheless the Governor did not abandon his segregationist scheme. Appealing to commercial firms to make grants for the white man's church he compelled, through the Legislative Council, the 'pagans', Christians and Muslims of Southern Nigeria to contribute half of the £10,000 appeal for, in Macaulay's words, 'the spiritual needs of their European Detractors'.[4]

Instead of Europeans being flattered by their imitation of them, educated Africans saw themselves the laughing stock of all classes of Europeans, including the missionaries. They were ridiculed as mere imitators who in trying to be what they could not be also lost the virtuous characteristics of the uncontaminated tribesmen. 'His European master and teacher has so stripped him of his own skin,' said an official of the educated African, 'so robbed him of his own soul and language, so daubed him over with spots and stripes of his own veneer, so tall-hatted and befrocked him, that he has turned him into an unrecognizable human being.'[5] By 1895 many educated Africans

1 C.O. 520/79, Egerton to C.O., 25 Aug. 1909.   2 Ibid.
3 *Nigerian Chronicle*, 9 Apr. 1909.   4 Ibid. 8 Oct.
5 *West African Mail*, 14 May 1909.

had begun to believe that this allegation was true. In the new world of European civilization they could find no firm footing. Missionaries could not provide them with a substitute for what they had lost, namely, membership in a group with clear moral standards and obligations. They found themselves isolated individuals without the moral and social solidarity of the tribal life. This lack of corporate feeling was a constant and pathetic note in the Lagos press throughout the period.

It was natural, then, that in response to the ridicule of Europeans educated Africans should fall back on their customs and institutions. They now argued that there were certain 'laws of nature',[1] dictated by the West African environment, which demanded a peculiar form of existence. In aspiring to become Europeans, they now realized, they were flying in the face of Providence and the ruinous effects of their unnatural cravings were already manifesting themselves. Physically, they believed, they were not as robust as the uncontaminated Africans in the interior; morally they deplored the existence of crimes like immorality, stealing, forgery and lack of respect for elders which, as a general rule, were absent from the traditional society; economically, some argued, educated Africans were deriving no intrinsic benefits from contact with Europeans, for they were reduced to the position of producers for Europe and thus lost the economic independence of the traditional society. Although no scientific evidence was produced for all these assertions the belief in the moral and physiological superiority of the uncontaminated Africans in the interior to the educated Africans was widely held by well-intentioned administrators like the much-revered Pope Hennessy[2] and Carter, apart from Blyden and James Johnson.

What was clear to all observers in Lagos was that after sixty years' aspiration of the educated Africans to assimilate European civilization they did not become Europeans, nor could they be described as Africans, at least not as tribal Africans. They remained a *tertium quid* between the two. Consequently by 1900 Lagos society was culturally in a state of fluidity. Its artificiality was described as follows by G. Neville, the founder of the Bank of British West Africa and member of the Legislative Council: 'Lagos has become a bazaar—that is, a place for exhibition and show—for temporary glitter and not solid progress.'[3] It is remarkable that the educated Africans found themselves 'stranded and floundering in the aggravating haze of semi-civilization',[4] while a newspaper defined a 'Europeanized African'

1 *Lagos Weekly Record*, 27 July 1895.
2 C.O. 267/317, Pope Hennessy to Kimberley, 31 Dec. 1872.
3 *Lagos Weekly Record*, 5 June 1898.   4 Ibid. 20 Aug. 1898.

as 'a geographical, a physiological and a psychological monstrosity' and went on, 'we are like pictures in a phantasmagoria'.[1]

While it cannot be over-emphasized that the cultural awakening among the educated Africans in the period under examination did not owe its origins to any external influence but was spontaneous and consequent on the factors mentioned already, a much-valued impetus was given by the writings and lectures of the intrepid, medium-sized, frail-looking Mary Kingsley. She first went to West Africa in 1893, principally to collect fish. With the insight of the anthropologist she studied missionary enterprise at first hand. While giving the missionaries credit to a certain extent she did not admire their denationalizing tendency. She joined the educated Africans in attacking missionaries for the 'delirious view' of the Africans they had fed the English public with, and venerated customs and institutions which missionaries were wont to disparage. While making converts, she said, they rendered the latter useless, lazy, cunning and timid.[2] It was Mary Kingsley who suggested the advisability of founding an African Society to study 'Africa as it is, from its backhair to its burial customs, from its soil to its statistics'.[3] Not realizing that she had the worst epithets for them, educated Africans respected her for advocating the cause of African culture, reviewed her books, reproduced her speeches and constantly employed her ideas as a bludgeon against missionaries.[4]

Before examining efforts made to rehabilitate specific customs and institutions it is pertinent to emphasize that the intense pride of educated Africans in their culture was not merely sentimental, but in many cases was solidly based upon detailed investigations. Apart from individual researches that will be touched upon presently, it may be mentioned that in 1903 was founded 'The Lagos Native Research Society', under the secretaryship of the Reverend H. Atundaolu.[5] Their discoveries led them to conclude that their cultural heritage was not only a thing to be proud of, but was in many ways superior to European culture.[6] Their reverence for their culture was based on the following rationalization. The institutions and idiosyncrasies of a people were a sacred gift to be cherished and nurtured

1 Ibid. 13 Mar. 1896.
2 M. H. Kingsley, *West African Studies*, London 1901, pp. 274, 320–3.
3 *Liverpool Daily Post*, 13 July 1898, reproduced in *Lagos Weekly Record*, 20 Aug. 1898.
4 *Lagos Weekly Record*, 21 Mar. 1896, 6 Apr. 1901.
5 *Lagos Standard*, 11 Nov. 1903.
6 This was a current idea. Cf. *Lagos Weekly Record*, 15 Aug. 1896: 'There is no African custom which is not for this continent superior to anything Europe can give us; and today if Europe could she would take many a leaf from Africa's social and domestic regulations.'

to the highest development by the people. Their institutions were their finest treasures through which they could express racial distinctiveness and fulfil their racial genius. The reason why they were being castigated by their European traducers was because they were imitative and not creative. They could create and demonstrate their racial distinctiveness only by studying their institutions and culture. By doing this they would excite the curiosity of outsiders and thus compel respect from other races. From the study of their culture fresh ideas would spring to their minds and these they would use to educate other peoples. Also, by placing the results of their researches at the disposal of the world Africans would be adding their quota to the common pool of world culture and knowledge.

The first African voices against the denationalizing methods of Christian missions in West Africa were those of James Johnson and Blyden. It was with a view to putting an end to what the latter later on termed as 'a terrible homicide' that both of them advocated in 1872 the foundation of a university in West Africa. James Johnson interviewed the Earl of Kimberley, the Secretary of State for the Colonies, in 1873.[1] The idea was to put an end to the presence of white missionaries by staffing the university with American Negroes and producing African graduates who would ultimately displace Europeans. Africans would be prevented from studying abroad so that their racial characteristics might be preserved. They expected the proposed university to lead to 'formation of a national intellect from which respect for the race has not been eliminated'.[2] In his famous correspondence with Hennessy James Johnson criticized missionary activity in West Africa in a language that demands long quotation:

> In the work of elevating Africans, foreign teachers have always proceeded with their work on the assumption that the Negro or the African is in every one of his normal susceptibilities an inferior race, and that it is needful in everything to give him a foreign model to copy; no account has been made of our peculiarities; our languages enriched with traditions of centuries; our parables, many of them the quintessence of family and national histories; our modes of thought, influenced more or less by local circumstances; our poetry and manufactures, which though rude, had their own tales to tell ... God does not intend to have the races confounded, but that the Negro or African should be raised upon his own idiosyncrasies ... the result has been that we, as a people ... have lost our

1   C.O. 267/325, James Johnson to C.O., 3 Nov. 1873.
2   *The Negro*, 16 Apr. 1873.

self-respect and our love for our own race, are become a sort of nondescript people ... and are, in many things, inferior to our brethren in the interior countries. There is evidently a fetter upon our minds even when the body is free; mental weakness, even where there appears fertility.[1]

Although James Johnson advocated cultural nationalism throughout his life and carried his crusade to the Pan-Anglican Conference in 1908, by far the most prolific apostle of cultural nationalism was Edward Blyden. Fondly remembered by present-day West African statesmen as their inspirer, his career and writings show clearly that his contribution to African nationalism, surprisingly, did not lie in the distinctly political but in the cultural sphere. An exponent of the view that the different races of the world had special talents distributed among themselves on racial lines, he believed that Africans were not marked out by Providence for either political or scientific achievements.[2] It is nothing to wonder at then that he welcomed the Partition of Africa by the European powers, to whom political talents were given, as an event 'ordained of God',[3] and urged Africans to accept European rule with good grace because it would conduce to their 'ultimate good'. Nor should educated Africans aspire to participating in the administration of their country or even ask for the franchise. Economically the purpose of their existence was that they should 'speak to the soil'. But above all to them and the Jews were given the spiritual gifts, hence Africa was 'the first home of God'.[4] Therefore Europeans were spiritually unqualified to Christianize Africans who did not need their theological interference, for 'the creeds formulated in Europe are not indispensable to Africa's spiritual development'.[5]

Hypnotized by the profound spirituality of Africans he directed his shafts at Christian missions and the destruction of African customs and institutions their methods implied. For Blyden believed that no greater calamity could befall a race than the loss of its culture: 'the soul of the race finds expression in its institutions and to kill those institutions is to kill the soul—a terrible homicide'.[6] Blyden's vitriolic denunciation of European civilization which, he said, involved 'derogatory aberrations'[7] for educated Africans, was born out

1 *The Negro*, 1 Jan. 1873.
2 E. W. Blyden: *Africa and the Africans*, London 1903, p. 44. Holden Manuscripts, Blyden to Professor Camphor, 22 Sept. 1899, pp. 1129–31.
3 *West Africa*, 22 Aug. 1903.
4 E. W. Blyden: 'West Africa Before Europe', *Journal of African Society*, 1903, pp. 361–5.
5 Ibid.   6 Ibid.   7 E. W. Blyden: *Africa and the Africans*, p. 43.

of a close study of both African and European cultures.[1] With the
contented life, solidarity and well-knit social system of the tribal life
before his eyes, he saw nothing profitable resulting from the impact
of European culture on the educated Africans. In place of the moral
purity ensured by polygamy in the indigenous society he saw immorality prevailing among the so-called monogamist converts; in place of
the well-ordered, dovetailed economic system of tribal society in
which every man had enough and not many too much, he noticed
individualistic, selfish economic competition among educated Africans and concentration of wealth in the hands of a few, while
concerted action in any scheme was impossible and distrust of one
another prevalent.

In his incessant plea to Europeanized Africans Blyden called for
emancipation from mental and cultural slavery in which, he said,
they were by adopting foreign culture. Europeanized Africans were
living in a no-man's-land, were incapable of formulating ideas and
could not give practical shape to their own conceptions on their own
initiative. This was because they were living in a borrowed atmosphere and were subsisting on the thought and ideas of others. In
practical terms the vandalism of Christian missions should be
arrested by the establishment of an African Church based upon the
Bible alone, for 'the Christ we worship must be an African . . . the
Christ revealed in the Bible is far more African than anything else.
Hence all the pictures drawn by Europeans to represent Him are false
to us.'[2]

Nevertheless too much credit cannot be given to either James
Johnson or Blyden, for neither of them put his convictions into practice. In spite of ridicule by white missionaries in England James
Johnson never wore African clothing, while he refused to throw away
the name which a German missionary had given to his father. In the
same manner Blyden never really identified himself with African
customs but enjoyed European civilization to the full, while no one
more than himself was in mental slavery. The fountain of his knowledge throughout his life continued to be Western literature, which he
said ought to be proscribed in an ideal national African education
programme. He regarded English as the most precious treasure in the
world,[3] and there is no evidence that he studied or spoke any African
language.

The only educated African who approximated to a practical cultural nationalist was D. B. Vincent, leader of the Native Baptist

1 E. W. Blyden: *African Life and Customs*, London 1908.
2 E. W. Blyden: *The Three Needs of Liberia*, London 1908, p. 32.
3 *West Africa*, 12 Oct. 1901.

Church. From 1891 onwards he refused to work for any Christian mission in spite of high positions promised by Bishop Tugwell.[1] Convinced that it was a 'curse' to depend on foreign missions, 'doing the baby for aye',[2] he preferred to be poor but independent. In 1894, while in Liberia, he changed his name to Mọjọla Agbebi. He cast off European clothing and was daring enough to wear his voluminous *agbada* in the cold weather of Britain and America. Agbebi had contempt for the Negro settlers in Liberia because they were Americans in Africa, and he asked them to disperse into the interior and be absorbed into the culture there.[3] From 1903 to 1904 he toured Britain and the U.S.A., lecturing on African customs. Repelled by American civilization, which he described as a 'snare', and its Christianity, which was a 'counterfeit',[4] he left a cultural legacy among the Negroes of Yonkers in Agbebi Day, 11 October, which the Negroes promised to observe in remembrance of African customs and institutions and in support of his evangelistic exertions in Southern Nigeria. When in 1900 he betrothed his daughter, Ibironkẹ, he did it in the traditional way.[5]

Unlike all the so-called African Christians Agbebi tried to reconcile Christianity and Nigerian institutions. He attempted to evangelize the interior through the chiefs and collected African gods for study.[6] He instructed his converts in the Ekiti country and in the Niger Delta not to use foreign songs for seven years and appreciated African art represented in the images. Mọjọla Agbebi was so carried away by his veneration of African institutions that in the Senate House, University of London, at the Universal Races Congress in 1911, he defended such institutions as secret societies, human sacrifice and cannibalism.[7] In his most famous address, reproduced throughout West Africa and London, he urged all Africans at the anniversary of the Bethel African Church in 1902 to make distinctions between 'essentials' and 'non-essentials' of Christianity. He declared:

> Prayer-books and Hymn-books, harmonium dedications, pew constructions, surpliced choir, the white man's style, the white man's name, the white man's dress, are so many non-essentials, so many props and crutches affecting the religious manhood of the Christian African. Among the great essentials of religion are that the lame

1 Roberson Collection, Extracts, W. A. Amakri to C. Roberson, 27 July 1955.
2 B. Vincent, op. cit.   3 *Lagos Weekly Record*, 13 Oct. 1894.
4 *Lagos Standard*, 7 Dec. 1904.   5 *The Wasp*, 17 Apr. 1900.
6 *West Africa*, 22 Aug. 1903, pp. 211–14 for some of the gods collected.
7 G. Spiller (ed.): *Inter-Racial Problems*, London 1911. Agbebi's paper was 'The West Africa Problem', pp. 341–8.

walk, the lepers are cleansed, the deaf hear, the dead are raised up, and the poor have the Gospel preached unto them.[1]

And yet Agbebi's strong cultural nationalism notwithstanding, the cultural rehabilitation engendered by missionary enterprise was never a complete one. By accepting Christianity—and no one rejected it completely—they had ceased to be Africans. Their ideas and mental outlook remained essentially European. They knew more of the histories of England, Greece and Rome than they did of Nigeria and spoke more of English than any vernacular. They had greater respect for Queen Victoria than for their chiefs. Ironically they remained revolutionaries visualizing a society radically different from the traditional one. The Nigerian society of their dream was not to remain relatively self-contained and isolated as it had been for centuries, but was to maintain economic links with the outside world. All of them advocated an economic revolution by which Nigerians would produce cocoa, coffee, rubber and cotton for Europe and become economically dependent. It is astonishing that none of them, including Agbebi who actually sponsored cash crop economy, observed that outside economic forces were already contributing to the undermining of Nigerian culture and the upsetting of the society. As leaders of an entirely new religion the cultural nationalists sought to supersede the tribal priests and usurped the spiritual functions of the chiefs. In appropriating this important sphere in the life of Africans they diminished respect for the chiefs who, like the masses, now looked to them for political guidance. Surely there was a contradiction in terms in Agbebi's cultural nationalism and his admission that Christianity was the 'grandest of all revolutions'.[2] In an unguarded moment Blyden spoke the truth when, in a letter to the Earl of Kimberley in 1873, he advocated establishment of schools by the British Government throughout West Africa. The education that would be given would result in 'a new world' and raise Africans into 'new habits of thought and new modes of life'.[3] At best, then, rehabilitation of Nigerian institutions and culture could not be more than a tinkering; the forms were rehabilitated but not the substance, the shell but not the kernel. It is vital to bear this fact in mind in estimating the concrete cultural achievements of the nationalist movement.

The earliest success of cultural nationalists was enacted in 1881

1 *Report of Proceedings of the African Church Organisations for Lagos and Yorubaland, 1901–1908*, Liverpool, 1910, p. 91.
2 *Sierra Leone Weekly News*, 5 Mar. 1892.
3 C.O. 267/325, Blyden to Earl of Kimberley, 22 Oct. 1873.

when the Lagos Government, attempting to regulate and control to a certain extent education in the Colony, passed its Education Bill. In a manner characteristic of the attitude of the age the Bill took no cognizance of the vernacular, the one thing, incidentally, in which missionaries were interested. It declared that all teaching from the lowest class to the highest must be done in the English language before a Government grant could be obtained. Apart from the obvious fact that such a measure could not in practice be carried out, educated Africans, engineered to a certain extent by the missionaries, protested to the Colonial Office successfully.[1] The Lagos press saw the Bill as a subtle cultural imperialist move and editorialized:

> Is the ulterior object of the Education Bill to promote the Conquest of West Africa by England morally through the English language and secure that morally which African fevers perhaps prevent acquiring physically. . . . We shall not sit tamely to witness the murder, death and burial of one of those important distinguishing national and racial marks that God has given to us. . . . Surely the way to elevate a people is not first to teach them to entertain the lowest ideas of themselves and make them servile imitators of others.[2]

But the first real stirrings of cultural nationalism did not occur until the nineties. The first popular movement was that of assumption of African names by important educated Africans of the second generation. Their feelings of gratitude to white missionaries could not have been as strong as those of the liberated Africans. Yet observers in Sierra Leone and Lagos, who noticed that the Yoruba were addicted to some of their customs more than any tribe, did not notice them retaining their African names.[3] A clear example of the importance attached to alien names was that of the *Saros* in Abẹokuta, many of whom, we have noticed, accepted titles with 'heathenish' rites and relapsed to undiluted 'paganism'. Not a single one of them renounced his alien name. Apart from converts like Moses Ladẹjọ Stone, David Brown Vincent and Dandeson Coates Crowther who assumed the names of their benefactors, it was the fashion among educated Africans to look for high-sounding or polysyllabic names such as James Penson Lablo Davies and Joseph Pythagoras Haastrup, or the alliterative James Johnson or Jonathan John Thomas or Richard Beales Blaize.

From the nineties onwards important figures in the nationalist

1   *Lagos Times*, 9 Aug. 1882.   2   Ibid. 12 July 1882.
3   S. Clarke: *Sketches of the Colony of Sierra Leone and its Inhabitants*, London 1863, pp. 11–12. C. Fyfe, op. cit., pp. 378–9.

movement discarded their foreign names. To name a few, David B. Vincent became Mọjọla Agbebi; the Rev. J. H. Samuel, Secretary of the Lagos Institute founded in 1901, became Adegboyega Ẹdun, Secretary of the independent Ẹgba United Government, 1902–14; Joseph Pythagoras Haastrup became Ademuyiwa Haastrup, while George William Johnson of the Ẹgba Board of Management became Oshokale Tẹjumade Johnson. Most of those who cast off alien names did so because these names reminded them of the days of slavery when their fathers were given the names, a history they wanted to forget. Others did so because alien names separated them in feeling from their own countrymen, encouraging to make them 'strangers in our own country'.[1]

The most important factor that made them decide to assume African names was that they saw themselves bearing meaningless names in a society that attached a great deal of importance to names. For among the Southern Nigerian tribes names are not mere emblems for distinguishing one person from the other. They are often a memorial of family incidents, showing the circumstances of the family when the child was born or showing whether the child hailed from a reigning family; names may also indicate the incidence of the birth of the bearer, showing whether a child was born with a cord around his neck (Ojo), or with the face turned downwards (Ajayi), whether twins, or whether the family had experienced repeated infantile mortality. Names may also tell the story of the occupation of the family or tell the family gods being worshipped. This is the meaning behind the Yoruba adage that says 'Ile ni a wo ki a to sọ ọmọ ni orukọ', that is, 'the condition of the family of a child is borne in mind before any name is bestowed on it'.

Educated Africans saw that they lost more than the circumstances of their birth. They also lost the much-to-be-valued knowledge of the extended family of infinite degrees. In Yorubaland, for example, there are totems and cognomens, apart from the usual names. The totem is the common possession of the extended family by which relationship is indicated and consanguinity established. The value of this when marriage issues arise is obvious: it makes possible observance of the law forbidding marriage by members of the same blood group. Since educated Africans could not have totems, breaches of this sacred tribal law were quite possible. One other loss suffered by educated Africans bearing alien names was the knowledge of 'Oriki Idile'—a sort of blank verse—often lengthy—transmitted from generation to generation by rote, depicting the characteristics and events in the extended family's history, and always a source of inspiration to

1 · *Sierra Leone Weekly News*, 12 Nov. 1892.

the members of the family whenever it is recited. The realization of such losses was sufficient to impel thoughtful Africans to renounce foreign names.

Significant as assumption of African names was, not all cast off their foreign names. This was probably because those who renounced foreign names did not return completely to the traditional naming system. For example, many who were not of royal blood attached to themselves names and cognomens suggestive of such a pedigree, an innovation that has persisted ever since among educated Africans. Others outraged the traditional system by adopting their father's name or by giving their own name to the children. In Yoruba society there is nothing like the surname, and traditionally a father's surname was held so sacred that no younger members dare mention it even after a father's death. Today the European custom of the surname has been practically accepted throughout Southern Nigeria, and this has in consequence diminished the reverence and respect given to elders and parents by children. In this period an educated African who refused to change his name or cast away European dress was stigmatized as 'a nondescript, a libel on his country and a blot on civilization'.[1] If he refused to join the cultural nationalists he was pitied for the incubus of slavery that had deadened his intellect and made him continue to abide by 'the fashion gee-gaws of his former master'.[2]

It is clear from the foregoing that as far as discarding of foreign names was concerned the attitude and efforts of cultural nationalists were positive and constructive. They retained parts of indigenous culture that were deemed valuable and borrowed judiciously from the European civilization they so much execrated. Realizing that complete cultural independence was impossible, they evolved a new synthesis which was neither reactionary traditionalism nor European-imitative but sufficiently African in appearance to satisfy their race-pride and sentiment. Moreover their new synthesis was a product of their own interest. Adoption of surnames was compatible with British law of property and inheritance in the Lagos Colony which they had accepted without questioning. It fitted in well with the individualism towards which each Christian family was groping—the idea of a family consisting of a man, his wife and children in place of the extended family, embracing many of such Christian families, which was the traditional basic social unit.

Probably the greatest positive achievement of cultural nationalism is historiography. For the first time there arose a desire among

1 *Lagos Standard*, 13 Mar. 1896.   2 Ibid.

educated Africans to chronicle the history and institutions of their country. Much of remembered history and oral traditions which might have been lost was consequently salvaged, and the Lagos Government was pressed to substitute West African history for Imperial and British history in schools. It was J. A. Otunba Payne who set the trail with his annual *Lagos and West African Almanack*, the first of which appeared in 1874. How much he cherished his effort is shown by the fact that he presented a copy as the best gift he could offer to Queen Victoria at her first Jubilee.[1] Acknowledged as the best informed on the social, ecclesiastical and political history of Lagos, which he knew before the 1861 cession, and with which he was intimately and continuously connected until his death in 1906, his knowledge was useful to many Governors. His *Table of Principal Events in Yoruba History*, published in Lagos in 1894, became a textbook for all lawyers and judges in Lagos during this period. Bishop Phillips recorded the history of the Ondo, their customs and traditions, and the elaborate Ondo title system which he drew up is of the highest value for any study of Ondo history.

Attempts were made to find out the origins of the Yoruba and the route of their migration to their present habitat. One such investigation was the series of lectures delivered in 1884 and 1885 by J. O. George at the Breadfruit Church, later on published bilingually as *Historical Notes on the Yoruba Country and its Tribes*.[2] Another effort worth noting was 'A Short History of the Ijeshas and other Hinterland Tribes', serialized in six articles in the *Weekly Record* in June and July 1901 by H. Atundaolu. Written with a view of promoting unity among the Yoruba tribal groups, it has the merit of a king-list of the Ijẹsha dating from 1425. By far the most comprehensive work of scholarship was the *History of the Yorubas* by Samuel Johnson. Although the manuscript was completed in 1897 it was not until 1921 that it was published. In 1898 the C.M.S. rejected it because it was not merely a chronicle of missionary enterprise. It is significant to note that Johnson wrote the book from 'a purely patriotic motive'.[3] In spite of the criticism of the work as being Ọyọ-biased, it remains the only monumental contribution to the history of the Yoruba and nothing strikingly different from Johnson's recording have been revealed so far by the Yoruba Research Scheme.

It was natural that national awakening should extend to indigenous religion. In a characteristic manner a retired American Baptist missionary wrote of the Yoruba during the nineties, 'In religious

1 A.P.S., J. A. Payne to Queen Victoria, 16 Feb. 1887.
2 Published by E. Kauffman, Lahr. Baden (undated).   3 Preface.

things, their minds are a desert, a wilderness.'[1] Ironically, about the same time, thoughtful educated Africans were becoming worried about the sort of Christianity that was being propagated in the country, and, for the first time, began to look into indigenous religion to remove their anxieties. The Christianity brought to them, they began to complain, was not that of the Bible, but that which Europeans had formulated for themselves. They did not see a Church national to Nigeria as the Church of England was to England, the Kirk to Scotland and Gallicanism to the French people. In all these places the Church expressed national distinctiveness in organization and forms of worship.

More serious was the fact that what was called 'European Christianity' became completely discredited. All Europeans, whether merchants or civil servants or missionaries, were lumped together as 'Christians' and their actions interpreted as a demonstration of their religion. Observed to be working hand in hand in many cases, the missionary's purpose in Nigeria from the nineties onwards was believed to be other than spiritual. He was in Nigeria 'to provide subsistence for men of his colour before the true religion of God he professes to teach'.[2] Ousted from their once profitable trade by European firms who now went into the interior and by the railways which put the producers directly on to the European traders, educated Africans saw dangled before their eyes enormous trade and prosperity which they could not share. This, in their view, was the white man's religion in action, hence, as the local press put it, 'Christianity' was only another word for 'exploitation'.[3] Viewed in the same light were the administrators who passed unpopular measures such as the Forest Ordinance and the Native Councils Bill, expropriated lands belonging to Africans, and attempted to force direct taxation upon an unwilling people.

Nor was the conviction of Africans that all white men in Nigeria were one body irrespective of their vocation, without some foundation. They noticed Bishop Tugwell, Governor Egerton and the merchants co-operating in the erection of the white man's church in 1910, as has been noted. Then, in 1914, when feelings were running high against the Lugard administration, educated Africans were incensed to see Bishop Tugwell improperly securing a vote of confidence in the administration in the Anglican Synod. Even non-converts knew that no distinction should be made between one white man and another. In 1904 the Ekumeku rebelled again against the cultural and

1 R. H. Stone: *In Afric's Forest and Jungle*, New York, p. 37.
2 *Nigerian Chronicle*, 29 May 1914; *Lagos Standard*, 2 Apr. 1902.
3 *Lagos Weekly Record*, 8 June 1901.

religious intrusion into their territory by Christian missions; they pulled down churches, burned schools and either killed or drove away Africans who had accepted the Christian faith. Roman Catholic and C.M.S. missionaries were fortunate to escape with their lives but their work in Issele-Uku, Akwukwu, Onitsha-Olona and Atuma was destroyed. The Ekumeku soon regretted their rashness. With troops the administration compelled them to receive back members of their tribe who had betrayed their culture, forced them to rebuild the schools and churches and taxed them to replace all property lost or destroyed. Small wonder then that the churches became more filled with converts than before.[1] In the same manner the estimated 6,000 delegates from all parts of Iboland to the Industrial Exhibition of 1905 at Onitsha saw what Tugwell described as 'true Empire-building'. The delegates had brought it to their notice that the Exhibition was not merely for the display of their artistic genius but an occasion for them to hear about the Christian faith. The exhibition was opened with prayer by Bishop Tugwell and missionaries were asked to preach the Gospel to the people in every camp.[2]

In 1910 all the African members of the Wesleyan Mission witnessed what 'European Christianity' could mean in the action of the Reverend O. Griffin, Chairman of the Mission. It will be remembered that according to the Wesleyan regulations no member of the staff, European or African, could be disciplined by the Chairman; all cases had to be brought before the annual District Synod. In the past no European had been guilty of any misbehaviour that required the action of the Synod, whose decisions were, according to regulation, decided by casting votes. In this year, as in many previous years, cases of immoral incontinence occurred, involving Fashọrọ, an African minister, and S. P. Hadley, the European Superintendent of Shagamu. Moreover the European missionary was notorious for 'over-drunkenness', and on one occasion he experimented with his gun on two African children, wounding them seriously. In order to hush up Hadley's misdeeds Oliver Griffin sent him away to England before the meeting of the District Synod. In explaining why he had sent Hadley prematurely back to England Oliver Griffin asked the Foreign Board in London to discountenance the charges of immorality against the white missionary on the grounds that his accusers were Africans, although he, Griffin, had evidence to show that Hadley had been guilty of 'indiscretions' in 'a hundred ways', including acts such as making improper demands from African

1 C.M.S. G3/A3/09, J. T. Dennis to Baylis, 2 Feb. 1904. W.E.B., Copland-Crawford to Tugwell, 5 Mar. 1904.
2 C.M.S. G3/A3/010, Tugwell to Nott, 19 Dec. 1905.

women and disguising himself in pyjamas and blanket at night when he moved about.[1] Nevertheless, contended Griffin, the white missionary must be given 'the benefit of the doubt'. After Hadley had been 'censured' and sent to a college for further training by the Home Committee Oliver Griffin admitted that Hadley had been definitely guilty of the charge of drunkenness and could no longer be sure whether he was not guilty of the charges of immorality as well, although the gun-affair was no more than 'a case of thoughtlessness'.[2]

In September, three months before the Synod met, J. D. Fashǫrǫ resigned. The whole affair might have ended there, but the Chairman would not be satisfied with anything short of a public humiliation of the African minister. Therefore when the Synod met he brought up Fashǫrǫ's case and asked that a resolution of dismissal be formally passed. The enraged African members, who were incidentally in the majority, refused to take any action unless Hadley was removed from the College to which he had been sent in England and brought to the judgment seat of the Synod. Griffin saw himself 'rough-handled' and the Synod had to break up in confusion. As another European missionary observed, Africans could not understand why there should be separate laws for white and black. Without reflecting at all on the moral implications of his action Oliver Griffin dilated on the defeat he had suffered from African opposition as follows:

> We have to bear in mind that our Native brethren have but recently come into anything like civilization and their experience of Christian teaching, duties and responsibilities does not extend over many years. Only 60 years ago this country was steeped in heathenism and ignorance of the deepest nature. There are many times when they regard themselves as great men and embodiment of all wisdom.[3]

Indeed by 1902 European Christianity had become a 'dangerous thing', 'an empty and delusive fiction',[4] debauching Africans with alcohol, promoting immorality, deceit, hypocrisy and indulging in 'swine's flesh'. It had become a 'religion which points with one hand to the skies, bidding you "lay up for yourselves treasures in heaven", and while you are looking up grasps all your worldly goods with the other hand, seizes your ancestral lands, labels your forests, and places your patrimony under inexplicable legislation'.[5] There was no

1   M.M.A., O. Griffin to Brown, 10 May 1910.
2   Ibid. O. Griffin to Perkins, 8 Oct. 1910.
3   Ibid. O. Griffin to Perkins, 1 Mar. 1911.
4   *Lagos Weekly Record*, 25 Apr. 1903.
5   *Report of Proceedings of the African Church*, p. 91.

thought of questioning Christianity itself, but cultural nationalists sought to discover the 'pure milk of the Gospel' and give it characteristics of the Nigerian situation. When discovered, they argued, Africans should 'demonstrate in practice the Christianity which the white man only theorizes'.[1]

Moreover, the West African press apart, leaders like James Johnson, Mọjọla Agbebi and Otunba Payne, who took the new creed seriously, were much concerned about the superficiality of Christianity in West Africa. It was no more than a veneer. The Church was valued mainly for its social advantages; it afforded for the converts the pleasant instrumentality for marriages, christenings and funerals, with their opportunity for pomp and display. Patently lacking however were the intense zeal, devoutness, devotedness and spontaneity that characterized the unsophisticated African and which educated Africans were rapidly losing. This failure of Christianity to be deeply rooted in the people impelled educated Africans to study their religion in order to see how much features of indigenous worship could be grafted on the 'pure milk of the Gospel'.

Blazing the trail, Mọjọla Agbebi wrote in *Africa and the Gospel*: 'To be successful (as missionaries) we have to study the names, designs, and influences of the stone and wooden gods of our fathers. . . . The lives and doings of our heathen sages, the origin of the several gods of whom our brethren worship will be useful instruments in the hands of the aggressive missionary.'[2] This was a radical attitude to indigenous religion. From 1890 onwards useful researches were made into Yoruba mythology, philosophy of religion and the metaphysics of *Ifa*. In 1896 appeared the Reverend Moses Lijadu's *Yoruba Mythology* in which Ifa and the legend of creation, not dissimilar to the Scriptural version, were examined. The Rev. H. Atundaolu went to Ile-Ifẹ to study its groves.[3] In 1899 James Johnson published his *Yoruba Heathenism*, a philosophical analysis and appreciation of the religion of the Yoruba.[4] Fascinating is the closeness of *Ifa* to Christianity, as revealed by Phillip M. Meffre, an Ijẹsha emigrant from Brazil, who until his conversion was an Ifa diviner.[5]

Studies of indigenous religion led to the foundation on 12 April 1901 of 'The West African Psychical Institute Yoruba Branch',[6] for the purpose of encouraging the study of comparative religion,

1 *Lagos Weekly Record*, 25 Apr. 1903.
2 Reproduced in *Lagos Weekly Record*, 6 Nov. 1897.
3 M.M.A. Minutes for 1901, Appendix A.
4 Published in Exeter, pp. 51–4.
5 J. O. George, op. cit.; cf. 'Odu Ofunsa' pp. 57–8 by Meffre.
6 *Lagos Standard*, 17 Apr. 1901.

philosophy and science, especially the psychic laws known to *babala-wos* (Ifa priests) and secret societies. The most anthropologically informative material was produced by the Reverend E. T. Johnson of the Wesleyan Mission, who under the pseudonym 'Adesola' wrote a series of articles entitled 'Yoruba Burial Customs' in the *Nigerian Chronicle* in 1908 and 1909. Based upon original research, the articles remain the best and most detailed sociological investigation of Yoruba deities—*Eluku*, *Oro*, *Egungun* and *Adamu-Orisha* concerned with burial and religious concept of the Yoruba on death.

Educated Africans were amazed at their discoveries: they saw that after all, the gap between the so-called pagans and Christians was not as wide as they had hitherto imagined. They and the missionaries had been living in the 'valley of delusion'[1] by assuming that Christians were higher exponents of the Deity than the Nigerian 'pagans'. It was quite clear that, had they studied indigenous religion they, the missionaries, would have condemned 'paganism' much less than they had been doing. In spite of his bigotry James Johnson was dumb-founded at the moral code of Yoruba religion which 'only waits for the superior enlightenment of Christianity to raise it to higher plane'. As Agbebi discovered, 'a redeemer remains hidden in the mystic rites of the palm-god (*Ifa*) and under the rubbish of idolatry the son of God is hailed'.[2] Indeed the success that attended the efforts of the only European missionary who based his evangelistic methods upon close understanding of Ibo religion indicates what might have been achieved by other missionaries. Bishop Shanahan of the Society of the Holy Ghost Fathers was perhaps the greatest evangelist the Ibo have ever seen. This brave Irish priest who arrived in Onitsha in 1902 went from village to village on foot, ate the people's food, shared the same shelter with them and spoke to them in a language they could understand. Deeply impressed by the religious instincts of the Ibo, he saw that what Ibo religion wanted was not 'destruction' but 'transformation'. Hence he made them understand Mass in terms of spirit worship and the Supreme Being in terms of *Tshuku*.[3] Shana-han's understanding of the Ibo religion undoubtedly contributed to the stupendous outstripping of the Protestant missions by the Catho-lics in the Ibo country, in spite of the fact that the former preceded the latter by forty years.

In fact the pull of indigenous religion was so strong among the converts outside Lagos that Christianity and some aspects of indigen-ous religion had to live side by side in their lives. In Lagos, too, by

1 *Lagos Weekly Record*, 6 Nov. 1897.
2 Agbebi, op. cit.
3 P. J. Jordan: *Bishop Shanahan of Southern Nigeria*, Dublin 1949, pp. 122–39.

1914, the movement among the educated Africans for accommodation with indigenous religion had reached a stage which made an intelligent African minister attempt a union of Christianity and African religion, and in an ostentatious manner. This dualism of traditional religion and Christianity was chiefly due to the politico-religious institutions known as secret societies, and the title system among the Yoruba and Ibo. The situation could not have been otherwise because, unlike the situation in late nineteenth-century Europe, there was no departmentalization in the social, political and religious lives of Africans. Hence Christian missions had to contend with the *Ogboni* among the Yoruba, with the *Owu-Ogbo* among the Ijaw and the *Egbo* among the Efik and Ibibio. In all respects Nigerian converts exhibited a vigorous resistance in defence of these institutions and Christian missions had no choice but compromise. Largely because of the strength of these institutions missionaries did not press their opposition too far, except with respect to the *Ogboni* with which we shall be predominantly concerned.

It was only in Onitsha that missionaries came across the secret society known as the *Mo*,[1] members of which controlled the government of the country. So important was this society in the eighties that the converts dared not mention its very name outside the Church. Both missionaries and converts recognized the fact that to discuss the society openly, let alone to declare opposition to it, would stir up much hostility and so result in the effacement of Christianity on the Niger. Therefore the matter was dropped and was never raised again in the period covered by this survey.

In the Niger Delta the African missionaries were very cautious in their attitude towards the *Owu-Ogbo*, the freemasonry of the Ijaw. As a result of the success of Christianity in Bonny the free-born converts and chiefs, headed by George Pepple, of their own volition, reformed the cult. All forms of sacrifice were consequently abolished, and also the pouring of *tombo*, a kind of alcohol, on some object at the beginning and end of the play by masqueraders. The Christian members of the cult also claimed that they were able to check excessive drinking of alcohol at meetings. In 1884 the African missionaries excommunicated a few converts from the Church until the Christian members of the cult could convince the missionaries that the cult '*is now altogether renovated*'.[2] Once the required assurance had been given by George Pepple I, that the institution had been reduced to 'an innocent gathering for harmless amusements', the missionaries per-

1 Cf. papers on this cult by Harford Battersby and Julius Spencer in C.M.S. G3/A3/05.
2 *The Delta Pastorate Chronicle*, 1897, cf. Boyle to King George, 12 Oct. 1884.

suaded the members, hitherto only freeborn, to admit slave converts into the society.[1] In this way the social gap between slaves and freeborn was narrowed further. Henceforward slaves could participate in the administration of Bonny, a milestone in the social and political history of the city-state.

In Yorubaland no easy comprise was achieved with *Ogboni*. This is not the place for the fascinating conflicting theories of the origin and development of *Ogboni*.[2] It suffices to note that in the nineteenth century it was an ancient institution deeply rooted in Yoruba country but most powerful and prominent among the Ẹgba and Ijẹbu. As an indigenous freemasonry the Lagos Government viewed *Ogboni* with suspicion and hostility. Probably aware of the subversive activities of freemasonry in eighteenth- and nineteenth-century Europe and its suppression by the enlightened despots,[3] the Lagos Government regarded the *Ogboni* Society as a potential danger to the pacification of Yorubaland. Hence the first task of Governor Carter in 1892 after the Ijẹbu Expedition was himself to supervise the destruction of the *Ogboni* house in Ijẹbu-Ode.[4] This institution was completely ignored by the administration as its rule spread over the country. This outlawing, so to speak, of the *Ogboni* Society in the administration of the Ẹgba in 1898 when Governor MacCallum compelled the Ẹgba to form the Ẹgba United Government, constituted a revolution in Ẹgba history. It therefore appeared that this most effective engine of government, law and order in the country would die a natural death. It was at this juncture that the Reverend T. A. J. Ogunbiyi saved it from crumbling, resuscitated it, gave it a new complexion and made it the nationalists' answer to the spread of foreign freemasonry in Nigeria.

No foreign institution succeeded in captivating so completely many of the leading educated Africans as Masonic Lodges. To be a freemason was considered the highest social achievement and a partaking of the highest values that European civilization could offer. As a benefit society freemasonry was seen as encouraging understanding, co-operation and respect among members and was described as 'this noble institution'.[5] What made it specially attractive to the educated

1 Ibid. p. 35. Decision was taken on 1 Oct. 1897.
2 For the various theories cf. Froebenius, *The Voice of Africa*, Vol. 1, pp. 60 ff. S. O. Biobaku: 'Ogboni, the Egba Senate', *Proceedings of the C.I.A.O.* (International West African Conference), Ibadan 1949, published in 1956. E. B. Idowu: *Olodumare God in Yoruba Belief*, London 1962, p. 24.
3 J. T. Lawrence: *Freemasonry: Its History, Principles and Objects*, London 1909, pp. 33–8.
4 C.O. 147/85, Carter to Knutsford, 20 June 1892.
5 *The Mirror*, 3 Nov. 1888.

Africans was that both they and European members regarded themselves as brothers and the racial feelings that permeated the Church and the Civil Service were conspicuous by their absence in the Lodge. Moreover unlike the Church where the European missionaries insisted on controlling the Church government and could not bear African leadership, European officials who were freemasons accepted with good graces African leadership in the Masonic Lodges in Lagos. On this phenomenon a newspaper remarked, 'the control and management of these institutions [Masonic Lodges] will develop capabilities of self-government'.[1]

The first Masonic Lodge was established in Bamgbose Street in 1868.[2] It soon had a building of its own and had among its members nearly all the African leaders including J. B. Benjamin, editor of the *Lagos Observer*, Otunba Payne, who ultimately became the Worshipful Master of the Lodge and also the Chief Ranger of the Ancient Order of Foresters, which was founded in 1890. In the nineties new members included religious and nationalist leaders like Herbert Macaulay, Sir Kitoyi Ajasa and Sapara Williams. Even Mọjọla Agbebi joined the Society of Oriental Mystics, Saskatchewan-on-Hudson. Of the greatest interest for us is the fact that many Anglican and Wesleyan European and African missionaries were prominent members. There were for example the Reverend L. Nicholson, Secretary of the C.M.S. in Lagos from 1868 to 1872, and Archdeacon G. T. Basden, of the Niger Mission, both of whom were Europeans; and among Africans, the Rev. A. W. Howells, the Rev. J. H. Samuel, the Rev. W. Euba and the Rev. S. A. Coker.[3]

No one ever questioned the spiritual side of European freemasonry in Nigeria. In fact the Protestant missions patronized it by allowing Masonic festivals and services in churches. The fact that the transition from operative to speculative freemasonry in England from 1722 onwards also resulted in substitution of Deism for Christianity[4] hardly occurred to the non-initiates and probably passed unnoticed by many freemasons themselves. For freemasonry has from the earliest times been historically and ritually connected with Christianity. Up to 1730 operative freemasonry was connected with temple or church building while notable figures like Noah, Solomon and John the Baptist have their place in the Masonic concept. The Masonic ritual was worked in the spirit of a solemn religious ceremony; the candidate for initiation took his oaths kneeling, with one hand on the open

1   Ibid.   2   Ibid. 24 Nov. 1888.
3   *Lagos Weekly Record*, 29 Aug. 1891.
4   D. Knoop and G. P. Jones: *Freemasonry and the Idea of Natural Religion*, Manchester University Press, 1942, pp. 3–8, p. 16.

Bible and the 'Deacons' crossing their hands above his head. It was a frequent custom to sing hymns at the opening and closing of the Lodge, candles were lighted before the three pedestals and the Bible was always open before the Worshipful Master. The Lodge must be opened and closed with prayer, which was also offered for the candidate at his initiation, passing and exaltation. The Grand and Royal Sign was accompanied by the exclamation 'All glory to the Most High'. The places where Lodges met were known as temples, a word strongly associated with worship and religion.[1] Like other Lodges, the Nigerian Lodges had their regular chaplains and organists.[2] Although the Roman Catholic Church has consistently anathematized freemasonry, the Church of England, undoubtedly aware of the dire consequences that might result, has never investigated the theological implications of freemasonry, nor attempted to proscribe it, although elements in the Church have opposed freemasonry and attempted to secure such investigations.[3]

But it was not until the last decade of the nineteenth century that freemasonry as a part of European cultural imperialism, began to spread at an astonishing rate in West Africa. This was mainly due to the fact that British administration was extending and, thanks to the conquest of malaria, white officials flocked to West Africa as never before. These officials and merchants, soldiers and technicians, represented the rising middle class in Britain for whom freemasonry was a mark of social importance. For at the end of the century, freemasonry became popular in England as it never had been before. It is recorded that in the first nine years of this century no less than 1,000 new members were being added to the register of the Grand Lodge of England every month and no less than 600 Lodges were founded.[4] This phenomenal growth was reflected in Nigeria. In 1897 Macdonald Lodge, a branch of the Grand Lodge of Ireland, was established in Old Calabar, and the New Calabar Lodge in 1910. Between 1893 and 1904 two more Masonic Lodges were founded in Lagos and in 1908 Northern Nigeria had its first Lodge in Kaduna.[5] In consonance with the spirit of the age Europeans now came to dominate the Lodges and in 1904, St George's Lodge in Broad Street, Lagos, was founded exclusively for Europeans.[6]

1 A fascinating work on freemasonry is W. Hannah: *Darkness Visible*, London 1952.
2 *The District Grand Lodge of Nigeria Masonic Directory*, 1951 (in the British Museum).
3 Controversy over freemasonry in the Church of England raged as late as 1962, cf. *Church of England Newspaper and the Record*, 6 and 13 July 1962.
4 J. T. Lawrence, op. cit., p. 5.
5 *Nigeria Blue Book* (1938) gives a full list of the Lodges in Nigeria up to that year.
6 *Lagos Standard*, 26 Jan. 1898; *Nigerian Times*, 19 July 1910.

It was this spread of foreign freemasonry and the seizure of control by Europeans that impelled nationalists to begin to advocate the kind of indigenous freemasonry represented by the secret societies. They now emphasized their usefulness and found in them stimulation for 'national aspirations'.[1] Secret societies inculcated the spirit of brotherliness as they embraced people of all creeds. Every member was expected to be a man of respect and integrity, must confide absolutely in all members and help members in distress. They had their signs, passwords and testwords. There were several carved images in their conclaves which were both symbolical and instructive. Secret societies served many useful purposes. The Ogboni House for example was the school of oratory and jurisprudence. Among the Egba and Ijebu, *Ogboni* fulfilled the role of the national court of appeal, tried criminals and executed them. The Ogboni House also served as a form of prison for the state. In the absence of standing army or police such a function was absolutely necessary. The institution also fulfilled a most desirable constitutional role. By the checks it placed on the monarchy it prevented absolute rule, while its power prevented the masses from being lawless. Among the Ibibio there was the *Ebre*, a secret society of women by which women maintained discipline among themselves and punished offenders such as thieves. These were the good elements in the traditional freemasonry that educated Africans could not ignore.

It is on record that an attempt was made in the last quarter of the nineteenth century in Abeokuta to Christianize *Ogboni* by founding a 'Christian Ogboni Fraternity'. The key figure was Isaac Olufusibi Coker, alias 'Aderupoko' and other chief members were Daddy Beckley and Daddy Peters. The fraternity withered away before the end of the century. For in 1904 Isaac Coker was given the title of Ntowa of Itesi of the 'pagan' *Parakoyi* and Oluwo (President of *Ogboni*) of the Itesi conclave of the traditional *Ogboni*.[2] For so vital was the Ogboni institution in Egba politics that the condemnation of European missionaries by the C.M.S. in 1861 notwithstanding, such white missionaries as Townsend, Faulkner and Wood, noting that they could wield no influence unless they were members of the cult,[3] joined it with its 'heathenish' rites. Ademuyiwa Haastrup joined the *Oshugbo*[4] in Shagamu and his influence was utilized by the Wesleyan

1 *Lagos Standard*, 26 Jan. 1898.
2 Egba Archives, 'Alake's speech at the unveiling ceremony of the photograph of the late Mr Isaac Olufusibi Coker, on Monday 3rd June, 1935'.
3 R. E. Dennett, 'The Ogboni and other secret societies in Nigeria', *Journal of African Society*, October 1916. Quotes Ogunbiyi.
4 Ijebu word for *Ogboni*.

Mission in the evangelization of the Ijẹbu Rẹmọ district. But the man who determined to put into action the desire of nationalists was the Reverend T. A. J Ogunbiyi.

Ogunbiyi's background prepared him for this step. We are fortunate in having his autobiography.[1] According to him Christianity came upon him by accident. In his youth he had hoped to be either a tailor or a carpenter and then end up as a farmer. His father, Chief Jacob Ogunbiyi, was the first Lagos indigenous chief to be converted, and in appreciation of his new faith Chief Ogunbiyi built a church at Ebute-Ero in Lagos, the first Native Pastorate Church. He intended his son for the Church but found it difficult to persuade him to accept a religious vocation. Jacobson (T. A. J. Ogunbiyi) was therefore articled to R. B. Blaize as a printer. He consequently became 'converted' partly because of James Johnson's efforts,[2] but mainly because his father promised to send him to Fourah Bay College if he agreed to be a minister. Having attended the C.M.S. Training Institution from 1886 to 1889, he was sent to Ondo as a teacher. In 1893 he was sent to Fourah Bay and obtained a theological diploma. His inclinations for Yoruba institutions were not affected by his education. As a boy he had been initiated into *Adamuorisha* secret society, a cult peculiar to the indigenes of Lagos and connected with ancestral worship.[3] This is a point of great significance, in view of the features common to both *Ogboni* and *Adamuorisha* societies. *Adamuorisha* as a traditional cult had three grades, grips and passwords, and laid emphasis on elaborate expensive obsequies in which members of *Ogboni* Society used to take part. In 1900 Ogunbiyi had attempted to found 'Christian' *Ogboni* but was dissuaded by other Anglican ministers. A trip to the Middle East and England in 1912, and what he saw of freemasonry in these places, convinced him of the advisability of taking the long-contemplated step.

It is worthy of note that he first joined one of the Masonic Lodges in Lagos and was by 1914 its district chaplain.[4] He saw the unnaturalness of this foreign institution and decided to 'reform' indigenous *Ogboni*. In December 1914 he, the Rev. W. Euba of the Wesleyan Mission, Dr Ọbasa and other 'Christians' took the momentous step. Indigenous brethren of the cult in its raw 'pagan' form were invited to initiate these educated Africans into the cult and its ceremonies. The Society was stated to be for Christians only. A

1 In C.M.S. G3/A2/o6, dated 10 Oct. 1892.
2 *Lagos Standard*, 16 Mar. 1903.
3 He actually wrote a pamphlet entitled *Adamuorisha* in 1912.
4 *The District Grand Lodge of Nigeria Masonic Directory*, from 1913 to 1915.

sensational service was held at Ebute-Ero Anglican church and nationalists hailed the foundation of the 'Christian Ogboni Society' as a nationally significant step.[1] The point must be emphasized that the founders of this new society were not ordinary figures in the Lagos community. Euba was principal of the Wesleyan Boys' High School from 1895 to 1912 and was a B.A. of London. In the latter year he had resigned from the Wesleyan Mission because of a clash between himself and Oliver Griffin. How far the bitterness engendered by the quarrel affected his attitude to European Christianity is not clear. He became the Society's secretary. Akinṣẹmọyin, a member of one of the royal families in Lagos, was a lawyer, while Dr Ọbasa was a prominent lay leader of the Wesleyan Mission who married one of the daughters of R. B. Blaize. Like his colleagues in the Civil Service he had resigned in protest against the discrimination against Africans in the institution. He established the Ogboni conclave in his home town, Ijero, in Ekiti country in 1915.

It is interesting to note that Ogunbiyi was convinced that he was taking a step in the right direction, spiritually and culturally. He conducted research into the origins of indigenous *Ogboni* and claimed that those who had the best knowledge of the institution related to him the story of Cain and Abel.[2] The word *Ogboni*, they told him, derived from the club with which Cain beat Abel to death. The Yoruba word for club is *Ogbo*. When Cain was asked by people what he had killed Abel with, he answered '*Ogbo ni*', that is, 'It is a club'. This is probably the explanation for the fact that members of the society that contravened its regulations used to be beaten to death with clubs. It may be pointed out that European freemasonry also traces its origin to Adam. Ogunbiyi was elated at finding the cult the *Bene Esse* of the Yoruba. In fact he looked into the Scriptures for a justification of the 'Christian Ogboni Society' and discovered two apposite passages which authorized the foundation of such a society and in one, Ezekiel 23 : 23, in the Yoruba Bible, of course, the word 'Ogboni' occurs. The second one, Nehemiah 10 : 29 is worth quoting in full:

> They clave to their brethren, their nobles, and entered into a curse, and into an oath, to walk in God's law, which was given by Moses the servant of God, and to observe and do all the commandments of the LORD our Lord, and his judgments and his statutes.

In the opinion of Ogunbiyi's lieutenant, Chief Olubọbokun of Uyin, near Igede-Ekiti, whom the writer met on 9 May 1961,[3] this

---

1 *Lagos Daily News*, 20 Apr. 1932.   2   R. E. Dennett, op. cit.
3   This chief was then 84 years old. He worked hand in hand with Ogunbiyi and it was he who introduced the 'Christian Ogboni Society' to Ado in 1916. The

passage made clear the religious motivation of the Society in 1914. Here, for them, was an unequivocal Scriptural command that Jehovah should be worshipped by oath-taking, so that Christians might be a united people. In their judgment, like indigenous religion, the passage justified enforcement of religion and worship by fear. In order to inculcate this fear terrible oaths are taken by initiates and so dreadful are the oaths that no one has ever divulged their content to non-members. Ogunbiyi's intention, then, was to enforce the moral code of Christianity and genuine brotherliness by fear, which code and brotherliness institutionalized Christianity in Yorubaland could not enforce. Moreover the convivialities, the feastings and rituals of *Ogboni*, smacked of characteristics of indigenous religion which Christianity failed to embody through the Church. Indigenous religion had colour and ceremonialism, and was full of festivities at the annual festivals. All this institutionalized Christianity seemed to lack. For the social agglomerations of Christian groups were unnatural and lacked cohesion when wakes, wailing at death and elements of fear, such as taboos, were removed. Christian missions, for instance, did not make burials as attractive as the traditional ones, and these Ogunbiyi and his followers restored in elaborate forms. Then there was the fact that the hierarchical apparatus of offices of Christian missions were not as elaborate and attractive as the traditional ones. This the Christian *Ogboni* provided in a pyramid of six rungs.[1] It should be noted that foreign Masonic Lodges did not present an adequate hierarchy with their three grades.[2]

Ogunbiyi attempted to synthesize Christianity and traditional religion in the following manner. Only Christians were to be members. As Ogunbiyi said, it was his objective to purge ' this wonderfully helpful craft' of its 'decidedly objectionable heathenish customs', and thus convert it to 'a precious jewel compared with the same jewel in the dust'.[3] However, the oaths taken were 'pagan' and were administered by covering the initiate's face while his hands were tied at the back. He was made to kneel three times before the two *Edan* (brazen) images of the traditional type who carried on their hands a bowl

---

chief said that members of the society heartened themselves with the Ezekiel passage, hoping that, in the words of the passage, *Ogbonis* would become noble and inherit the Kingdom of God. Chief Olubọbokun informed the author that God had already spoken to him in a dream to this effect.

1 There are six degrees: *Ọmọ, Awo, Ogboni, Ẹgan Arin, Ẹgan Oke* and *Iwarẹfa*, then there were thirty titles listed in the Constitution of the 'Reformed Ogboni Fraternity' which the writer saw. Cf. Appendix for the distribution of titles on 18 December 1914 by the founders of 'Christian Ogboni Society'.

2 First Degree, Fellow craft or Second Degree and Master Mason or Third Degree.

3 Dennett, op. cit.

called 'ọpọn epe', that is, 'the wooden bowl of oaths', containing human blood. The novice dipped a piece of white kola-nut into the human blood, the person officiating pronouncing at the same time certain words which the novice was not allowed to understand.[1] The spot on which the oaths were taken was called 'oju iku', that is, 'the spot of death', while the object of worship in *Ogboni* house is *Iledi*. The Bible was enclosed in a calabash and 'Christian' songs and prayers began and ended meetings. One of the signs of the cult is a three-finger salute which outsiders are made to believe stands for the Trinity.[2] Like the Bible which is laid in the so-called altar in the European Lodge, and is used in initiation, the Bible was kept in the 'calabash' as a ritualistic accessory without any intrinsic value of its own.

That indigenous religion and Christianity should jostle together was clear from the initiation of a 'heathen' chief as an 'associate' to act as a 'link' with the traditional cult, thus making the traditional and the 'Christian Ogboni Society' members common members of one Body, in the adoption of the *Ẹdan* images, of the signs and passwords, the calabash and the exact title of the traditional *Ogboni*. The adoption of the symbols did not render those symbols Christian in character but indicated the reality of the bond which united the two Bodies of which those symbols thus became a common possession. Nor was the placing of the Bible in the 'Calabash' (the *ọpọn epe* mentioned above) more than a window-dressing, for its significance was shown in the words, 'Dare you look at it?'[3] said to the initiate. To Christians this was irreverence if not profanity.

But the 'Christian Ogboni Society' did not see itself heathenizing Christianity but vice versa. Christianity was looked upon as the 'mother' of *Ogboni*, and the members of this Society believed that they were the best exponents of the right doctrine of Christianity. By adopting the symbols and signs of indigenous *Ogboni*, declared Euba, the symbols and signs had lost their original 'heathenish' connotation 'but in their new light have shed lustre on our most holy religion' (Christianity). The object of the Society was stated to be 'the amelioration of our race and the uplifting of our brethren in the interior. It believes that by the exercise of Christian influence a brother-hood of love will be formed throughout the length and breadth of Nigeria.'[4]

1   C.M.S. CA2/096, J. B. Wood to H. Venn, 5 Sept. 1861.
2   Hint by Chief Ọdọfin Olubọbokun.
3   Encyclical by Bishops Tugwell and Oluwọle in 1916 entitled 'The Christian Reformed Ogboni'.
4   N.A. Ibadan C.M.S. Y1/5 File 10, Rev. W. Euba to Mackay, 19 Oct. 1916.

Bishops Tugwell and Oluwọle were suspicious of the new Society and sought to crush it. Ministers who had joined it were asked to leave it (a thing they could not do) and Ogunbiyi was asked to give up his effort in spite of his declaration in his parish magazine that the new Society stood 'on all fours with any recognized fraternity'. In point of fact the Church Missionary Society had pronounced against *Ogboni* as early as 1861, and the hope was cherished that the institution 'must be exterminated by the Gospel'.[1] But the revivification of this cult and the attempt to 'Christianize' it raise a number of questions which would be difficult to answer in face of the non-proscription of European freemasonry by the Church.

One of the problems presented to Christian missions was the issue of title-taking by Christians. How far would it be consistent for Christians to take titles and become chiefs without at the same time running into the spiritual dangers of the 'heathenish' rites that went along with these titles? This question was most important among the Ondo and the Ibo. Every Ondo man must take a title before he could claim a recognized position in the community. Among the Ibo, authority and prestige varied according to the grades of title taken.[2] Everybody who was anybody must take *Ọzọ* title if he were to take part in the administration of the village. After the conquest of Iboland the administration had to recognize the importance of the *Nditchie* (those who look after things) who constituted the executive council and selected Warrant Chiefs appointed to represent towns and villages through them, the *Nditchie*.

If Christians were to be debarred from taking titles or becoming chiefs, how would Christians become important in Nigerian society? Would evangelization not be thus hampered and important men and chiefs become alienated from Christianity? If the chiefs who wielded political power were alienated against Christianity, what hope would there be for permanence of this creed in Nigeria? Christian missions did not ask these questions. Rather, on the whole, they were pragmatic, allowing circumstances to direct their decision. The C.M.S. advised the Ondo to consider the problem according to individual conscience. In Iboland the Ibo agents of the C.M.S. Mission defended title-taking vigorously[3] and the court clerks produced by missions took titles without any desire to request the guidance of the white missionaries. In Old Calabar the United Presbyterian Mission recognized the right of Christians to become members of *Egbo*, leaving

1 C.M.S. CA2/o68 Maser to Henry Venn 10/9/1861.
2 J. I. Orakwe: *Onitsha Custom of Title Taking*, Onitsha; R. N. Smith: 'The Ibo People', Ph.D. Cambridge 1929, pp. 159–69.
3 *The Church and Native Customs*, C.M.S. Press, Lagos, 1914.

judgment to individuals. In the Niger Delta the African missionaries, as has been mentioned, encouraged the converts to join the *Owu-Ogbo* cult and thereby become a wholesome influence on the society. By discouraging Ogunbiyi, who suspended his activities until 1932, *Ogbonis* were driven into the African Churches, who readily recognized them and accepted them into full membership.

There were very important economic factors that could not detach converts in Ibibioland, Old Calabar and Iboland from their secret societies and title-taking. In the cases of *Egbo*, *Ekpe* and *Ozo* title-taking, membership was a guarantee of economic security for the aged, who benefited from the high fees which new members paid at initiation. These societies therefore performed in a sense the functions of insurance companies in European countries. There was also the fact that members of *Egbo* had separate lands and palm trees to which non-members could have no access. Furthermore in the case of *Egbo* and *Ozo* titles property could be inherited only by the children who had joined the society or had taken titles themselves. It is plain then that if Christians would join these societies and take titles, Christianity would spread, for Christians could bring their progressive ideas forward in the meetings of the Ibo villages. Also missions could have stressed the honourable side of the title system, in expanding and developing higher ideals, such as fines imposed upon members who stole, or in the *Ebre* among the Ibibio, fines imposed upon any men who showed discourtesy to women. The title system and the secret societies would have been made instruments, rather than impediments, of Christianity.

Ogunbiyi's step is of the greatest importance in the social history of Nigeria. If he did not renounce his membership of the Masonic Lodges, he at least encouraged *Ogboni* to supersede foreign freemasonry numerically. Africans who would have joined foreign Lodges patronized Ogunbiyi's *Ogboni*. That he ultimately succeeded is shown by the fact that Masonic Lodges are now confined to centres like Lagos, Ibadan, Jos, Kano, Kaduna, Enugu and Port Harcourt, places where white officials are concentrated. On the other hand what is now known as the 'Reformed Ogboni Fraternity' has spread throughout Nigeria. By 1951 the number of Masonic Lodges in Nigeria was sixteen only, while the Reformed Ogboni Fraternity conclaves were 124, including one in London. By being scattered all over the country the *Ogboni* cult has attempted to promote, and claims to have promoted, brotherhood among the important tribes of the country such as the Yoruba, Ibo, Hausa, Efik and Ibibio—tribes whose parochialism hitherto hindered brotherly contact with one another. Though traditionally a Yoruba institution, it has broken tribal frontiers and has imposed a brotherliness that surpasses natal brotherliness. Thus Ogunbiyi as the Olori Apena, General Secretary, conferred Iwarẹfa[1] titles on members of the different tribes. The cult is also a brotherhood that transcends political affiliations, according to Clause 18 of the Fraternity's constitution. Since the majority of the élite such as lawyers, ministers of religion, magistrates, politicians, merchants and contractors are members of the Reformed Ogboni Fraternity, what happens in effect is that a cultural unity is achieved among them. A few nationalistic aspects of the cult are clear from its regulations. The clothing used at meetings is Nigerian and the language employed at meetings and for passwords Yoruba.

It should not be supposed that Ogunbiyi completely resuscitated the indigenous *Ogboni*. Membership of the indigenous cult was mainly for important people, chiefs and their children, and they were predominantly illiterate. They had no written constitution and the institution was political, administrative and judiciary. The so-called Christian Ogboni was for a new class of people, the educated Africans who in the traditional setting, would not have qualified for membership. It had no political, judicial and administrative powers but is of great cultural importance. The point should be emphasized that it has however surpassed the indigenous one and educated Africans retain the leadership to which kings and Ọbas submit.

In 1916 there were three conclaves only. These were in Lagos, Ijero-Ekiti and Ado-Ekiti. In face of the objections raised by Bishops Tugwell and Oluwọle in 1916 Ogunbiyi suspended his activities for over fifteen years. It was not until November 1932 before the fourth conclave appeared, in Benin City. In the next twenty years 123 conclaves were founded. Ogunbiyi resumed his activities after 1930, after he had fallen out with the Church Missionary Society and his licence as an Archdeacon had been withdrawn on the instruction of the Government. Ogunbiyi retorted by founding his own church at Ikeja. He seems to have enjoyed the sympathy of many of the African ministers, who refused to ostracize him ecclesiastically and therefore invited him frequently to participate in their church services. He came back to favour when, in the forties, L. G. Vining became Bishop, later Archbishop, of the province of West Africa. Vining was himself a freemason and he became convinced that *Ogboni* was no more than freemasonry. The movement changed complexion when it ceased to be a 'Christian' cult but assumed the name of Reformed Ogboni Fraternity, embracing 'Christians', 'pagans', Muslims and all classes of religious creed. It is paradoxical that the cult today numbers many of the high divines of the Anglican Church

1 The highest grade in the *Ogboni* hierarchy.

in Nigeria and ministers of other denominations. In fact this writer has been reliably informed that there are dioceses in Nigeria today where ecclesiastical promotion in the Anglican communion is no longer based on spiritual and academic ability, but depend solely on membership of this decidedly anti-Christian cult. In the main the prophecy of the Reverend W. Euba in his letter to a missionary who sympathized with the 'Christian Ogboni Society' in 1916 has become true. 'The fraternity will be found as time goes on, not a vicious and dangerous movement,' pronounced Euba, 'but as a handmaid, a loyal and faithful ally of all missionary enterprise and an indispensable auxiliary to Christian efforts.'[1]

The place of cultural nationalism in the evolution of modern Nigeria must be strongly emphasized. With Ethiopianism it provided sufficient scope for articulation of nationalist sentiment among the educated Africans, which unpreparedness for political control could not make them turn to a distinctly political demand. The importance attached to cultural nationalism was shown by the fact that practically all important figures, except Herbert Macaulay who had to advocate it in later years, during the period being investigated either returned to some African customs, however incompletely, or advocated return.

This was why all administrative measures from 1900 to 1914 were criticized in the light of preservation of indigenous culture and institutions. Governor Macgregor was compelled to defend his Forest Ordinance and Native Councils Bill on the cultural plane in the bar of British public opinion, represented by the Aborigines Protection Society, who accused him of assaulting immemorial vital institutions. The former was criticized by nationalists on the grounds that indigenous forest regulations were being upset and Yoruba land tenure being violated. The latter, which sought to give the Governor authority to appoint rulers, was condemned as an unsolicited blow on the indigenous democratic procedure of election of chiefs and on the traditional form of administration.[2]

Cultural nationalism was at the root of the opposition of all Africans to the attempts of the Lagos Government to provide electric light and 'pure water supply' for Lagos. Their opposition was not just a 'protest movement'. Nor was it one of implacable aversion to the taxation that the acceptance of the two schemes would imply. For, amusing as it may seem to us, educated Africans were genuine in their belief that European civilization was responsible for

1 N.A. Ibadan, C.M.S. Y1/5 File 10, Rev. W. Euba to Mackay, 19 Oct. 1916.
2 *Lagos Weekly Record*, 7 and 21 Sept. 1901.

the brevity of life among themselves; that the high rate of infantile mortality was to a great extent caused by the European clothing heaped upon children; that the white man's alcohol brought sterility upon their women, and that European civilization destroyed the commercial instinct of Africans in contact with it. Their conviction was reinforced by statistics which indicated that in spite of sanitary measures by the administration to improve the healthiness of Lagos, the mortality rate rose from 10 per thousand to 40 per thousand between 1881 and 1908.[1] It is nothing to wonder at therefore that when in 1908 Egerton brought forward his scheme for a 'pure water supply' on the grounds that it would help to reduce the death-toll, the local press commented, 'If the effort to procure an improved or "a pure water supply" should take the same trend that other measures of improvement appear to have taken it would amount to the people being taxed in order to improve themselves off the face of the earth—a consequence which as everybody knows has not been wanting in the wake of European civilization in more than one instance.'[2]

On the whole evidence shows that uncontaminated Africans, though dazzled by the white man's technical marvels, were not enamoured of European culture as it manifested itself in Nigeria. The Lagos chiefs who marched to Government House in 1895 with native lamps believed that, for them, these lamps were better than the European electric light the Government promised to supply[3] and they refused to have it after an electric plant had been installed. Although Governor Macgregor explained to Ibadan chiefs that they would benefit and then progress would be brought to Ibadan if their land was surveyed, yet he failed to persuade them to accept a surveyor. Intensely suspicious of any innovation they had no reason for rejecting the Governor's dangerous gesture other than that 'their forefathers had no surveyors'.[4]

The rise of cultural nationalism showed educated Africans seizing leadership in the cultural as in the political and economic activities. On the political plane they were becoming the spokesmen for all Nigeria, while in economic activities it was the Christians who took the initiative in the cultivation of cash crops like cotton, cocoa and rubber. In the same manner they were destined to determine the cultural pattern which Nigeria has since evolved—an amalgam of the traditional and alien, the components of which vary with particular

1 Ibid. 4 Sept. 1909.
2 Ibid.
3 Ibid.
4 C.O. 147/155, Macgregor to Chamberlain, 26 May 1901.

custom and institution. In clothing, name-pattern, education, greater respect for the English language than for the vernacular and in narrow concept of family and its obligations, it was the Christians—not the chiefs or 'pagans'—that set the example for the others to follow.

On them [Christian missions] the future of Africa mainly depends. British occupation and British mercantile operations have not of themselves done much, nor can they of themselves do much, for even moral and social progress.

African Times,
1 April 1878

9 The Missions and Education

The greatest weakness of the cultural nationalists was that they emphasized only the negative results of missionary enterprise on Nigerian society. But the Christian missions were more than destroyers; they were builders as well and, to some extent, preservers. Upon the Christian missions devolved the task of preserving the vernacular against the wishes of their converts and the indifference of the administrators who preferred the English language. By their efforts the main languages of Nigeria have been preserved as a lasting legacy to the Ibo, Yoruba, Efik, Nupe and Hausa. For the reduction of these languages into writing has resulted in a linguistic homogeneity that never existed in these tribes. The importance of this in the awakening of tribal consciousness cannot be overestimated. Take for instance the 'Union Ibo' into which the Bible was translated in the opening years of the century. A synthesis of three almost indistinguishable dialects, it has become the Esperanto of the Ibo, a common vehicle of expression, the language of literature and a bond unifying the third largest tribe in West Africa.

But apart from their linguistic efforts the supreme importance of Christian missions in the evolution of modern Nigeria lies in the fact that it was upon them almost entirely that the social and moral development of the Nigerian peoples fell in the period ending in 1914. This is not to say that British administration had no moral purpose for its presence in Nigeria. But, until the days of Lugard, the moral purpose of British administration in our period was purely negative. The administration justified its presence by creating law and order in place of intertribal wars and anarchy, and by suppressing 'abominable crimes' repugnant to Christian morality. The immense value of this effort on the part of the administration is not to be underrated. It not only facilitated mobility and intertribal mingling, but also made it safe for anyone to travel about freely without the risk of being enslaved in Yorubaland or killed in Iboland. But the administration was mainly engrossed with economic matters—the development of the 'imperial estate'. Never within his experience, declared

Sir Walter Egerton, had he witnessed such 'extraordinarily rapid' economic transformation as that which Southern Nigeria underwent in the first decade of this century.[1]

It is against this background that the efforts of Christian missions in the elevation of the moral and intellectual condition of the Nigerian peoples can be clearly appreciated. They adopted a two-fold attitude to the society. On the one hand they sought to effect a moral and social regeneration through their churches and schools. On the other they exerted themselves to prevent the demoralization of the society by the white man's 'fire-water', liquor. On these two issues, education and anti-liquor agitation, they won the universal approbation of the nationalists in principle. As time went on, however, differences began to occur between the missions and nationalists over the aims, purposes, quality and content of education to be given, and the extent to which anti-liquor agitation should be pursued in the context of the Nigerian situation.

Before 1900 the Western form of education was appreciated and patronized in two areas in Nigeria—in the Niger Delta and in Lagos. In the Delta, long contact with European traders and the usefulness of English and accountancy to the Ijaw and Efik traders made the latter eager to have their children literate. Consequently there arose a few élite, educated in Britain for an average period of eight years. Bonny was perhaps the most zealous in this respect in the nineteenth century, producing George Pepple I, the erudite and sophisticated king about whom much has been said in an earlier chapter; Charles Pepple, the king's brother who joined the civil service of the Gold Coast and Herbert Jombo, who was educated in Liverpool College. One of Jaja's sons, Sunday Jaja, was trained in both Liverpool and Glasgow. In Lagos the educated Africans looked upon Western education as the only agency that could bring about the social revolution they envisaged for Nigeria—that in which literacy would prevail and a host of clerks, technocrats, doctors, lawyers, ministers of religion and educated traders would flourish. By 1900 all these professions were represented in Lagos society.

It is not surprising, then, that in both places mission schools were eagerly welcomed. But in the Delta, patrons of education had to be content with an elementary form of education until the foundation of the Hope Waddell Institute in 1895. This was partly because, in the absence of effective British administration, there was little demand for clerks in the Delta, a demand that made it imperative for missions and educated Africans to concern themselves with secondary education.

It is essential to emphasize that, generally speaking, outside

1 C.O. 520/65, Egerton to Earl of Crewe, 14 Sept. 1908.

284

Yorubaland, the missions did not consider it their business to provide the higher form of education, and opinion varied from mission to mission as to the form and quality of elementary education that should be imparted to their Nigerian converts. Naturally, to all the missions, the main object of all education was religious instruction, especially of the young children who could be weaned easily from the 'pagan' ideas and prejudices of their unyielding parents. The elementary day schools were an evangelistic agency of the highest importance. All the knowledge that was considered really essential to impart was the three R's with particular emphasis on the Bible and religious tracts translated into the vernacular. Great emphasis was placed on character training and spiritual development, rather than on the raising of the status and material standing of the pupils and converts in society. The ideal of many of the missions was to make their converts spiritual and moral automatons, to live literally as the 'unlearned and ignorant' apostles of old, according to the tenets of the new faith. To this end the children were overdosed with religious instruction and all their behaviour watched and frequently corrected. The children were expected to grow up in an intensely spiritual atmosphere; traditional amusements such as *Egbo* play and dances were discouraged. Moral lapses were not expected and when they began to occur, were severely punished.

It is clear from records that ideally Christian missions wanted to make Nigeria a veritable 'Christian' country. Even though they endeavoured to Europeanize their converts, most of the missionaries deplored the moral effects of European Christianity and denounced Europeans in Nigeria who were not a credit to the Christian faith. Christian missions could hardly favour the nominal Christianity exemplified by many Europeans in Nigeria. To some extent the universal denunciation of their converts by the missions from the eighties onwards, noted already, was not motivated by racial pride alone but also by a genuine indignation that their Nigerian converts were not *par excellence* the moral beings of their imagination. Many of the European missionaries, such as Wilmot Brooke, Bishop Tugwell, Thomas Harding, Oliver Griffin and Walter Miller, left behind unquestionable records of morality, dedication and devoutness. They had their African counterparts. The austere-looking ascetic 'Holy' Johnson thundered vociferously from the pulpit against the moral lapses of his age; Bishop Crowther led a transparently devout and guileless life, while Bishop Charles Phillips lamented that 'my kinsmen (educated Africans) according to the flesh are still guilty, very guilty, inexcusably guilty'.[1] It is easy, then, to understand why the

1 C.M.S. G3/A3/06, Report for July to December 1894.

Protestant missions held a fanatically spiritual concept of their schools and training institutions, and why they were unduly sensitive about 'secular' education. The C.M.S. viewed with horror inspection of their schools by Government officers (Europeans) whom they feared would 'infect' their pupils with their 'loose and secular orientation'.[1]

This fanatical religious concept of schools by Christian missions was central to the development of education in the period covered by this book. It defined the limited scope of their contribution to education during the period and affected vitally the development of secondary schools; it emphasized their view of the proper Nigerian citizen, the Christian, and explains why they wished forcible conversion of 'pagans' and elimination of Islam; it was the basis of divergence between most of the Protestant missions and Government, a factor which retarded the development of education in the period; it conflicted with the wider views of the educated Africans and the masses about education. With the exception of the Presbtyerian Mission and the Society of the Holy Ghost Fathers, Christian missions in Nigeria continued to look at education from the strictly evangelistic viewpoint throughout the period. There was no question of wholehearted patronage of an educational system that would emphasize the social and material needs of their converts and prepare them adequately for various walks of life. Their training institutions were established with the sole purpose of rearing schoolmasters who were to graduate to catechists, deacons and then priests, while girls' schools were established mainly for the wives and fiancées of their male workers.

Outside Yorubaland, until the nineties, the missions were reluctant to give higher education to their converts and many did not believe that their African lieutenants should be given any formal education. In the Niger Mission Bishop Crowther discovered that the best people for the spread of Christianity were those who lacked literary pretensions. They were mainly middle-aged shoemakers, shingle-makers, carpenters, farmers, bricklayers, Government messengers and stewards on board ships, people who had no formal education of any kind or very elementary education for two or three years in a mission school.[2] They were most useful for spade work. What they lacked in formal education they had in wisdom which grew with their age, and tactics which enabled them to deal successfully with the chiefs. They were unsophisticated folk who took the Bible seriously and treated it with deep, pious reverence. In the judgment

1   C.M.S. G3/A2/013, Memorandum of Conference, 22 June 1908.
2   C.M.S. CA3/04 (b), Bishop Crowther, *Journals* Report for 1877.

of all the missions such men lived Christ more than they talked Him. If they needed any training at all, all they were given were periodic courses in Bible study. Even in the more enlightened Yorubaland many missionaries doubted the utility of training institutions. The C.M.S. Training Institution in Lagos provided a three year post-primary course for schoolmasters who were ultimately to become priests. They were not taught the classics, higher mathematics, natural science and higher theology. 'I have very little confidence in Training Institutions in our stage of Christian work and growth,' declared Henry Townsend, 'what I want is a man or rather men who can read the Scriptures in his own tongue and preach the gospel among the heathen as a brother; I don't want a youth confined by intellectual culture till he becomes an individual of superior caste and must carry with him wherever he goes the comforts and show of civilized life.'[1]

In fact, apart from the Wesleyan and C.M.S. Missions, no other mission had institutions for formal training of their employees. The Church Missionary Society was by far the most liberal in matters of higher education for a selected few of their African agents, many of whom were trained at Islington in England and at Fourah Bay College, an institution that was affiliated to Durham University in 1876 and which until the establishment of University College, Ibadan (now University of Ibadan) in 1948 was the main nursery of Nigerian principals of secondary schools and Church leaders. The Wesleyans followed the Anglicans in a relatively poor way. Up to 1914 they produced only one graduate, the Reverend W. Euba, and one matriculant, John Henry Samuel, who, it will be recollected, became Adegboyega Ẹdun. The other missions had nothing to show at all. The Southern American Baptist Mission refused to encourage any of their agents to go to the United States even for advanced courses in theology. The only outstanding Nigerian connected with that Mission is Nathaniel David Oyerinde, who, out of his personal savings, made his way to the United States in 1906 and was made to fend for himself until 1916 when he returned to Nigeria. In 1867 the United Presbyterian Mission scorned the idea that a training institution should be established among the Efik.[2]

The spiritual conception of schools was in the period under survey stretched to the utmost limits by the Society of African Missions in Mid-Western Nigeria in the first decade of this century. Having discerned the fact that many of the converts of the Mission were after education primarily to improve themselves socially and materially,

1 C.M.S. CA2/085 (a), Townsend to Wright, 20 Dec. 1875.
2 U.P. Minutes, 31 Dec. 1867.

Father Zappa, the Prefect of the Mission, became inveterately opposed to schools on the grounds that the true purpose of all education, from the Christian viewpoint, was to develop the moral and spiritual fibres of the converts. In his judgment Christian missions would be committing a 'crime against the souls'[1] of the converts and pupils who employed their acquired knowledge for social services primarily.

From the mission viewpoint, higher education was not conducive to the spread of Christianity in Nigeria. This was because, in the circumstances of a pacified Nigeria, many of the mission agents found one excuse or the other to resign their appointment in mission work in order to take employment in Government services or in commercial establishments. In Bishop Crowther's experience most of the agents who had grammar school education ultimately went over to the Royal Niger Company or became traders on their own account. In 1900 the C.M.S. Training Institution at Asaba, which had been established as a nursery of the Niger Mission in 1895, had to be closed down because most of the trainees left the Mission for secular appointments. It is significant to note that one of the trainees was Obed Azikiwe, father of Dr Nnamdi Azikiwe, President of the First Republic of Nigeria, who in 1899 resigned his appointment as a Junior schoolmaster in Onitsha waterside for a secular post.[2] In Yorubaland also it was not difficult for African agents to find convenient excuses for leaving mission for Government jobs. Henry Carr, the earliest African educationist in Nigeria, left his teaching position in the C.M.S. Grammar School, Lagos, for a brilliant and more lucrative career in the Civil Service. When in 1902 the Reverend J. H. Samuel was 'scorned' by his colleagues for accepting the honorary post of Secretary to the Lagos Institute, a literary discussion institution founded in the previous year, he made it an excuse for throwing away the £100 per annum mission job and took up the secretaryship of Egba United Government, a post for which he was paid a yearly salary of £250. As at present the Civil Service was more lucrative than the Church. A clerk, if he had sufficient intelligence, could rise to a scale of £300 per annum, as opposed to the ordained man in the Church whose maximum yearly earnings were about £100. Also, as at present, the legal and medical professions were most rewarding. In 1914 a lawyer hardly made less than £500 a year, while there were many who earned as much as £1,800. Medical practitioners made only a little less than the lawyers.

However, it would be untrue to say that none of the Christian

1 J. M. Todd: *African Mission*, 1964, p. 122.
2 C.M.S. G3/A3/08, Dennis to Baylis, 15 Sept. 1899.

missions saw the urgency of higher education for the Nigerian peoples, or that they did nothing at all in educating many converts for various walks of life. In fact, through the efforts of educated Africans, the C.M.S. founded a Grammar School in 1859 and the Wesleyan Mission, the Methodist High School and Training Institution in 1877. Both of them were to a great extent clerk-making machines. The Wesleyan High School taught book-keeping, mathematics, shorthand, accountancy and penmanship. In the eighties both the Society of African Missions and the American Baptist Mission followed suit and established St Gregory's College and the Baptist Academy respectively. But they argued, rightly of course, that advanced education was not their business but the Government's. In 1882 the C.M.S. were prepared to teach chemistry, mechanics, drawing, French and scientific farming if the Lagos Government would provide sufficient grants. They also suggested the cultivation of rubber and indigo in Yorubaland and urged a Nigerian naval engineering and shipbuilding yard.[1]

But, as will be shown presently, from the eighties onwards the missions were no longer interested in grammar school education, which devolved entirely on the peoples themselves. Elementary schools became their real concern, especially in the interior after 1900. These schools became the most effective agency of evangelization, as *Pax Britannica* shattered the indigenous world, created new values, new tastes, new standards of life, new hopes and new vistas. Education became the greatest boon that could be conferred on the masses. The rapid economic development, the establishment of 'Native' Courts and Councils, Posts and Telegraphs, the introduction of the bicycle and commercial lorries, construction of motor roads and the 'iron horse'—all these introduced a new wealth, opened up countless opportunities, excited immeasurable hopes and created fresh values. To the masses education was the only key that could unlock the mysteries and prosperity of the new world being created. In Yorubaland the prestige of the chiefs fell sharply and passed on to the white man's scribblers, the clerks who could appropriate other people's wives with impunity or to the converts who could elope with ladies of their own choice without paying dowry. So high did the prestige of learning become that, as it was recorded, it was *infra dig.* for a man who knew how to read or write to carry any load of any kind, including Bibles and hymn-books which had to be carried for the Christians.[2] In Iboland the court clerk became the most influential person in the village. He was even more important

1 C.M.S. G3/A2/01, J. A. Maser to R. Douglas, 25 Oct. 1882.
2 C.M.S. G3/A2/012, Report of visit for April and May 1900 by Bishop Tugwell.

than the European administrator who did not understand the vernacular and had to rely on the often misleading and false interpretation of the clerk.

This was the tempting environment that made the elementary school of the highest importance in the strategy of the Christian missions. For the first time, outside Lagos, Abẹokuta and the Niger Delta, village upon village hankered after missionaries, were prepared to erect buildings for teachers and pay the cost of educating their children. In Yorubaland demand for the white man's education was confined mainly to the Ẹgba and Ijẹbu. In the far interior there was little inducement to seek education. As has been pointed out in an earlier chapter, the administrative machinery set up was not only gradual over Yorubaland but was not as elaborate as in Eastern Nigeria. Traditional contempt for the 'book' people continued, and the chiefs in Ọyọ, Ibadan, Isẹyin and Shaki preferred to hand over slaves to the missionaries to be 'spoilt' rather than to part with their own children. Time and again many chiefs complained that education was of no use to them because once educated their children would run away to Lagos. In later years, as the writer's knowledge of the Ọyọ and Isẹyin situations reveals, the chiefs were to regret that their deliberate unkindness to the unprivileged children they handed over to missionaries resulted in the social advancement of the children, many of whom became council clerks and ministers of religion and wielders of strong political influence in independent Nigeria.

In Abẹokuta where the Ẹgba United Government was being directed to a great extent by the *Saros*, the local Anglican community and the local government patronized education with a renewed vigour. In 1904 it was estimated that there were not less than 2,000 schoolchildren in Ẹgba schools. In 1908 the Ẹgba Anglicans, aided by patriotic non-Christians, demonstrated self-effort by founding the Abẹokuta Grammar School, the first secondary school in Nigeria that was not directly founded by an alien Christian mission. The Ijẹbu became the most enthusiastic patron of elementary education. Literacy spread among them to the extent that the C.M.S. Bookshop had to restrict the quota of books to the Ijẹbu, whose avidity for learning made them buy up most of the books at the expense of the rest of Yorubaland. The unintentional monopoly of the Ẹgba and Ijẹbu in the patronage of education is a decisive factor in the development of Western Nigeria, for these two tribal groups have since 1900 produced the largest number of well-educated people in the Government services, in politics and in mercantile establishments.

It was in Iboland that an insatiable desire for education rose to fever pitch. Once the religious cohesion provided by the Long Juju

had been demolished, the traditional intervillage and interclan warfare that had been the main feature of these atomized people was
transformed into rivalry for the white man's education. Having
tasted the military power of the white man most of all the Nigerian
peoples, the village world collapsed much more quickly than the
urban world of the Yoruba. Thousands rushed into the village school
where missions made acceptance of religious instruction the only
condition for admission. The desire of the Ibo for education compelled the Society of the Holy Ghost Fathers to revolutionize its
evangelistic strategy. The man who saw the necessity for doing this
was Father (later Bishop) Shanahan, perhaps the best known missionary to the Ibo. Hitherto Roman Catholic missions throughout
the world had carried out their activities by the strategy of the
'reductions', or Christian villages. By this system slaves were purchased and settled around the priests, completely cut off from the rest
of the community. This system, which had proved a great success in
Paraguay, Father Shanahan observed, could not work among the
Ibo, and was the main reason for the slender rewards this Society had
received after twenty years of hard work. For freemen regarded
Christianity as a religion for slaves. Now that the freemen wanted
schools, they were not opposed to their children being given religious
instruction so long as education was provided. The Society thus took
the Christian faith to the Ibo people through the village school,[1] and
together with the Church Missionary Society prepared the Ibo
people for 'catching up' with the Yoruba, who had the advantage of
missionary enterprise fifty years earlier than they.

Christian missions were to a certain extent disappointed in their
schools, which could not fulfil completely the moral and spiritual
purpose they expected of them. In a way they defeated their own
ends because the Christianity inculcated in their elementary schools
could not strike deep roots in the absence of an intellectual development that could match the principles of the new faith. Their converts
could not accept the Bible in the simple manner the Christian
missions expected. The examples of European officers, traders and
educated Africans were a greater lesson than the precepts the missionaries were imparting. The material wealth and social advantages
of the new world in which the masses found themselves were a greater
appeal than abstract Christian morality. The masses were not ready
for the moral programme of the missionaries; rather, in effect,
together with other agencies, Christian missions destroyed the high
morality of indigenous religion without succeeding in replacing it
with Christian morality. Manifestations they did not bargain for

[1] P. J. Jordan, op. cit., pp. 91–4.

were the results of the education they gave. Sexual immorality in Nigeria began earlier among the so-called Christians than among the 'pagans' and was common among the African staff. The mission pupils became arrogant, disrespectful and dishonest. Most of the parents in the interior of Yorubaland regretted that they ever allowed their children to be 'educated'.

Nor were the school children interested in the vernacular education, the real object of the mission schools. Outwardly the pupils conformed to the compulsory routine of worship at school but only wanted English education. Outside the school the children neglected the vernacular Bible and literature. Ibo children went to the extent of complaining to the C.M.S. that they had enough religious instruction in the church and Sunday schools and wanted to have no more of it at school.[1] Thus, much against their intention, the C.M.S. had to provide English education to Iboland so that they might not lose ground to the Roman Catholics and contact with the people.

The educated Africans regarded education as the greatest social blessing of missionary propaganda to Nigeria. Like the missions they believed that secular education alone was a dangerous thing that would destroy the traditional morality without replacing it with any other kind of purposeful morality. It is essential to emphasize that it was upon them and the converts, rather than on the missions, that the financial responsibility for both elementary and secondary education fell. In Lagos the C.M.S. established a local School Board in 1876 to relieve Salisbury Square of financial responsibility gradually. By 1882 the School Board financed nine elementary schools with 814 scholars at an expense of £370 3s, while the C.M.S. retained seven elementary schools, three higher schools and a staff of twenty-one teachers at the cost of £1,274 9s 9d. In 1910, of the 120 schools in the Yoruba Mission, only nine were directly under the C.M.S. and looked to the Society for financial support. By 1880 the Lagos Circuit of the Wesleyan Mission was responsible for all its day schools.

Within their financial capacity the efforts of the people were most liberal. In Lagos the schools and teachers were maintained from regular Sunday collections, special fees, school fees and the paltry but significant Government grant. Fees in the elementary schools varied from 4d to 6d monthly, and in the non-boarding secondary schools from £4 4s to £6 6s a year. In the interior of Yorubaland fees ranged from 3d to 6d a month, while in Iboland those who wanted English education paid in advance a graduated fee from one to two shillings per quarter. From 1911 onwards Ibo children had to pay all the salaries of their teachers and for the equipment used in the school.

1   C.M.S. G3/A3/011, Memo. on education for committee, by J. Brandreth.

From the eighties the interest of Protestant European missionaries in the secondary schools in Lagos was virtually dead and their control passed to Africans. From the beginning the C.M.S. had left the principalship and teaching in their Grammar School to the Africans. Until his death in 1878 Babington Macaulay, a son-in-law of Bishop Crowther's and founder of the school, was the principal. The principalship passed on to Henry Johnson, M.A., from 1878 to 1880, to Isaac Oluwọle, one of the first graduates of Fourah Bay College with B.A. Durham, from 1880 to 1893, and then to Fanimokun, also a Fourah Bay College graduate, until the end of our period. Likewise the Wesleyan Mission handed over their High School to H. Samuel and W. Euba, and the Baptist Academy was headed by a Negro, S. M. Harden. Even the Wesleyan Girls' High School was handed over to an African lady principal, Mrs Juliana Campbell, until 1892, when the school was closed down for twenty years because the Wesleyan Mission had no interest in it and the Africans could no longer maintain it.

The motives behind the missions' waning interest in secondary grammar schools should be clearly grasped. These schools were serving no evangelistic purpose because the students were already Christians. Moreover, since in the case of the Wesleyans and C.M.S. the grammar schools had training sections as well, it was clear to the missions that the best students concentrated on the secular subjects with the hope of ending up with a career other than that of the Church. This meant that the less clever students were those who concentrated on religious instruction. Even by 1891 it was becoming clear that unless the missions removed their training departments to the interior they would soon begin to lose even the less clever people. With the encouragement of the administration, which by the Education Ordinance of 1891 sought to encourage professionalism in teaching by supplementing salaries of teachers, the brighter pupils could earn the Government certificate.

Apart from other factors, then, it was this unsatisfactory nature of the grammar schools in Lagos, from the evangelistic viewpoint, that made both the Wesleyans and Anglicans decide to found training colleges. Opinion was in favour of colleges that would be located far in the interior, which would produce evangelist-teachers who would help in the spread of Christianity in the ever-widening missionary field. The Church Missionary Society blazed the trail with the Ọyọ Training Institution, conceived in 1893 and born in April 1896. It began with ten students, one of whom lived into the present decade. The following year it became a fee-paying institution. Students were to pay £6 per annum and were expected to serve the Mission for not less than five years after the completion of their course. The important feature of the institution in its early days was that it set out to produce vernacular preachers, rather than professional teachers, until 1900 when a separate institution was founded in Oshogbo for vernacular evangelists. Nevertheless, until the end of our period the institution, which became the famous St Andrew's College, did not produce professional teachers, but amateurs who looked to the priesthood as their ultimate profession. In 1895 the C.M.S. also established the Asaba Training Institution, the aim of which was to produce vernacular preachers who would remain primitive cultivators as well and live on the same material level as the people they were to Christianize. But, as mentioned already, this institution had to be closed down in 1900 because the students conceived the institution in terms other than those on which it had been founded. Other missions established their own. In 1896 the Baptists laid the foundation of what flowered into the Baptist College, Iwo. In 1901 the Wesleyans succeeded in putting their long-standing ideas into action by establishing in Ibadan what was to become Wesley College. The Society of African Missions, typically, waited until 1922 before establishing a training college in Ibadan.

The withdrawal of all interests in secondary school education by Christian missions was the primary reason for the impoverishment and the unsatisfactory condition of the secondary schools in Lagos. Statistics which have survived show clearly that the largest source of income was fees which more than maintained the poorly paid unqualified teachers. The Government grant was no more than one-fifth of the fees[1]. Moreover, by the way the Government gave grants after 1881—payment by results—the schools were tempted to multiply subjects in order to earn the largest grant. The standard of education was consequently very low. Teachers were inefficient and often resigned to seek better employment with the Government or commercial houses. For instance between 1897 and 1908 twenty-four teachers resigned from the C.M.S. Grammar School, Lagos. So bad was the situation that in 1898 the Lagos Government, with the approval of the educated Africans, offered to assume responsibility for and control of secondary education, leaving primary education to the missions. The latter, however, for fear of secularism, spurned the offer. A Lagos Governor observed that most of the clerks supplied by these secondary schools were 'illiterate and ignorant' and that 'a radical change was imperative'.[2]

1 Cf. Reports on C.M.S. Grammar School and Girls' School in C.M.S. G3/A2/012 and G3/A2/013.
2 C.O. 147/132, H. MacCallum to Chamberlain, 1 May 1898.

The consequences of the inadequacy of secondary education and the missionaries' emphasis on education for spiritual ends were considerable. While the lower posts in the Civil Service and mercantile establishments were filled by the products of these schools—the demand for clerks was never satisfied—the higher posts went not only to Europeans but also to Sierra Leonians and West Indians. In 1914 ninety per cent of the African clerical staff in Northern Nigeria were non-Nigerians. Henry Carr was compelled to press in 1914 for 'importation from outside the country of a large number of suitable and competent men for service as clerks if not as schoolmasters'.[1]

Furthermore the missions monopolized the intelligentsia of the country for a long time, for the priesthood was the only lever for the poor to higher education in Fourah Bay and Britain. Between 1878 and 1908 there were twenty Anglican Yoruba sent to Fourah Bay by the Lagos Church and the C.M.S. for degrees in theology and arts. In spite of a poor salary—many of them started on £36 per annum— all of them stayed within the missions. The Wesleyans had only one man with a degree, W. Euba. He remained in the Mission until 1912 when he resigned and founded his own secondary school. In the same period only eight educated Nigerians had families rich enough to send them to Fourah Bay College as a preliminary to medical and legal studies in Britain.[2] The concentration of intellect in the Church provided a moderating influence to Nigerian nationalism. The Church intelligentsia devoted themselves primarily to the all-absorbing problems of the rapidly expanding missions. Radical nationalism was consequently confined to very few professionals who, though important Church office-bearers, had more time for purely political matters. Among these were Herbert Macaulay, a professional surveyor, Dr. O. Johnson, brother to the Reverend Samuel Johnson, the historian and Sapara Williams, the most popular lawyer in Nigeria before 1914. Nevertheless these professionals had to sink their radical views and concede leadership to the Church dignitaries. James Johnson remained the most respected nationalist and was made, as pointed out already, President of the local auxiliary of the Anti-slavery and Aborigines Protection Society, which he guided on an ethical basis, dismissing Macaulay, the Secretary, in 1913 when the latter was found guilty of fraud.[3] Until 1914 the Vice-presidency was occupied by Mojola Agbebi, leader of the Native Baptist Church.

1 L.P., 'Education in Colony and Southern Provinces of Nigeria', by Lugard, quotes Henry Carr.
2 C.O. 520/65, Report on Education by H. Carr, enclosure in Despatch No. 609, 14 Sept. 1908.
3 A.P.S. G232, J. Johnson to Dr Agbebi, 11 July 1913.

One aspect of the missions' education programme about which relatively little is known, and for the supposed absence of which they have often been criticized, is industrial education. It is generally remarked that mission education was not related to the real social and economic needs of the society; that the school in the village ought to have concentrated on improvement of agriculture and handicraft, rather than on literary subjects which only produced people who nursed contempt for farming and manual labour, and who usually left the village in search of white-collar jobs in administrative towns.

A close study reveals, however, that the missions made some effort at providing industrial education, but that the prospect of such education flourishing in the circumstances of Nigeria was very remote indeed. Take the latter point first. Indigenous handicraft had very little hope of survival in face of superior imported foreign articles like chairs, tables, drawers, plates, umbrellas and printed cloths, which people generally preferred to indigenous articles. It was, as it still is, out of the question that traditional handicraft could compete economically with the much cheaper and more attractive imported goods. In fact the only room open to the missions, as to the Nigerian Governments today, was to attempt to teach their converts superior European craftsmanship in brick-making, cabinet-making, tailoring, coopering, boat repairing and masonry. This involved importation of tools, a very expensive undertaking.

Moreover, even if the majority of people desired, as they still desire, to have superior technical skill, the resources available to missions were severely limited, while most Nigerians lacked the means to afford superior houses or purchase the necessary tools for scientific cultivation. In places where the missions established industrial schools there is no record that people around the schools expressed any eagerness to abandon the traditional for the superior European skills. In any case, even in Lagos where industrial education might have been expected to be successful, the evidence available shows that the skilled artisans and craftsmen found it difficult to earn a good living, that imported articles were cheaper than locally made goods (a problem still facing local industries in Nigeria today), and that the demand for skilled artisans by the people was very small indeed.[1] Moreover, as is the case in many developed countries today, there was less respect for technical workers than for clerks, lawyers, ministers of religion and medical practitioners.

In Yorubaland industrial education was provided on a limited

1 C.O. 520/65, Report by Henry Carr, Acting Director of Education, 28 Aug. 1908, enclosure in No. 609 of 14 Sept. 1908.

scale at Topo, near Badagry, by the Society of African Missions and at Agbọwa, a small village in Ijẹbu Rẹmọ, by one Ricketts, a West Indian connected with the Colwyn Bay Institute.[1] The former concentrated on coconut, the proceeds of which helped in the expansion of the Mission. At Agbọwa many acres of cocoa and Liberian coffee were planted, but the scheme came to an end within six years for lack of adequate funds. Individuals, traders and the Lagos Government also did something about industrial education. In 1903 the most industrially-minded educated African, R. B. Blaize, committed a substantial part of his fortune to the Industrial Institute which was in that year established at Abẹokuta. Apart from giving elementary training to its Nigerian employees in the Railways, Survey, Public Works and Marine Departments, the Lagos Government for many years gave £500 annually to the Hussey Charity Institution, where renegade boys in Lagos were taught smithywork, carpentry and joinery. But carpentry, masonry and handicrafts did not appeal to most people. What did appeal to a large number of people was the cultivation of export crops such as cocoa, rubber and cotton. Abẹokuta, Ijẹbu-Ode, Ondo and Benin became centres of one or more of these export crops. The Ẹgba in particular received stimulus for the cultivation of cotton by the British Cotton Growing Association which sent one Hoffman to supervise the cultivation on the spot.

Industrial education was no less encouraged in Eastern Nigeria. In 1897 an Industrial Institution was opened in Brass by the Church Missionary Society, and another in Onitsha in the following year. In the former boys of sixteen years of age were accepted for a period of five years' apprenticeship in carpentry. Throughout their training they were boarded free and given allowances. At the end of their training each apprentice was given £4 worth of tools with which to start on his own. The Onitsha Industrial School taught masonry, brickmaking and carpentry. Its students erected many mission houses and made furniture for the Protectorate administration.[2]

But perhaps the most ambitious and most comprehensive industrial education scheme was that drawn up by the United Presbyterian Mission in the last decade of the nineteenth century. Hitherto the missionaries had introduced Liberian coffee, cocoa, arrowroot, paw-paw, ginger, tomato and other fruits, but no Efik cultivated these crops on a commercial scale. In 1893 Dr Robert Laws of the Livingstonia Mission, who had already made a name for his industrial

1 C.O. 147/145, Macgregor to Chamberlain, 16 Nov. 1899.
2 C.M.S. G3/A3/07, Executive Committee, Minutes, 3 Nov. 1897; G3/A3/08, Annual Letter, 1898–99, by Dennis.

school in Central Africa, was sent out to the Efik country to survey Efik industrial needs.[1] The result was the Hope Waddell Institute, a unique institution which had many departments—industrial, teacher training and secondary. Under the superintendence of the Reverend W. R. Thomson, who had been in an industrial institute in Jamaica, the Institute was founded in 1895. Courses were offered to boys in carpentry, masonry, blacksmithing, coopering and naval engineering, and for girls in domestic science and dress-making.

Although the brickworks established at Okorofiong in the hinterland seemed flourishing—88,000 bricks having been made in 1897 and Government orders being substantial—yet the Mission's interest in brickmaking soon waned and in that year it was decided to sell the business to the Niger Coast Protectorate. Perhaps the most successful department was the carpentry department, which obtained apprentices from various villages in the interior and ultimately brought to an end the situation by which Accra carpenters did all important work in Old Calabar.

It is essential to make a brief survey of Government contribution to education in the period with which this work deals, in view of the fact that the largely indirect efforts of the administration have not received due recognition. Moreover, had the Protestant missions co-operated with the administration more than they actually did, the pace of education in Nigeria would have been faster. This is not to arrogate to the administration more credit than it deserved. Until the days of Lugard's second administration (1912–19), administrators took little direct interest in education, while any proposals they made were killed in the Colonial Office. Hence it was not until after 1900 that the Government began to establish schools here and there, and its only secondary school, King's College, Lagos, was founded in 1909. As late as 1914 only slightly more than one per cent of the country's revenue was spent on education, including grants to mission schools.

The first Government financial aid to Christian missions was the sum of £30 distributed equally among the Anglicans, Wesleyans and Catholics in Lagos in 1872. In the following year no grant was made, but in 1874 the grant swelled to £100 to each of the three Missions, and to £200 two years later. The importance of this grant, small as it was, should not be overlooked. For the C.M.S., the largest of the missions, it was only £40 less than the Society's total expenses in 1876, the very time when the Society wanted the Lagos Christians to bear entirely the burden of the primary schools. The significant thing

1   U.P. Minutes, 30 May 1893, cf. Report attached.

about these grants up to 1881 was that no strings were attached to them.[1]

A different situation arose in May 1882, when the first Ordinance by the British administration in Nigeria was promulgated. The implications of the Ordinance for the missions and the future development of education in Nigeria were far-reaching. By declaring religious neutralism in matters of education the administration dealt a potential blow at the very basis of education in the country before 1882. Henceforward the missions became apprehensive of Government avowal of interest in education and whatever financial help it offered. The religious clause of the Ordinance marked the beginnings of the divergence of opinion between Government and missions on the content and purpose of education, a phenomenon that persists to this day. The 1882 Ordinance also saw the administration setting down the conditions upon which it would unloose its purse strings—payment by results. The system of payment by results indicated Government desire to foster intellectualism and not spirituality, the basis on which mission education had hitherto reposed.

But no administration dared brush aside the agitation of the missions for the maintenance of the religious principles on which their schools had been founded. Administrators who perceived education in social welfare terms, rather than in missionary or religious terms, had to deal with a parsimonious Colonial Office and the pressure of the influential Church Missionary Society. Consequently until the first decade of this century the administration could not implement any education scheme, except with the participation of the missions, on the latter's terms. All that the administration could do in 1891 and 1898 was to revise the 1882 Ordinance by making capitation grants on the average attendance of individual pupils or students in the school, in addition to special grants on industrial subjects and the qualification of the teachers assessed by Government examinations.

The official records show in bold relief the bewildering reluctance of the administration to spend liberally on education. In 1899 the three governments of Nigeria—the Lagos Colony and Protectorate, the Niger Coast Protectorate and the Northern Nigerian Government—found it financially impossible to establish a 'Normal School' at a capital cost of £12,000 and an annual current expenditure of £2,075. The scheme, which on paper was designed to train annually twenty-five youths from each region as 'certificated teachers' and 'superior officers', was thrown aside by the Colonial Office on the

1 C.M.S. G3/A2/01, 'The Lagos School Board', Wood to Hutchinson, 27 Apr. 1881.

grounds that the missions would frown at the establishment of such an institution![1] In the same year Henry Carr's proposal to the Lagos Government that the Government should train four Nigerians annually in Fourah Bay College at an estimated annual cost of £500 received no attention.[2]

Nevertheless, the administration showed keener interest than is appreciated. While it did not wish to undertake capital expenditure on buildings and provide teachers, evidence shows that from 1900 onwards attempts were made to increase grants, improve the efficiency of the mission schools and increase its financial responsibility. In 1903 the Southern Nigerian administration offered to assume responsibility for all schools in Eastern Nigeria and in 1910 in Yorubaland, in terms of grants and promotion of efficiency.[3] But these offers were rejected by the C.M.S., by far the largest and most important of the Christian missions in Nigeria, because vital missionary interests were involved in the attempted secularization of education by the administration.

It was unfortunate that the administration in theory scared off the Protestant missions with the conscience clause that was causing an unpleasant relationship between Church and State in England. In its various ordinances the administration harped on the clause at a time when the people (except Lagos Muslims) gave no thought whatsoever to the religious aspect of education. The Government made religion an optional and not an obligatory subject. In practice, as the wiser Roman Catholic missions knew, the clause was of no effect in the interior. No one was aware of its existence; no one objected to his children being taught the white man's faith. In fact, even in Lagos, at the turn of the century, Muslims began to send their children to mission schools.

The real point of dispute between the administration and Protestant missions was one of attitudes and clash of aims. To the missions, as has been mentioned, vernacular education with emphasis on religious instruction was the most important thing. Promotion from one class to the other was determined by knowledge of the Bible and not by ability in the secular subjects. In the C.M.S. Mission in Iboland there was a regulation that children who consistently absented themselves from religious studies and vernacular education should be dismissed, and religious studies took about half the entire

1 C.O. 147/145, Macgregor to Chamberlain, 4 Dec. 1899, and minutes on it.
2 C.O. 147/150, Carr's Education Report enclosed in Denton to Chamberlain, 23 July 1900.
3 C.M.S. G3/A3/010, R. L. Antrobus to C.M.S. Secretary, 28 Mar. 1905.
   C.M.S. G3/A2/013, Minutes of Executive Committee, 14–26 Jan. 1910.

curriculum. On the other hand the administration laid emphasis on the teaching of English and pressed it to the exclusion of the vernacular. In fact Government code pressed the teaching of English to a standard much higher than the C.M.S. felt necessary. Grants were given for secular subjects upon which promotion was to be based. The administration did not care whether its clerks were 'pagan' or Muslim or polygamists, so long as they could write and speak good English, write ornately and make simple calculations. But as far as the Church Missionary Society was concerned the Bible, which by 1910 was being translated into Union Ibo at great cost in time and money, was the main book which the Society wanted its pupils in Iboland to read, and not the English version. This meant that emphasis must be placed upon the vernacular, which the administration did not recognize. It was clear that should the children be allowed to concentrate on the secular subjects they would neglect religious studies.

Fundamental too was the clash of views on the spiritual and financial status of the teachers. For missions the teachers were not professionals but spiritual agents with the priesthood as their ultimate goal, and salaries were so regulated that their teachers were the lowest paid and priests the most highly paid. Schoolmasters became catechists after six years of good conduct and devotedness. Mission workers were taught to receive low salaries as spiritual workers and thus lay up for themselves treasure in heaven. Schoolmasters rose from £1 10s to £3 on becoming Catechists Class II, and to £3 10s as Catechists Class I. After many other years of spiritual devotedness they became deacons and earned £60 per annum. When finally ordained as priests they began at £70 per annum and reached a bar at £80. On the other hand, by its codes, the administration sought to make teachers professionals. Their academic qualifications and efficiency were tested by examinations and Government certificates of three grades awarded to qualified teachers. Then the administration made the financial position of these teachers much better than that of their spiritual superiors. For instance a Government Certificated teacher was started on £60 and Grade I on £80. Should missions accept Government education codes and grants they would be compelled to raise the salaries of Catechists and priests on a considerable scale, a burden they could not bear. In such a situation the missions would not be able to obtain workers as evangelists and priests, for the material appeal of teaching would be too strong for the workers to resist.

The rejection of Government grants by the C.M.S. affected the development of education among the Ibo. But for opposition by

Salisbury Square the first secondary school among the Ibo would have begun as early as 1899. Mission teachers were inefficient and the standard of education was very low. The mission was aware that it was opposing the material and social purpose that was behind Ibo yearning for education. The mission drew up its own code in 1905, revised it in 1910 and set up an Education Department in Onitsha in 1911.[1] How far Government grant would have aided C.M.S. education expansion among the Ibo is illustrated by the rapid development of education under the Society of the Holy Ghost Fathers which depended almost entirely (except for the salaries of the priests) on a Government grant. In 1908 the Society earned £3,077, that is, more than twice of what all the Christian missions in Lagos received for their elementary and secondary schools in that year. The result of acceptance of a Government grant by this Catholic mission is clearly illustrated in its statistical success. In 1906 the Society had 2,057 Ibo pupils and the C.M.S. only 651; in 1909 the figures stood at 2,591 and 1,478 respectively; 6,578 to 4,066 in 1912, 13,158 to just over 6,000 in 1915. In 1918 the Catholic mission registered 22,838 pupils. In 1913 the C.M.S. had 45 schools while in 1918 the Catholic mission had 355 schools.[2] Consequently by 1914 the Catholic adherents had already outnumbered the Protestant adherents in the Ibo country, a factor of the greatest significance in the political and social history of Eastern Nigeria.

Then the substantial financial support given by the administration to the Hope Waddell Institute demands mentioning. Between 1895 and 1900 the Presbyterian mission spent £5,000 on buildings alone and £2,000 every year on maintaining its efficient European staff. By 1899 more than 136 students were in the institution as apprentices. In the following year the Foreign Mission Board decided to add a secondary school section to the Institution for fear that the administration might anticipate the missions and establish 'a purely secular system of education, which will take the children and youth of Old Calabar out of our hands as a Church, and away from the religious instruction and moral influence, which from our own point of view, are the one thing needful, not only for the saving of souls, but for social development'.[3] Consequently the mission and the Southern Nigerian administration were able to reach a convenient agreement in 1902. The Government conceded to the mission that 'religious teach-

1 Cf. Codes in C.M.S. G3/A3/010 and G3/A3/012, Minutes of Executive Committee, August 1911.
2 Statistics of the Society of Holy Ghost Fathers in Jordan, op. cit., p. 140. Statistics of the C.M.S. Niger Mission in G3/A3/013.
3 U.P. Minutes, 26 June 1900.

ing shall have a prominent place throughout the curriculum'. The mission was to continue to provide all staff and admit students from all over the Protectorate. Henceforward, apart from grants based upon efficiency and results and £10 per child sent by the Government to the school, the Government undertook to erect additional buildings to the tune of £10,000—an astonishing undertaking in those days, fulfilled within three years.

The year 1914 marked the end of an era and the beginning of another in the history of education in Nigeria. Up to this year the missions and Government, the two agencies on whom the development of this most important social service depended, seemed to be drifting apart in their conceptions of education. But both agencies needed each other, as has been shown. In 1914 the beginnings of a fruitful co-operation between the two bodies were symbolized in Lord Lugard, whose concern for the development of education in this country is still to be fully appreciated. Indeed the Memorandum on Education in Nigeria which he drew up at the outbreak of the First World War[1] remains the best of such documents which ever emanated from a colonial administrator and in its idealism and boldness remains a challenge to all the Governments of the Federal Republic of Nigeria. Lugard sought to co-operate with the missions on terms acceptable to the latter by fostering the teaching of non-denominational Christianity in 'pagan' areas, by increasing grants to the missions and by setting up an efficient inspectorate that would recommend grants on the moral behaviour of pupils and the sanitation observed in each school.

Lugard's education programme ideally would have brought about a transformation of rural economy and would have modernized village life to the level of rural life in contemporary Europe. Village schools, he said, should be introduced all over the country. Peasants would be taught the three R's, up to Standard Three level, so that they might understand Government legislation and the proceedings of the so-called Native Courts he was establishing. They were to be given simple instruction on rotation of crops, manuring, marketing and cultivation of cash crop economy. Promising children in the rural schools should be given higher technical education on scholarship. The towns should become centres of literary education to produce the much-needed qualified clerks. Scholarships were to be given to clever but poor boys in secondary schools and the children of chiefs should be specially encouraged to go to secondary schools, 'with a view to improving the next generation of school rulers'. Had the First World War not intervened, and had ample funds been available,

1 L.P., 'Education in Colony and Southern Provinces of Nigeria'.

it would not have been difficult for the administration and the missions to work together in the implementation of the scheme.

For a long time to come education remained virtually in the hands of the missions. And whatever the defects of their education Nigeria owes them an incalculable debt of gratitude for preparing her peoples to adjust themselves to the new environment created by *Pax Britannica*. Even to this day the great majority of Nigeria's leaders in politics, in medicine, in law, in the civil service and in education itself owe their beginnings and their positions in Nigerian society to their education in a mission school. In this respect the observation made in the Lagos press in 1894 about missionary enterprise—'of all the agencies which have contributed to the regeneration and development of our country, missionary effort has been the most potent'—is an axiom.[1]

1 *Lagos Weekly Record*, 6 Jan. 1894.

The whole subject of the attitude of the philanthropist towards liquor and sanitation in this country [of Nigeria] is of intense interest to the philosopher. But it is of the deepest importance to the administrator, who cannot but look long for the Madhi or Moses that will turn the minds of earnest philanthropic, and benevolent men from the liquor phantom to sanitation.

Sir William Macgregor
in a paper read to the
Lagos Institute in 1901

10 The Triumph of Gin

The social and moral problem that attracted the greatest attention in Nigeria, Britain and international conferences of European Powers in the period covered by this work was the liquor traffic. For the administrators in Nigeria it was 'the vexed subject' that dragged them before the tribunal of British public opinion from time to time; for the educated Africans the traffic was a calculated attempt by the 'godless' European merchants to destroy the Negro Race; for the illiterate masses in the interior of Yorubaland, gin was equivalent to 'death' and was the cause of sterility among women; for the Niger Delta tribes it was an indispensable evil; for Christian missions it was the greatest danger that hung over Nigeria and the greatest impediment neutralizing their 'civilizing' efforts; for Mary Kingsley and the Liverpool traders it was a salutary prophylactic for the Nigerian peoples; for the humanitarians in Britain it was a 'grave scandal to our boasted civilization and Christianity'; for Lugard and Goldie the liquor trade was unethical and opposed to sound commerce.

In dealing with this most controversial and richly documented subject the unwary historian can easily be carried away on the one hand by the excessive emotionalism, zeal and obsession of the anti-liquor movement in Nigeria and Britain, and on the other by the specious and often deliberately twisted facts marshalled by the administrators who were placed in a most difficult situation. The leaders of the anti-liquor crusade, it must be emphasized, were moral and spiritual zealots who wanted to see Nigeria a teetotal state. They were often guided by fancies and not by facts. All the evils under the sun were ascribed to the liquor traffic—military expeditions, depopulation, infantile mortality, brevity of life among Africans and Europeans, crimes and assumed laziness of Nigerians. They went to the ridiculous extent of claiming that the European 'fire-water' was causing mental and physical degeneracy among the people while drunkenness had infected babes and school children. But the administrators, while accepting that ideally liquor was best prohibited, had their vital interest, revenue, to defend. They minimized the evil of the

307

traffic and employed false arguments for the consumption of the British public.

Trade in spirits by Europeans with West Africa was by no means new in the nineteenth century. It had been one of the most important commodities since the beginnings of the slave trade. Up to the sixties of the nineteenth century, almost the entire spirit trade in the Nigerian coast was in the hands of English manufacturers who exported Jamaica rum. But the absence of customs duties and restrictions of any kind to regulate the quality of the spirit imported enabled the French and Germans to supplant the English manufacturers with an inferior and cheaper spirit, and West Indian rum disappeared altogether. By the end of the century all the gin exported to Nigeria was a concoction of potato spirit, prepared in the cheapest way possible and with no attempt to clear it from impurities. Much was manufactured in Germany and Holland, but most of it was carried by British vessels to the order of British merchants. The wholesale varied from 9d to 1s 6d a gallon, and it could be retailed in Nigeria at a great profit after duty had been paid at 6d a quarter, or less.

It was the coastal areas that were mainly affected by this trade, especially the Niger Delta. It was computed that nowhere else outside Europe and the U.S.A. was this traffic so concentrated as in the Niger Delta. European liquor became an essential element in their marriage, burial and religious rites. According to Sir Ralph Moor, it was the 'chief inducement'[1] to oil production in the interior. In Yorubaland it was confined to the Mahin, Egun, Egbado and Egba, and was becoming a substitute for the traditional kola-nut in entertaining visitors. The point to emphasize is that their addiction to spirits, apart from their pestilential environment, contributed to the 'inferiority' of the coastal tribes to the interior peoples, universally commented upon by contemporary observers.

And it should be added that the imported spirits were not considered good for Europeans; indeed, importation of such spirits to Britain was absolutely prohibited. The Europeans in West Africa in the nineteenth century were as a rule drinkers, and believed that unless they partook regularly a moderate quantity of liquor as a stimulant and preventive they would succumb to 'fever'. But they did not take the spirits imported from Germany and Holland, but the selected ones from Britain.[2]

That trade in liquor increased in proportion to the establishment and extension of British administration in Nigeria is beyond dispute.

1 F.O. 2/84, R. Moor to F.O., 13 Aug. 1895.
2 *West Africa*, 26 Apr. 1902.

But the administration was not responsible for it and could not be charged with not preventing it; liquor was so deeply rooted in the European trade with West Africa that to ask the administration to prohibit it was asking for the impossible. The main fault of the administration between 1861 and 1905 was that it did not regulate the quality and strength of the spirits imported. In Britain the proof standard was 50 degrees trailles measured by Sykes hydrometer, that is, liquor mixed with less than 12½ per cent alcohol. But the administration in Nigeria charged duties on gallons only, whatever the strength. This was an opportunity for the traders who imported over-proof spirits, at times pure alcohol, which after dilution could amount to two or more gallons per gallon. In the light of this fact statistical evidence up to 1905 was not a correct indication of the quantity of gin actually distributed in the country. The quantity might be more than double the official statistics. According to official statistics over one and a half million gallons a year were imported into the Lagos Colony and over two million gallons a year to the Niger Coast Protectorate.

The social effects of this enormous import of over three and a half million gallons on an estimated population of about six million cannot be assessed *per capita*. Only the very few people who possessed the means indulged in it as a luxury. There are records of chiefs in Abẹokuta spending over £500 on gin alone at funerals. Most of the people spent the greater proportion of their wealth on liquor, instead of on useful manufactured goods that would have increased their taste for cotton and other articles that could improve their standard of life. Moreover the distribution of liquor was limited to a relatively small area until the construction of roads and railways made its distribution into the far interior easier, quicker and cheaper. Nor was there any substance in the contention of the administrators that if drinking of imported liquor was prohibited, the people (who were believed to have become addicted to drinking beyond redemption) would develop indigenous liquor. The latter was also falsely believed to be ruinous. If indigenous liquors of palm wine and ọtika made from guinea-corn were as intoxicating or more intoxicating than European liquor, as traders and administrators alleged, then foreign liquor could not have found a ready market.

Except for Mary Kingsley, who was not concerned with the moral aspect of the liquor traffic, the opinion of administrators and independent observers were unanimous that the traffic was doing a great deal of harm to the Nigerian peoples. R. Burton believed that it was a worse thing than the slave trade for the Yoruba. Joseph Thomson was horrified at the effects of liquor in Lagos and the Niger Delta, and observed that it was driving the people to 'a tenfold deeper slough of moral depravity'.[1] Worth quoting is the observation recorded by Major F. D. Lugard in 1895 after his extensive journey in the interior of Yorubaland to Nikki. He wrote:

> The Yorubas amongst whom the poison [liquor] is distributed are a singularly industrious people, eager to engage in trade of all kinds—a people who should long ago have reaped the benefit of their energy and industry in an increase of comfort, and an improvement in social and agricultural appliances, had it not been for the sterilizing and strangling influence of the liquor traffic on all forms of legitimate trade.[2]

As the champion of morality and humanitarianism where Negroes were concerned in the nineteenth century, Britain could not remain indifferent to the ravages of the liquor traffic. Since the anti-liquor movements in Britain and Nigeria were inseparable, a brief look at the crusaders in Britain is essential. Britain assumed the leadership of an international anti-liquor crusade from 1884 onwards. At the Berlin West African Conference Sir Edward Malet, the British chief delegate, was a lonely voice in the wilderness when he urged international control of the liquor traffic. The other delegates were more concerned with the sharing of the African continent and peoples. Both Goldie and Salisbury Square were concerned about the possibility of the Niger basin being flooded with gin. The latter asked the British Government to annex the area at once because, as it claimed, a Hamburg firm was already making preparation to start a liquor trade on the Benue 'and thus a great impetus will be given to this traffic in the article so demoralizing to these uncultured savages, exciting them to carry on to a yet greater extent their dreadful practices of human sacrifices and cannibalism'.[3]

Henceforward the anti-liquor movement gained accelerated momentum. In 1886 the C.M.S. enlisted the support of the Wesleyan Missionary Society and the United Presbyterian Mission, all of whom formed a committee that tried to exert pressure on the British Government to do something to check the flow of the traffic into Nigeria. In March 1887 the Native Races and Liquor Traffic United Committee held its inaugural meeting under the presidency of the Duke of Westminster. In the same year James Johnson held a meeting

1 J. Thomson: 'Mohammedanism in Central Africa', *Contemporary Review*, December 1886, p. 881.
2 F. D. Lugard: 'British West African Possessions', *Blackwood's Magazine*, p. 977.
3 *Church Missionary Intelligencer*, January 1885, p. 52.

with the M.P.s in the Committee Room of the House of Commons, and gave addresses throughout the length and breadth of England. The Archbishop of Canterbury addressed special letters about the traffic to his lieutenants all over the world. On 24 April 1888 the House of Commons unanimously adopted a motion pledging support for the Imperial and Colonial Governments in their efforts to suppress a traffic which was having 'disastrous physical and moral effects' on the benighted peoples.[1] On 4 May 1889 the German Reichstag followed suit.

At the Brussels Conference of 1890 Lord Vivian, the British delegate, incarnated the idealism which had infected the Salisbury administration. He emphasized the high importance Britain attached to the matter and proposed that the distribution and consumption of alcoholic liquors should be absolutely prohibited over all the portions of Africa within European spheres of influence in which their use was not yet established. He also recommended a high tariff, 7s per gallon, to be rigidly imposed wherever the traffic existed. The first proposal was accepted and an area of prohibition was drawn, affecting Muslim Northern Nigeria. As a tariff of 7s a gallon would have crippled, if not killed, the French and German trade with Africa neither of the two powers would agree to a tariff higher than 6d a gallon. The Salisbury administration regretted this and protested that '*Her Majesty's Government are convinced that a duty so low will prove an insufficient and useless check upon the increased consumption of strong drink by the natives of Africa*' and hoped that the British proposals would in future '*serve as bases for negotiations which may be crowned with success*'.[2] This hope was never even half-fulfilled.

The anti-liquor movement in Britain decided to give the Brussels agreement which came into force in 1892 a trial. It was hoped that if the tariff did not prove a sufficient deterrent, subsequent Conferences which would revise the agreement every six years, would ultimately put matters right. The attention of the humanitarian organizations and the Native Races Committee was fixed on the anti-liquor movement in Nigeria and especially on the Bishop of Western Equatorial Africa, Herbert Tugwell. He was looked upon for regular reports on the behaviour of the administration in implementing the Brussels agreement and on its practical results. It is essential to bear in mind that no one as yet, except 'Pope' Johnson and Bishop Tugwell, considered absolute prohibition as within practical politics. Bishop Tugwell did not disappoint the anti-liquor crusaders. But before surveying the movement led by Tugwell it is essential to have a short look at the use Goldie made of the anti-liquor movement in Britain in

1   A.P.S., 'Poison of Africa Papers', No. 2, August 1895.   2   Ibid.

order to discredit the Brassmen who, as Dr Flint has clearly analysed, attacked the Royal Niger Company's establishments at Akassa in early 1895.

A tactician and strategist of uncommon shrewdness, Goldie, having assessed the strength of the anti-liquor movement in which the Church Missionary Society were the most outspoken, paraded himself and his Company, with maximum publicity, as enemies of the liquor traffic.[1] The supposedly anti-liquor policy of the Niger Company also became the most convenient weapon which he used with effect to discredit the Liverpool traders of the Niger Delta who wished to participate in the trade of the Company's territory. When therefore the Brassmen fell on Akassa on 28 January 1895, actually ate a number of the African employees and drank from the enormous stock of spirits in the Company's store, they did not reckon with Goldie and the use he could make of anti-liquor agitation in Britain. The Brass rising ceased to be a localized issue. Both the Lagos Government and the Niger Coast Protectorate administration were dragged in and the whole question of the principles of administration of 'backward peoples' raised up in Britain by the British press, the Aborigines Protection Society, the Native Races and Liquor Traffic Committee, the Church press and the Colonial Office. For the first time British administration in Nigeria was put on trial and its moral purpose defined. Everything revolved on liquor. On its rocks the hopes of Brassmen foundered while the Lagos and Niger Protectorate administrations were condemned as enemies of the people they were governing and of missionary enterprise.

Goldie brought about this situation in the following manner. While the news of the cannibalism of the Brass raiders was still fresh and the real causes of the 'revenge' not yet known, Goldie chose to speak to the Native Races and Liquor Traffic Committee on 28 February. He sent copies of his carefully prepared address to 'all the leading papers',[2] including *The Times*. Goldie was not the man to miss such a psychological opportunity as that afforded by the death of Lord Aberdare, Chairman of the Company, a day before he gave his address. He harped upon it that it was evidence of the Company's anti-liquor policy and the importance it attached to it that such tragedy as had befallen the Company by the Chairman's death did not deter him from giving the address. His trump card was an extract from a speech made by the deceased in 1890 after the Brussels

1 Goldie, Taubman to Salisbury in *African Times*, 1 Sept. 1887. A.P.S., Goldie to Fox Bourne, 11 Nov. 1889. *Church Missionary Intelligencer*, 1887, p. 75; cf. also p. 711 of 1890 issue.
2 L.P., Goldie to Miss Shaw, 15 Mar. 1895.

Conference, illustrating that the Company was the first body to protest against the traffic in Nigeria. On the whole Goldie's speech was a masterpiece of rhetoric and rational argumentation calculated to whip up all the idealism of which his audience was capable. He declared that the Brussels Agreement of 1890, upon which the Committee pledged itself, was a 'dismal failure'; no time was more propitious for an international agreement to bring about, not a raising of duties, but total prohibition and he quoted from debates in German Parliament to show that Germany, the greatest dealer in vile spirits exported to Africa, was ready for such an agreement; he detailed geographical facts to illustrate that all talk of smuggling, usually employed by other administrators in Nigeria as unpreventable, was nonsense, and wondered why Britain, the custodian of morality and vanguard of humanitarianism that had employed the West African Squadron to suppress the slave trade, should not be able to spare a few ships to patrol West African ports and thus prevent the accelerated demoralization of Africans. While commending the efforts of the Committee he was surprised that they were not zealous enough and he urged them to move the whole of Britain into doing something about the 'poison'. Having sufficiently worked up the emotion of his audience he declared that his Company was the only administration throughout the colonial world which ameliorated the conditions of its peoples by completely prohibiting the importation of liquor into nine-tenths of its territory; this was the main reason, he said, why the Company was unpopular and why the Brassmen had attacked its establishments! Hitherto he had advocated the impossibly high duty of 10s 6d a gallon, now he threw down a gauntlet which the wildest anti-liquor maniacs in Britain could never pick up—absolute prohibition.[1]

The effects of his address and the use he made of it were electric. Never had feelings been stirred on this issue as Goldie stirred them up in 1895. The grievances of the Brass traders were no more than the anti-liquor regulations of the Company. This was even sufficient to win to Goldie's side so dangerous a pen as Miss Flora Shaw, later Lady Lugard.[2] Not even in 1908–09, the time when the Commission of Inquiry was set up, did Britain witness such emotionalism and vigour on the part of anti-liquor advocates. Completely taken in and using the data and arguments supplied, in many cases

1 Copy of speech in L.P. (S. 58).
2 L.P., Goldie to F. Shaw, 4 Feb. 1895. Same to same, 15 Mar. 1895. In the latter Goldie rejoiced that he did not miscalculate: 'Let the spirit traffic people abuse the Niger Co. as they wish so long as its policy on this question wins the day as it shall.'

retaining the very words, *The Times* wrote in a leading article on 4 March:

> The rising which has taken place at Brass in the Niger Protectorate, relatively insignificant as it has proved in itself, calls attention to a question which is by no means insignificant. It is the question of the liquor traffic with native races. There is not a doubt left in the minds of intelligent, experienced, and practical men that the supply of intoxicating liquor to the native races is equivalent to the demoralization and degradation of the races concerned and that the first condition of progress in the habits of orderly and industrial existence is to keep the poison of alcohol from their reach. It is not a temperance fad nor a mere philanthropic counsel of perfection. It is the sober decision of unromantic men of business, from one end of Africa to the other, that an essential preliminary to successful administration is to prevent the sale or supply of spirits to the native.

Indeed Sir George Goldie could rightly jubilate in the success of his skill. There was some truth in his observation in June 1895 that the liquor question was '*by far the most important African question of the day*'.[1] On 3 May, he was especially invited by the anti-liquor crusaders to speak at Grosvenor Square and he made the best use of the occasion to discredit both the Lagos Government and the Niger Coast Protectorate. This was the moment seized by Carter to engage in acrimonious correspondence with Bishop Tugwell in *The Times*. Carter and his administration were not only condemned by the British press but also by the Colonial Office, who reproved him for so indiscreetly airing a pro-liquor view. The Aborigines Protection Society actively joined hands with the Native Races and Liquor Traffic Committee, and in August a series of widely circulated 'Poison of Africa Papers', ten in all, painted in the blackest colour the unmitigated wickedness being perpetrated by British administrators who were allowing 'fire-water' to be imported into their territories in the name of revenue. Views of educated Africans like those of James Johnson and R. B. Blaize, were quoted. The British public could not have been unmoved by the appeal of Maliki, the Emir of Bida, to Bishop Ajayi Crowther to petition Queen Victoria to put a stop to liquor which '*has ruined my people very much; it has made my people become mad*'.[2]

Apparently unaware that they were dancing to Goldie's tune, this

---

1 A.P.S., Goldie to Fox Bourne, 20 June 1895, quoted in No. 6 of 'Poison of Africa Papers'.
2 'Poison of Africa Papers', No. 8.

was the time when the anti-liquor agitation in Nigeria reached one of its peaks. Goldie's speech of 3 May was quoted and his arguments were supported. A Lagos newspaper editorialized: 'But for the introduction of this trade in spirits, nearly every producer in the Interior would have been comparatively rich.'[1] Carter's views were disowned. Never in the history of Lagos had African opinion been so strong and unanimous as in the months when anti-liquor hysteria saw the Muslims concerting with educated Africans and Lagos chiefs on 15 August at a rally in which James Johnson, Chief Taiwo, J. S. Leigh and others spoke strongly. Johnson moved the motion, which was unanimously adopted, that

> That this meeting recognizing that the Traffic in spirits, that is, Gin, Rum and other poisonous liquors, introduced into Western Equatorial Africa, is working immense harm, physically, morally and spiritually amongst every section of its communities, and further recognizing that the time has come when a decisive blow should be dealt with against the Traffic, pledges itself to support every effort which may be made in Africa or Europe to suppress it.[2]

This hysteria was contagious. In Abẹokuta 8,207 signatures of Muslims, Christians and 'pagans' were collected and sent to Britain on sheets said to be 250 feet long.[3] Signatures were also collected in Lagos, Ọyọ and Ogbomọshọ.

The man who captured the limelight both in Britain and in Nigeria after 1895 was the austere, gaunt, most vociferous and one of the most devoted ecclesiastics Britain ever sent to West Africa, Bishop Herbert Tugwell. He deserves some analysis. Bishop Tugwell looked upon himself in Nigeria in the spectacles of the medieval popes. For him British administration in Nigeria was expected by the 'Christian Nation' of Britain to fulfil primarily 'Christian' moral and social obligations to Nigerians, in the latter's interest. It was the administration's divine task to aid the Church in promoting 'purity and righteousness'.[4] This included maxims and seven-pounders for the 'pagans' who resisted peaceful entry of missionaries and the Fulani who had supposedly imposed Islam on unwilling Northern Nigerians. No greater blessing was in store for the Nigerian peoples than the British Raj, if its representatives discharged their duties faithfully. Hence Governor Carter was regarded as the right type of governor when he destroyed the anti-missionary Ijẹbu kingdom, but betrayed Britain when he not only attended the opening ceremony

1 *Lagos Weekly Record*, 22 June 1895.   2 Ibid.
3 *Church Missionary Intelligencer*, June 1896.   4 *London Record*, 30 Oct. 1896.

of the Shitta Bay Mosque in 1894 but also pronounced favourable views on Islam. Actually the religious indifference of the European community filled him with dismay and he did compel his countrymen to erect 'Colonial' Churches. Governors could neglect going to church regularly only at the risk of having themselves castigated from the pulpit and being reported as unworthy of their post in the British press.[1]

Bishop Tugwell spared no one, black or white. Horrified by the venereal disease which, he said, was spreading among Europeans in Lagos he forced them to agree to put an end to employment of African women in their 'factories'.[2] Having noticed that the seamen who anchored in Lagos from time to time ran after women and spirits he borrowed over £1,000 to erect the Sailors' Institute to correct their morals.[3] He bullied administrative officers whom he noticed were oppressing the people as if the officers were small children. Even Lugard, when Governor General of all Nigeria, was not spared when during his episcopal tour of the 'pagan' Bauchi Province he came across Muslim officers working there. Lugard had to remove them.[4]

For Bishop Tugwell all other considerations had to be brushed aside where moral principles were concerned. He did not care whose horse was gored, whether the administrators who mistakenly thought they could placate him or the educated Africans, his wards, for whom he had the most potent epithets when they refused to follow him on moral questions. No one could doubt the devotion of this wonderfully energetic man, who sacrificed every personal interest to his episcopal duties. For all his brilliant qualities, however, Herbert Tugwell had a weakness—a mercurial temperament which when added to his fanaticism on moral questions made his actions often theatrical.

It can then be imagined how such a man would lead the anti-liquor crusade. He threw himself into the movement with the verve of an actor. He came to see everything in the spectacle of the liquor traffic. Better Britain had never come to Nigeria, better no pacification, better no trade, no roads and no railways, than to see Britain's representatives allow traders to destroy the souls of innocent Nigerians with 'fire-water'. It is not surprising that Mary Kingsley, the arch-defender of merchants and the liquor traffic, was scandalized by

1 *Lagos Standard*, 14 Oct. 1896; *Modern Society*, 12 Sept. 1896; *Liverpool Mercury*, 2 Sept. 1895.
2 C.M.S. G3/A2/012, Tugwell to Sir Alfred Jones [undated: 1906].
3 M.P., John Holt to E. D. Morel, 21 Jan. 1909.
4 C.M.S. G3/A9/02, Tugwell to Lugard, 3 Jan. 1913 and 4 Feb. 1913; Lugard to Tugwell, 15 Jan. 1913 and 6 Feb. 1913.

Bishop Tugwell and his followers, whom she described as 'a set of wild emotional, vain, cruel, shocking creatures'.[1]

All administrations in West Africa in our period found in liquor the best source of revenue. Without it revenue would be insufficient to run the government. For reasons that will be examined shortly, no administration that did not want a bloody rebellion dared essay direct taxation until after our period. Tax on liquor had every advantage. It was a tax on wealth; it was morally defensible, for the higher the tax the less the quantity of liquor imported would be; so the Brussels Conference and the anti-liquor agitators in Britain and Nigeria imagined. It was also welcome to the administration because, as it was paid through customs, it made collection easy and cheap. In the last decade of the nineteenth century more than 90 per cent of the revenue of the Lagos Government and the Niger Coast Protectorate derived from customs on liquor. In 1906 it was 55·15 per cent and in 1908 49·8 per cent of the revenue. For the administration this revenue was useful for salutary moral and social measures such as railway and road buildings, maintenance of law and order and suppression of 'absurd superstitions'.

For Bishop Tugwell such ratiocination was the crudest of nonsense. How could evil beget good? Judgment must be based on fundamentals—'on grounds of morality'—whether liquor *per se* was good or bad. An administration based on liquor was 'absolutely dishonest'.[2] The liquor traffic was the greatest obstacle to the 'religious and social progress' of Nigeria and could best be described as 'a scandal and disgrace, a dark blot on an otherwise splendid system of administration'.[3] Asked to read a paper on sanitation at the inaugural meeting of the Lagos Institute in 1901 this was how he saw it:

> The greater the import of Spirits the richer the Treasury: and the richer the Treasury the more rapidly we can advance in matters of Reform. We import Spirits for the purposes of Revenue. How is the Railway being built? By Gin. How was the Carter-Denton Bridge built? By Gin. How is the town lighted? By Gin. And now if it be asked How is the Town to be drained, or how are we to secure a good supply and good pure water? The answer is, with Gin.[4]

Bishop Tugwell's crusade was fought by mobilizing the opinion of

1 L.P., Mary Kingsley to F. D. Lugard, 31 Dec. 1897.
2 *The Lagos Institute*, Proceedings, Lagos 1901, p. 29.
3 H. Tugwell: *A charge delivered in St Paul's Church, Breadfruit Lagos on 21st January, 1902*, p. 17.
4 *The Lagos Institute*, Proceedings, Lagos 1901, p. 29.

Christians, 'pagans', chiefs and Muslims of Yorubaland, by speeches at conferences and synods in Nigeria, by speeches at Grosvenor House in London and by articles in *The Times*, which, as said already, had become a convert to the crusade by 1895. The next peak of anti-liquor agitation in Nigeria was reached in 1899. Following an article by the Bishop in *The Times* of 27 March 1899, describing how in his 1,000 mile episcopal tour (mostly on foot) he discovered that 'at every centre in response to my enquiries, I ascertained that drunkenness is on the increase', the merchants in Lagos prosecuted him for libel. For in the same article he also ascribed 75 per cent of deaths among Europeans in West Africa to liquor. He was sensationally arrested just as he was to embark in Lagos for the centenary celebrations of the foundation of the Church Missionary Society. The traders thought that he would be silenced by such a lesson. But they misunderstood their man who was delighted at an event that seemed to him ordained 'of God' who had a 'special purpose to effect by this means'. Moreover he came to be regarded as a martyr by the people and chiefs of Lagos and by the temperance movement in Britain. Never would the Lagos Government forget how embarrassed they had been by the action of the traders. Although the Bishop was prepared to face the court and financial and legal help had been obtained from Britain, the administration judged that the best thing to do was to prevent the court action taking place. No time could have been more ill-chosen by the merchants. The humanitarian pulse in Britain quickened and Chamberlain, the Secretary of State for the Colonies, found himself besieged by anti-liquor crusaders, who quoted from Tugwell's letter to *The Times* and castigated the British Government for allowing 'a public scandal',[1] liquor traffic, to be pulling down the moral and religious edifice missionaries were erecting in Nigeria. The memorialists, including the Duke of Westminster, urged the Government to prohibit liquor in Northern Nigeria and to make stringent regulations that the Lagos railway, which would soon be opened, should not carry liquor at all. Furthermore the British Government was urged to exhort all the other Powers at the forthcoming Brussels Conference to increase the tariff to a prohibitive level.

In the circumstances Chamberlain had to make humanitarian pronouncements and placate the prohibitionists with the assurance that the new Governor of Lagos, Sir William Macgregor, who was just being transferred from New Guinea, would abolish the nefarious traffic as he had done in the latter territory. These proceedings, reported in the Lagos press, stirred up the Lagos masses again. Macgregor, who had been able to prohibit liquor in New Guinea by a

1 Cf. copy of Memorial in C.M.S. G3/A2/09.

14s 6d per gallon tariff, found himself in an entirely new situation in Lagos. The traffic, he noticed, was 'deeply rooted'[1] and to prohibit it would mean suicide to the administration. The Lagos masses, white cap chiefs and Muslims besieged him in Government House and urged him to raise duties from 2s to 5s per gallon at least; to prohibit overproof spirit absolutely; to legislate against railways carrying liquor and to tighten up the ordinances relating to the granting of spirit licences. Absolute prohibition must be his objective, said the mass assembly, if he was to live up to his earlier pronouncement that 'from the first to the last the dominant note of your administration will be to do justice to the aboriginal population [and] to make the natives useful to themselves and others'.[2]

The difficult position of the administration can be best appreciated by the fact that in the nineties and first decade of this century the traders did not willingly acquiesce in the duties levied on their goods. The administrators, who had to take the discontent of the traders into consideration, did not like the rapid rise of duties on liquor which they were instructed to raise from time to time as the anti-liquor crusaders put pressure on the Imperial Government. The Brussels minimum of 6d was more than exceeded. In 1895 duties rose to 2s and in 1899 the Lagos Government could not escape increasing tariff. It actually rose to 3s the next year. Furthermore in 1900 the Lagos Government increased the *ad valorem* duties on all goods from five to ten per cent. The traders, always selfish to the finger-tips, considered themselves being bled white by merciless, overpampered administrators, whose presence at all in Nigeria was inimical to trade. The administrators, they thought, were 'a contemptible lot of lazy parasites'[3] and were 'overpaid, underworked, extravagant and luxurious officials'.[4] The traders' view was well expressed in John Holt's letters to Morel, their spokesman, and one may be quoted. He wrote thus in 1901 of the administration of Southern Nigeria:

Truly our rulers are very Shylocks! Can you tell us what this government has to shew for the £1,327,546 customs duties paid it since it started in 1891 up to 31 March 1900? They have no great interior roads made open and secure for trade. They have a few fine houses such as would delight the heart of Major Ross. They have a beautiful yacht called the Ivy to buy and keep, and what else? Let the decreased trade since their advent answer. It is positively disgraceful.[5]

1 *Lagos Weekly Record*, 3 June 1899.   2 Ibid.
3 M.P., John Holt to Morel, 14 Aug. 1905.
4 Ibid. Same to same, 10 Sept. 1908.
5 M.P., Holt to De Ville, 23 Apr. 1901.

Tugwell continued his campaign, but not until 1908 did he secure what he had wanted and what the administration had always dreaded—a full-scale Royal Commission of Inquiry to investigate the whole question. From 1900 to 1905 the South African War, the question of the Chinese coolies in South Africa and domestic issues like the Education Bill and Free Trade versus Protection, over-shadowed the liquor question in Britain. Moreover the administration in Nigeria was able to put its house in order in 1905 by regulating the quality and strength of liquor. The tariff rose to 4s per gallon in 1905 and to 5s in 1908, just as the Commission was about to be set up. In order to diminish the consumption of potent liquors, a sliding scale of duty was adopted. For every degree or part of degree over 50 per cent trailles there was a surcharge of $2\frac{1}{2}d$ and a rebate of $1\frac{1}{4}d$ for every degree under that strength, subject however to a minimum of 3s 6d in 1905 and 4s in 1908. The result was that the liquor imported steadily declined in strength until about 90 per cent of the imports were about 28 degrees under proof.[1] Then, at the same time, the Egba and Ibadan governments imposed respectively 1s and 9d per gallon duty on spirits imported into their territory, while over-proof spirits were absolutely prohibited.

It would therefore be expected that the anti-liquor agitators would relax their efforts after 1905. In Nigeria this was what happened. Apart from the measures taken by the administration there were other reasons why the anti-liquor movement in Nigeria lost considerable support. These reasons will be examined presently. But in Britain the period 1905 to 1908 saw resurgence of a vigorous anti-liquor movement. This resurgence was not an isolated one, but was part of the strong humanitarian climate that characterized the Britain of the first decade of this century. Imperialism, it came to be clearly appreciated, had a moral side to it; acquisition of territories did not mean only exploitation of their material resources by the Imperial Government but implied moral responsibility to the governed as well. Hence Milner was censured for sanctioning the flogging of the Chinese and their recruitment was denounced; the atrocities of the Leopold regime in the Congo gave birth to the Congo Reform Association which compelled Britain to see that the territory was taken over by the Belgian Government; the opium question which had slumbered for eleven years was reopened in the House of Commons in 1906 and the Liberal Government had to accept the moral challenge of having it gradually abolished in Hong Kong by arrangements with China.[2]

1   C. P. Lucas: *A Historical Geography of the British Colonies*, Vol. III, Oxford 1913, pp. 210–13.   2   M. Perham, op. cit., pp. 319–74.

It was unthinkable that the liquor question should be forgotten in such a political climate. From 1905 onwards the prohibitionists were again on the warpath. The Archbishop of Canterbury and many members of Parliament raised the question oftener than before. A valid point was made in the fact that the Lagos railway, which could not have paid its way if it had not been carrying spirits, was to reach Ikirun in 1908. As Ikirun was close to the prohibition zone demarcated by the Brussels Conference of 1890, the spectre of 'fire-water' invading Northern Nigeria from Ikirun was raised. The railway, it was contended, was not a blessing but a curse. For while liquor got to the far interior in trickles before the *Pax Britannica*, it was now becoming a flood spreading ever wider over a wide area as a result of cheaper railway transport. No amount of guarantees and argument could convince the prohibitionists, except an investigation on the spot, to show that Britain had not been breaking an international agreement.

The Liberals who were swept into power in 1906 partly by nonconformist and temperance votes could not avoid responding to the demands of these moral enthusiasts. Worried and quite against its wish, the British Government had to agree in August 1908 to the principle of a Royal Commission of Inquiry to investigate the whole question. This decision was inescapable in the atmosphere of the Pan-Anglican Conference that was taking place, and the representations made in July by a deputation which included Bishops Tugwell, Johnson and Oluwọle, who described in lurid phrases the untold miseries of the liquor traffic in Nigeria. In May, Bishop Tugwell spoke before a large and credulous audience at Grosvenor House in so damaging a manner that the Governor, Sir Walter Egerton, had to summon an emergency meeting of the Legislative Council and denied the charges in an extraordinary *Government Gazette* in September. In October the Autumnal Conference of the Church of England Temperance Society met at Leicester at which inflammatory speeches were made against the Southern Nigerian administration. On November 14 *The Times* published Bishop Tugwell's lengthy reply to Egerton, an article which incensed both Egerton and the Colonial Office. The composition of the Commission, which would have included representatives of the Christian missions, was changed at once to exclude them and people who were obliged to back up the administration were nominated.[1] Even Morel whose paper, as noted

1 C.O. 520/67. Minutes on Egerton to Earl of Crewe, 17 Nov. 1908 by Antrobus, 24 Dec. 1908. Originally the Committee was to have been made up of 1 Chairman, 4 Government officials, 3 Missionaries, 3 Merchants, 4 Natives and 1 (Mr Welsh).

elsewhere, had been campaigning against missionary propaganda in Nigeria, was seriously suggested. Egerton found himself lambasted as the worst enemy of the Nigerian peoples. Said the Bishop:

> Is he (Egerton) satisfied that it is right and equitable to export from the country valuable products such as palm oil, palm-kernels, in thousands of tons per annum, rubber, ivory, mahogany, cotton, and maize to the greatest benefit of Great Britain and Europe, and to suffer to be imported in exchange for such products, for the sake of revenue, millions of gallons of vile Hamburg spirit to the infinite injury of a people and country committed by God to our care?

Since Egerton and the Legislative Council had failed in their imperial duty to the Nigerian peoples, he had no alternative to appealing to Britain to repair the damage done. He went on:

> I cannot believe that as a nation we have become so Godless and callous. And therefore failing to receive the help we ought to command at the hands of the Legislative Council which appears to be unable to face the situation with courage or ability or with regard to the best interest of the people, I appeal to all in England who regard our possessions in West Africa as a sacred trust to raise their voices in the name of Him whom we profess to serve against this pernicious and ungodly traffic, and demand its immediate and entire suppression.

The Commission of Inquiry, which did not set out until April 1909, was, from the official viewpoint, no more than a futile exercise to please the 'faddists'. No one in the Colonial Office thought of prohibition, as this would mean the administration either imposing direct taxation on the Nigerian peoples at the risk of violence, or asking the British people to finance the administration of Nigeria, a preposterous idea. The membership was pruned from twenty-one to four, the main aim being to spend the least amount of money. The Chairman of the Commission, a retired distinguished lawyer, Sir M. D. Chalmers, who had served in many legal positions in Britain, Gibraltar and India, had indicated that he would not take a penny for his services. In fact the total cost of the Commission to the Imperial Government was estimated at £671 1s.[1] The three other members of the Commission were chosen for their pro-Government biases. Captain Elgee, the District Commissioner in Ibadan, we will remember, was decidedly anti-missionary; A. Cowan, a Lagos trader, was a dealer in gin traffic. Thomas Welsh, the fourth member, was a

1   C.O. 520/86, Francis J. S. Hopwood to Secretary to the Treasury, 24 Feb. 1909.

retired trader who claimed he had never traded in gin but believed that the anti-liquor agitators overstated their case. It is essential to note that before the Commission set out the Colonial Office was in possession of certain facts which were deliberately suppressed and not made available to the Commission itself. It was clear that in certain parts in the Niger Delta, particularly in the Brass district, many of the so-called Native Courts were receiving fines in gin, the standard currency in the Brass district since the last decades of the nineteenth century.

For lack of space we cannot delve into the manoeuvres of the Imperial Government designed to produce a pro-Government Report; the efforts of Morel to damage the case of the prohibitionists and turn the British press against them by raising the matter into an international issue and the efforts of administrative officers to prevent witnesses speaking against the trade in Nigeria. It suffices to mention here that 171 witnesses were examined, of whom 83 were Africans and that the Commissioners visited Lagos, Abẹokuta, Ibadan, Ọyọ, Ogbomọshọ, Brass, Bonny, Opobo and Old Calabar. Their Report denied entirely the allegations of the prohibitionists and came to the conclusion that 'the people generally are a sober people, who are able to drink in moderation without falling into excess'. It also mentioned that drunkenness was on the increase only among the Christians.[1]

One must not, however, ignore the final reaction of the Nigerian peoples on which the anti-liquor campaign foundered and the division that occurred in the ranks of the Christian missions. Nothing is more astonishing than the inactivity of the anti-liquor movement in Nigeria after 1905. The Commission was then not a product of the Nigerian atmosphere, and it evoked indifference and hostility from many sections of the Nigerian community.

The educated Africans and the Lagos press represented the greatest opposition to Bishop Tugwell and his co-fanatics. As has been shown in a previous chapter missionaries had become unpopular with cultural nationalists by 1900. Bishop Tugwell was already at this date a *persona non grata*. So far as the educated Africans were concerned his record had not been edifying since 1892. They could not forgive his part in bringing about the Ijẹbu Expedition; he was held responsible for the forcible conquest of the Fulani Empire: he had condemned their Christianity as only skin-deep and had denounced cultural nationalists from the pulpit. Then in 1901 his impatience, tactlessness and impetuosity had incensed the founders of the Bethel African Church who seceded from the Breadfruit

1 For details cf. (Cd. 4906) *Report of the Committee of Inquiry into the liquor Trade in South Nigeria*, Part i (Cd. 4907) Part ii, *Minutes of Evidence*.

Church. In April 1909, the very month that the Commissioners were expected, he was supporting segregation of white and black in the Church. In the eyes of the educated Africans, the Bishop's greatest crime was his relentless advocacy of 'direct taxation' as the solution to the liquor problem. This was touching the educated Africans and the illiterate masses on their tenderest spot. Direct taxation was their bugbear.

The aversion of Africans to direct taxation before the First World War was proverbial. In dispatches and minutes the Governors and officials in the Colonial Office attributed this aversion to lack of patriotism and unwillingness of the people to pay for services and local administration that would have given the educated Africans an opportunity to have a measure of self-government. This explanation is at best only partly true. The real point is that the educated Africans did not see in the administrators benefactors but leeches. In their opinion there was no justification for an additional financial burden when the 'colossal revenue' through the customs for which they, the people who bought imported articles, paid, was not deployed in their interests. This was a view shared by some European traders and administrative officials.[1] Sapara Williams, an educated African and an unofficial member of the Legislative Council, was held by his colleagues as a pro-Government man and yet, he recorded privately on the Egerton administration which lasted from 1903 to 1912, 'There is no doubt that the country has fallen upon evil times under the present administration'[2] and, 'personally I am friendly to Sir Walter, but that does not blind my eyes to the fact that under his Administration Native and Native interests count for nothing'.[3] They, the educated Africans, had to pay for educating their children, while there was little to show of social services by the administration. In their view the administration was spending the revenue on passages and leave, on magnificent quarters and recruitment of European officers for jobs that could be more ably and more cheaply done by competent educated Africans.

Nor were they impressed by the huge public works such as the dredging of the Lagos harbour, road construction and the building of the railways which in effect denied to them the middleman's profits on which 80 per cent of them depended. The total value of Lagos trade rose from less than £4 million in 1903 to over £11 million in 1912. But, contended the educated Africans, Britain was the real gainer. 'You exploit the country with foreign capital,' burst

---

1 M.P., Holt to De Ville, 30 Oct. 1901; *West African Mail*, 28 Mar. 1907.
2 A.P.S., Sapara Williams to John Harris, 21 Mar. 1910.
3 Ibid. Same to same, 2 May 1910.

out a nationalist, 'and you say you have developed its resources; when capital has deducted its principal and interest, and the shipping its profits, precious little is left for the country, and it is that little that is the local wealth ... to a poor country like our own where the money comes from abroad, and both the principal and interest will have to go out, I see no advantage, I see impoverishment.'[1] Moreover, richer as the Protectorate became every year, the educated Africans became poorer and poorer. 'The halcyon days of enormous profits in business are gone, never to return,' lamented the Lagos press in April 1907, 'the ones who do anything like a profitable business are the members of the big European firms, who are thus able to get a reduction in prices.' European competition 'has practically ousted the Native out of the field of commercial enterprise'.[2] 'Under existing circumstances,' echoed Morel in his *African Mail*, 'the intelligent native is very heavily handicapped in the race for wealth ... without the assistance of the whiteman, he can never hope to attain any great measure of success.'[3] Consequently the educated Africans were very much on edge by 1907. The situation was not one in which they could be favourably disposed to the moral question of the liquor traffic, when its prohibition would mean direct taxation. Already in 1907 there was universal apprehension that the Lagos Government was contemplating a water rate. Government House was besieged by a large crowd and some stones were cast. Public opinion was whipped up by the pamphlet, *Governor Egerton and the Railway*, published by Herbert Macaulay in September 1908. In it he alleged that there had been misappropriation of funds in connection with the railway and that this was plunging the administration into 'the hopeless abyss of a gigantic Public Debt which will create a good cause for Land and Capitation Taxes in the near future'. The people were likely in such an eventuality to be asked to bear 'the nasty brunt of an imminent HEAVY PUBLIC DEBT with all its concomitant political evils'.

This was the stony ground upon which the moral issue of the liquor question fell. Fearing the logical consequences of prohibition the Lagos press had denounced the leaders of the Nigerian antiliquor movement in Britain as early as October 1908 as 'the blatant ecclesiastics from this country who have been howling themselves out of breath quite recently in England'[4] over the liquor question. Bishop Tugwell chose the moment to renew his bitter attacks against

1 *The Lagos Institute*, Proceedings, Dr O. Johnson, p. 26.
2 *Lagos Standard*, 10 Apr. 1907.
3 Ibid. 24 July 1907, quotes from *African Mail*.
4 *Lagos Standard*, 14 Oct. 1908.

the educated Africans in Lagos for not being willing to bear the burden of direct taxation which, in his judgment, was 'a product of Civilization based upon a spirit on Christian Patriotism'. 'The people of Lagos,' he wrote in April 1909, 'have been thriving on the impoverishment and demoralization of the people in the Interior [and] that all the improvements enjoyed in Lagos have been largely purchased at their cost, and that such a condition of affairs is intolerable.'[1]

Bishop Tugwell went into the interior to mobilize the chiefs and people of Abẹokuta, Ibadan, Ọyọ and Ogbomọshọ against the traffic. Whilst there is evidence to show that the rulers of Abẹokuta, Ibadan, Ọyọ, and many towns in the Ijẹbu territory regarded the liquor trade as a danger to their people, it is not clear whether they would sanction Tugwell's extreme views. Set against Tugwell was Macaulay, whose vitriolic denunciations descended on the Bishop and whose views were circulated in the interior. Although a total abstainer, Macaulay repeated the danger of direct taxation which would mean 'hut Tax, Land Tax, Income Tax, Poll Tax, Export Tax, and ... What does it not mean?'[2] This was a message well understood by the people. Moreover the administrative officers threatened that in places like Ọyọ and Ibadan, where spirits were being boycotted due to Tugwell's efforts, opposition to the liquor traffic also meant opposition to the administration. Chiefs actually sent heralds round the towns to abjure people from taking the white man's wine. Bishop Tugwell's prestige fell sharply, to Egerton's delight.

The differences that occurred among the Christian missions were indeed amusing. After 1888 concerted effort by them had ceased. Although the United Presbyterian missionaries acknowledged the fact that drunkenness was leading to violence among the Efik and that the liquor traffic was the 'great enemy of African Missions', their protests hardly went beyond their headquarters in George Street, Edinburgh. So far as the Wesleyans were concerned their interest in the liquor traffic dwindled after 1901, when the Conference in Great Britain had spoken on the 'ravages of the liquor traffic' in Nigeria. The Roman Catholic missions had never taken part in the movement. The anti-liquor movement had dwindled into a one-mission show, that of the Church Missionary Society. The Roman Catholic missions refused to volunteer to appear before the Commission until their heads were begged to give evidence. They held the view that the Nigerians were a sober people. Particularly fascinating

1   *Nigerian Chronicle*, 26 Mar. 1909.
2   Ibid. Supplement to 2 Apr. 1909 issue.

was the behaviour of the Wesleyan missionaries. In spite of appeals by the Government for Wesleyans to give evidence, the African clergymen declined to give evidence at first, and those who did so later emphasized that the evils of alcohol had been unduly exaggerated. The Chairman of the mission, Oliver Griffin, was of the same view and had always stated in England that the Yoruba 'are the most sober people on the face of the earth'.[1] He did not consider the Commission necessary or of practical value and therefore went off to Britain a few days after the Commission began sitting. Of the four remaining European missionaries three refused to give evidence. The fourth who volunteered to appear before the Commission was Walton, himself a drunkard. In fact so notorious was he that in July 1909 he had to be recalled to England for drunkenness.[2]

So far as the Nigerian peoples were concerned the anti-liquor movement had collapsed deservedly like a house of cards (although that was not the end of the matter with the Imperial Government, the administration in Nigeria and the prohibitionists in Britain). Its fall was an outright rejection of the puritan moral codes which well-intentioned but visionary missionaries wanted to impose upon the Nigerian peoples. As we have seen this was happening in the field of education also. Western materialism of an unprecedented kind which opened the eyes of the people to European social and economic notions and standards was becoming a much stronger force than the abstract moral principles of the Christian missions. In the circumstances of the first decade of this century Nigeria could not be Calvin's Geneva of the sixteenth century, or the traditional Puritan Massachusetts of the seventeenth century. For good or ill, the moral aspects of contemporary European civilization, which the Christian missions did not wish to flourish in Nigeria, were to be more and more firmly entrenched in a society that was already losing its indigenous and effectively high, if 'pagan', morality.

1   M.M.A., Oliver Griffin to Perkins, 1 Mar. 1911.
2   Ibid.

Native custom has the privilege of *melior conditio possidentis*. Before in
effect decreeing its eventual suppression the missionary must prove
that it is indissolubly linked with error, or immorality or absurd
superstition. In so far as this proof is not made, custom holds. It has
the force of law. It possesses legal right.

Pope Pius XII, 1950

11 The Missionary Impact on Society

Apprehensions about the effects of missionary activity on West African society have been expressed for wellnigh a century. From the sixties of the nineteenth century to the second decade of the present century well-known erudite critics of Christian missions like Edward Blyden, Mary Kingsley and Edmund Morel, spilled much ink in their effort to direct public attention to the 'denationalizing' results of missionary propaganda in this part of the continent. The substance of their allegation was that missionary activity was a disruptive force, rocking traditional society to its very foundations, denouncing ordered polygamy in favour of disordered monogamy, producing disrespectful, presumptuous and detribalized children through the mission schools, destroying the high moral principles and orderliness of indigenous society through denunciation of traditional religion, without an adequate substitute, and transforming the mental outlook of Nigerians in a way that made them imitate European values slavishly, whilst holding in irrational contempt valuable features of traditional culture.

For many reasons missionaries' contributions to the instability of African society in general, and of Nigerian society in particular, have never been historically assessed. Prejudice has weighed heavily against the missions. There was the fact that in the opening years of this century the administration, hiding under the umbrella of their supposed Indirect Rule, attempted to exonerate themselves from all blame for the disconcerting state of affairs and posed as preservers of all healthy customs and institutions. Even when unpopular measures like the hut tax in Sierra Leone in 1898 and fear of tax by Aba women in 1929 led to violent uprisings against the administrators there were not wanting people who affected to believe that the risings were a direct consequence of missionary activity.[1] Moreover, even to this day, missionaries who have tried to refute the various charges levelled at them have attempted to do so only apologetically and mission conferences have tended to endorse the popular views on the

1 N.A., *Report of the Aba Commission of Inquiry* (Lagos 1930).

denationalizing results of their activity on purely hypothetical grounds. Lastly there is the fact that in these days when the African heritage is being studied sympathetically the anthropologists and sociologists, whose purpose differs widely from that of missionaries, cannot resist the temptation to give missionaries a hard knock for ignoring, misconceiving or misconstruing the salutary functions of some customs and institutions in the stable traditional society.

No attempt should be made to undermine the sociological aspect of missionary teaching. The missionary was necessarily a revolutionary on a grand scale. No society could be Christianized without its being upset to a considerable extent. Ideologically, in point of time and to a certain degree in actuality, missionaries began the process of disintegration of Nigerian society. In a 'pagan' society it was the missionary's task to overturn and, given a suitable environment, the missionary knew how to do this. The incitement of the slaves against their masters in the Niger Delta in the nineteenth century may be recalled.

No one can argue against the fact that the Christian missions broke into tribal solidarity with their denominational varieties and rivalries. Moreover each mission had regulations and worked on principles which threatened the traditional society. Take for instance the preposterous regulation that polygamists who wanted full membership and privileges of the Church must first disown all wives but one. In a polygynous community this regulation could upset the society if there were many polygamist converts disposed to listen to the missionaries. More fundamental was the fact that the missions' basis of conversion emphasized and exalted the individual. For the missionary it was the relationship of the individual to God that mattered. He, not the family or the group, must make the decision. Consequently individuals and not social units like the family were converted. But indigenous Nigerian society was communal, perhaps more so than the Greek *polis*. Every member of the group, village or tribe, from the highest to the lowest, was no more than a unit in an organic whole controlled by an ironbound code of duties, taboos and rights, on the faithful performance of which by every individual the cohesion, order and welfare of the group depended. It was only as a unit in the organic whole that he must think, speak, believe and act. The individual had to submit to the collective will and authority of the community in this manner because it was only in this way that he and the community could live.

When a missionary converted individuals in a community he removed units from an organic whole and thereby undermined the monolithic structure of the community. The converts not only imbibed a new set of religious beliefs but began to nurse alien ideas, economic ambitions and political aspirations of their own, detrimental to the welfare and solidarity of the community. In a country where religion was the cement of the society, the guarantor of moral principles and the basis of secular authority, renunciation of the traditional religion implied renunciation of the moral, civil and political obligations to the community as well.

But the revolutionary doctrine of the missionary and its subversive potentialities should not be emphasized at the expense of facts—a mistake made by educated Africans and administrators in the period before the First World War. After all, ideas alone do not make a revolution. Indeed, before the *Pax Britannica* Christian missions in Nigeria had no scope for upsetting the society as they wished but had to suspend their revolutionary programme. Under the patronage of the chiefs missionaries could not change customs more than society would approve. And, as should be clear from the opening chapter of this book, the society in the interior of Yorubaland approved of no tampering with vital customs and institutions. Rather, it was the missionaries who had to compromise their culture and Christian principles by joining *Ogboni*, by giving polygamists positions of responsibility in the Church and by allowing their wards to take 'pagan' titles.

A brief survey of missionary enterprise *vis-à-vis* slavery and polygamy will illustrate the limitations of missionaries in the implementation of their idealistic social programme in Nigeria before the establishment and consolidation of British rule. Whether in the Niger Delta or in the Ibo country or in Yorubaland, slaves were a principal source of investment in which wealth consisted. Also the possession of slaves added dignity to a man and gave him position among his neighbours. In the Niger Delta most of the trade was conducted by slaves, whilst in Yorubaland farming, trading and household functions were mostly performed by these 'living tools'. According to the records, most of the slaves in the Niger Delta were of Ibo origin and by the middle of the nineteenth century had out-numbered the Ijaw and Efik, twenty times in the Efik society.[1] In Yorubaland the population was dominated by slaves and the well-to-do had an average of 250 slaves each, mostly of Hausa stock.[2]

Although Protestant missions detested slavery none of them had a convenient environment in which to disseminate anti-slavery propaganda, how much less of forcing society to set their slaves free. In

1 Hope Waddell: Journals, Waddell to Somerville, 22 Jan. 1855; Waddell to Blythe, March 1855.
2 C.M.S. CA2/056, James Johnson's Annual Report for 1879.

Mid-Western and Eastern Nigeria the Roman Catholic missions were very sympathetic to slavery, which they found an institution by which proselytes could be easily made. With the 20,000 francs granted annually to the Society of the Holy Ghost Fathers by Rome, specifically for the purchase of slaves, the Society encouraged the institution by buying slaves from eager Ibo sellers.[1] These slaves were settled in Christian villages and they constituted the nucleus of the Catholic community in Eastern Nigeria. In Yorubaland neither the Southern American Baptist Mission nor the Wesleyans made any fuss about the institution. It was only the Church Missionary Society that attempted to persuade its agents and adherents to desist from using slave labour. In 1879 and 1888 the Society drew up regulations, according to which slaveholders were not to be accepted into full Church membership. In the former year, interpreting the Bible in the light of European economy and social system, the Society delivered the following lecture to unwilling ears: 'We venture to maintain that slavery in any shape or form, as distinguished from voluntary hiring and service, is thoroughly alien from the spirit of the Gospel. . . . As the law of gravitation determines the descent of heavy bodies, so, as its necessary result, the spirit of the Word of God has eliminated slavery from Christianity.'[2]

The Society's adherents did not accept this view. They were fully convinced that the institution of slavery was not a crying evil, that it was indispensable in the context of Nigerian community and that all that they could do was to heed the Pauline advice that Christian slave-owners should be kind, just and liberal in the treatment of their slaves. Not only did the Christians remain slave-owners but they warned the Society that anti-slave propaganda in the interior of Yorubaland would result in 'a wholesale slaughter of the Native Christians, the plundering and expulsion of our beloved white missionaries, and a total extirpation of Christianity'.[3]

Slavery seemed in fact to be of evangelistic value in Nigeria before the establishment of British rule. In pre-colonial days freemen nursed contempt for Christianity. To become a Christian meant a complete dissociation of oneself from the family compound, and consequently loss of social family privileges and undesirable estrangement. Hence, strong as missionary influence was in Abẹokuta, conversions among the non-immigrant freemen were few and far between. Indeed until after 1900 only one chief, John Okenla, was converted in Ẹgbaland, although many gave up their children for the white man's education. In Ibadan it was a social stigma to be a

1 Jordan, op. cit., pp. 86–93. 2 *Church Missionary Intelligencer*, 1880, p. 399.
3 C.M.S. G3/A2/o5, C.M.S. Agents to the Secretaries, 14 June 1889.

Christian, for, as mentioned earlier, Christians were poor fighting material and were therefore not helping in fulfilling the purpose of the military state. Even in Bonny where Christianity made the most astounding success in the Niger Delta the chiefs and nobility refused to become Christians, though they patronized the faith with zest.

In Yorubaland Christian converts, mostly liberated Africans, allowed their slaves to become Christians and most of the increases reported in missionary journals were due to conversions of this kind. In Ibadan impertinent slaves were sometimes given to missionaries as pawns. In times of distress many chiefs pawned their children to the relatively wealthy missionaries. The people so pawned became servants of the creditors and worked for them until those who pawned them had refunded the money loaned. In most cases the money was not refunded for years. The advantages of this situation for missionary enterprise were many. The pawns became converted, thereby swelling the ranks of Christians, in many cases redeemed slaves became zealous evangelists after redeeming themselves, and as has been noted, it was such converted slaves, bought by missionaries in Ibadan and Abẹokuta, who pioneered the Christian evangelization of the Ekiti country. More important still for missionary enterprise was the fact that without slaves and pawns no schools or churches could be erected in Yorubaland. For no Yoruba would work for anybody for wages, this being considered a most disgraceful thing. Without slaves missionaries could not have had house servants. Also missionaries were compelled to grant loans to the chiefs in order to ingratiate themselves into their good graces, whilst in this process to have refused to take in return pawns from the chiefs would have been regarded by the society as an anti-social behaviour. In the circumstances, too, to have refused to lend a borrower money would not only have been uncharitable but would have resulted in sending the borrower and his family into the slave market.

There was another reason why the Yoruba Christians could not have renounced slavery in the pre-colonial era. Inheritance was attached to it, and as inheritance was a family issue, 'pagan' and Muslim relatives had an interest in the preservation of the institution. By Yoruba custom relatives, not children of the deceased, inherited a man's property and Christians could not unilaterally set inherited slaves free, except with the approval of the members of the extended family among whom were often 'pagans' and Muslims. This would involve the customary form of manumission—giving of money to the owner by the slaves themselves in the presence of the relatives, and the owner giving due shares to the relatives.

In the circumstances all that the Church Missionary Society could do was to set up a Court of Redemption in Abẹokuta in 1881 for the redemption of slaves by the Society along traditional lines. After 1890 the C.M.S. made no more reference to this institution which was destined to die a natural death as British administration became firmly rooted and as the traditional economic pattern began to be modified and transformed. The economic reasons for the existence of slavery were gradually removed by the introduction of silver coinage, the rise of paid labour, attachment of dignity to industry and the introduction of cash economy.

The demise of slavery was hastened by the administration which instructed the soldiers to set free 'oppressed' slaves without payment of redemption fees[1] such as the Missions had been paying. This was a revolutionary anti-social measure. Slaves were set free in large numbers by the series of military expeditions in Southern and Northern Nigeria, sometimes on a scale embarrassing to the administrators themselves. Over 1,000 slaves were set free in a single day after the bombardment of Ọyọ in 1895. The social chaos which might result from a sudden liberation of a large number of slaves in Northern Nigeria became the preoccupation of Lugard to the extent that he drew up a very moderate regulation on the institution, as the Southern Nigeria government had to do about the same time. In Northern Nigeria Freed Slave Homes had to be established in many centres of the territory.

It is clear from the foregoing that in a matter of a few years, so far as slavery was concerned, the administration brought about a social upheaval greater than the missions had been able to do in the pre-colonial times. In the same manner it can be shown that in matters of education, marriage, the lowering of the prestige of the chiefs in the eyes of the masses and in recruitment for labour the administration disturbed the society more than missionary enterprise did.

The attitude of Christian missions to polygamy is fascinating for its revelations. Polygamy remains one of the African institutions on which Christian missions have up to date refused to compromise. At the epochal Conference of the Protestant missions in Le Zoute, Belgium, in 1926, the missions apologetically blamed their qualified success in Africa on the lack of understanding and unwillingness to adopt 'everything that is good in the African's heritage'. And yet they outlawed polygamy, declaring that 'this conference is convinced that the Christian society must be built on Christian family life and that the ideal of the Christian family life can only be realized in monogamy'.[2]

1 C.O. 147/121, MacCallum to Chamberlain, 20 Dec. 1897.
2 E. Smith: *The Christian Mission in Africa*, 1926, p. 51.

Nevertheless this uncompromising attitude of the missions must remain the most baffling problem to the student of missionary enterprise in Africa. For, unlike all other customs and institutions, polygamy (not to be confused with marriage) is unique in African society because it bears no religious or 'heathenish' tincture. It is not a moral issue either. It is this fact, more than anything else, that explains the zest and apparent conviction with which cultural nationalists defended the institution. A close study of the arguments of both the exponents and opponents of polygamy in Nigeria leaves one with the impression that neither on scriptural, nor on rational, nor on hypothetical basis was the attitude of the missions defensible. Consequently practically all Christian missions saw their churches filled with a majority of polygamists, whose money they could not reject, while the African Churches increased their number considerably by accepting polygamists into full membership. In most churches of Christian missions not a few of the professed monogamists kept secret wives, and such a practice was not absent among the African clergy.

It is important to bear in mind the position of polygamy in Nigerian society in order to understand why the institution remained an essential part of Nigerian Christianity throughout the period covered by this book. Polygamy was a product of the economic, social and political circumstances of the indigenous society. Essentially an agrarian society there was plenty of land for everybody. Standard of living was more uniform than it is now; there was no social or economic reason to make birth control a rational proposition. With a very high infantile mortality there was need for a multitude of wives to ensure a large number of children, who in turn would ensure adequate productivity by the family. On reaching manhood a child would have his own farm and slaves and thus increase the economic potentiality of the family. Socially parents were very keen on having a large number of children so that at death expensive and elaborate obsequies, lasting many weeks, might be observed, a custom to which much importance was attached, as it meant that parents buried in such a manner would occupy a high status in the other world. Also the number of wives a man had corresponded with his social standing and no man, however wealthy, would be regarded as a social and political figure if he did not add wife to wife. This was why it was the kings and chiefs who possessed the largest number of wives, some being reported as having over five hundred. There was, too, the fact that polygamy was a way of dispensing social justice to women by providing husbands for all women. The idea of an unmarried woman which now exists among the Christian élite was completely absent in the traditional society. There is some truth in the following syllogism by a leading member of the African Church: 'The celibate is selfish and lives for himself. The monogamist is better, he serves the other although to the exclusion of all others. The polygamist is the best, because he lives a life of sacrifice for providing homes for others, more or less comfort, they say, for himself.'[1]

Perhaps the strongest case for polygamy was the fact that it guaranteed an incredibly high moral tone in the traditional society. As a general rule sexual misbehaviour was absent in the traditional society. The rarity of sexual irregularity was not due only to the fear of punishment, in many cases death, by the society for offenders, or the permanent disgrace attached to sexual lapses, but the satisfaction of sexual urge derived from numerous wives. It may be observed here that in the traditional society children were not weaned until after two years, and throughout that period physical relations with the wife was by custom forbidden. In such circumstances plurality of wives was the only practical solution. The high sexual morality that prevailed in the traditional society was upset by Western civilization and its conception of monogamy, missionary enterprise beginning the process in the greater part of Southern Nigeria.

Non-African observers should disabuse their minds of the assumption that women in the traditional society did not like polygamy and that quarrels among the wives, and with their husband, were bound to be endless. As a general rule harmony prevailed because the exact position and duties of each wife and the code of behaviour that should subsist between the one and the other were clearly defined by tradition. In the indigenous setting women liked an institution from which they derived several advantages. The woman first married was pleased to see her husband take a second wife. For her it meant an improvement in her position, as in this way she became the chief wife and mistress of the house, exercising supervision over other wives. With her husband she had a privileged position, and generally enjoyed his confidence in a particular way. At the same time it meant for every individual woman a relief from work, for this was now divided among several, and every one had more time for her own affairs. The point being emphasized here is that the wives of a polygamist in the traditional society did not feel themselves injured or denied of any freedom. Nor were they unhappy with their lot. The modern European concept of equality of the sexes did not exist; women accepted it as a law of nature that ultimate wisdom and guidance belonged to men, a concept held in the Pauline epistles.

1 Ayọ Ajala: 'African Communion its Aims and Objects', *The African Church Chronicle*, April–June 1936.

Even in European society in our times equality of the sexes remains an ideal. It is not surprising that as late as 1934 a Leverhulme researcher into the Ibo society observed that the uncontaminated Ibo women regarded 'Christian' marriage as a 'prison', and she commented:

> I am inclined to think that the women who have no contact with Western opinion are satisfied with a polygamous order and can derive some vanity from it. The more wives a man has, the more she feels that she has married somebody of importance, and if by her capacity as a manager she can save enough money to pay the dowry of yet another wife, she has the supreme satisfaction of hearing the latter say: 'this is the woman who made it possible for my husband to pay my dowry, greatly will I honour her'.[1]

Missionary doctrine of monogamy effected only a minor disruption of society, compared to the administration's marriage regulations. In their treatment of polygamists the missions were compelled to be pragmatic. Except the educated Africans the majority of the illiterate converts ignored, as they still ignore, the so-called Christian form of marriage. On the other hand the population could not ignore laws made by the administration. Take, for instance, the divorce laws introduced by the administration in the 'Native Courts'. These laws upset many homes by encouraging divorce and by making it easier. In indigenous society marriage was not the affair of a man and a woman as individuals, but of two extended families the members of which guaranteed the welfare of husband and wife. Divorce was very rare and it needed the commitment of the gravest of crimes by the husband—not poverty or misfortune—before the consent of all members of the wife's extended family (without which divorce could not take place) could be obtained for such a disgraceful decision. But the administration legislated that ability to pay from £5 to £12 to the husband of a woman was the only condition necessary for divorce.[2] Thus a woman could henceforth decide on her own, for trivial reasons, to leave her husband for a more well-to-do man. Divorce cases increased as wealth became easy to acquire. The administration, and not the missions, must bear responsibility for a state of affairs which progressively worsened until today when special 'Customary' Courts are established throughout Southern Nigeria, specifically to grant divorce on the basis enunciated by the late British administration.

1 Sylvia Leith-Ross: *African Women—A study of Ibo of Nigeria*, London 1938, pp. 125–6.
2 C.M.S. G3/A2/015, Jones to Tugwell, 30 Jan. 1912.

There were many ways in which administrative measures disturbed the society more than did the missions, whilst in many cases the administration also consciously encouraged the missions to accelerate the process of disturbance which the latter had begun. Paradoxically the first major disturbers of the Nigerian society were the soldiers, particularly the Hausa soldiers, who were supposed to maintain law and order in the interior after pacification. In many places the administration forced the Hausa troops to recover debts for individual favourites, an action often accompanied by outrages by the soldiers.[1] So exasperated were the Ekiti chiefs that they began to wonder whether they were not paying too high a price for the administration's termination of the Yoruba civil war. So terror-stricken were the Ibo after the Aro Expedition that people used to flee into the bush at the sight of anyone in English dress.[2] In Southern Nigeria there were universal complaints of the Hausa troops commandeering food and burning down villages for amusement. In many places they seized political control and judicial functions from the chiefs and prevented parents from admonishing refractory children, except with their (the soldiers') permission. The appropriation of seven wives of the *Balẹ* of Ogbomọshọ by some Hausa soldiers in 1897 was by no means exceptional.[3]

Another element which undermined society were the Travelling Commissioners, mostly military men, located in the interior after pacification. They treated the chiefs in the most contemptuous manner, thus lowering the prestige of the latter in the eyes of their subjects. The result was that young people became insubordinate and disobedient, aware that the chiefs could no longer inflict traditional deterring punishments like mutilation, flogging and death. They also knew that, for lack of adequate personnel, no administrator was near to enforce obedience to the traditional authorities. In Ilesha Captain Ambrose handcuffed chiefs and cast them into prison because they had flogged their wives.[4] In 1899 Major Tucker of Ondo sent carriers to plunder and beat up chiefs for 'disobeying orders' and threw many of them into prison.[5] Many people actually left the town while the Osemawe, it is said, committed suicide because of the humiliation administered to him by the Commissioner. The Awujalẹ was the most humiliated of the Yoruba rulers. In 1896 he was told that the so-called Christians were no longer his but 'British subjects', and that if

1   N.A. Ibadan, Phillips Papers, C. Phillips to Captain Hawtayne, 20 Sept. 1893. *Lagos Weekly Record*, 9 Jan. 1897.
2   C.M.S. G3/A3/09, James Johnson to Baylis, 3 Nov. 1903.
3   *Lagos Standard*, 23 Mar. 1897; *Lagos Weekly Record*, 27 Feb. 1897.
4   *Lagos Weekly Record*, 23 Apr. 1904.   5   Ibid. 20 Jan. 1900.

he continued to show hostility to the latter, who openly jested at the tribal groves, ridiculed him and took cases to their teachers, then the British Government would be compelled to declare that 'he was not a fit person to be entrusted with the high authority vested in him, and other arrangements would have to be made'.[1] For the administration, he was no more than 'a bigoted, obstinate, cantankerous drunkard' and he was threatened with deposition in 1903 if he did not stop drinking. In 1896 he was beaten up by carriers who were asked to fetch him to the soldiers' camp by a white military officer.[2] Consequently, in Yorubaland, the greatest upheaval occurred in the Ijẹbu territory.

Then there was the disturbing element of requisition for labour in and out of season by the administration and merchants for the building of roads, railways and the cultivation of rubber, coffee and cocoa. Practically throughout Yorubaland the most enterprising people, dazzled by the phenomenal wealth which could now be acquired in cash, left farming for wages. Nigerian labour was recruited for the Gold Coast railways and plantations in Fernando Po and the Belgian Congo. Between 1892 and 1897 3,000 Yoruba left for the Congo, while in 1901 alone over 4,000 Nigerians left for the Gold Coast to build railways. Many of the labourers did not return to their villages and those who did so returned wealthier than their chiefs and parents. They returned with a new set of ideas and outlook on life, and an implacable contempt for the traditional religion. For in the conglomerate artificial society in which they had worked religion was of little importance, and they saw the educated Africans and white masters violating with impunity moral laws which the tribal priests had taught them not to break if they wanted no calamity to befall them. These labourers had probably imitated with impunity the educated Africans and white officials. It was natural they lost faith in the moral teachings and religion of the traditional society. It therefore needed no missionary propaganda to wean people from the traditional religion with all its consequences.

The administration was as much responsible as the Christian missions for the unsatisfactory human product of the mission schools. The Government encouraged missions to carry out an educational programme beyond the latters' intentions and thus converted the schools into clerk-making machines. It was the administration that compelled the missions to lay emphasis on English and that wished the vernacular were dead. 'The sooner we can make English—even if it must be "pidgin English"—the common speech of W.A., the

1 C.O. 147/112, enclosure in Denton to Chamberlain, 19 Jan. 1897.
2 *Lagos Weekly Record*, 9 Dec. 1896.

better,'[1] commented an official in the Colonial Office with levity on James Johnson's petition for emphasis on vernacular education in 1909. If it is true that, in Lugard's words, 'the language of a people is the expression of its soul, by which alone a key to their thoughts could be found',[2] then the administration must bear the responsibility for the 'terrible homicide' which the discouragement of vernacular education implied.[3]

Indeed, far-reaching though it was, there is temptation on the part of unwary observers to overemphasize the intrinsic spiritual and cultural conquest of missionary propaganda in Nigeria. If Christian missions completely converted a locality, then, they would have succeeded in establishing their millennium, a new moral and social basis. But nowhere in Nigeria was this the case. Christian ethics and the kind of European civilization they wanted to establish remained an ideal, whether in Lagos or Abẹokuta, Bonny or Old Calabar. To all outward appearances the Christians tended towards the individualist conception of Europeans, but they retained strong attachments to their extended family and their hearth; Christianity seemed to be embraced with zest and churches were filled to capacity, but reliance was placed more on the jujuman's charms for protection against unseen evil influences than on supplications to the Christian's God; European culture was apparently appropriated with gusto but emotionally-charged traditional customs and institutions still exerted a greater appeal.

For the Christians to be really dug up from their roots in the manner the missions wished they would have needed to shift to Nigeria the European environment—material prosperity, technological advancement, its long history and the instincts and attitudes of its peoples. But this environment could neither be shifted wholesale to Nigeria, nor acquired by the Christian converts in a matter of years or generations. In fact, at best, only a caricature of the European environment could be imported into Nigeria. The environment in which the missions worked was predominantly indigenous, 'pagan', agrarian and communal. Christian missions were scattered and numerically small. With few exceptions they were one or two in each extended family, few in the village, fewer still in the towns and districts, and only one to eighty in Southern Nigeria in 1914.

1 C.O. 520/89, minute dated 6 Feb. 1909, on James Johnson to Colonel Seely, 20 Jan. 1909.
2 D. Westermann: *The African Today and Tomorrow*, O.U.P. 1949, p. vi.
3 For the social and political disturbance which the British administration introduced into Ibo Society with the Warrant Chiefs, cf. A. E. Afigbo: 'The Warrant Chief System in Eastern Nigeria 1900–1929', Ph.D. (Ibadan) 1964.

But statistics are not a true guide to the social and political influence of missionary propaganda in the development of Nigeria. The extent of the spiritual achievement of the missions will never be known. Socially the process of disintegration continues; culturally the indigenous and the European continue to jostle together, mixing in a way that defies analysis. Politically, even before 1914, Nigeria's independence was already foreshadowed in the appointment of mission-trained Nigerians to high posts, though mostly subordinate, in Church and state. In the period surveyed by this work, in no other non-white colony outside West Africa were the natives appointed to such high posts as in the Civil Service of Nigeria; before the thirties in no other British mission field were natives raised to the rank of 'half Bishops'. Well could Esien Esien Ukpabio, the retired Efik pastor already mentioned, visualize 1 October 1960 before his death in 1902 when he observed:

> From near and far come calls from Government for native junior officials. An excellent sign! The administration now leans upon sons of the soil; and here is a sure path in which our lads may lessen our doubts and add to the small volume of growing respect in others. My young countrymen are now on trial: more the whole scheme of self-government is at stake. The scheme in its present form is a momentous experiment, and one which no one wants to fail. The British do not want to occupy our country, they are teaching us to govern ourselves.[1]

After 1914, the last year of the period covered by this book, the missionaries' direct political influence in Nigeria declined rapidly. This was largely because British sovereignty, which many chiefs and Emirs had feared would follow missionary activity like cause and effect, and which they had resisted, was already accepted by all sections of the Nigerian community with equanimity, by some with gratitude. In this year the last relic of indigenous authority in Nigeria, the attenuated independence of the Ẹgba, was taken over by the British, at the invitation of the Alake himself. During the First World War, the Northern Nigeria Emirs not only showed loyalty but voted money to the British 'infidels' for a war which was also being waged against their spiritual overlord, the Sultan of Turkey. Even the educated Africans, critical as they were of specific measures of the administration, hailed British rule as salutary and indispensable in the evolution of modern Nigeria. 'We are to a man proud today ... that we are subjects of the British Crown,' declared the emerging

1 Esere, op. cit., p. 63.

341

fiery nationalist, Herbert Macaulay, in 1913.[1] Demand for political independence remained outside the programme of the nationalists for the next thirty years.

Henceforward the missions which, apart from the independent African Churches, numbered fifteen at the end of the First World War, devoted their energies to evangelization. Nevertheless their activity continued to produce political results, indirectly, through their schools, which continued to serve as nurseries for practically all nationalists of note in Southern Nigeria until the achievement of independence. It was not an accident that when in 1923 the elective principle was introduced into the Legislative Council of Nigeria only the élite in the citadels of Christianity, Lagos and Old Calabar, were given the franchise. It was also in the logic of things that all the Nigerian sixteen elected and twenty-seven nominated members of the Council from 1923 to 1946 were professed Christians, including many ministers of religion and journalists who fanned the embers of national awakening in the country. Even until this day the development of the Southern half of this country is largely in the hands of Christian adherents.

There was another way in which missionary enterprise contributed to the nationalist movement after 1914. Even more than before the Christian communities began to produce journals and magazines which enjoyed wide circulation. In 1917 appeared the first issue of *In Leisure Hours*, an Anglican organ which is still alive, and *African Church Gleaner*, an organ of one of the African Churches, which did not live long. In 1919 appeared the *African Hope*, and in 1922 the first issue of the *Nigerian Baptist*. In 1925 and 1946 the Wesleyans launched respectively *The Nigerian Methodist* and the *Nigerian Methodist Review*, whilst by 1936 the Roman Catholics had begun the *Catholic Herald* and *Catholic Life*. A particularly significant journal was the *African Church Chronicle* which appeared in 1936 but ceased to exist after a few years, during which important articles were published by the élite of the African Church. The important feature of most of these Church news media was that they made observations on political events in the country, though to a much lesser extent than the national newspapers.

It is important to note, however, that after 1914, even more than before, the human products of the mission schools, whatever their career, did not make Christianity the determinant of their nationalist struggle and attitude towards national issues. Their attitude had to become increasingly neutral and secular with the formation of political parties seeking the support of all classes of the country's population.

1 A.P.S. G230, Proceedings of deputation to Lugard, 28 Feb. 1913.

Also for several years after 1914 cultural nationalism in Nigeria ceased to be pursued with much vigour. The African Churches remained predominantly alien in their forms of worship, although attempts were made to introduce native airs into services, and polygamists and members of the Ogboni cult continued to be fully recognized in the Churches. It was not until the early fifties that most of the political leaders began to revive cultural nationalism in matters of clothing and the patronage of the Reformed Ogboni Fraternity.

Apart from the schools, the missions came to exert some impact on the Nigerian community through hospitals. By 1914 there had been founded the C.M.S. Iyi Enu Hospital near Onitsha, the Baptist Hospital in Ogbomọshọ, the Wesleyan Guild Hospital in Ilesha and the Sacred Heart Hospital of the Society of African Missions in Abẹokuta. But these medical centres did not begin to flourish until after 1914, when European medical science came to be progressively appreciated by the rapidly swelling number of Christian adherents. For a long time, according to the records, European medical science did not commend itself to large sections of the Nigerian population because the people, as in many other things, were suspicious of European medical skill and continued to have a much greater faith in indigenous medical facilities.[1]

In statistical terms and in the desire to appropriate all the material and social opportunities that missionary enterprise could afford, it is the Ibo people who have responded most enthusiastically to Christianity.[2] By 1910 the number of Christian adherents in Eastern Nigeria had outstripped that in the area west of the Niger. In 1910 there were 18,500 in the former and 17,000 in the latter. Ten years later the figures stood at 514,395 and 260,500 for Eastern and Western Nigeria respectively. In the present decade there are about four million Christian adherents in Eastern Nigeria, as opposed to about a million in the area west of the Niger. The reasons for the stiffer resistance of the Yoruba to Christianity than the Ibo's are not difficult to perceive. In the first instance, in the urbanized community of the Yoruba traditional religion remains strong still in the majority of households, whilst the torch of Christianity is still very dim in the rural areas. This situation contrasts with that in the village community of the Ibo where the mission school became from

1 *Sudan Leaflet* No. 18. A.P.S., 'Colonial Medical Appointments in West African Colonies' by Dr O. Sapara, who regretted that medical practitioners had to 'contend with bush doctors who have the advantage of hoary-headed superstition behind them'.
2 Statistics taken from Table 11 in J. S. Coleman, op. cit., p. 95.

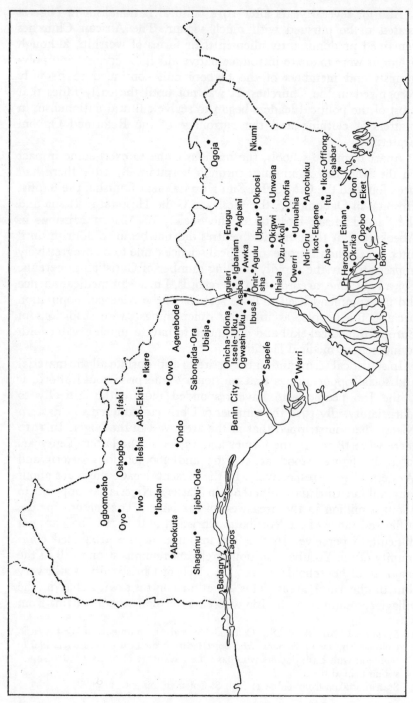

Southern Nigeria: The Key Mission Stations in 1928

the beginning of this century the instrument for the conversion of children for more than a generation. Moreover, Islam, which, it will be remembered preceded Christianity in Yorubaland, is still a strong competitor with Christianity in the territory. This also contrasts with the situation in Iboland where Islam has made a negligible impact.

In Northern Nigeria Islam remains the religion of the majority in the far north. Even in the area known as the Middle Belt, where Christian missions have had a chance of working among the over sixty-five 'pagan' tribes of the dissected Bauchi plateau, Christianity is facing strong competition from Islam. In this physically difficult area, which sprawls across a wide belt between Pankshin, Shendam and Langtang in the West and to the Adamawa hills in the East and North, southwards to Kaltungo and Zinna, the traditional religion and customs of the fierce 'pagan' tribes die hard. In 1953 only 3·3 per cent of the less than a million inhabitants of the plateau had been converted to the Christian faith.

As this work goes to press missionary enterprise in Nigeria remains an active force in the lives of villagers, out of the main highways where the administration has not established schools. In these places mission schools, churches and medical institutions, most of which the writer saw in his extensive tour of the country in 1961, are still beacons shedding light on the people around them. But in the increasingly large number of urban agglomerations the influence of Christian missions is to a large extent being neutralized by other agencies among which may be mentioned secular education, administrative establishments, gambling houses, drinking centres, prostitution, obscene literature, politics, emergent labour organization, irreligion and increasing materialism. All combined, they present the Christian community of the Republic of Nigeria with a formidable challenge. In the writer's view this challenge is still to be fully appreciated and accepted by the Church of Christ in Nigeria if Christianity is not to become a spent force in the years that lie ahead.

Bibliography

PRIMARY SOURCES

A. Mission Sources

These are by far the most useful sources, particularly for the period before 1900 when the British administration was not yet established in the interior. No serious study of the political and social history of Southern Nigeria can be attempted without these immensely rich sources. After 1900 the missionaries reported less eagerly and less frequently than before, except when particular issues of contention arose between them and the administration.

I. CHURCH MISSIONARY SOCIETY ARCHIVES at Salisbury Square, London, E.C.4.

Of the missions the C.M.S. was by far the most important, not only in terms of staff, number of converts and territorial extent but also in terms of its peculiar connection with the administration. In Yorubaland the C.M.S. was regarded as *Ṣọsi Ijọba*—the Government Church—and no administration in our period could brush aside the Society's or its missionaries' representations with impunity.

All in-coming and out-going letters from 1842 to 1914 were carefully studied, as well as the personal files of individual African and European missionaries who figured prominently in the political and social questions of the period. These individual files are classified under CA2/o and CA3/o for the Yoruba and Niger Missions respectively. After 1880 the Yoruba Mission is classified under G3/A2/o, the Niger Mission under G3/A3/o and the Hausa Mission under G3/A9/o. Before 1900 there was no Hausa Mission administratively but papers dealing with Northern Nigeria before then are to be found in the Niger Mission papers.

The outgoing letters are classified as CA2/L/o and CA3/L/o for Yoruba and Niger Missions respectively. All out-going letters for the Hausa Mission continued to be in the Niger Mission letter books until 1912 and in the Yoruba Mission letter books after 1912.

In many cases the individual files of the Bishops and some missionaries in the Sierra Leone Mission were consulted. These come under the CA1/o series. Yorubaland was until 1894 (and Lagos until 1898) part of the Sierra Leone Diocese and matters dealing with the Yoruba Mission were classified under the individual files of the Bishops. The files of James Johnson and Edward

Blyden in the Sierra Leone Mission are of vital importance in understanding the background and ideas of both of them before they came to exert influence in Yorubaland.

Private Papers

The C.M.S. archives is still in the process of building up, and the private papers of important missionaries in Nigeria are being collected. The Dennis papers are of value, in view of Dennis's significance for the Ibo peoples as the translator of the Bible into 'Central Ibo' and as an enthusiast for the education of the Ibo. But the most valuable papers are Brooke's. They not only throw new light on the 1890–91 crisis in the Niger Mission but contain valuable materials on the political situation in the Fulani Empire from 1889 to 1892. The diaries and journals are extremely fascinating.

Annual Letters

The Annual Letters, published every year in one volume, were the annual reports by individual missionaries. Since many of the native missionaries rarely corresponded directly with Salisbury Square after 1880 in any other manner, the *Annual Letters* contain useful information which cannot otherwise be obtained.

Journals

These journals, all published in London, were intended for the Society's subscribers. Sometimes they contained articles on political and social questions in Africa in general and West Africa in particular. They are useful also for the understanding of the changing attitude of Salisbury Square to the Negro Race with particular reference to West Africa during the period. The most informative up to 1893 was the *Church Missionary Intelligencer* which became *Church Missionary Review* in 1907. In 1893 the *Yoruba and Niger Notes* was founded specifically for the Nigerian Mission field.

2. WESLEYAN MISSIONARY SOCIETY ARCHIVES, 25 Marylebone Road, London W.1.

All in-coming and out-going letters, reports and minutes of conferences from 1842 to 1914 were used. The papers of the Primitive Methodist Mission, which reunited with the Wesleyans in 1932, are also in these archives.

The chief journals consulted are *The Wesleyan Missionary Notices, Work and Workers* and the *Primitive Methodist Missionary Records*.

3. UNITED PRESBYTERIAN MISSION, 121 George Street, Edinburgh.

All manuscripts have been transferred to the National Library of Scotland. The most valuable of these are the Hope Waddell

Journals. The Mission cannot account for the terrible loss of all the in-coming letters from Old Calabar in the period. Fortunately the Foreign Mission Board used to meet frequently and its minutes fill up the missing gap to some extent. Oftentimes the Board discussed matters raised by the Presbytery of Biafra (Old Calabar) and letters were either summarized or partially reproduced.

The Mission's main Journal was the *United Presbyterian Record*. In 1901 the United Presbyterian Mission joined with the United Free Church of Scotland Mission, following the union of the two Churches—United Presbyterian and Free Church—of Scotland.

4. SOUTHERN AMERICAN BAPTIST MISSION, Richmond, Virginia.

The necessity of going to the U.S.A. was obviated by the enormous collections on this Mission by the Rev. Cecil Roberson who was in Ijẹbu-Ifẹ when he kindly allowed me to go through his collections. He has not only collected letters, journals and reports of the most important missionaries but has copied as well the bulk of materials of the headquarters in the United States. The Rev. Roberson has also stimulated a growing enthusiasm for the writing of local histories by many of the Baptist churches in Nigeria. A rich source of information is the Mission's main journal, *Foreign Mission Journal*.

5. SOCIETY OF AFRICAN MISSIONS ARCHIVES, Rome.

The papers of this Catholic Mission, based in Lyons, are of immense value. All the incoming letters have been carefully preserved and filed either under individual names of the fathers or local superior in Lagos. They throw a great deal of light on the political situation in Yorubaland and on the Niger, and indicate the intensity of the French patriotism of the priests (all French) and the depth of French influence in Yorubaland, particularly in Abẹokuta. It was fortunate that this Mission did not impose the hundred-year ban which other Catholic societies, following the regulation of the Vatican, adopt. Consequently I was allowed to see all materials up to 1914. A few letters in Vol. I of Father Planque's Letter Books were also found highly revealing. The Mission's activities in Nigeria were published in *Les Missions Catholiques*, a journal of the *Propaganda de Fide*.

Two Missions—one Protestant and one Catholic—refused to open their archives to me. The former, the Qua Iboe Mission, whose headquarters is Belfast, claims to have manuscripts dating to the earliest times (1887) but would not allow any outsider to see them. The Society of the Holy Ghost Fathers of Paris, in spite of exertion by the Education Attaché of the Nigerian Federal

Government in London, warded me off with the hundred-year ban. It established itself on the Niger in December 1885.

There was no necessity to use the archives of the Sudan United Missions (headquarters, Portland Street, London) in view of the fact that the manuscripts covering this period were sent to Salisbury Square. At its inception in 1904 the C.U.M.P., later merged with the S.U.M., elected to be under the patronage of the C.M.S. Moreover during the last war the Mission's headquarters was bombed and all its early records were destroyed.

I could not go to Toronto in Canada, the headquarters of the Sudan Interior Mission, the other Protestant Mission that began work in Northern Nigeria in 1899. In this period it was a small Mission and avoided collision with the Northern Nigeria administration.

B. Government Records

The official records are indispensable to this investigation not only because they make possible the checking of the accuracy of Missions' reports but also because they enable one to see and assess the official views on the political and social questions of the period. As the footnotes should have indicated, neither the missionaries nor the administrators told the whole story of events, but by using their reports with the other sources mentioned below the fullest account is at the disposal of the historian.

1. PUBLIC RECORD OFFICE

C.O. 147	1861–1907	(Lagos series)
C.O. 446	1898–1900	(Northern Nigeria series)
C.O. 520	1907–1912	(Southern Nigeria series)
F.O. 84	1865–1891	(Slave Trade Series)
F.O. 2	1891–1900	(Oil Rivers and Niger Coast Protectorate series)

2. SENATE HOUSE LIBRARY
Parliamentary Papers
Africa (Consular)

Volume LVI	(1854–1855)
Volume XLIV	(1857)
Volume LXX	(1860)
Volume LXIV	(1861)
Volume LXI	(1862)
Volume LXXI	(1863)

3. NIGERIAN NATIONAL ARCHIVES
   Ibadan, CSO 1 Series 1900–1914
   Enugu, Intelligence Reports
   Kaduna, G.O.K. 1/0 series
4. ẸGBA ARCHIVES, ABẸOKUTA
   Miscellaneous papers covering the period 1891–1914, apart from Minutes of the Ẹgba United Government and G. W. Johnson's letters.

C. Private Papers

1. RHODES HOUSE, OXFORD
   The Lugard Papers
   The Aborigines Protection Society Papers
2. UNIVERSITY OF IBADAN LIBRARY
   G. W. Johnson's papers
3. MACKAY HOUSE, OSHOGBO
   The Phillip Papers, now in the National Archives, Ibadan.
4. UNIVERSITY OF IBADAN, HISTORY DEPARTMENT
   The Fombo Collection

D. Printed Primary Sources

(a) Newspapers
   1. Published in Lagos
   Anglo African, 1863–1865
   Lagos Times, 1880–1883
   Lagos Observer, 1882–1888
   The Mirror, 1887–1888
   The Eagle and Lagos Critic, 1883–1887
   Lagos Weekly Record, 1891–1914
   Lagos Standard, 1895–1914
   Nigerian Chronicle, 1908–1914
   Daily News, 1932
   African Church Chronicle, 1934–1950
   2. Published in Sierra Leone
   The Negro, a few copies, 1873
   Sierra Leone Weekly News, 1893–1894
   3. Published in London
   African Times, 1870–1898
   West Africa, 1900–1903
   West African Mail (later *African Mail*), 1903–1910

(b) Books

AFRICAN CHURCH. *Report of Proceedings of the African Church Organization for Lagos and Yorubaland 1901–1908*. Liverpool 1910.

ANTHROPOLOGICAL SOCIETY. *Memoirs read before the Anthropological Society of London, 1863–4*. London 1865.

BLYDEN, E. W. *The People of Africa*, New York 1871.

— *The West African University*, Freetown 1872.

— *From West Africa to Palestine*, Sierra Leone 1873.

— *Christianity, Islam and the Negro Race*, London 1887.

— *The African Problem and other Discourses*, London 1890.

— *The Lagos Training College and Industrial Institute*, Lagos 1896.

— *Africa and the Africans*, London 1903.

— *West Africa Before Europe*, London 1905.

— *African Life and Customs*, London 1908.

— *The Three Needs of Liberia*, London 1908.

— *The Arabic Bible in the Soudan: A Plea for Transliteration*, London 1910.

BOOCOCK, N. *Our Fernandian Missions*, London.

BOWEN, J. W. E., ed. *Africa and the American Negro*, Atlanta 1896.

BOWEN, T. J. *Central Africa. Adventures and Missionary Labours in Several Countries in the Interior of Africa from 1849 to 1856*, Charleston 1857.

BURDO, A. *A voyage up the Niger and Benueh*, London 1880.

BURTON, R. F. *Abeokuta and the Cameroons Mountains*, Vol. 1, London 1863.

— *Wit and Wisdom from West Africa*, 1902.

C.M.S. *The Yoruba Missions*, 1906.

— *The Niger Mission*, 1909.

— *The Church in the Yoruba Country*. Proceedings of the Diocesan Conference at Lagos, April, 1887.

CLARKE, R. *Sketches of the Colony of Sierra Leone and its Inhabitants*, London 1863.

COKER, J. K. *The African Church*, Lagos 1913.

COKER, S. A. *The Rights of Africans to Organize and Establish Indigenous Churches*, Lagos 1917.

CROWTHER, S. A. and TAYLOR, J. S. *The Gospel on the Banks of the Niger*, London 1857.

CUST, R. N. *Essay on the Prevailing Methods of the Evangelization of the Non-Christian World*, London 1894.

— *The Gospel Message*, London 1896.

— *Africa Redivivia*, London 1891.

DAVIDSON, R. T. *The Lambeth Conferences of 1867, 1878 and 1888*, London 1896.

DENNIS, J. S. *Christian Missions and Social Progress*, London and Edinburgh 1899.

ESERE. *As Seen Through African Eyes*, 1916.

FAULKNER, R. E. *Joseph Sydney Hill*, London 1898.

[FREEMASONRY] *The Secret Warfare of Freemasonry against Church and State*, London 1875.

— *The District Grand Lodge of Nigeria*, Masonic Directory 1951.

GEORGE, J. O. *Historical Notes on the Yoruba Country and its Tribes*, Baden, undated.

GOLDIE, H. *Calabar and Its Mission*, London and Edinburgh 1901.

GOUDIE, W. *Report of Visit to West Africa*, 1915.

GRIFFITHS, S. *Trips in the Tropics*, London 1878.

HAMILTON, A. *The River Niger and the Progress of Discovery and Commerce in Central Africa*, London 1862.

HANNAH, W. *Darkness Visible*, London 1952.

HARRIS, J. H. *Domestic Slavery in Southern Nigeria*, London 1912.

HODGKIN, T. *Nigerian Perspectives*, London 1960.

HODGSON, W. B. *Notes on Northern Africa, the Sahara and the Soudan*, New York 1844.

HUTCHINSON, E. *The Lost Continent: its Rediscovery and Recovery*, London 1879.

HUTCHINSON, T. J. *Ten Years' Wanderings Among the Ethiopians*, London 1861.

— *Impressions of Africa*, London 1858.

JOHNSON, C. R. *Bryan Roe: A Soldier of the Cross*, London 1896.

JOHNSON, JAMES. *Yoruba Heathenism*, London 1899.

KINGSLEY, H. M. *Travels in West Africa*, London 1897.

— *West African Studies*, London 1901.

KNIGHT, W. *Memoir of Henry Venn*, London 1882.

KNOOP, D. *University Masonic Lodges*, Sheffield 1945.

— *The Masonic Word*.

KNOOP, D. and JONES, J. P. *Freemasonry and the Idea of Natural Religion*, Manchester University Press 1942.

LAWRENCE, J. T. *Freemasonry: Its History, Principles, and Objects*, London 1909.

LEONARD, A. G. *The Lower Niger and Its Tribes*, London 1906.

— *Islam, Her Moral and Spiritual Value*, London 1909.

LUGARD, F. D. *The Rise of Our East African Empire*, Edinburgh and London 1887.

MACARTHY, J. A. *The Prospects of Christianity in West Africa*, London 1887.

MARKE, C. *Africa and the Africans*, London 1881.

353

MARXWELL, J. R. *Advantages and Disadvantages of European Inter-course with the West Coast of Africa*, London 1861.

MARWICK, W. *William and Louisa Anderson*, Edinburgh 1897.

M'KEOWN, R. L. *Twenty-Five Years in Qua Iboe*, London and Belfast, 1912.

MOCKLER-FERRYMAN, A. F. *Up the Niger*, London 1892.

OMONIYI, B. *A Defence of Ethiopian Movement*, Edinburgh 1908.

PAGE, J. *The Black Bishop*, London 1908.

PAYNE, J. A. O. *Table of Principal Events in Yoruba History*, Lagos 1894.

PHILLIPS, S. C. *The Heathen Cult called Reformed Ogboni Society*, Ibadan.

PINNOCK, S. G. *The Romance of Missions in Nigeria*, Richmond 1918
— *The Yoruba Country, its People, Customs and Missions*, London 1893.

READE, W. *Savage Africa*, London 1863.

ROBINSON, C. H. *Nigeria our Latest Protectorate*, London 1900.

ROE, H. *West African Scenes*, London 1874.

STOCK, E. *History of the Church Missionary Society*, Vols. 3 and 4.
— *Are Foreign Missions Doing Any Good?* London 1894.
— *Foreign Missions and Home Calls*, London 1893.

STONE, R. H. *In Afric's Forest and Jungle*, New York 1899.

TALBOT, P. A. *The Peoples of Southern Nigeria*, Vol. 1, O.U.P. 1926.

TUCKER, A. R. *Eighteen Years in Uganda and East Africa*, London 1911.

TUCKER, MISS. *Abẹokuta or Sunrise Within the Tropics*, London 1858.

VENN, H. *Notices of the British Colonies on the West Coast of Africa*, London 1863.

WADDEL, AGNES. *Memorials of Mrs Sutherland of Old Calabar*, Paisley 1883.

WADDELL, H. M. *Twenty-Nine Years in the West Indies and West Africa*, London 1863.

WARNECK, G. *Modern Missions and Culture: Their Mutual Relations* (translated by T. Smith), Gemmel 1883.

WILLOUGHBY, I. H. *Polygamy in West Africa*, Reading 1887.

(c) Articles

JOHNSTON, H. H. 'British Missions in Africa', *Nineteenth Century*, Vol. 4, 1887.
— 'Are our Foreign Missions a Success?' *Fortnightly Review*, Vol. 45, 1888.

KINGSLEY, H. M. 'Liquor Traffic with West Africa', *Fortnightly Review*, Vol. 63, 1898.

LUGARD, F. D. 'British West African Possessions', *Blackwoods Magazine*, Vol. 157, 1895.
— 'Liquor Traffic in Africa', *Nineteenth Century*, Vol. 43, 1897.
THOMSON, J. 'Mohammedanism in Central Africa', *Contemporary Review*, December 1886.

SECONDARY SOURCES

(a) Books

AJISAFE, A. K. *History of Abeokuta*, Bungay 1924.
ANENE, J. C. *Southern Nigeria in Transition 1886–1906*, Cambridge 1966.
BAETA, C. O. *Prophetism in Ghana*, S.C.M. 1962.
BANE, M. J. *Catholic Pioneers in West Africa*, Dublin 1956.
BASDEN, G. T. *Among the Ibos of Nigeria*, London 1921.
BAUDIN, P. *Fetichism and Fetich Worshippers*, New York 1885.
BELLO, SIR AHMADU. *My Life*, Cambridge 1962.
BIOBAKU, S. O. *The Egba and their Neighbours*, O.U.P. 1957.
BOIS, D. B. *The Negro Church*, Atlanta 1903.
BUEL, R. N. *The Native Problem in Africa*, New York 1928.
BURNS, SIR A. *History of Nigeria*, 4th edn., London 1948.
CARY, J. *Britain and West Africa*, London 1946 (pamphlet).
C.M.S. *Nigeria: The Unknown*, 1918.
COLEMAN, J. S. *Nigeria, Background to Nationalism*, California 1958.
CROCKER, W. R. *Our Governing Colonies*, London 1947.
CROOKS, J. J. *A History of the Colony of Sierra Leone*, London 1903.
DAVEY, C. J. *The Methodist Story*, London 1955.
DAVIS, J. M. *The Economic and Social Environment of the Younger Churches*, London 1939.
DELANO, I. O. *The Soul of Nigeria*, London 1937.
DELANO, I. O. *One Church for Nigeria*, London 1945.
DIKE, K. O. *Trade and Politics in the Niger Delta*, O.U.P. 1956.
DUVAL, E. M. *Baptist Mission in Nigeria*, 1928.
EGHAREVBA, J. *A Short History of Benin*, Ibadan University Press 1960.
— *Some Tribal Gods of Southern Nigeria*, 1951.
ELLIS, A. B. *The Land of Fetish*, London 1883.
EPELLE, E. M. T. *The Church in the Niger Delta*, Port Harcourt, 1955.
— *The Church in Opobo*, Aba 1958.
FARROW, S. *Faith, Fancies and Fetich*, London 1926.
FINDLAY and HOLDSWORTH. *The History of the Wesleyan Methodist Missionary Society*, Vols. I and II.

FLINT, J. E. *Sir George Goldie and the Making of Nigeria*, O.U.P. 1960.

FORDE, D. *Efik Traders of Old Calabar*, O.U.P. 1956.

— *The Yoruba-speaking People of South-Western Nigeria*, London 1951.

FORDE, D. and JONES, G. I. *The Ibo and Ibibio-speaking Peoples of South-Eastern Nigeria*, O.U.P. 1950.

FYFE, C. *A History of Sierra Leone*, O.U.P. 1962.

GAIRDNER, W. H. T. *Edinburgh 1910*, Edinburgh and London 1910.

GEARY, G. W. M. *Nigeria Under British Rule*, London 1927.

GROVES, C. P. *The Planting of Christianity in Africa*, London, Vols. II and III.

GWYNN, S. *Life of Mary Kingsley*, London 1932.

HALLIGEY, J. T. F. *Methodism in West Africa*, London 1907.

HARGREAVES, J. D. *A Life of Sir Samuel Lewis*, London 1958.

HARRIS, J. H. *Dawn in Darkest Africa*, London 1914.

HAYFORD, C. M. *Mary H. Kingsley from an African Standpoint*, London, undated.

— *West Africa and Christianity*, London 1901.

HEWETT, J. F. *European Settlements on the West Coast of Africa*, London 1862.

HOBSON, J. A. *Imperialism: A Study*, London 1902.

HODGKIN, T. *Colonialism and Nationalism in Africa*, London 1956.

HUNTER, J. H. *A Flame of Fire*, Aylesbury and Slough 1961.

IDOWU, E. B. *Olodumare God in Yoruba Belief*, London 1962.

JOHNSON, SAMUEL. *The History of the Yorubas*, Lagos 1921.

JOHNSON, T. S. *The Story of a Mission*, London 1953.

JOHNSTON, H. H. *The Story of My Life*, London 1923.

— *The Opening up of Africa*, London.

JORDAN, J. B. *Bishop Shanahan of Southern Nigeria*, Dublin 1949.

KENYATTA, J. *Facing Mount Kenya*, London 1938.

KIMBLE, D. B. *A Political History of Ghana*, O.U.P. 1963.

KRAEMER, H. *The Christian Message in a Non-Christian World*, London 1938.

LATOURETTE, K. S. *A Story of the Expansion of Christianity*, London (5 vols. 1938–46), Vol. 5.

LEGUM, C. *Must We Lose Africa?* London 1954.

LEITH-ROSS, S. *African Women*, London 1938.

— *Beyond the Niger*, London 1951.

LETHBRIDGE, A. *West Africa the Elusive*, London 1921.

LUCAS, C. P. *A Historical Geography of the British Colonies*, Vol. III, Oxford 1913.

LUCAS, C. *The Partition and Colonization of Africa*, London 1922.

LUCAS, J. O. *History of St. Paul's Breadfruit*, Lagos 1952.

LUGARD, F. D. *The Dual Mandate*, London 1922.
MACAULAY, H. *History of Missionary Work in Nigeria with Special Reference to the U.N.A.*, Lagos 1942.
MACDONALD, A. J. *Trade, Politics and Christianity in Africa and the East*, London 1916.
MACFARLAN, D. M. *Calabar*, London 1946.
MALINOWSKI, B. *Freedom and Civilization*, London 1947.
— *The Dynamics of Culture Change*, Yale University Press 1945.
MAXWELL, J. L. *Half a Century of Grace*, London.
MILLER, W. R. S. *Reflections of a Pioneer*, London 1936.
— *Have We Failed in Nigeria?* 1947.
— *An Autobiography*, Zaria 1953.
— *Yesterday, Today and Tomorrow in Northern Nigeria*, 1938.
MOREL, E. D. *Nigeria, Its Peoples and its Problems*, London 1911.
— *Affairs of West Africa*, London 1902.
— *Africa and the Peace of Europe*, 1917.
MUMFORD, B. W. *A Comparative Survey of Native Education in Various Dependencies*, London 1937.
NASSAU, R. H. *Fetichism in West Africa*, London 1904.
NEWBURY, C. W. *The Western Slave Coast and its Rulers*, Oxford 1961.
OGLIVLE, J. N. *Our Empire's Debt to Missions*, London 1924.
OLDHAM, J. H. *Christianity and the Race Problems*, London 1924.
OLIVER, R. *Sir Harvey Johnston and the Scramble for Africa*, London 1957.
— *Missionary Factor in East Africa*, London 1952.
— *How Christian is Africa?* C.M.S. 1956.
OLIVER, R. and FAGE, J. D. *A Short History of Africa*, Penguin 1962.
ORR, C. W. J. *The Making of Northern Nigeria*, London 1911.
PARRINDER, G. *African Traditional Religion*, London 1954.
— *West African Religion*, London 1961.
— *Religion in an African City* (Ibadan), 1953.
PERHAM, M. *Native Administration in Nigeria*, 1937.
— *Lugard, The Years of Adventure*, London 1956.
— *Lugard, The Years of Authority*, London 1960.
— *The Colonial Reckoning*, London 1961.
PLATT, W. J. *From Fetish to Faith*, London 1935.
PLESSIS, J. DU. *The Evangelization of Pagan Africa*, Cape Town 1929.
— *Thrice Through the Dark Continent*, London 1917.
PRICE, T. *African Marriage*, London 1954.
READ, M. *Africans and their Schools*.
— *Mass Education in African Society*, 1943.
ROOME, W. J. W. *Can Africa Be Won?* London 1927.

RUXTON, F. H. *Missions in Africa. Their Political Necessity*, undated.

RYAN, I. *Black Man's Country*, London 1950.

SADLER, G. W. *A Century in Nigeria* (Baptist), Nashville, U.S.A. 1950.

SCHAPERA, I. *Married Life in an African Tribe*, London, 1940.

— *Livingstone's Missionary Correspondence 1841–1856*, London 1961.

SCOTT, H. S. *Native Authorities and Education*, undated.

SMITH, E. W. *The Golden Stool*, London 1927.

— *The Christian Missions in Africa*, International Missionary Council 1926.

— *African Idea of God*, London 1950.

SOUTHON, A. E. *The Whispering Bush*, London 1929.

— *Ilesha and Beyond*, undated.

STAUFFER, M., ed. *Thinking with Africa*, London 1928.

STEWART, J. *Dawn in the Dark Continent*, London 1906.

STODDARD, L. *The Rising Tide of Colour against White World Supremacy*, London 1922.

SUNDKLER, B. G. M. *Bantu Prophets in South Africa*, London 1948.

— *The Christian Ministry in Africa*, London 1960.

TEMPLE, C. L. *Native Races and their Rulers*, Cape Town 1918.

THORP, E. *Ladder of Bones*, London 1956.

THORTON, M. D. *Africa Waiting*, London 1897.

THWAIT, D. *The Seething African Pot*, London 1936.

TOWNSEND, M. *Asia and Europe*, Westminster 1901.

TRIMMINGHAM, J. S. *The Christian Approach to Islam in the Soudan*, O.U.P. 1948.

VILDER, R. A. *The Church in an Age of Revolution*, Penguin 1961.

WALKER, F. D. *The Romance of the Black River*, London 1931.

— *The Call of the Dark Continent*, London 1911.

— *Africa and Her Peoples*, London 1924.

— *A Hundred Years in Nigeria* (Methodist), 1942.

WARD, E. *The Yoruba Husband-Wife Code*, 1938.

WASHINGTON, B. T. *The Story of the Negro*, New York 1909.

WATT, E. S. *The Quest of Souls in Qua Ibo*, London and Edinburgh 1951.

WEBSTER, J. B. *The African Churches among the Yoruba 1888–1922*, O.U.P. 1964.

WELBOURN, F. E. *East African Rebels. A Study of some Independent Churches*, London 1961.

WESTERMANN, D. *The African Today and Tomorrow*, O.U.P. 1949.

— *Africa and Christianity*, O.U.P. 1937.

— *The Missionary and Anthropological Research*, O.U.P. 1932.

WHEARE, J. *The Nigerian Legislative Council*, London.

WRONG, M. *Five Points for Africa*, London 1942.

(b) Articles

AJAYI, J. F. A. 'Henry Venn and the Policy of Development', *Journal of the Historical Society of Nigeria*, Vol. 1 No. 4, December 1959.
— 'Nineteenth Century Origins of Nigerian Nationalism', ibid., Vol. 2 No. 2, December 1961.
AYANDELE, E. A. 'An Assessment of James Johnson and His Place in Nigerian History, 1874–1917: Part I, 1874–1890', *Journal of the Historical Society of Nigeria*, Vol. 2 No. 4, December 1963.
— 'An Assessment of James Johnson and His Place in Nigerian History, 1874–1917: Part II 1890–1917', *Journal of the Historical Society of Nigeria*, Vol. 3 No. 1, December 1964.
CLINTON, J. V. 'King Eyo Honesty II of Creek Town', *Nigeria Magazine*, No. 69, August 1961.
DIKE, K. O. 'Beecroft 1835–49', *Journal of the Historical Society of Nigeria*, Vol. 1 No. 1, December 1956.
FLINT, J. E. 'Mary Kingsley—A Reassessment', *Journal of African History*, Vol. 4 No. 1, 1963.
GERTZEL, C. 'Relations between African and European traders in the Niger Delta 1880–1896', ibid., Vol. 3 No. 2, 1962.
RYDER, A. F. C. 'Missionary Activities in the Kingdom of Warri to the Early Nineteenth Century', *Journal of the Historical Society of Nigeria*, Vol. 2 No. 1, December 1960.
— 'The Benin Missions', ibid., Vol. 2 No. 2, December 1961.
SMITH, H. F. C. 'The Islamic Revolutions of the 19th Century', ibid., Vol. 2, No. 2, December 1961.

Unpublshed Theses

ADERIBIGBE, A. A. B. 'The Expansion of the Lagos Protectorate 1861–1900' (Ph.D. London, 1959).
AFIGBO, A. E. 'The Warrant Chief System in Eastern Nigeria 1900–1929 (Ph.D. Ibadan, 1964).
AJAYI, J. F. A. 'Christian Missions and the Making of Nigeria 1841–1891' (Ph.D. London, 1958).
AJAYI, W. 'A History of the Yoruba Mission (C.M.S.) 1843–1880' (M.A. Bristol, 1959).
ALI, M. M. 'The Bengali Reaction to Christian Missionary Activities, 1833–1857' (Ph.D. London, 1963).
ANENE, J. C. O. 'The Boundary Arrangements for Nigeria, 1884–1906: An Objective Study in Colonial Boundary Making' (Ph.D. London, 1960).

BIOBAKU, S. O. 'The Egba State and its Neighbours 1842–1872' (Ph.D. London, 1951).

FADIPE, N. A. 'The Sociology of the Yoruba' (Ph.D. London, 1940).

GERTZEL, C. 'John Holt: A British Merchant in West Africa in the Era of Imperialism' (D.Phil. Oxford, 1959).

GRAHAM, SONIA F. 'History of Education in Relation to Development of the Protectorate of Northern Nigeria, 1900–1919' (Ph.D. London, 1955).

HERSKOVITS, J. F. 'Liberated Africans and the History of Lagos Colony to 1886' (D.Phil. Oxford, 1960).

IFEMESIA, C. C. 'British Enterprise on the River Niger 1830–1869' (Ph.D. London, 1959).

INYANG, P. E. M. 'The Provision of Education in Nigeria with reference to the work of the Church Missionary Society, Catholic Mission and the Methodist Missionary Society' (M.A. London, 1958).

MCINTYRE, W. D. 'British Policy in West Africa, the Malay Peninsula and the South Pacific during the Colonial Secretary-ship of Lord Kimberley and Lord Carnavon, 1870–1876' (Ph.D. London, 1959).

NORTHCOTT, W. C. 'Life and Work of Robert Moffat with particular Reference to the Work of Missions and White Settlements North of the Orange River 1817–1870' (Ph.D. London, 1961).

SMITH, R. N. 'The Ibo People' (Ph.D. Cambridge, 1929).

TAMUNO, S. M. 'The Development of British Administrative Control of Southern Nigeria, 1900–1912: A Study in the Administration of Sir Ralph Moor, Sir William MacGregor and Sir Walter Egerton (Ph.D. London, 1962).

WALSH, M. J. 'The Catholic Contribution to Education in Western Nigeria' (M.A. London, 1951).

Index

Atundaolu, Rev. H.: incident at Ilesha, 166; Secretary Lagos Native Research Society, 251; historical writings, 260; study of groves, 264

Awka, 115

Awo, 273

Awujalẹ, King of Ijẹbu: anti-missionary policy, 35, 156; Moloney defers to, 37; and J. B. Wood, 40; won over by French, 50, 58-9; missionary hostility to, 57; admits a missionary, 58; Denton's visit, 59; Carter demands apology, 61; Tugwell's insult, 64; sacred name of, 68; power reduced, 69, 173; compared with Jaja, 156; humiliated by British, 338-9. *See also* Ademiyẹwo *and* Tunwase

Axim, 130

Ayesan, 35, 37

Azikiwe, Dr Nnamdi, President, 288

Azikiwe, Obed, 288

Azumini, 106

Babalawos (Ifa priests), 265

Babamubọni, *see* Ifamubọni

Badagry (map, p. 344)
    Political and Social: situation on advent of missionaries, 5; traditional rulers of, 5, 6; slave-dealing, 6; influx of *Akus*, 7; Commissioner Tickel, 48-49; Islam in, 117
    Missionary activity: advent of missionaries, 5, 9; pro- and anti-missionary factions, 6; protection of Christians, 8; anti-missionary party expelled (1851), 9-10; white men in, 31; Topo Industrial School, 297

Balẹ, chief of Ogbomọshọ, 14, 169, 338. *See also* Bashọrun

Ballot, M., 53

Bambuk, 120

Bank of British West Africa, 250

Baptism: infant, 49; public, of eminent persons, 110; incident at Zaria, 148; of polygamists, 199; baptismal names, 244

Baptist Academy, Lagos, 289, 293

Baptist Church, Native, 194, 197-202, 205; Agbebi leader of, 180, 254-5, 295; Hill Report, 229

Baptist Mission, Southern American: at Ogbomọshọ (1855), 14; Church, 67; Bowen's attempt at Ilọrin, 117; and Royal Niger Company, 118; Foreign Mission Board, 118; in Ijẹbuland, 156; at Ọyọ and Pinnock affair, 166-168; secession, birth of Native Baptist Church, 197-201; attitude to polygamists, 201; Africans in majority, 241; training of agents, 287; Academy at Lagos, 289, 293; College at Iwo, 294; attitude to slavery, 332; Hospital at Ogbomọshọ, 343

Baptist Missionaries, British, 224

Baptist Yoruba Association, 201

Barika, convert, 14

Barleycorn, Napoleon, 102

Barth, Dr Henry, 120

Basden, Archdeacon G. T., 268

Bashọrun, 169-70. *See also* Balẹ

Battersby, European missionary, 220

Bauchi: Plateau, 125, 345; province, 316

Baylis, F., 143

Beckley, Daddy, 270

Beecroft, John: attitude to Efik chiefs, 17, 18; appointed Consul (1849), 18; lands missionaries at Old Calabar (1846), 18; and Eyo II, 21; member S.A.I.S.C., 21-2; fines Efiks for insulting missionaries, 22; and Spanish settlements, 102; Foreign Office and, 105

Belfast, 115

Belgium, 320, 334. *See also* Congo, Belgian

Bell, Sir Hesketh, 148-9, 171

Bello, Mohammed, 121

Bende, 115

Benin (map, p. 344)
    Political and Social: trade with Mahin, 36; Overami of, 113; fetish defiled, 113; expedition of 1897, 158; export crops, 297
    Missionary Activity: early Christianization, 3; C.M.S. move towards, 115; apathy to Christianity, 158; schools, 158; church, 158-9; James Johnson, 236; Reformed Ogboni Fraternity in, 277

Benin, Bight of, 3, 6, 56, 71, 77, 94

Benjamin, J. B., 65, 197, 268

Benson, Archbishop of Canterbury, 227–31, 233, 237
Benue, 208
Benue, R.: information on, 32; Islam on, 117; exploration of, 208; liquor traffic, 310
Berlin: West African Conference (1885), 310
Bethel African Church, 156, 201–2, 234, 236–7, 255, 323
Biafra, Bight of, 3, 56, 71, 77, 94
Bible: teachings of, 62, 72, 176, 197, 235, 261, 287, 301; Edward VII's gift of, 69; and Emma Jaja, 81; and Sword, 113, 159; and African Church, 254; converts' acceptance of, 286, 291; and African religions, 264; and freemasonry, 269; and oath-taking, 272; and Christian Ogboni Society, 272, 274; and slavery, 332. *Vernacular*, 292, 301; Arabic, 118, 150; Hausa, 124; Fula, 218; Yoruba, 272; Union Ibo, 283, 301
Bickersteth, Rev., 57, 67
Bicycle, introduction of, 289
Bida (map, p. 119), 114, 131, 133; war against, 125–6; Toronto Industrial Mission at, 142; C.M.S. at, 142; Resident of, 143; Emir of, 118, 142–3, 215, 217, 314
Bingham, of Sudan Interior Mission, 122
Birmingham, 176
Birth control, 335
Blackall, Governor of Lagos, 185
Blaize, Richard Beales: founder, *Lagos Times*, 65, 271; finances deputation to Ijẹbu-Ode (1892), 180; leader of educated Africans, 196; his name, 257; and Dr Ọbasa, 272; finances Abeokuta Industrial Institute, 297; and anti-liquor movement, 314
Blyden, Edward Wilmot: Negro writer, authority on Islam, 120, 217–18; supports Venn's policy, 183; welcome in Lagos (1890), 217, 219; formation of African Church, 218; birth and education, 218; cultural nationalism, 220, 245, 250, 252–4; diplomat, 230; critic of missions, 329
Boer War, 130, 188
Boler, Captain R. D., 82

Bolton, 122
Bonny (maps, pp. 91, 344)
Political and Social: power of ruler, 30; civil war (1869–73), 72; English firms in, 76; trade with New Calabar, 76; palm oil, 77; George Pepple I and Jaja compared, 77–82; political upheavals in, 81, 83, 92; Court of Equity, 82, 86; *Owu-Ogbo* influence, 84, 266–267; Jaja's influence, 92–4; chiefs depose George Pepple I, 93; British recognition of George Pepple I as king, 95; slavery abolition, 96; unity supervenes, 99; era of prosperity, 110, 224; Native Council, 111
Missionary activity: status of missionaries, 30; era of activity, 71–7; William Pepple invites Presbyterians, 71–2; slave-converts in, 84–90, 96; chiefs refuse C.M.S., 93; British support Christianity, 94; protests at Crowther's ill-treatment, 217; St Stephen's Church, 220; Committee of Delta Pastorate, 236; education of élite, 284; and liquor traffic, 323; chief's attitude to Christianity, 333; and European civilization, 340
Bonnymen, 109
Books, 290
Bornu, 118; Shehu of, 121
Bororos, 123
Bowen, Rev. T. J., American Baptist, 117
Bower, Captain, 167
Boyle, James, 232
Bradlaugh, Charles, M.P., 92
Brand, Consul, 12
Brass
Political and Social: early slave trade, 3; power of ruler, 30; French seek to annex, 33; political upheavals in, 81, 83; traders in, 82; *Owu-Ogbo* influence, 84; socio-political revolution in, 84–5, 86, 88; slavery in, 96; Native Council, 111; officials' neglect of Sunday observance, 160–1; cannibalism, 211; attack on liquor store, 312–14; Native Courts, 323; Royal Commission on liquor traffic, 323
Missionary activity: status of missionaries, 30; response to, 68, 71;

becomes Christian state, 85; Archdeacon Crowther at, 93; British support Christianity, 94; C.M.S. failure in, 231; Industrial Institution (C.M.S.), 297

Brassmen, 312–13

Brazil, emigrants from, 264

Breadfruit Church, Lagos, 185, 189–90, 196, 201–2, 235, 260, 323–4

Brickworks, Okorofiong, 298

Britain

British Government Policy: early reaction of rulers, 5–14; secular arm and protection of missionaries, 5, 7–8, 33, 35, 37, 45; Ijaye war, 12–14; in Yorubaland, 15, 29–30, 33–40, 66; destruction of Old Town, 22, 24; missionaries as pathfinders, 29–30, and source of intelligence, 32; Halligey incident, 48; Viard affair and French rivalry, 49–54, 58–9; Ijẹbu Expedition, 54–69; support missionaries in Bonny, 194; back Harry Johnson against Jaja, 103–10; anti-Islamic feelings in, 118; indifference of officials, 158–61; Ord Commission, 182; and Native Pastorate, 187, 194; and Ethiopianism, 202–3, 205; discrimination against Africans, 234; Africans' acceptance of British rule, 242; white officials flock to West Africa, 269; education in, 295; anti-liquor movement in, 307–8, 310; Flag, Union Jack, 24, 62, 67, 97, 113

Consuls and Agents: in Lagos, 6, 11–13, 16; in Niger Delta, 17, 21–3; and humanitarian treaties, 21; mildly imperialist tone, 32; Lokoja, 32; Brass, 84–5. *See also names of individuals*

Press and Public Opinion: and George Pepple I, 90; and Bonny politics, 92; on Islam, 118; and events in Kano, 135; on Fulani, 139; and Indirect Rule, 151; and Yorubaland unrest, 163; and indigenous culture, 278; on liquor traffic, 307, 312, 314, 323; and church-going, 316. *See also Times, The*

Citizenship, Subjects: status and protection, 7–8, 11, 32, 38; Pinnock renounces, 168; attitude of educated Africans to, 247

See also: Ashanti Confederacy; Colonial Office; Foreign Office; Lagos Government; *Pax Britannica*; Treaties; Trade; Traders; Slave Trade; Slavery; Navy, British

British Cotton Growing Association, 138, 297

Brooke, Graham Wilmot: and Sudan Party, 120–2; 124, 224–5; on Bishop Crowther, 213; overzealous evangelist, 213–14; character, 214, 245, 285; member Finance Committee, Lagos, 215, 220–1; hated by Delta chiefs and converts, 217; Blyden's praise for, 219

Brussels, Conference and Agreement (on liquor traffic), 1890, 311–13, 317–319, 321

Buganda, Mutesa I of, 80

Burdon, Major, 133, 142–3, 147

Burial rites and customs, 243, 251, 335; Egba, 12; in Ogbomọshọ, 14; in Henshaw Town, 86; Yoruba, 265, 271; liquor in, 308–9

Burton, Consul R. F., 21, 186, 210, 216, 244, 309

Bussa, 50

Butter, P., 108

Cairo, 122, 147, 150

Calabar, New (map, p. 91)

Political and Social: early slave-trade, 3; dispute with Bonny, 75, 89, 93; political upheavals, 81, 83; traders in, 82, 90; civil war, 85–6; Jaja's influence supreme, 85, 92; accepts Protectorate Treaty, 98

Missionary Activity: response to, 71; expulsion of African missionaries, 86; abolition of slavery in, 96; C.M.S. mission reopened, 98; and Independent Delta Church, 224

Calabar, Old (map, p. 193)

Political and Social: early slave trade, 3; Efik of, and attitude to European civilization, 3, 16, 111, 340; chiefs and super-cargoes, 17; British influence in, 19–22, 98; humanitarian treaties with, 21; vulnerability, 22; power of ruler, 30; traders in, 82; Consular authority, 84, 86, 111;

socio-political revolution, 85–6; Jaja's influence, 109; Macdonald Lodge, 269; title system, 275–6; franchise, 342

Missionary Activity: propaganda, 4–5, 8; H. Waddell in, 7; protection of Christians, 8, 32; Beecroft lands missionaries, 18; Waddell on revolution in, 18; S.A.I.S.C., 21; converts, 26; status of missionaries, 30; British support Christianity, 94; abolition of slavery in, 96; Presbyterian mission, 112, 192–4, 298; James Johnson visits, 236; U.P.M. education policy, 302–3; liquor traffic, 323

Calvin, 195, 327

Cambridge, 121, 124, 213; University Mission, 142, 213–14, 221

Cameroons: territory, 200, 203, 208; chief in Brass, 85

Campbell, Mrs. Juliana, 293

Canada, 122, 146, 205, 245

Cannibalism: in Okrika, 90, 112; Ijaw, 113; Northern Nigeria, 130; Brass, 211; defended by Agbebi, 255; and liquor traffic, 310; at Akassa, 312

Canterbury, Archbishop of, 172, 227–231; 233, 237, 311, 321

Cape Coast, 236

Caravans, 130; routes, 195

Cardew, Sir Frederick, 234

Carr, Henry, 288, 295, 300

Carter, Guilbert Thomas (later Sir): signs 1893 treaty with Ẹgba; Ijẹbu Expedition, 55, 59 n., 267, 315; background and attitude, 60, 128; handling of Ijẹbu, 61–2, 64; goes to Ondo 63; receives mandate to attack Ijẹbu, 64; his Ẹgba policy, 66; separates Ibadan and Ilọrin, 68; and James Johnson, 188; at Bishop Crowther's funeral, 226; and educated Africans, 250; destruction of Ogboni House, 267; anti-liquor movement, 314–15

Carter-Denton Bridge, 317

Catechists, 181, 211, 286, 301

Catholic Church, Roman, and freemasonry, 268

Catholic Herald, 342

Catholic Life, 342

Catholic Missions generally: outstrip

Protestants in Iboland, 265; competition with Protestants, 292; government grants and educational progress 300–3; and liquor traffic, 326. *See also:* S.M.A.; Holy Ghost Fathers; Christian Villages

Central Africa, 177, 202, 203, 298

Chad, L., 118, 226

Chalmers, Sir M. D., 322

Chamberlain, Austen, 318

Champness, Rev. Thomas, 57

Chaplains, Colonial, 39, 248–9

Chausse, Father, 49, 51

Cheetham, Bishop, 196

China, 11

Christ Church, Lagos, 185, 212, 248–249

Christian Ogboni Fraternity, 270

Christian Ogboni Society: 271–5, 278; foundation of, 271–2; rituals, 273–4; objects, 274; suspended until reformed (1932), 276; members driven into African Churches, 276. *See also:* Ogboni *and* Reformed Ogboni Fraternity

Christian Party, Abẹokuta, 44–7

Christian villages: Shurẹn, 47; Catholic policy, 49, 291, 332; Gimi, 150

Christianity: and progress, 4, 112; and social reform, 8; and Yoruba unity, 11; and British flag, 24; recognized in Abẹokuta, 46; Ijẹbu attitude to, 56–57; and George Pepple I, 77–8; and House Rule, 83–4; British support of, 94; Jaja's fear of, 100; and Islam in Northern Nigeria, 113, 117–52; and African nationalism, 186–7; Abẹokuta citadel of, 195; number of Christians, 241; and Nigerian institutions, 255, 340; 'European', 261–4; 272, 285; and *Ifa*, 264; and African religion, 266; and freemasonry, 268–9; Christian Ogboni Society, 274; 'a religion for slaves', 291; and liquor traffic, 307; and slavery, 332; success of in Bonny, 332; leaders mostly Christians today, 342; massive response of Ibo, 342–5; the challenge to, 345. *See also:* Conversion; Civilization; missionary propaganda, etc.

Church Committee, Lagos, 190, 235

Church Missionary Intelligencer, 32 n., 236
Church Missionary Society, *see* C.M.S.
Churches and Chapels: in Ekiti camp,
43; Egbaland, 50; Bonny, 73, 82, 87–
88, 92, 97, 220; Okrika, 90, 93, 112;
Santa Isabel, 101–2; Uranta, 110;
Opobo, 110; Aba, 110; Benin, 158–9;
Imuku and Isire, 160; Lagos, 160,
183, 189–91, 248–9, 271; Ora, 164–5;
Ọyọ, 168; Yorubaland, 183; Ogbo-
mọshọ, 200
Churches, Christian, generally: cradle
of Nigerian nationalism, 175–6; and
Ethiopianism, 177–8, 205; educated
Africans' attachment to, 178–9;
church government, 179–81, 183,
191, 194–5, 197, 203; foster sense of
unity, 180; church property, 190–1;
Church attendance, 88–9, 96–7, 160–
161
Churchill, Lord Alfred, 210
Civil Service, Servants: European and
Christian example, 261; and freemasonry, 268; discrimination in, 241,
247, 268, 272; salaries of, 288; shortage of clerks, 295; Nigerians in, 178,
187, 304, 341
Civilization, European: Efik attitude to,
3; and Niger Delta, 4; missionary belief in, 8; one of the three Cs, 8; and
Yoruba unity, 11; unedifying manifestations, 31; Carter on, 60–1;
George Pepple I's conversion to, 77–
78; Jaja's acceptance of technology,
80; Bell on, 149; and Christianity,
105, 242–5; Blyden's denunciation of,
253; educated Africans' resistance to,
278–9; a missionary ideal, 340
Clapham Sect, 180
Class dues, 195
Clerks, 4, 284, 288–90, 295–6, 301,
303
Clothing, *see* Dress
C.M.S. (Church Missionary Society)
   Politics and Society: and Ijaye war,
12; Divorce Court and Christians,
Abẹokuta, 47; Court of Redemption,
47, 333–4; Viard affair, 51; and
George Pepple I, 90–2; journals, 90,
92; and Bonny Protectorate Treaty,
95; and Jaja, 99; seek military inter-

vention, 136–7; anti-Fulani propaganda, 138; Kent incident, 160;
alarm at nationalist movement, 185;
and polygamists, 201; missionaries
escape from Ekumeku attack, 262;
and *Ogboni*, 270, 275; and title-taking,
275
   Missionary Work: Ondo mission,
33–5, 37; Ijẹbu Ode, 58; New Calabar, 98; Opobo, 110; Onitsha, 115;
Lokoja, Egga, Kipo Hill, 118; Arabic
Bible, 118; Northern Nigeria, 120,
125–8, 135–6; Sudan Party, 121;
Hausa Association, 124–5; Kano, 129,
142, 146, 150; Lugard's encouragement, 129; Zaria, 132–3, 140, 142–3,
147; prevent Miller becoming Resident, 141; lost opportunities, 142,
146; Pategi, 142; Bida, 142–3; Yorubaland, 155; and Ọni of Ifẹ, 156;
Benin, 158; Brass, 160–1, 231, 297;
anti-liquor agitation, 171, 310, 312,
326; Ibo pastors, 176; pro-Crowther
'rebellion', 180; and Henry Venn,
180, 183; Lagos Church, 181, 183,
185, 189–91, 295; and James Johnson, 186–8, 194–6; Lagos School
Board, 190, 292; promotes African
agency, 198; Wood Report, 209–
210; Special Sub-committee, 220–
223; Africans 'revolt', 221–4; deputation to Lagos, 225–6; Hill Report,
228–9; failure on Niger and in Delta,
231; Delta Pastorate, 231–3, 235–7;
on Nigerian names, 244; Press in
Lagos, 246 n.; and Ogunbiyi, 277;
Centenary, 318; Onitsha hospital,
343
   Education: early scheme ends, 146;
Grammar Schools: Sierra Leone,
178; Lagos, 228, 288–9, 293–4; reject
S. Johnson's *History of Yorubas*, 260;
Training Institutions: Lagos, 271,
287; Asaba, 288, 294; Ọyọ, 293;
Oshogbo, 294; schools policy, 286,
291; Bookshop, 290; Christianization
of Ibo through schools, 291–2; Lagos
School Board, 292; disinterest in
secondary education, 293–5, 302;
Fourah Bay, 295; Industrial Institu-
tion, Brass, 297; reject government

grants, 299–303; Education Department, Onitsha, 302; outpaced by Catholics, 302

Parent Committee and Salisbury Square H.Q.: 16 n.; influence on Colonial Office, 37, 146–7, 161, 299; J. B. Wood and Yoruba war, 40; Bishop Tugwell and Ijẹbuland, 64; receives Alake, 69; Brass chief's idols sent to, 85; and Bishop Crowther, 87, 207, 212, 216–17, 220, 222–5; and Hausa Mission, 124; Lord Salisbury and, 137; resolution on Lugard's resignation, 143–4; Pinnock affair, 168; and Venn's Pastorate scheme, 181–5; and James Johnson, 187–9, 194–6; Mann's warning to, 191; and E. T. Phillips, 210; and anti-Negro attitudes, 211; and E. W. Blyden, 218–19; Delta Pastorate, 231

Cocoa-growing, 156, 164, 256, 279, 297, 339

Coconut, 297

Coffee-growing, 164, 256, 297, 339

Cognomens, 258–9. *See also* Names

Coinage, *see* Currency

Coker, Isaac Olufusibi (Aderupọkọ), 270

Coker, J. K., 234, 236

Coker, Rev. S. A., 268

Cole, William Emmanuel, 201

Colonial Chaplains, 39, 248–9

Colonial Hospital, Lagos, 247

Colonial Office: and *Akus*, 7; recalls Glover, 31; Moloney and, 37; Ijẹbu policy, 59–61, 63–4, 173; C.M.S. pressure on, 37, 146–7, 161, 299; relations with Girouard, 148; and Lugard, 150; Indirect Rule, 151; reports from Nigeria, 165–6, 168; and James Johnson, 188, 340; C.M.S. in Brass and Abonema, 231; Civil Service, 247; chaplaincies, 248–9; Lagos Education Bill, 257; refuse aid for education, 298–9, 340; and anti-liquor movement, 312, 314, 321–4

Colwyn Bay Institute, 297

Commerce: early European interest, 3; missionary belief in, 8; one of the three Cs, 8; and British flag, 24, 62; with Ijẹbu, 54–6, 64; the *Pampas*, 59;

the Parakoyi, 61; Lagos Chamber of, 64–5; and education, 71; prosperity under Jaja, 81–2; factor in Jaja's fall, 103; Morel and, 171; European versus Africans, 205, 241, 261, 325; and 'white' churches, 249; and educated Africans, 288, 325

Commons, House of, 311, 320

Communications: in Yorubaland, 10; in Nigeria, 289. *See also:* Railways; Roads; Trade Routes

Communion, Holy, 197, 211

Congo, Belgian, 188, 202–3, 320, 339; — Reform Association, 320

Congo R., 120

Congregationalists: Mission to Qua Ibo, 115; system of church government, 197–8, 200

Conversion to Christianity: of Efik, 17–26, 176, 255; and detribalization, 30; of Ijẹbu, 36, 67–8, 156; of Alake, 69, 156; Jaja's attitude to, 78–80, 94; mass, at Nembe and Tuwon, 85; and polygamy, 87, 330; and education, 105; in Northern Nigeria, 118, 120, 122, 133, 139, 149, 151; in Ondo, 156; in Ekitiland, 156–7; in Brass, 161; European missionaries' attitude to, 183, 286; of Ẹgba and Ibadan, 194–5; in Lokoja, 215; forcible, 286; and indigenous society, 330–3; of slave-pawns, 333; spiritual conquest incomplete

Converts, Christian: in Niger Delta demand annexation, 42; Manilla Pepples, 72; in Henshaw Town, 74–75; George Pepple I, 77; slave converts, 82–90, 95, 333; disobedience to chiefs, 163, 172; Ukpabio, first Efik, 176; take over power, 241; Europeanization of, 243–5, 285; among Ekumeku, 262; defend secret societies, 266; Chief Jacob and T. A. J. Ogunbiyi, 271; gain prestige, 289

Corruption, 166, 220

Cotton-growing, 256, 279, 297

Courts: Divorce, 47, 337; Consular, 86; Maliki, 125; Ogboni, 270; Native, 289, 303, 323, 337; influence of clerk, 289–90; 'Customary', 337

185; Lagos School Board, 190, 292; in Yorubaland, 194; industrial, 230, 296–8; Blyden's national programme, 254; Agbebi on; means of regeneration, 284; western form patronized in Delta and Lagos, 284, 290–1; élite educated in Britain, 284; elementary, 284–5, 289, 290–1; higher and technical, 285–9, 303; and mission policy, 286; grammar schools, 288–90, 293; boon to masses, 289, 292; vernacular, 292, 300–1; financial responsibility, 292–3; fear of secular, 292, 302; and Calvinism, 327

Secular, Government policy: grants to missions, 249, 289, 294, 298–303; Lagos Education Bill withdrawn, 257; Ordinances: of 1882, 299; of 1891, 293, 299; of 1898, 299; Government contribution to, 298–303; examinations for teachers, 299; Lugard's Memorandum (1914), 303; Inspectorate, 303; and disturbance of society, 334, 339; influence of secular, 345

See also: Schools; Teachers, Religious instruction; Training Institutions

Ẹdun, Adegboyega, *see* Samuel, Rev. J. H.

Edward VII, king, 69

Efik (map, p. 193)

Political and Social: chiefs, 3, 9; customs and institutions, 3–4; society, 4; refuse European settlement, 4; destruction of Old Town, 16; united under Egbo, 17; slave trade, 17; and Eyo Honesty II, 19; and Consul Hutchinson, 24; traders, 55, 82, 284; religion and politics, 74; effect of consular authority, 84; kinship with Santa Isabel, 101; trade with neighbours, 111; secret society, *see* Egbo; language, preservation of, 283; crops, 297; industrial needs, 298; slavery among, 331

Missionary Activity: protection of missionaries, 8, 22; missionary involvement in politics, 8; interest in Christianity, 9; education and conversion of, 18, 20; last resistance to missionary change, 24; authority flouted by missionaries, 25–6; Ukpabio the first convert, 176, 192–4; Reformed Ogboni cult, 276; U.P. Mission, 287, 326; and liquor traffic, 326

Ẹgan Arin, 273 n.

Ẹgan Oke, 273 n.

Ẹgba, Ẹgbaland

Political and Social: slave trade, 6; position in Yorubaland, 6; desire for white man's friendship, 7; British aid to, 8, 9, 11–12, 14; Ijaye war (1860), 11–13; and *Ogboni,* 11, 267, 270; attitude to *Saros,* 11–12, 14–16; and to education, 12, 290; war with Ibadan, 13, 33; Glover's aggressive policy, 14–15, 31; human sacrifice, 20; Sixteen Years' War, 33, 35, 39, 48; end of independence (1914), 43, 54, 341; fear of British influence and pro-French leanings, 44–5; Ogundipę uncrowned king of, 45–6; Commissioner Tickel and Flag affair, 48–9; French designs and Viard affair, 49–52; in Lagos, 50; waning authority of chiefs, 53–4, 94–5; commerce, 56, 65; trade routes, 60–2, 65–6; political revolution, 68–9, 79, 172; Pope Hennessy's policy, 184; cotton growing, 297

Missionary Activity: welcome to early missionaries, 6; Townsend and, 7, 11–12; involvement in politics, 8, 39–40, 68–9; disinterest in Christianity, 9; Wood and, 39–40; and his great influence, 46–7; Halligey incident, 47–8; S.M.A. mission, 58–9; Alake goes to church, 69, 156; and James Johnson, 194–6; demand for village education, 290; and liquor traffic, 308, 320; conversion in, 332

Ẹgba United Board of Management/Government, 14, 69, 258, 266, 288, 290

Ẹgbado, 50, 308

Egbo: hallowed position of, 4; Efik united under, 17; Waddell on authority of, 18; and Eyo Honesty II, 20–1, 84; abolition of slave-immolation, 20; trial of criminals, 21; and S.A.I.S.C.,

21-2; and S. Edgerley, 22-3; 'illegal' immolation in Old Town, 23; and Mission House, 25; authority flouted by missionaries, 26; Sunday processions banned, 26; in Duke Town, 74-5; deprived of authority, 111; and Christian missions, 266, 275; titles, 276

Egbosha, 114

Egerton, Sir Walter: Kent incident, 160; and Laseinde, 165; Pinnock affair, 168; and Morel, 171, 173; Civil Servants, 247; segregation, 248-249, 261; Lagos water supply, 279; economic progress under, 284; and anti-liquor movement, 321-2, 324

Egga, C.M.S. mission at, 118

Egun, 308

Egungun (masquerade), 163-4, 265

Egypt, 122, 147, 202

Ejinrin, 56

Ekanem, Rev. Asuqua, 192

Ekiti, Ekitiland: missionary success in, 156-7; anti-missionary unrest, 162-3, 338; Tucker Travelling Commissioner, 166; Morel on converts' attitude to chiefs, 172; educated Africans, 179-80; nationalism in, 200; *Ogboni* in, 272; slave converts, 333

Ekiti Confederation (*Ekitiparapo*), 34-5, 38-41, 43

Ekitiparapo, see Ekiti Confederation

Ekpe (title), 276

Ekpeyong (god), 20

Ekumeku, 114, 261-2

Elder Dempster and Co., 248

Electricity supply, Lagos, 278-9, 317

Elgee, Captain, 164-5, 322

Elgin, Lord, 148

Eluku (god), 265

Emin Pasha, 118

Emirs: of Northern Nigeria, 122, 129, 134, 140-2, 146, 148, 151-2, 341; of Kano, 124

England: Alake visits, 69; Jaja refuses to visit, 75; George Pepple I's visit, 76, and education in, 77; public's view of Africans, 250; Africans' knowledge of, 256; Grand Lodge of, 269

England, Church of, *see* Anglican Church

English language: 'Pidgin', 3, 339; early use in Calabar, 3-4; Ijebu attitude to, 56; in Santa Isabel, 101; Hausas to study, 124; medium of teaching, 206, 257, 292, 301, 339-340; Blyden on, 254; educated Africans' preference for, 280; administrators' preference for, 283, 339-40; traders' use of, 284

English Town, Badagry, 6

Enugu, 276 (map, p. 344)

Enyong, 111

Epe, 36, 57

Epelle, Chief Samuel Oko, 110

Ephraim, Duke, 25, 30

Episcopal Church, 198

Equity, Court of, 82, 85-7

Eruwas, 52

'Esere', *see* Ukpabio, Rev. E. E.

Esere beans, 4, 21, 24-5

Ethiope (ship), 18

Ethiopian, 178

Ethiopianism: defined, 177; identity with Negro race, 178, 194, 196; sense of oneness, 180; and Christianity, 202; and British policy, 202-203; success and failure, 205-38; Bishop Crowther's attitude to, 207; Madeira Conference, 210; Blyden's rôle in, 218-20; Special Sub-committee Report offends, 221; and C.M.S. deputation, 226; and Hill Report, 227; and Delta Church, 231-232; James Johnson leader of, 235-6; becomes spent force, 237-8; and cultural nationalism, 278

Etinam, 115 (map, p. 344)

Euba, Rev. W., 268, 271-2, 274, 278, 287, 293, 295

E.U.B.M., *see* Egba United Board of Management

Exeter Hall, 121, 137, 148

Export: of slaves, 3; of Bonny, 110; crops, 297

Eyamba V, King, 3-4, 17, 19, 20

Eyo Honesty II, King: his European clerk, 4; rise and character, 18-21, 98; travel abroad, 20; attitude to missionaries, 20-3, 30; challenged by S.A.I.S.C., 21-2; protests at interference, 22; and Edgerley's indis-

373

6, 15, 20; abolished in Old Town, 24, 266; missionaries immune from, 32; and Ijẹbu, 60, 68; in Ondo, 68; by Jaja, 73, 104; in Delta society, 87; absent in Islam, 136; European name a protection from, 244; defended by Agbebi, 255; and liquor traffic, 310

Humanitarian treaties, 21, 51

Humanitarianism, 66, 283, 307, 310, 313, 318, 320

Hunt-Grubbe, Rear-Admiral Sir W., 109

Hussey Charity Institution, 297

Hutchinson, Edward, 207–10

Hutchinson, Consul T. J., 24–5, 186, 210, 244

Hygiene and Sanitation, 145, 279, 303, 317

Ibadan (map, p. 334)
Political and Social: hostile state of, 6; defeated in Owiwi war, 7; Ijaye war, 11–13; Muslim state, 12; *Saros* in, 15; British influence, 33; Sixteen Years' War, 33–5, 38; Ilọrin wages war on, 39, 41, 63; end of independence (1911), 43; war and peace with Ijẹbu, 44, 55, 57, 61–4, 67–8; and Dahomey, 47; fear of British Government, 68; travelling commissioner at, 68; Fuller Resident at, 155; slavery in, 157, 333; chiefs and land ownership, 168–70; Masonic Lodges in, 276; chiefs and land survey, 279; University of, 287; Captain Elgee District Commissioner, 322
Missionary Activity: receives missionaries, 10; Anglican churches in, 16; Daniel Olubi, 39, 43; Wesleyans in, 47; S. G. Pinnock, 58; Harding's visit, 62–4; S.M.A. in, 158; converts' attitude to chiefs, 172; missionaries and independence, 173; and James Johnson, 195; African majority in church councils, 241; University College, 287; chiefs' attitude to education, 290; Wesley College, 294; and liquor traffic, 320, 323, 326; Christianity in, 332

Ibẹrẹkodos, 51

Ibibio, 30, 115, 276

Ibo, Iboland
Political and Social: markets, 97; educated Africans from, 100, 186; strife in, 111; Aro Expedition, 113–114, 175 n., 338; Western Ibo penetrated, 114; Onitsha Industrial Exhibition (1905), 262; title system, 266, 275–6; safety of travellers, 283; influence of Court clerk, 289; slavery in, 331–2; women and marriage, 337; British disturbance of society, 340; negligible impact of Islam, 345
Missionary Activity: missionary designs on, 90, 113, 117; Lokoja S.M.A. retire to, 136; response to, 156–8, 343–5; officials' neglect of Sunday observance, 160–1; desire for education, 171, 290–2; first pastors, 176; and James Johnson, 180; Niger Mission, 206; Native Pastorate, 241; religion and Christianity, 265; school fees, 292; C.M.S. education policy, 300–2
Language: preservation of 283; Bible in Union Ibo, 283, 301

Ibrahim, Malam, 149–50

Ibuno, 98

Ibusa, 114 (map, p. 334)

Icarus, H.M.S., 108

Idah, 117

Ides of March, by Agbebi, 200

Idolatry, 15, 85–6

Idoma, 117

Idua Oron, 98

Ifa (palm-god), 264–5

Ifamubọni (Babamubọni), 157

Ifẹ: Ọni of, 155; Treaty, 41

Ifọle (expulsion of European missionaries): 14–15, 39; stopped by Ogundipẹ, 45–6; and annexation of Ebute Metta, 48; chiefs regret incompleteness of, 48; effect of Viard affair, 51; Glover on Ijẹbu part in, 57

Igalla, 111

Iganmu, 65

Igbogun Island, 37

Igede-Ekiti, 272

Iguana (totem), 73, 75, 95

Ijaw (map, p. 34): urged to expel white men, 35–6, 57; and Royal Niger Company, 111; cannibals, 113; work

Industrial Exhibition, Onitsha (1905), 262
Infanticide, 21
Infantile mortality, 279, 307, 335
Ingham, Bishop, of Sierra Leone, 47, 225, 248
Inheritance, 333
Ipokia, 5
Ireland, Grand Lodge of, 269
Isẹ, 163
Isẹyin, 41, 47, 117, 290
Ishẹri, 65
Isire, 160
Islam, Islamic, 202; revolution of nineteenth century, 4; converts to, 4; chiefs replaced by white men, 5; Muslim state in Ibadan, 12, 15, 43; and Christianity in Northern Nigeria, 117-52, 213-15, 345; contempt for *kafiris*, 121, 133, 140, 215; unifying effects of, 136; Burdon's support of, 142-3; Girouard's tenderness for, 148; Blyden's fear of, 219; Christian missions desire elimination of, 286; Tugwell on, 315; Carter and, 315-316
Islington, C.M.S. Training College, 287
Issele-Uku, 114, 262 (map, p. 334)
Itebu, 35, 37
Itẹsi, Ntowa of (Isaac Coker), 270
Itibọ, 51
Itoiki, 62
Itsekiri, 180; Nana of, 113
Itu, 115 (map, p. 334)
Iwarẹfa, 273 n., 277
Iwo, 117, 157, 294 (map, p. 334)
Iyi Enu Hospital (C.M.S.), 343
Iyin, 157

Jagunna, of Abẹokuta, *see* Ogundeyi
Jaja, King of Opobo: political stature, 71; and Manilla Pepples, 72-7; hatred of Bishop Crowther, 74, 93, 99-100; comparison with George Pepple I, 77-82; attachment to indigenous religion, 79-80, 89, 109; instinct as ruler, 83; influence in New Calabar, 85, 92, and in Bonny, 86, 89, 92-4, 99; fall predicted, 94; fortunes wane, 95-7; loyalty to Britain, 97-8, 107; 'envelopment' by missionary pro-

paganda, 98; objects to 'black' missionaries, 99-100; his patriotism, 99; fear of Christianity, 100-1; reluctantly accepts Protectorate Treaty (1884), 101, 109; challenged by Primitive Methodists, 101-3; conflict with H. H. Johnston and Bonny, 103-110; his fall discussed, 103-9, 224; his charm and hospitality, 107-8; summoned to Johnston's gunboat, 108; humiliated and exiled, 109-10; nationalists oppose his removal, 175 n.
Jaja, Emma (Miss White), 81
Jaja, F. D., 110
Jaja, Mac Pepple, Amanyanabo of Opobo, 110
Jaja, Sunday, 81, 109, 284
Jamaica, 188, 192, 298; rum, 308
Jebba, 128, 131
Jedda, 126
Jews: Blyden on, 253
Jihad: Fulani, 4, 39, 117, 136, 149; Alafin, 41
John, as African name, 244
Johnson, Rev. E. T. ('Adesola'), 265
Johnson, George William ('Reversible'), alias Oshokale Tẹjumade Johnson, 11; leads anti-missionary group, 14; career, 45-6; opposes Ogundipẹ, 46; Flag affair, 49; begged to return to Abẹokuta, 53; sides with James Johnson, 196
Johnson, Archdeacon Henry: his opinion of Muslims, 135; spokesman of educated Africans, 184; at Breadfruit Church, 196; supports Bishop Crowther, 209, 212, 215, 247; Principal, C.M.S. Grammar School, Lagos, 293
Johnson, Bishop James ('Holy'): proposed episcopate under, 16; and Ijẹbu Expedition, 55, 60; mission in Ijẹbu-Ode, 58, 59 n.; his reputation, 67; Aro Expedition, 114; in Benin, 158; parentage, 180, 186; and Native Pastôrate, 181-3, 186-92, 212; transfer to Lagos, 185-6; education and character, 186-8, 214, 285; his nationalism, 186-9, 191, 194, 206-7, 217-19, 245, 253-4; summoned to London, 189; carries Ethiopianism

into interior, 194–6; his removal, 195–6; leads revolt against C.M.S., 221–2, 225; and Independent Delta Church, 224, 230; conducts Bishop Crowther's funeral service, 226; refuses to be 'half bishop', 228; and Hill Report, 228–9; negotiations with C.M.S., 231; accepts junior bishopric, 233; his consecration, 233–4; received by Queen Victoria, 233; Bishoprics Fund, 234; the 'idol of Lagos', 235; Ethiopian leader, 236–238; and Nigerian names, 244; and European missionaries, 247; and educated Africans, 250; plan for African University, 252; on missionary activity, 252; as cultural nationalist, 253–4, 295; dress always European, 254; his name, 257; on superficiality of Christianity, 264; writes *Yoruba Heathenism*, 264; surprise at Yoruba moral code, 265; and Ogunbiyi's conversion, 271; and anti-liquor movement, 310–11; 314–15, 321

Johnson, Dr O., 221, 241, 295
Johnson, Opobo, 81
Johnson, Rev. Samuel, 32, 39–41, 260
Johnston, H. H.: on missionary propaganda, 30, 60; becomes Acting Consul, conflict with Jaja, 163–4; his character, 104–5, 128; attitude to missions, 104–5, 210–11, and to Jaja, 105–6; friendship with George Pepple I, 106; disagreement with naval officers, 107; summons Jaja, 108; exiles him, 109; leads missionaries into hinterland, 109–10; on African missionaries, 211–12
Jombo, Herbert, 284
Jones, A. L., 65
Jos, 276 (map, p. 119)
Journalists, 342
'Joyful News' branch of Wesleyans, 58, 166–7
Jujuism, 340; Ijẹbu, 60, 68; in Bonny, 73, 75, 87, 89, 97; Jaja's in Opobo, 76, 79–81, 101, 106, 109; in New Calabar, 85; Nana's, 113; in Aro Chukwu, 113; Ibo, 290–1
Jukun, 117
Jumbo, Herbert, 92

Jumbo, Oko, 72–4, 83, 89, 92–3, 95–7
Jurisprudence, 147

Kaduna, 269, 276
Kaduna River, 132
Kaffraria, 192
Kalabari, *see* Calabar, New and Old
Kaltungo, 345
Kanawa, 121, 135
Kano (map, p. 119), 122, 132; proposed missionary college at, 124; C.M.S. school in, 125; object of C.M.S. enterprise, 129; misguided march to, 130–6, 235; contemptuous reception, 134–5, 138; Emir of, 135, 149–50; origins of expedition, 135; failure of mission, 139, 141, 146–7; Arabs in, 141; London and Kano Company, 147; the Maguzawa, 149; the Ansa, 149–50; grand durbar at, 150; railway advocated, 175 n.; Masonic Lodges in, 276
Kanuri, 118
Katsina, Emir of, 133, 142
Kayọde, 155
Keffi, 125–6
Kent, Dr Hugh, and incident, 160
Ketu, 48, 117
Khalifa, 118
Khartoum, 118, 129–30, 135
Kimberley, Earl of, 251, 256
King's College, Lagos, 298
Kingsley, Mary: anti-missionary attitude, 128, 171, 329; speaks for traders, 139; champions indigenous religion, 159; anthropological work, 211, 244, 251; attitude to liquor traffic, 307, 309, 316–17
Kipo Hill: C.M.S. mission at, 118, 215
Kiriji, 38, 40
Kirk, James, 208–9, 247
Knutsford, Lord, 60, 64–5
Koeffe markets, 93
Kola-nut, 62, 164, 274, 308
Kontagora: Emir of, 142–3; Resident in, 143
Koran, 124–5, 133, 135–6
Kosọkọ, ruler of Lagos: leads anti-missionary faction, 5, 9, 55; deposes Akitoye, 9; removal demanded, 10; his Ẹpẹ desperadoes, 36

329–45; small scattered force, 340; decline of influence, 341–3; the press, 342–3; and Ibo, 343; hospitals, 343. *See also* Missionary propaganda

Missionaries, African: imperialist tone of, 32; rôle in Yorubaland, 38–40; indiscretion in Ijẹbuland, 58; conflicting loyalties, 66–7; and Jaja, 80, 99–100; and slave converts, 83; expelled from New Calabar, 86; replaced in Bonny by Europeans, 93; in Ekitiland, 157. *See also under individuals' names*

Missionary Conference, 218

Missionary journals, 6, 32, 45, 56–7, 90, 92, 221; contribution to Nigerian press, 342. *See also under of titles of journals*

Missionary propaganda: introduction of, 4–5; reaction of rulers to, 5–6; political effects of, 8; and Ẹgba, 10; Efik, 17, 84; and occupation of Yorubaland, 29–30, 33, 42; British influence, 29–30, 66; power of chiefs, 30; Ijẹbu and Mahin, 36–7, 55–7, 60–1; and African missionaries, 66–7; effects greatest among Ijẹbu and Ẹgba, 68–9; in Yorubaland interior, 71; Jaja's hatred of, 72, 92–3, 98, 100; a danger to traders, 82; and society, 83; championed by George Pepple I, 90; extended to Okrika, 90, 93; development of Opobo, 98; ascendancy of in Bonny, 110; and Islam in Northern Nigeria, 137–42, 345; Girouard's opposition to, 146–8; and Indirect Rule in Northern Nigeria, 150–2; Educational side of, 156–7, 179, 292–3; Morel campaigns against 322–3, 329; critics of, 329; disruption of tribal society, 330–1; attitude to slavery, 331–4; and to polygamy, 334–7; and traditional moral code, 339; spiritual conquest incomplete, 340–1; active force in villages, less in towns, 345

Mississippi, 198

Mọ, 266

Mockler-Ferryman, Army officer, 213

Modakẹkẹ, 155

Moloney, Alfred, Governor of Lagos, 36–7, 200; Viard affair, 50; and Ijẹbu relations, 59–60; and James Johnson, 188

Monarchy, 188, 270

Money economy, 8

Moor, Sir Ralph, 96, 160–1, 308

Moore, C. B., 65, 69

Morality: and polygamy, 336

Morel, E. D. (De Ville), 138; editor, *West African Mail*, 159, 321, 325; anti-missionary campaigner, 171–3, 321, 329; attacks prohibitionists, 171, 323

Morland, Colonel, 131

Morocco, 147

Mortality rate, 279

Mosẹlẹkatse, 80

Mosques, 125, 147, 316

Motor transport, 289

Munchi, 175 n.

Muslim, *see* Islam

Mutesa I of Buganda, 80

Mythology, Yoruba, 264

Nagwamanchi, Emir of Kotangora, 132

Names: African, 243–4; 257–9; European, 254–5, 280

Nana of Itsekiris, 113

Nassarawa, 142

Nationalism, Nigerian, generally: in Southern Nigeria, 80, 173–203; ideology of, 176; Dosunmu's movement alarms C.M.S., 185; engenders Native Baptist Church, 198; Agbebi articulates African feelings, 200; Bishop Crowther symbol of, 205–7, 217; E. W. Blyden and, 217–20, 253; and Special Sub-committee Report, 221–3; Hill Report, 227–9; Bishop Crowther's successor, 229–31; growth of political organizations, 238; anti-missionary feeling, 241–8; contributions of J. Johnson, E. Blyden and M. Agbebi, 253–6; against liquor, 284; effect of shortage of intellectuals, 295; aims cultural not political, 342. *Also see next entry.*

Nationalism, Cultural: 241–280; African's veneration of cultural heritage, 242; Europeanization repudiated, 243–6; racial segregation, 247–9;

communal society, 330; polygamy in society, 335–7; acceptance of British sovereignty, 341; leaders today mostly Christians, 342; the Christian community in the Republic, 345. *See also under names of regions*

Nigerian Baptist, 342
Nigerian Chronicle, 265
Nigerian Methodist, 342
Nigerian Methodist Review, 342
Nikki, 128, 310
Nile railway, 146
Ningi, 150
Nlado, 53
North Africa, 122, 141, 147
Northern Nigeria (map, p. 119): Islamic revolution in, 4; British sovereignty in, 44; Islam and Christianity in, 117–52, 315, 345; attraction of Christian missions, 118–20; pacification of, 129, 131, 133, 142; Indirect Rule in, 139–52; Northern Peoples' Congress, 176; Masonic Lodge, Kaduna, 269; non-Nigerian clerks in, 295; and liquor traffic, 311, 321; liberation of slaves, 334; loyalty of Emirs, 341
Northern Peoples' Congress, 176
Notsho, Ekike, 106
Nupe: kingdom, 100; Emirs of, and Bishop Crowther, 118, 135; war of 1897, 124; language, preservation of, 283

Oath-taking, 273
Obas: generally, 171; of Edo, 133
Obasa, Dr, 238, 271–2
Obiabutu, 75, 93
Obsequies, *see* Burial rites
Oca, Don Jose Montes de, 102
Ockiya, King of Brass, 85
Odo Otin, 68
Offa, 61, 63
Offerings, church, 206
Ogbomosho, 189 (map, p. 344): receives missionaries, 10; Christians expelled from, 14; Anglican churches in, 16; Wesleyans in, 47; Islam in 117; converts' attitude to chiefs, 172; nationalists build church, 200; anti-liquor movement, 315, 323, 326;

soldiers take *Bale's* wives, 338; Baptist hospital, 343; *Bale* of, 14, 169, 338
Ogboni: Townsend and, 11; Egba and, 12; *Saros* join, 15; Onlado head of, 45; J. B. Wood and, 46; advisers to Awujale, 61; destruction of Ogboni House, 68, 267; authority ended, 69; and Christian missions, 266–7; functions of Ogboni House, 270; Christianization of, 270–5; origin of word, 272; rituals of, 273–4; missionaries join, 330; accepted in African Churches, 343. *See also:* Christian Ogboni Fraternity and Society; Reformed Ogboni Fraternity
Ogedemgbe, 40
Ogunbiyi, chief Jacob, 271
Ogunbiyi, Archdeacon T. A. J.: resuscitates *Ogboni*, 267; founds Christian Ogboni Society, 271–5; dissuaded from first attempt, 271; his moral code enforced by oath, 272–3; meets objections by Bishops, 275–7; suspends activities, 276–7; founds Reformed Ogboni Fraternity, 276–7; leaves C.M.S., founds own church at Ikeja, 277
Ogunbona, 6
Ogundeyi, 49–51, 54
Ogundipe, uncrowned king of Egba; J. B. Wood's influence over, 40; character, 45–6; opposed by G. W. Johnson, 46; and Halligey incident, 48; admits Catholic missionary, 49; his death, 49
Oguntolu, D. O., 234, 236
Ohambele, 106, 109
Oil, *see* Palm oil
'Oil Rivers', 109, 113; Protectorate, 226
Ojo, 167
Oke Igbo, 33
Oke Ishokun, 167
Oke-Mesi, 163
Okenla, *see* Owolatan, John
Okeodan, 53
Okorofiong, 298
Okoyong: 'white queen' of (Mary Slessor), 114 (map, p. 193)
Okpanam, 114
Okrika (maps, pp. 34, 344); response to

Oyekan, 46
Oyerinde, Nathaniel David, 287
Ọyọ (map, p. 344):
    Politics and Society: domination of Dahomey, 5; dissolution of old empire, 10, 40; French designs on, 50; bombardment of, 166–8, 334; Alafin of, 38–41, 50, 58–9, 167–8
    Missionary activity: receives missionaries, 10; Anglican churches in, 16; and Samuel Johnson, 39, 41, 260; Matthews at, 58; C.M.S. Training Institute, 130, 293–4; S.M.A. in, 158; Baptist mission, 166; Pinnock affair, 166–8, 334; chiefs' attitude to education, 290; anti-liquor movement, 315, 323, 326
Ọzọ, (title), 275–6

Palm oil, in Niger Delta: change-over from slave-trade, 3, 17; oil markets, 73, 90; and Jaja, 76–7, 99, 106–7, 109; and liquor traffic, 308
Palm wine, 309
Palma Island, 55, 184
Pampas, 59, 61
Pan-Africanism, 187
Pan-Anglican Conference (1908), 253, 321
Pankshin, 345
Paraguay, 291
Parakoyi, 61, 270
Parliamentary government, 176, 179, 236
Pastorates, Native African: Venn's scheme, 181–3; 185–6, 206, 222, James Johnson and, 186–7, 189–91; Ibo (Onitsha) Pastorate, 241; Lagos, 156, 182, 185, 212, 224–6, 235, 271; Niger Delta, 115, 158, 188, 191, 221–222, 224, 227, 231–3; Sierra Leone, 182–3, 186, 224–6, 232
Pastors, African, 162–3, 166, 176, 178, 181, 192, 194, 211, 244
Partition of Africa, 253
Pategi, 142
Paul, Rev. Charles, 215–16
Pawns, 333
Pax Britannica: in Nigeria generally, 29–30, 172, 238, 289, 304, 331; in Old Calabar, 26; in Yorubaland, 54,

155; in Southern Nigeria, 112, 241; in Northern Nigeria, 137, 321
Payne, J. A. Otunba: and Ijebu Expedition, 58, 59 n., 62, 67; nationalist, 184–5, 221, 225; and *Lagos Almanac*, 200, 260; and E. Blyden, 217; and Bishop Crowther, 225–6; on superficiality of European Christianity, 264; a freemason, 268
People's Union, 238
Pepple, Charles, 89, 284
Pepple, George I, King of Bonny: accession, 74–6; comparison with Jaja, 77–82; supports missionary activity, 83, 90, 99; helps Archdeacon Crowther in Okrika, 90; deposed, 93, 96; faith in Britain 94; restoration 95–6; becomes an autocrat, 97; H. H. Johnston's friendship with, 106; advises Jaja's exile, 109; reforms *Owu-Ogbo*, 266; education, 106, 284
Pepple, William, King of Bonny, 71–2
Pepples: Annie faction, 72, 79; Manilla faction, 72–4; Warribo Manilla, 89, 93, 96–7, 110
Perekule, 93, 96
Peter, Pastor, 112
Peters, Daddy, 270
Phillips, Bishop Charles: and Ondo Mission, 8, 35, 39, 228, 230, 260; imperialist tone, 32; biographical note, 35 n., entreats Lagos Government, 36; rôle in Ondo war, 39–41, 43; reports Kayọde, 155; Hill Report, 228–9; consecration, 230, 233; history of Ondo, 260; laments Christian immorality, 285
Phillips, E. T., 210
Phillips, Consular official, 113
Pickles, Dr, 164
'Pidgin' English, 3, 339
Pinnock, Rev. S. G., 58, 166–8
Pioneer (paper), 246 n.
Poison, ordeal by, 4
Police, 270
Political parties, 342
Polygamy: as Islamic institution, 4, 145; Ẹgba on, 12; among *Saros*, 15; George Pepple I and, 77; slave converts reject, 87, 330; James Johnson on, 188–9; in African Churches, 197,

386

Ships: segregation on, 248; shipbuilding 289
Shitta Bay Mosque, 316
Shuren, 47
Sierra Leone, 39, 45, 109, 157, 175 n., 214, 216, 225, 246–7; exodus of *Akus*, 7; bishopric of, 47; governors of, 180, 184, 234; liberated Africans of, 100–1, 145, 180, 212, 231, 257; C.M.S. Grammar School, 178; Native Pastorate and Church, 182–3, 186, 225, 248; and James Johnson, 186–9; Church property in, 191; and Bishop Crowther, 217; Muslims in, 218; 'cabal', 231; C.M.S. in 232; James Johnson and, 234, 236; Wilberforce Memorial Hall, 234; Ijẹsha Association, 234; in Civil Service, 295; hut tax, 329
Sixteen Years' War, 33–8
Slave trade; in Niger Delta, 3; abolition of, 3; in Yorubaland and Dahomey, 6–8; the Ẹgba and, 6; the Efik and transatlantic, 17, 21; Bishop Crowther a victim of, 87; slave-dealers, 6, 65; slave-holders, 6, 215, 332; slave hunters, 6; slave raiders: Fulani, 127; and Emir of Kontagora, 143; in Ibadan, 169
Slavery: as social institution: and Ẹgba, 4; Islam, 4; Ẹgba, 12; Efik, 17, 84; in Ikalẹ and Ondo, 36; in Ijẹbuland, 60, 66; in Bonny, 78, 96; in Niger Delta, 83–4, 96, 182, 331; by Fulani, 127; in Iboland, 331; in Yorubaland, 283, 331–3; missionaries' immunity from, 32; C.M.S. resolutions on, 47–8 195, 332; Flag Affair, 49; and Catholicism, 49, 291, 332; humanization of, 96; J. Johnson on, 188; and African Church, 197; and European names, 244, 258–9; Blyden on mental and cultural, 254; of travellers, 283; Christianity and, 291, 332–3; Protestants' detestation of, 331; Catholics sympathetic to, 332; demise of, and liberation of slaves, 334. *See also:* Immolation; Redemption; Slave Trade; Slaves
Slaves: given refuge in Lagos, 15; Waddell on, 18; disobey Eyo II and

are converted, 22; female, 26; slave converts, 22, 26, 82–7, 90, 95, 333; and Union Jack, 67; Jaja a bought slave, 79; religious freedom for, in Brass, 85; George Pepple I and, 94; improved condition of, 96, 111; many freed in Asaba, 114; escaped, 124, 184; purchased by Catholic missions, 291; incited by missionaries, 330; slave pawns, 333; liberation of, 334. *See* Slavery
Slessor, Mary, 114
S.M.A. (Société des Missions Africaines): and French influence, 33; and Yoruba war 41; patronized by Ẹgba and Ijẹbu, 44; in Abẹokuta, 48–9, 158; at Ilaro, 50; Ijẹbu preference for, 58–9; in Lower Niger, 114; Lokoja, 136; Ijẹbuland, 156, 158; in Benin, Ibadan, Ọyọ, Oshogbo, 158; escape from Ekumeku attack, 262; education policy, 287–8; St Gregory's College, Lagos, 289; Training College Ibadan, 294; Topo Industrial School, 297; Sacred Heart Hospital, Abẹokuta, 343
Smallpox, 84–5
Société des Missions Africaines, *see* S.M.A.
Society for Abolition of Inhuman and Superstitious Customs (S.A.I.S.C.), 21
Society for Promotion of Religion and Education, Lagos, 185, 189
Sociologists, 330
Ṣodẹkẹ, 6–7
Sokoto: caliphate, 117, 122, 125, 132, 137, 139, 151; Sultan of, 38–9, 118, 121, 127–8, 132–3, 142–3, 148; mosque, 125; slavery in, 127
Soldiers, troops (Hause), 68, 167, 338
South Africa, 130, 177, 188, 194, 202–3, 320
South America, 59
Southern American Baptist Mission, *see* Baptist Mission
Southern Nigeria (map, p. 344): politics and society, missions and, 71–115; Indirect Rule in, 155–73; economic progress, 284; government and education, 300, 302–3; Holt on govern-

ment waste, 319; liberation of slaves, 334; 'Customary' Courts, 337; Hausa troops in, 338; few Missions numerically, 340; nationalists from mission schools, 342

Spain, 101. *See also* Fernando Po

Spiff, Chief, 85

Spirits, *see* Liquor

Stone, Moses Ladẹjọ, 198–9, 257

Student Volunteer Movement, 213

Sudan: Islamic Theocracy in Eastern, 188, 125–6; Northern Nigeria termed Central, 118; *Sudan leaflets*, 121, 123; Nagwamanchi of, 132; reconquest of Eastern and banning of missionaries, 146–7

Sudan Party, 121–3, 213–14, 221, 223–224, 226

Sudan Interior Mission, 149

Sudan United Mission, *see* Cambridge University Mission

Sunday observance: in Old Calabar, 3, 20, 86; in Creek Town, 26; by Ogundipẹ, 45; in Bonny, 73, 87–8; officials' neglect of, 160–1; chiefs' opposition to, 163

Sunday schools, 78, 292

Supercargoes, 17, 19, 24

Surnames, 259

Survey Department, 297. *See also* Land Survey

Sylvan products, 3

Taiwo, Chief, 315

Tariffs, 46, 311, 319–20

Taxation: direct versus indirect, 137, 170, 261, 317, 312, 324–6; exemption from, 145; educated Africans resist, 178, 278–9, 324–6; and representation, 236; unpopular, 329

Teachers: missionary, 178, 181, 192, 200, 211, 271, 288; Okrikan's request for, 90; salaries of, 195, 199, 292–3, 301; training of, 286–7, 293–4, 298–300; buildings for, 290; in Lagos, 292; imported 295; qualifications of, 299, 301; government, 301

Technical training, 183, 303. *See also* Education, Industrial

Temperance movement, 318, 321; Church of England T. Society, 321

Temple, C. L., 133, 147–8, 150

Theocracy, 11, 86, 144, 178

Thomas, Jonathan John, 257

Thomas, S. B., 234

Thomson, Joseph, 210, 309

Thomson, Rev. W. R., 298

Tickel, Commissioner, 48–9

Timber concessions, 156

Times, The, 78, 126, 312, 314, 318, 321

Titles, title system: Ondo, 260; Yoruba and Ibo, 266; advantages of, 275–6, 330

Tiv, 117

Tolls, 56, 62–3, 65

Tombo, 266

Tools, imported, 296

Topo, S.M.A. Industrial School, 297

'Topping', 96 *and* n.

Toronto Industrial Mission, 142

Torture, 85

Totems, animal: iguana, 73, 75, 95; python, 85; names, 258–9

Townsend, Henry: received by Ṣodẹkẹ, 7; influence in Abẹokuta, 11–12; and Ijaye war, 12–13, return to interior, 16; joins *Ogboni*, 270

Townsend-Wood Memorial Church, 69, 156

Trade: in sylvan products, 3; in Niger Delta, 42, 261; with Ijẹbu, 59–65; on Lower Niger, 111; Lagos 324; conducted by slaves 331; trade routes, 58–62, 65, 97. *See also* Eastern Route; Communications

Traders and Merchants: not necessarily 'civilizers', 4; European, and Ijẹbu, 54–6, 58, 62, 64; middlemen, 55–6 66, 82, 188; of Lagos, 56, 64–5; African, 58, 65; in Britain, 65–6; in Bonny, 72, 74, 82, 90; in Opobo, 76–7, 82, 90, 99, 100; in Southern Nigeria, 82, 111; oppose Bishop Crowther's mission, 82; against Jaja, 103–10, 138, on Lower Niger, 111; oppose, missionary intrusion, 137–9; Girouard's policy towards, 147; trading companies, 156; Europeans displace Africans on Niger, 209; Bishop Crowther dependent on, 212; as 'Christians', 261; use of English and accountancy, 284; European,